MOTHERHOOD AND SEXUALITY

Motherhood

and

SEXUALITY

Marie Langer

Translation, Introduction, and Afterword by
Nancy Caro Hollander

OTHER

New York

Library of Congress Cataloging-in-Publication Data

Langer, Marie.
    [Maternidad y sexo. English]
    Motherhood and sexuality / Marie Langer ; translation, introduction, and afterword by Nancy Caro Hollander.
       p. cm.
    Translation of: Maternidad y sexo.
    Previously published: New York : Guilford Press, c1992.
    Includes bibliographical references and index.
    ISBN 1-892746-64-6
    1. Women—Mental health. 2. Motherhood—Psychological aspects. 3. Sexual disorders. 4. Gynecology—Psychosomatic aspects. I. Title.

RC451.4.W6 L3613 2000
155.3'33—dc21

00-027427

Contents

Preface to the English Translation

NANCY CARO HOLLANDER

I began this translation of *Motherhood and Sexuality* with the idea that it would be but a brief interlude in my work on Marie Langer's biography. I was, however, to live with this book for several years as I struggled with the intricacies of transforming the substance and meaning of a text from one language to another. The task was complicated by my desire to remain faithful to what Langer wrote in 1951, even while I knew that some aspects of her analysis underwent changes in the years following the book's first publication. In addition, I could not resist the temptation to introduce English-speaking readers to Marie Langer, and so the project expanded to include a lengthy overview of her life and work, which is provided in a translator's Introduction and Afterword. Translator's comments throughout the text complement information in the Afterword to indicate the shifts in Langer's ideas about motherhood and sexuality. The few alterations that have been made from the original Spanish text are explained in the translator's Introduction.

Partial support for this project came from a Dean's Research Grant, School of Social and Behavior Sciences, California State University, Dominguez Hills, and from a travel grant awarded by the Plumsock Fund. I am appreciative of the ongoing partial research leaves from my teaching responsibilities at California State University, Dominguez Hills, which permitted me to focus more attention on this book. I am indebted to the faculty and clinical affiliates of the California Psychoanalytic Center of California, with whom I studied psychoanalysis.

I would like to thank my editor, Kitty Moore, for her support, good humor, and truly collegial exchange of ideas during the completion of this project. My heartfelt thanks as well to my North American colleagues and friends, Laurien Alexandre, Susan Gutwell, Lisa Aronson, and the members of my Psychoanalytic Writing Group, Maggie Magee, Diana Miller, and Bonnie Engdahl, who enthusiastically supported my work and generously gave of their time and talent to read and criticize initial drafts of the text; a special thanks to those—especially Jan Briedenbach, Stephen Portuges, Herb Schreier, Stephanie Soloman, and Judith Stacey—with whom I shared many exchanges into the wee hours about the perplexing relationships between radical politics, psychoanalysis, and feminism. I am most fortunate to have enjoyed the friendship and collaboration of my Latin American colleagues and *compañeros*, Julia Braun, Omar Cabezas, Nacho Maldonado, Juana Pereyra, Angela Pazarin, Janin Puget, Margaret Randall, Juan Carlos Volnovich, and Silvia Werthein, each of whom helped in one way or another to deepen my appreciation of Latin American political culture, to sharpen my understanding of the unique history of politics and psychoanalysis in the region, and to enhance my assessment of the life and work of Marie Langer.

I am grateful to my father, Maurice, for having bequeathed to me his love of Latin America and to my mother, Mildred, for having shown me the value of meaningful work. My special appreciation goes to my husband, Stephen Portuges, whose support, computer genius, and commitment to the values represented in this project have nurtured me throughout, and to our son, Rafael, who drew us both from the domain of theory to the daily politics of parenting and in the process taught us about the profound joy of motherhood and fatherhood.

As Marie Langer wished, the English version of *Motherhood and Sexuality* is dedicated to her daughters, Anna and Veronica.

My own contribution to this project is dedicated to my *compañera*, Marie, who will always be *presente*.

Preface to the First Edition

MARIE LANGER

This book is based principally on direct psychoanalytic observation of conflicts and difficulties experienced by women with respect to their femininity. Because this topic has always been of special interest to me, as a psychoanalyst I have paid special attention to the analysis of female reproductive disorders, first among my own analytic patients and later in the cases of other analysts who have consulted with me. In addition, many colleagues have shared with me psychoanalytic case material related to these disorders. This method of collecting clinical data is imposed by the nature of psychoanalysis, a discipline in which, because of the duration of treatment, the analyst treats far fewer patients than do other medical specialists.

The writings of Helene Deutsch and Melanie Klein have been especially useful in the theoretical conceptualization of female disorders. The important contributions of anthropologist Margaret Mead have helped me appreciate the extent to which these disorders may be culturally determined.

As I developed the basic idea for this book, it occurred to me that a specific theme needed to be elaborated because it formed part of my personal experience. Does a woman engaged in a professional career experience obstacles to her realization of motherhood and, if so, to what extent? Even in an era long since past, this question was a familiar one to me: During my adolescence it was a frequent topic of conversation among my girlfriends and comrades. Later I had to abandon the question at the theoretical level so that I might resolve it in practice. Only when I recently read a book with the alarmist title *Modern*

Woman, The Lost Sex [by Lundberg and Farnham (New York: Harper, 1942)], did I begin to think again about the possible incompatibility between motherhood and career. The authors of this book maintain that modern woman is losing her femininity because of changes in her role within the family and society. For them, the declining number of children and the increasing participation of women in the professional world represent a vicious circle that takes women further and further from their sexuality and, consequently, from their femininity. I began to struggle with this question—to observe, investigate, and analyze— and I came to the conclusions expounded at the end of this book.

It seems to me, however, that the essence of my conclusions belongs to this prologue. Biologically, women are capable of having a child every two years or at even briefer interludes. Women's instincts are biologically based. But, as in many other domains, our culture has alienated us from the full and direct gratification of our instincts. Thus, at the conscious level, women do not wish to have as many children as in previous eras. (I refer, of course, to women in our society.) The authors of *Modern Woman: The Lost Sex* are correct in arguing that although they are not often aware of it, women are frustrated in the gratification of their maternal instincts, which succumb to repression and are then later manifested in a variety of symptoms—frigidity, psychosomatic disorders and so on. But does the solution of this dilemma lie in returning to the large families of yesteryear and in once again reducing the arena of female activity exclusively to the home? Whether or not the idea seems attractive, it is not feasible to be diametrically opposed to the evolution of society. Another solution, fully in agreement with this evolution, would be to offer women the opportunity for sublimation in satisfying work, which would permit them to avoid the repression that is so prejudicial to part of their instincts. In other words, the remedy does not lie in suppressing their endeavors in the social sphere but, on the contrary, in educating women so that as adults they are capable of sublimating a part of their maternal instincts. Women would then accept their femininity and realize the gratification of instinctual life through sexual satisfaction and a more fulfilled motherhood, less encumbered by psychosomatic disorders.

While writing this book I became convinced of the need to provide a critical review of the psychoanalytic concept of femininity. My gratitude to Freud and to his great work—as with all psychoanalysts, my own experience has demonstrated to me the enormous benefits of health and knowledge offered by psychoanalysis—makes it seem in a way like a sacrilege to disagree with him on certain issues. However, what I question in this book are not fundamental viewpoints or concepts that Freud himself would have considered definitive. In one of his last and most important contributions to this subject, <u>Freud</u> characterizes psychoanalytic knowledge about femininity as "incom- plete and fragmentary," leaving the door open for new perspectives, concepts, and dialogue.

I wish to express my gratitude to all who helped me write this book: my husband, Dr. Max Langer, and Dr. Heinrich Racker, for their constructive criticism after reading the manuscript; Professor R. Rascovsky, for her linguistic corrections; Mr. D. J. Vogelman, for his technical assistance; and all my colleagues and analysands who, in one way or another, collaborated with me.

Buenos Aires
February 1951

Introduction to the English Translation

NANCY CARO HOLLANDER

Motherhood and Sexuality was first published in Buenos Aires in 1951. Its author, Viennese-born Marie Langer, had lived in Argentina for a little over a decade and, as one of the six founders of the Argentine Psychoanalytic Association in 1942, was a prominent figure in that country's psychoanalytic community. By the time the second edition was published in 1964, Marie Langer had become Latin America's foremost female psychoanalyst. *Motherhood and Sexuality* was read widely throughout South America by the lay public as well as her professional colleagues. A psychoanalytic study of psychosomatic disorders of female reproductive life, the book's central thesis represented a marked departure from contemporary mainstream psychoanalytic perspectives on femininity, which equated female mental health with the conservation of the traditional sexual division of labor. Langer argued that only when the economic institutions and cultural values of patriarchal society were altered to permit woman full participation in creative and productive activities beyond the domestic sphere would she be able to accept her maternal role without conflict and resentment.

In *Motherhood and Sexuality*, Marie Langer's discussion of psychoanalytic theory and presentation of clinical cases appeared within the context of a historical analysis of the economic, political, and cultural forces that have shaped and altered woman's unconscious life, reflecting Langer's attempt to integrate her political, feminist, and psychoanalytic understanding of the female experience. Indeed, her perspective anticipated by several decades contemporary feminist psychoanalytic endeavors to explain the social and psychological structures that reproduce female subordination and inhibit woman's satisfactory and nonconflictual realization of potential in every domain.

By the time *Motherhood and Sexuality* was translated for European distribution in the 1970s, Langer had become known internationally as a prominent spokesperson within the Latin American human rights movement, which opposed the traumatic policies of repressive Latin American military regimes. In the final years of her life her reputation as a Latin American psychoanalyst committed to progressive social change was further enhanced through her role as consultant to the Sandinista government's efforts to build Nicaragua's first national mental health care system. While Langer's passionate dedication to human emancipation found many different expressions from her youth until her death in 1987, she maintained a special commitment to understanding and challenging the social and psychological fetters that inhibit the realization of female desire and productivity.

It was during the last five years of her life, in the course of researching a biographical project on her life and work, that I came to know Marie Langer. Our collaboration on this and other projects emerged from our mutual commitment to radical social change, feminism, and a psychoanalysis dedicated to both personal and social transformation. Each of us had learned, through similar experiences in Argentina and Nicaragua, to appreciate the struggles of Latin American peoples to construct societies based on the principle of peace with justice. I visited Langer often in Mexico, where she lived in exile from the Argentine military government, and I had the opportunity to share many aspects of her personal, professional, and political life. I accompanied her to Nicaragua, where I observed her contributions to a unique convergence of psychoanalysis and radical politics. One could not help but be impressed by her strength, her consistency of values, and her ability to confront and accept contradictions in herself and others. In the process of working together on the biography, we decided that I should translate *Motherhood and Sexuality* so that it would be available to the English-speaking world.

This Introduction to *Motherhood and Sexuality* provides the reader with a sketch of Marie Langer's life from her birth until she wrote the book; it stresses those influences that helped to shape her approach to the subject of female psychosexual experience. In the Afterword, Langer's life following the publication of her book is examined, emphasizing the manner in which she subsequently elaborated its subject matter in light of her theoretical development and political experiences. Many of its psychoanalytic concepts she maintained intact; others she altered or abandoned in response either to the latest scientific discoveries or to new ideas emanating from the contemporary feminist movement or to lessons gleaned from her many experiences with women of various social classes, cultures, and political conditions. Until she died at the age of 77, Langer's political and professional engagement continued to deepen and alter her ideas about sexuality and motherhood. In both this Introduction and the Afterword all direct quotes, unless otherwise indicated, are taken from the more than 60 hours of interviews and conversations I taped with Langer from 1983 through 1987.

Vienna: The Formative Years[*]

Born Marie Lisbeth Glas in 1910, Marie Langer was the second of two daughters in a wealthy, progressive, and assimilated Jewish family in Vienna, Austria. Her father, Leopold, was a textile manufacturer whose frustrated intellectual ambitions had led to an interest in social movements and politics. Her mother, Margareth, was an attractive and volatile woman who as a young girl had been prevented from pursuing the studies she adored in favor of being groomed to make a good marriage. She was a "lady of leisure" who sustained herself while supervising the household's servants and mothering her two daughters by escaping into romantic and adulterous relations. Marie believed that she was "saved" from identifying with her mother because Margareth lavished special attention on her older sister, Gucki, who would grow up to embrace their mother's ideas about femininity and woman's role. "I can remember saying to myself, perhaps defensively, 'that's fine, I escape.' I left their domain and sought my own, perhaps out of fear of competing with them. . . . I developed a negative identification with my mother, rejecting all of the attributes I associated with her and Gucki, losing some of the positive ones in the bargain, like her love for music and ability to drive. But it permitted me the space to explore other interests." As a child Marie thought of herself as the privileged of the two sisters because she was the favorite of their father, for whom she was the son he never had.

Indeed, as a little girl, Marie believed that her family was characterized by two complementary dyads, a conviction reinforced as she grew older by the fact that her intellectual interests and professional aspirations seemed to be more understood and supported by her father than by her mother. It was Leopold, for example, who was

---

[*]All direct quotes, unless otherwise specified, are from taped interviews by the author with Marie Langer in Mexico and Nicaragua, 1983 through 1986, as part of the research for a biography of Langer.

responsible for the political discussions that highlighted the family's lively dinners with friends and relatives, especially after the Bolshevik Revolution, which he "viewed with a mixture of admiration and fear." Heated debates about the scandalous Alexandra Kollantay, a communist revolutionary and feminist who advocated free love, made a profound impression on the young Marie, as did the book she was given to read about Vera Figner, a Russian revolutionary who was also one of the century's first female doctors. It was these women who provided Marie with the first inkling of the possibility of an alternative to her mother's life.

But Marie would later conclude that much of her recollection of this family alignment was based on a wishful oedipal phantasy,* and she would come to appreciate how many of her choices as an adult had been based on an identification with her mother as well as with her father. For example, Margareth's life of domesticity generally hid her culture and talents, but these were mobilized when given the opportunity, as was the case during the First World War when Marie's father had gone to the front. Margareth seized the opportunity to put to use her notable cooking and organizational skills to establish a cafeteria in her home for Russian refugee children. It was a challenging charitable project, which she automatically abandoned when Leopold returned from the front, "as if she simply accepted without question that a wife did not do anything outside her domestic domain." Marie would come to say that in spite of all her mother's objections to her daughter's ambitions, "In some way I had her permission to dedicate myself to something meaningful beyond a woman's traditional role in the home, because when she thought she could do something else, she did it . . . perhaps I was for her, as well, the substitute son who had a right to do things."

---

*I have chosen to write "phantasy" in the tradition of English psychoanalysis rather than "fantasy" as is the custom in the United States for several reasons. Marie Langer was a follower of Melanie Klein, who believed that unconscious phantasy, the psychic representative of instinct as she saw it, is of central importance to infantile and adult mental life. Langer's concurrence with Klein's emphasis on the significance of unconscious phantasy will be apparent in her book. Some Kleinians have attempted to denote the difference between conscious daydreams or fictions and unconscious primary activity through the alternative spellings of "fantasy" and "phantasy" respectively. Langer was unable to employ this linguistic tool because in Spanish there is but one spelling, "fantasia." Rather than interpret which of the mental states Langer refers to throughout her book and alternating the spelling in the English translation, I use "phantasy" to avoid confusion and in order to represent her Kleinian orientation. I employ the same spelling in my Introduction and Afterword for the sake of uniformity. For an elaboration of the history of the concept and the implications of the alternative spelling, see J. Laplanche and J. B. Pontalis, The Language of Psychoanalysis (New York: W. W. Norton, 1973, pp. 314–319). For Klein's views of phantasy, see M. Klein, Envy and Gratitude and Other Works, 1946–1963 (New York: Free Press, 1975).

Moreover, Marie would come to attribute her interest in psychoanalysis and in psychosomatic disorders in part to her mother's own "intuitive grasp, though she had never read Freud, of the significant interplay between mind and body." Even when Marie was a child, for example, Margareth would explain her closer relationship to Marie's sister as a compensation for her emotional absence at the time of Gucki's birth due to her unhappiness in her marriage. Margareth seemed certain that Gucki had suffered as a result of not having been breast-fed and that, in contrast, her younger child, Marie, was extraordinarily strong and healthy because she had been more content when Marie was born and thus had breast-fed her for more than a year. Marie also grew up hearing the story of how her mother had developed a chronic heart condition; Margareth was fond of telling her that she, as a young girl, had been forced to end her studies in order to accompany her mother on a lengthy cruise and, in spiteful desperation, had responded with an acute attack of rheumatism, from which she suffered throughout her life. This tendency to understand her ailment as a response to an emotional upheaval was characteristic of Margareth, who inclined toward a psychological explanation of physical illness in general. Marie would recognize this quality in her mother as "an important element in my later interest in psychosomatic medicine," acknowledging, "For her attitude toward illness and health, I owe her a lot." As well, Marie's regrets for the confining limits of her mother's life—"She could have been Freud's Dora"—and her desire to repair Margareth's lost opportunities would be important elements in her commitment to feminism, through which she would be able to "reclaim the woman who was in my mother."

Growing Up: Politics and Psychoanalysis

These psychological insights concerning her mother's influence on her were not to come until adulthood. For the most part, during Marie's adolescence the struggles between mother and daughter were intense and occurred in the context of the exciting political and cultural milieu characteristic of the period between the two World Wars. Europe's only mass-based Social Democratic Party, which ruled "Red Vienna," made progressive advances in education, housing, social security, and health and fomented a cultural renaissance in which sexuality and the role of women were among the subjects frankly and critically treated in the theatre and the arts. At home the new values were given their more frivolous interpretation, as Margareth cut her hair, donned short skirts, took up smoking, and learned to drive a car. Books belonging to the new literature of open sexuality bedecked the reading tables of the family's living room, though Marie and her sister were expected to "save themselves for marriage." When Marie expressed the desire to abandon her traditional upper-class girls' school for one that would lead to a university education and ultimately to a profession, she and her father had to overcome her mother's stubborn resistance to the idea. Finally, Margareth agreed to allow Marie to enroll in the highly esteemed college preparatory *Schwarzwald Schule*, whose director and faculty were known for their active support of women's rights. One of her literature teachers would actually be a Social Democratic member of Parliament. Here Marie's Marxist and feminist instructors formally introduced her to a critical vision of the world and provided alternative role models to the limited life choices expected of women of her social class. Typical of the intellectual climate throughout Europe during this culturally fertile period, the academic environment encouraged students to investigate the sources of institutional and subjective limits on human productivity and pleasure and to envision a world less burdened by class antagonism and gender oppression. Students read Freud, exploring the provocative theories of psychoanalysis popular among intellectuals and artists of the era. While Marie did not devote her undivided attention to her classes—much of her curiosity was expressed in a girlish preoccupation with boys and "exciting but guilt-ridden" sexual experimentation—this remarkable education nonetheless represented the intellectual foundation of her radical view of the world and her subsequent professional and political development.

By the time Marie entered medical school in the early 1930s, political conditions in Austria were rapidly deteriorating and cultural experimentation was being choked by the rising tide of anti-Semitism and Austro-fascism. Her own life was deeply affected by a research semester she spent in Kiel, Germany, in 1932, during which she witnessed the mesmerizing effect of Hitler as he spoke at a Nazi mass rally. This experience would transform Marie's intellectually radical social analysis into a commitment to political activism. Following her return to Vienna she joined the Communist Party, convinced that "it was the only political party to comprehend the real danger of Nazism" and equally persuaded that "socialism was the only vehicle for the liberation of women from bourgeois morality and social and economic subordination." In the subsequent three years her life became a complicated jigsaw puzzle, whose professional and political parts were ultimately an unsuitable fit.

Absorbed in the increasingly dangerous struggle against the fascist attack on social democracy in Vienna, Marie simultaneously pursued her medical career. She had chosen to specialize in psychiatry, but because she was Jewish she was prohibited by Austro-fascist policy from acquiring clinical training in a hospital residency. It was through her continuation in the women's section of the medical school, where she worked with psychotic patients, that her interest began to shift toward psychoanalysis. She decided that a personal analysis would permit her to deepen her understanding of both her "own neurosis" and the suffering of her seriously disturbed patients. She approached her instructor, Heinz Hartmann, who referred her for analysis to Richard Sterba. After a year of analysis she applied to Freud's *Weiner Vereinigung Institut* to be trained as a psychoanalyst. Following an interview with Anna Freud she was accepted as a candidate and began her training, which included seminars with Helene Deutsch and supervision with Jeanne Lampl de Groot.

Marie endeavored to involve herself in her professional training, but did so at times with guilty feelings: "I was studying my umbilical cord while the world was blowing up around me." She felt increasingly pulled toward her antifascist political activities, even at the risk of her personal safety. Ultimately, living with psychoanalysis and· political activism proved to be an impossible task. As Austro-fascism became more repressive, the Vienna Institute grew alarmed, especially when psychoanalysis in Berlin came under attack by the Nazis for being a subversive ideology. Responding defensively, the Vienna Institute assumed a position of neutrality by passing a ruling prohibiting analysts and analysands from participating in clandestine organizations. Since Austro-fascism had already declared all political opposition—including Social Democracy itself—illegal, the ruling obliged all members to refrain from engagement in antifascist politics. It thus required that a choice be made between psychoanalytic training and political activism. Analysts were either forced to end the treatment of politically involved patients, therefore ignoring medical ethics, or patients who were political activists had to agree not to speak about politics during their analytic hours, countermanding the psychoanalytic rule of free association. After the institute's ruling Marie lived with increasing tension, worried that her activism would be discovered. She simultaneously felt disillusioned with the psychoanalytic community, which, from her perspective, had withdrawn from the challenge facing all democratic sectors of Austrian society to take a stand against fascist repression. Psychoanalysts, she believed, had acted naively, manifesting "psychological denial," as if refusing to respond to the persecution of Jewish analysts in Berlin and the elimination of all civil rights in Austria could assure survival of individual analysts or their profession. "I felt rage, I devalued psychoanalysis, and I knew that the Revolution was more important." Marie left the institute shortly afterward in order to finally immerse herself in the struggle against fascism.

By 1936 this struggle drew Marie to the Spanish Civil War, where she and Max Langer, a surgeon and her future husband, joined the efforts of the International Medical Brigades to defend the young Spanish Republic. In her first contact with Spanish political culture she marveled at its passion, joy, and comradeship, and was impressed by the respect afforded female political leaders. But soon the grim reality of war became devastating. She and Max spent months on the front operating on wounded and dying soldiers defending their country against the onslaught of Franco's forces. At first Marie worked as an anesthesiologist, but eventually she performed surgical procedures as well. One of the grueling frustrations was the number of amputations, without the possibility of prosthesis, that had to be performed. At the end of 1937 it was decided that Max and Marie would travel to France to buy machines for manufacturing prosthetic devices. When they were in France, word came that the Republic was beyond saving, and so they rejoined Marie's parents, who had moved to Czechoslovakia to be near her father's factory.

During those difficult years Marie had suffered several miscarriages. By the time she left Spain, she was seven months pregnant, and shortly after arriving in Nice, she went into premature labor; her baby girl, for lack of an incubator, died only three days after birth. Later in Czechoslovakia, Marie once again became pregnant; in her third month she began to hemorrhage so badly she had to be taken by ambulance to a hospital in the nearest town, Reichenberg. There, as she suffered another miscarriage, through the window of her room intruded the frightening sounds of a fascist demonstration, the loudspeakers blaring their intrusive messages of hatred and destruction. Nice and Reichenberg: the two most terrible times of Marie's life, filled with profound losses due as much to "the fear of bringing a child into a world torn apart by violence and death" as to her "unconscious ambivalence rooted in [her] complex relationship with [her] mother." In retrospect, Marie would see these painful experiences as pivotal to her subsequent professional interest in studying psychosomatic mechanisms in pregnancy, miscarriage, and premature birth.

This was to be the final chapter of Marie's life in Europe. With the triumph of fascism throughout the continent, she and Max, like tens of thousands more, fled the escalating holocaust. They emigrated to Uruguay, to be joined soon by her parents and sister. In the New World they found that European immigrants with skills, patience, and fortitude could begin again. Following several difficult and impoverished years, during which Marie and Max had the first two of their five children, they were able to move to Buenos Aires, the cosmopolitan capital city of Argentina, where Marie joined the small psychoanalytic community and resumed her professional interests. In 1942 she and five colleagues founded the Argentine Psychoanalytic Association (APA), destined to become Latin America's most prestigious center of psychoanalytic theory and practice.

Buenos Aires: Psychoanalysis in the New World

Buenos Aires was a propitious environment for the development of psychoanalysis. It was the most Europeanized center of Latin America, a huge metropolis whose ornate buildings, wide avenues, and cafe society were intended to be a faithful reflection of European tradition and culture. Anxious to emulate the latest in art, literature, and science on the continent, the Argentine intelligentsia had long been interested in psychology and psychoanalysis. However, with the establishment of the APA, psychoanalysis came to have a widespread impact on Argentine culture in general. A generation of practitioners built a rigorous training institute that welcomed candidates from many other Latin American countries and featured seminars and public lectures by prominent psychoanalysts from Europe and the United States. They also dedicated themselves to the dissemination of their discipline within scientific, artistic, and university circles, as well as through the mass media.[1]

During the next several decades Marie Langer dedicated her organizational talents to the development of institutionalized psychoanalysis in Argentina. She came to have a significant impact within her profession, not the least of which was due to her personal charisma. She was pretty and strikingly youthful, and her serious attitude toward work was embellished by her charming Viennese-accented Spanish, occasional coquettish behavior and a sense of humor that gently pointed up contradictions in herself as well as in others. She was an independent thinker, faithful to her understanding of the needs of her profession, even when she risked offending her colleagues.[2] Such was the case when she was instrumental in the establishment of the Argentine Association of Psychology and Group Psychotherapy, which many APA members opposed on the grounds that psychoanalysis could not be practiced in the group setting.[3]

Marie Langer's personal dynamism and skills as a clinician attracted a loyal following, which gave her voice considerable weight in the internal struggles within the APA that inevitably developed over the years.[4] In fact, the APA became for a time "a type of political activism, the only kind," said Langer, "I felt secure enough to engage in because of my immigrant status and the unpredictable nature of Argentine politics." Like many of her colleagues, Langer developed a Kleinian orientation in her work, especially with respect to Melanie Klein's ideas about female psychosexual development, which she found to be "an important corrective to the phallocentric aspects of Freud's ideas about femininity." Although Langer wrote and lectured on many topics, she became best known among colleagues throughout Latin America during the fifties and sixties for her work on various aspects of female psychosomatic disorders. International recognition of this work was won through presentation of papers at congresses of the International Psychoanalytic Association.[5]

Langer's success brought her family a comfortable life and a secure place within a tight-knit network of friends and colleagues. But difficult choices had to be made, and the hours dedicated to psychoanalysis meant time away from her husband and their children. Indeed, her husband assumed more than the usual fatherly interest in their children's schooling and social relations, taking up the slack created by their mother's full work schedule. Eventually, though, Langer learned to balance the demands of career and motherhood by confining professional engagements to the workweek and maintaining inviolate her weekends with family and friends at *Escobar*, the Langers' country house.[6]

The Psychosocial Contradictions of Femininity

Marie Langer's professional interest in the psychogenesis of psychosomatic disorders of female sexual and reproductive life emerged in the course of her reencounter with psychoanalysis. Because she was the only woman among the six founders of the APA and, in the formative years of the development of the field, one of the few practicing female psychoanalysts in Buenos Aires, colleagues tended to refer female patients to her, some of whom suffered from psychological difficulties related to infertility. Although Langer's treatment did not focus on these particular symptoms, a notable impact of therapy was the resolution of fundamental conflicts associated with motherhood, resulting in successful pregnancies. In her search for a theoretical framework within psychoanalysis that could adequately address this conflictual female state, Langer was led to reject Freud's ideas about female sexuality, which she "felt did not resonate with the clinical material derived from [her] female patients or effectively reflect the essence of [her] own experience as a woman."

Although Langer was influenced by the work of Helene Deutsch, Karen Horney, and other female psychoanalysts, it was during the course of supervising the translation of Melanie Klein's work from German to Spanish that Langer discovered another psychoanalytic approach to understanding femininity, one that, from her perspective, more adequately captured the nature of female identity and the sources of woman's psychological conflict. While critical of Klein's theory of female development for its failure to link unconscious mental states to social conditions and cultural values, she nonetheless found in Klein's ideas about female sexual development a challenge to the view that conceptualized female experience in the shadow of male development. In Klein, Langer found an acceptance of woman's innate reproductive capacity as the source of a particular feminine psychological identity and an exploration of a specifically female psychobiological experience, including unconscious phantasies and anxieties that exist from infancy on related directly to this latent reproductive ability. Furthermore, Langer was drawn to Klein's concepts of the infantile world, including her views of the central significance of the unconscious mechanism of projective identification; her emphasis on the importance of object relations as well as instincts in the formation of psychic structure; her view that the Oedipus complex exists in the first year of life, focused mainly around the infant's rivalry with father and siblings, born and not yet born, for mother's love; and her assertion that the female infant's unconscious angry attacks on the mother because of her nonexclusive love result in the female fear of the destruction of her internal organs due to mother's retaliation. For Langer, these ideas were an accurate representation of the intrapsychic condition that could produce woman's conflict about sexuality and motherhood. And although Klein painted a particularly violent portrait of the human infant's unconscious phantasy world, she also indicated that the severity of the infant's unconscious drama and its destructive effects could be gradually ameliorated if in reality a good and nurturing mother were the stimulus for strengthening the good internal objects. It was this assertion and the centrality of the concept of reparation that permitted Langer, always a firm believer in the ability of the human spirit to struggle for good, to accept Klein's view of unconscious mental life, which she believed she detected in her patients' associations and in their transference relationship to her. Langer was able to utilize Kleinian concepts to interpret the concrete issues emerging in the material of her female patients, who came from Argentina's bourgeois and middle classes. While her patients "often manifested penis envy, castration feelings and a masculine identification, [she] came to understand these phenomena as defenses against more profound conflicts related to their fears of the destruction of their femininity."

As a psychoanalyst Langer witnessed an intensifying conflict experienced by Argentine women with respect to their professional aspirations and maternal role. Since the 1930s economic and social developments in the country had created increasing possibilities for women in the wage-labor force. Industrial expansion in Argentina had advanced at such a rapid rate that by 1950 women had come to represent well over a quarter of the country's wage earners and salaried employees. In Buenos Aires alone almost one-half of the women between 18 and 29 years of age worked to sustain themselves or to contribute to family income.[7] Even though working-class women had found work alternatives to domestic service in the expanding industrial sector, they still provided the vast numbers of domestic servants that were needed by middle-class women who were rapidly entering the professional world. The ideological response to the changing role of women was reminiscent of prevailing attitudes in North American and European cultures. Like their counterparts elsewhere, working women in Argentina were blamed for a number of real and imagined problems in their country. Beginning in the 1930s notable intellectuals and political economists blamed those women working outside the home for what they viewed as a series of national crises, such as a declining birth rate, the deteriorating moral significance of the family, the increasing unemployment rate among men due to "unfair" competition of cheap female labor, and the consequent decline in the dominant position of the father within the family structure. This catastrophic view of the threat of female equality was countered politically and ideologically by the powerful Peronist movement, whose leader, Juan Peron, was president of Argentina from 1946 to 1955. Together he and his wife, the charismatic Evita Peron, advocated women's rights, legalized women's suffrage, and mobilized women nationally in the Peronist Women's Movement. While this movement appealed mainly to women of the working class, its progressive politics had a widespread impact on cultural attitudes toward women's participation in activities outside the domestic sphere.[8] Thus, many of the patients who sought psychoanalysis with Marie Langer manifested psychological conflicts about motherhood that were exacerbated by the new opportunities for women outside the family and by the contradictory attitudes and expectations in Argentine culture regarding woman's appropriate role in life.

In the late forties Langer read *Modern Woman: The Lost Sex*, by Ferdinand Lundberg and Marynia Farnham,[9] and was struck by the authors' depiction of a similar drama in the United States. Their argument that modern woman was losing her femininity because of her successful battle to achieve equality with males in the political, professional, and social arenas appeared to address much of what Langer had seen in her own clinical practice. But she rejected their prescriptive assertion that the endangered maternal instinct could only be protected through the return of women to the limited sphere of maternal domesticity, a perspective echoed in much of the psychoanalytic literature in the post–World War II period. Since Langer's psychological observation and understanding were framed by her feminist and politically radical intellectual formation, she advocated as the remedy for contemporary woman's conflict and diminished capacity to find fulfillment in motherhood institutional reforms that would facilitate the expansion rather than the restriction of the socially acceptable domains of female activity.

Langer's contribution to the discourse in the post–World War II era about the vicissitudes of contemporary female experience was *Motherhood and Sexuality*, in which she chose to focus on the psychosomatic disorders of female reproductive life. Her introduction elucidated the social, economic, and cultural forces that throughout history had framed female psychological experience. Because the various editions of the book contain two different versions of the introduction, the main arguments of both are integrated and summarized here.

Langer offered the following thesis in order to situate her historical discussion and clinical material. Until the 20th century, she wrote, woman had been subjected to social and sexual restrictions that had favored the development of her maternal functions. Narrow parameters had fostered repression of sexuality and creativity in general, resulting frequently in hysteria and other neurotic symptoms. Women seldom seemed to manifest psychosomatic disorders of reproduction. However, since the turn of the century, women in Western culture had acquired sexual and social liberties hardly imagined in earlier times. New economic and social imperatives had created a conflictual condition for women with respect to their maternal role. The general neurotic picture of hysteria had been superseded by a dramatic increase in psychosomatic problems of infertility among women who did not necessarily present a general picture of neurosis. Instead, they suffered a basic conflict with respect to their femininity.

Langer argued that Freud had misinterpreted the dilemma of woman in "Civilization and Its Discontents," his analysis of mankind's hostility to contemporary culture because of its repression of instinctual life. Freud explained woman's resentment toward civilization as a reaction to the manner in which society tended to draw the male away from the home into a world that she could not share because of her biological investment in her family. Thus Freud believed that woman resented society for robbing her of a partner, with little compensation in return. Langer saw this as a misreading of female discontent. She emphasized that woman's antagonism to contemporary culture is due to the fact that she herself is prohibited from expressing her creative capacity in the social sphere because it conflicts with her family duties and satisfactions. This dilemma—the conflict between social engagement and motherhood—had become more troubling in the modern era following the incorporation of women into the public sphere since the First World War. Popular culture was rife with the articulation of fears about woman's newfound political and economic gains, which were interpreted as a threat to social stability and the family. Why, asked Langer, should this predicament exist, and to what extent did this gendered division of labor, which allocated to woman a limited domain of expression along with a subordinate status, represent a universal condition? She sought the answer in the Marxist analysis of the historical origins of patriarchy and in the anthropological exploration of the impact of culture on gender roles.

Citing Friedrich Engels's theory of the origins of patriarchy, Langer suggested that the oppression of woman by man—the original class antagonism—had emerged historically with the human capacity to produce a surplus, the male's appropriation of that surplus and his wish to control woman so that he could guarantee legitimate heirs for his property. In this way patriarchy had been born, initiating the centuries-long tradition of socially imposed restrictions on woman's sphere of activity. The customary and legal inferior position of women had been justified historically through arguments related to female biology. However, the recent changes in woman's role had provoked anthropologists to question these arguments rationalizing female subordination. Their investigations indicated that, in all likelihood, prior to the development of patriarchy matriarchal societies had existed, in which the biological capacity of females to reproduce and nurture the young had won them social power and status instead of a position of inferiority.

In order to illustrate this point, Langer reviewed anthropological studies by Margaret Mead and Abraham Kardiner, which delineated the varied ways different cultures organize gender relations and define masculinity and femininity. She was also interested in demonstrating through selected examples from primitive societies the varied nature of the social organization of human psychic processes and the manner in which the components of psychic structure are mobilized so as to produce cultural and national difference as well as specific types of neuroses. First she described the Arapesh, whom she believed retain characteristics of matriarchal social patterns in that the male exercises dominance over the female through rituals and actions that emulate the nurturing and caregiving mother–infant relationship in the social sphere. It is, Langer wished to point out, the male's maternal relationship to the woman that legitimizes his power over her. Then she turned to an examination of the society of the Marquesas islands, where the role of women reveals similarities with that of women in contemporary Western culture.

In the Marquesas islands, women enjoy sexual and social equality, which is paid for, according to Langer, by the repression of their maternal instinct. Among the Marquesans, women are highly esteemed for their sexuality and prohibited from developing intimate relations with their infants, who in their fourth month of life are given over to others for caretaking. As a result, there is among women a rejection of pregnancy, expressed in the widespread practice of birth control, the frequency of abortion, and low birth rates. Moreover, pregnancy is considered to be very dangerous, a belief seemingly borne out in the surprisingly high rate of maternal deaths in childbirth.

Unconscious conflict among the women of the Marquesas islands, wrote Langer, is reflected in their mythology. The female experience of being frustrated by their mothers in infancy and of being deprived of their maternal functions by men in adulthood is manifested in two categories of supernatural beings. The *fanauas* are the spirits of dead men at the service of a specific woman, which can be sent to do evil to a hated rival by destroying the fetus in her womb or killing her during childbirth. The *vehini-hai*, or wild women, also destroy fetuses and steal little children in order to eat them. In this culture what the women fear most is suffering unspeakable aggressions from other women. Langer suggested that while these women, whose sexual and social equality exist alongside the renunciation of all maternal satisfaction, come from a completely different social organization from that of modern Western culture, they nonetheless share with modern woman an unconscious conflict about reproduction. In the Marquesans this conflict is manifested in the mythical *vehini-hai*; in contemporary Western societies, in female psychosomatic disorders. This argument would be demonstrated clinically in subsequent chapters, but first Langer turned her attention to the historical process responsible for the dilemma of contemporary woman.

She began by analyzing the legacy of the historical changes wrought by the French Revolution and the emergence of industrial capitalism. Asserting that the preindustrial family had been a unit of production and consumption in which female labor was acknowledged to be central to its survival and prosperity, she indicated how women had become marginalized from production with the advent of industrial capitalism and the separation of the home from the workplace, a process that had drawn the man of the family out into the factories to produce in the commercial sphere that which had traditionally been made within the family by women. Many women of the poorer classes had been drawn into factory labor as well, and for them the "double day," combining paid work with unremunerated work in the home, emerged as the typical burden of working-class women. Each additional pregnancy became a family crisis because it temporarily withdrew women from the wage-labor force. Women in the agricultural sector had experienced fewer immediate alterations in their traditional division of labor, being subject instead to a centuries-long process of alteration in land ownership that forced the migration of families from rural areas to urban centers, where their quality of life often deteriorated in the exploitative and corrupt city slums and shantytowns.

By the turn of the century, wrote Langer, by and large, middle-class women's lives had not changed, in spite of the feminist movement that had arisen to protest their legal and political subordination. It was, she claimed, the First World War that offered both the middle- and working-class woman the possibility to participate in the public sphere, a dramatic change that proved to be irrevocable. From her perspective, although women remained in the wage-labor force in both the United States and Europe, it was in the Soviet Union that the radical alteration of opportunities for women occurred, owing to the Socialist revolution and its Marxist ideology.

Langer challenged those social critics, including her psychoanalytic colleagues, who interpreted this historical process as a threat to the family and woman's natural role and who advocated a return to the past. For her, those who opposed change specifically when it altered woman's relationship to the family and the social sphere represented continuity with the traditional belief in the natural inferiority of woman, a view she believed to have many functions and to be sustained by social and psychological factors. The way she saw it, the latter stem from earliest infancy, in which the child resents the mother for its complete dependency on her and for her inability in phantasy or reality to satisfy its every need. According to Langer, this fear of dependency is complicated by the infant's unconscious rivalry, envy, and fear. These early sentiments remain as an unconscious fear of the omnipotent mother, which is expressed defensively within patriarchy through the social control of women. The psychological basis for maintaining women in a status of inferiority is rationalized through an ideological apparatus that induces an attitude of resignation among women toward the limited parameters of their lives. Deprived of socially acceptable avenues of discharge, women express their conflict within the family constellation. This division of labor, though detrimental to women, had maintained social stability and provided both male and female with a set of strictly defined and predictable expectations until the 20th century.

The preceding discussion has integrated the substance of the two different versions of the introductory chapter of *Motherhood and Sexuality*. However, the note on which Langer ended the 1951 version was polemical. She critiqued the feminist response to the historical changes affecting women since the turn of the century. In her estimation the feminist demand for women's equality with men tended to ignore the fact that the quality of life for most men in industrial capitalism was dismal and deserving of alteration rather than emulation. Bourgeois feminists demanded equal pay for equal work without critiquing surplus value, that is, the expropriation of labor power of the male working class by its capitalist employer. Moreover, bourgeois feminists demanded sexual equality for women without providing a critique of the quality of alienated sexuality underwritten by a male-dominated society. Langer also believed that while feminists had struggled for social reforms in general, they tended to emphasize the more narrow vindication of their rights with respect to men, whom they resented and simultaneously admired. Furthermore, she wrote, the focus of feminist energies on the struggle for suffrage from the turn of the century through the 1920s had resulted in acquisition of women's political rights without having resolved the fundamental sociopsychological conflicts of modern woman.

Langer continued her argument, positing that Marxism helped to explain how woman's dependency was the consequence of relations based on private property, which was the basis of patriarchy. The majority of women found themselves in a situation, therefore, that is identical to that of any person deprived of the means of production and exploited by those who own them. The Marxist view that woman was in the same position as the worker pointed to a struggle to modify the destiny of both. From the Marxist perspective, the theoretical issue was not sexual difference but class struggle, which included the fight for economic, political, and sexual equality for women. Langer postulated that in the Soviet Union, for example, legislative and social reforms undertaken by the government to conserve the family had created the possibility for women to be mothers and also participate in social labor, which was reflected in the country's rising birthrate. She saw the Socialist program as the most adequate attempt thus far to facilitate woman's "masculine" needs and ambitions without prejudicing her femininity. Admitting that it was too soon to judge the social changes occurring in the Soviet Union, she nonetheless supported what she interpreted to be their attempts in practice to do everything possible so that woman could satisfactorily integrate her political participation, work life, and maternal functions.

Langer concluded the 1951 version of *Motherhood and Sexuality* by distinguishing her perspective from those she had reviewed. On the one hand, she disagreed with the conservative psychoanalytic position regarding the conflict of modern woman, which from her perspective was based on a narrow conceptualization of the feminine and an unrealizable and absurd phantasy of turning back the historical clock to a time in the past when women were ostensibly happier and less conflicted about their femininity. She also disagreed with the feminist vision, which she believed denied sexual difference, as well as with the anthropological inclination to consider masculinity and femininity as human attributes arbitrarily determined by culture. Both male and female, she insisted, must be understood in terms of their biological, psychological, and reproductive imperatives, all of which form a gendered character with the capacity for multifaceted creative expression.

In the 1964 version Langer ended the introductory chapter on a much gentler note, eliminating the more politically radical aspects of her conclusions in the earlier edition. This decision was in part due to the pressure exerted by a publisher who was intimidated by the unpredictable political climate in Argentina and to Langer's wish to see her book once more in print. But she was also willing to write a new ending because in the intervening years she had grown cynical about the nature of socialism in the Soviet Union and about the possibility that socialism would automatically liberate women, especially without the existence of a strong women's movement. Thus, in the 1964 version she focused on the anxieties suffered by contemporary women attempting to integrate the multiple demands of motherhood and career.[10]

Langer expressed her agreement with psychoanalytic and other observations that increasing opportunities for women had resulted in a confusing array of expectations. For middle-class married women, the norms of conduct were no longer well defined. The combination of maternal and professional aspirations represented complex new pressures. The female was now expected to bear and raise children, retain a job with hours and duties like those of her husband, be responsible for housework, maintain her physical attractiveness, remain psychologically available for her husband, and successfully negotiate the vaginal orgasm, sexual proof of her mature womanhood. Langer thought that these multiple roles, presented as new possibilities for self-realization, in reality resulted in increasing demands with a built-in guarantee of failure. Any woman in this situation was destined to feel inadequate in every domain and vulnerable to blaming herself for her perceived failure. On the other hand, the middle-class married woman who was exclusively a homemaker found her work increasingly devalued because of its invisibility, with the concomitant result that she felt less interesting and useful than her husband and women in the professional world. Moreover, in a highly mechanistic society, often women did not know how to enjoy mothering, fearing that their love could do harm to their infants. It was ironic, Langer pointed out, that the job of the psychoanalytically oriented pediatrician was to authorize the mother to love her baby and follow a natural rhythm rather than a rigid feeding and changing schedule imposed by some scientific "expert" in child-rearing.[11]

Langer related these conditions to the intensification of conflictual attitudes toward mothering. Women suffered from increased difficulties in their reproductive life, some could not become pregnant at all, and many had problematic relationships with their children. Each of these conditions was a manifestation of woman's rejection of motherhood, indicating a discordance with her sex and thus with her very existence. But, asked Langer, was it necessary that women become mothers in order to fully realize themselves, or, put another way, was maternity a fundamental aspect of female instinctual life? In woman, she argued, there exists a constant interrelationship between biological and psychological processes. During the period from menarche until menopause—the most important of female life—biological processes destined for maternity are developed; each month a woman's body is prepared to receive the fertilized egg and to harbor the fetus. Langer referred to the works of Benedek and Rubenstein,[12] which had demonstrated that psychological changes accompanied these physiological rhythms and were reflected in alterations of the intensity of sexual desire and manifested in dream content. Langer indicated that possibly women who use birth control, consciously discounting the possible consequences of coitus, unconsciously relate sexual pleasure to the phantasy of pregnancy and childbirth. And to the assertion that many women appear to be happy and capable of a satisfying sexual life without ever having been mothers, she maintained that this happiness is often based on a repression of the conflict that would succumb later on to menopausal depression when the woman realizes she has definitively lost her possibility of being a mother. While Langer recognized that a woman who does not have children could be happy if she managed a satisfactory sublimation of her maternal instinct, she believed contemporary woman would be most satisfied with her life if she lived by the old Chinese proverb: "To be able to calmly confront old age and death, one has to have had a child, planted a tree, and written a book." A woman who arrived at this transcendent position, at peace with herself, would raise and nurture happy children, giving them in infancy the basic sense of internal security that would enable them to live a satisfying and productive life in a very insecure world.

The introductory chapter established the context for the subsequent chapters, in which Langer presented a review of the psychoanalytic literature on female sexuality and her detailed analysis of woman's unconscious conflict as manifested in psychosomatic disorders related to menstruation, pregnancy, infertility, labor, lactation, and so on. In 1972, when another edition of the book was to be published, Langer wrote a prologue in which she questioned whether the social changes that had taken place during the decade since its last publication, as well as the modifications in her own thinking about different aspects of sexuality and motherhood, did not, in fact, require a complete revision of the book. She went on to write that in order to update her analysis she would have to address many issues not included in the prior editions and also to suggest the ways in which she had changed her mind about some of the theories she had previously argued. She would, she asserted, have to alter the material on the vaginal orgasm and frigidity so as to include the contemporary thinking about female orgasm resulting from the Masters and Johnson research and the feminist critique of Freud; she would be obliged to reconstruct her psychoanalytic arguments, situating them within the class and social determinants of woman's unconscious conflicts; and she would need to address the history of women's struggles for liberation from the fetters of patriarchal culture. But, she demurred, such an endeavor would require a great deal of thought and time, "and in Argentina, in 1972, there was very little opportunity for either." So she had agreed to the new edition of the book, believing that even without any changes in the text, its psychoanalytic content was essentially still accurate. She ended the prologue by promising the reader to write, as soon as possible, a study that would address the important questions omitted in *Motherhood and Sexuality*.[13]

Notes

1. Interviews with Argentine psychoanalysts Arnaldo Rascovsky, Jorge Mom, and Mauricio Abadi, Buenos Aires, August, 1990.

2. Interviews with Argentine psychoanalyst Juan Carlos Volnovich, Miami, December 1989 and Buenos Aires, August, 1990.

3. M. Langer, "La mujer, la locura y la sociedad," in S. Marcos (ed.), *Antipsiquiatria y Politica* (Mexico: E. Extemporaneos S.A., 1978, pp. 181–193).

4. Interviews with Argentine Psychoanalysts Mauricio Abadi and Edwardo Zimmerman, Buenos Aires, August, 1991.

5. See, for example, M. Langer, "Envy and Sterility," *International Journal of Psychoanalysis, 34* (pts. 2–4, March–August, 1958): 139–143.

6. Interviews with Marie Langer's sons, Tomas Langer and Martin Langer, Buenos Aires, August 1991.

7. N. C. Hollander, "Women Workers and the Class Struggle: The Case of Argentina," *Latin American Perspectives,* issues 12 & 13, nos. 1 & 2 (1977): 180–193; for a more extensive discussion of the history of women in the labor force and their political response, see N. C. Hollander, "Women in the Political Economy of Argentina," (Ph. D. diss., University of California, Los Angeles, 1974); also see M. Carlson, *Feminismo!* (Chicago: Academy Chicago Publishers, 1988).

8. N. C. Hollander, "Si Evita Viviera...," *Latin American Perspectives 1,* no. 3 (1974): 42–57; see also N. Fraser and M. Navarro, *Eva Peron* (New York: Norton, 1980).

9. M. Farnham and F. Lundberg, *Modern Woman, the Lost Sex* (New York & London: Harper and Brothers, 1942).

10. Interview with Marie Langer, Mexico, December 1986.

11. It might be pointed out that while Langer agreed with other psychoanalysts in the object relations tradition within psychoanalysis on the primary influence of the mother–child relation on psychosexual development, she did not, like her counterparts in the fifties, privilege the preoedipal period only to then lay complete responsibility—and blame—on women for their children's psychological destinies. Throughout the text of *Motherhood and Sexuality* Langer reminds the reader that social constraints on women lead to their difficulties in mothering and thus to possible psychological disorders in their daughters. For a feminist discussion of the prevailing themes in the psychoanalytic literature about women during the fifties and sixties, see B. Ehrenreich and D. English, *For Her Own Good: 150 Years of the Experts' Advice to Women* (New York: Anchor Books, 1979).

12. T. Benedek and B. Rubenstein, *The Sexual Cycle in Women: The Relation between Ovarian Function and Psychodynamic Processes* (Washington, DC: National Research Council, 1942); see also T. Benedek, *Psychosexual Functions in Women* (New York: Ronald Press, 1952).

13. M. Langer, Prologo, *Maternidad y Sexo* (Barcelona: Ediciones Paidos, 1972).

Review of the Psychoanalytic Literature on Femininity

This book is about the conflict of modern woman and its manifestation in psychosomatic disorders of female reproductive life.[*] In this chapter I shall explore the contributions of the science of psychoanalysis toward a profound understanding of female conflict and its symptomatology. I begin with a review of Freud's ideas about femininity as elaborated in his writings from the early decades of the 20th century on, after which I trace the evolution and modification of his thought in the work of other important psychoanalytic thinkers.

---

[*]Langer conceptualizes the psychosomatic symptom in reproductive disorders as a physiological manifestation of unresolved conflicts of femininity whose etiology can be traced to frustrations in the early preoedipal relationship to the mother. This view—that psychosomatic illness develops with an underlying neurotic structure based on conflicts of the preoedipal phases, with fixation points and regression to the oral and anal phases of development—is shared by others within psychoanalysis; see, for example, M. Sperling, *Psychosomatic Disorders in Childhood* (New York: Jason Aronson, 1978). D. Pines, in a recently published article, "Pregnancy, Miscarriage, and Abortion: A Psychoanalytic Perspective," *International Journal of Psychoanalysis* 71 (1990), pp. 301, 306, echoes Langer's perspective in stating that many women who suffer from psychogenic infertility "may have unconsciously somatized their childhood emotional difficulties by using their bodies to avoid unconscious affects and fantasies which have felt overwhelming to the young child's ego . . . Mind and bodily changes influence each other in a woman's monthly and developmental cycle and the intimate link between them allows a woman unconsciously to use her body in an attempt to avoid psychic conflict." However, it is important to note that some investigators have developed specific subcategories within the general area of psychosomatic disorders. For example, recurrent multiple somatic complaints of several years' duration that

First and foremost, Freud studied the development of infantile sexuality in the male. For him, the "standard" sex was masculine. He attributed the same development to women, until the fateful moment when the girl realizes the anatomical difference between the sexes. According to Freud, this recognition generally occurs when the little girl reaches 3 or 4 years of age. He argues that the girl always reacts to this discovery with an immediate feeling of inferiority, an envious desire to possess the masculine genitalia and a devaluation of her own sex. Her interpretation of her lack of a penis is that she has suffered a genital mutilation. This psychological process is assumed to be independent of the girl's social environment. With the first disillusionment behind her, the girl slowly and with great conflict reconciles herself to her own sex, although throughout her life she will experience a certain degree of resentment because of her femininity. Furthermore, says Freud, the lack of a penis, considered by the girl to be an almost organic inferiority, may result in a psychological, cultural, and moral inferiority.[1] And since characteristics of each sex exist in both man and woman (concept of bisexuality), this inferiority is not contradicted by the emotional and intellectual qualities of some superior women,

---

cannot be explained by a physical disorder, including those of a reproductive and sexual nature, are included in the category of "somatization disorders" (American Psychiatric Association, *Quick Reference to the Diagnostic and Statistical Manual of Mental Disorders*, third edition, revised, Washington, DC, APA, 1980, pp. 139–140). In the past several decades psychosomatic illness has been studied in order to differentiate its specific qualities from both neurotic and psychotic dynamics. In France, P. Marty and M. de M'Uzan have suggested that the "psychosomatic personality" is marked by what they call "operatory" thinking, a pragmatic and affectless way of relating to oneself and others in which the body manifests what the individual is unable to feel and communicate in any other way. *Alexithymia* refers to the character of such an individual who has no words to describe her emotional states, either because she is unaware of them or because she is incapable of distinguishing one emotion from another, thus communicating through the body that which can be expressed in no other way. From Joyce McDougall's perspective (*Theaters of the Body: A Psychoanalytic Approach to Psychosomatic Illness*; New York: Norton, 1989), it is important to distinguish between patients with a neurotic psychic organization, in which psychologically disturbing thoughts and feelings have been denied or repressed and thus unconsciously registered, and psychosomatic patients, in whom there is a regression to more primitive forms of relationship between body and mind that produce somatic reactions as an expression of a struggle to protect oneself from archaic libidinal and narcissistic longings felt to be life-endangering. Here there is a distinction made between the symbolic nature of hysterical and obsessional symptoms and the primitive psychic message of warning to the body that bypasses the use of language so that the danger cannot be thought about. We shall see that Langer did not make such a distinction but, rather, viewed disturbances in sexuality and reproduction as the bodily (symbolic) representations of primitive conflicts rooted in the unsatisfactory infantile relationship to the mother and the consequent inability to identify with a nurturing and life-giving maternal imago.

because their capacities are simply a manifestation of masculine tendencies. Woman's inferior condition results from her psychobiological development and is, therefore, somewhat independent of family and cultural environment.

This concept was accepted by Freud's early collaborators and still characterizes much psychoanalytic thought today. However, it is not by mere coincidence that it has been mainly female psychoanalysts, younger than Freud by several decades, who have discovered the defensive character of penis envy. The first to investigate this subject, although with a certain polemical tone, was Karen Horney. Afterward, using the concept of unconscious phantasy to study the psychological experiences of the first year of life, Melanie Klein and her school were able to demonstrate that from virtually the beginning of life both girls' and boys' experiences are framed by their sex and their biology.

Melanie Klein and other female analysts were able to go further than was possible for Freud with regard to feminine psychology, thanks to him and his ingenious discoveries. Important as well is the fact that these female psychoanalysts already belonged to another era, and neither they nor the female patients they studied were hampered by negative assumptions about female inferiority.

I shall now review the psychoanalytic literature on femininity, which will serve as a foundation for the analysis of the clinical material that follows. But first a summary of Freud's concept of infantile sexuality is in order because it led him to include a group of instinctual manifestations not previously considered to be part of the concept of "sexuality."

By 1905 Freud had described the development of infantile sexuality in broad strokes in "Three Essays on the Theory of Sexuality." The conclusions of his study were obtained through the analysis of adults, that is to say, through a somewhat speculative procedure. However, when some years later he had the opportunity to directly observe the development of an infantile neurosis in a young child, whom he cured completely by intervening through the father ("Analysis of a Phobia in a Five-Year-Old Boy"), Freud proved the veracity of the concepts developed through his analysis of adults. This child, who appeared to be perfectly normal during the entire time he was making himself ill with a phobia, already had a rich sexual life expressed through feelings, urges, and conflicts.

This first direct psychoanalytic observation of a child was done with a male. In "Three Essays on the Theory of Sexuality," Freud also dedicated his principal interest to the evolution of male sexuality. Later he would complete his theory with contributions on the evolution of female sexuality. I will base my own discussion on Richard

Sterba's summary of Freud's thought in *Introduction to the Psychoanalytic Theory of the Libido* and on Karl Abraham's conceptualization of the two stages of each phase of development in "A Short History of the Development of the Libido."

The sexual pleasure corresponding to the "first oral phase" is sucking. The child feels as much pleasure in sucking at the maternal breast and swallowing the milk, thereby satisfying her nutritional needs,* as she does in sucking her finger or a pacifier, thus stimulating the oral mucosa without assuaging her hunger. So, too, in the rest of the phases it can be observed that the child experiences sexual satisfactions in the very organs and zones that fulfill an important function of self-preservation. But the search for pleasure usually becomes independent of the need for self-preservation, sometimes to such a point that it often turns into the opposite of self-preservation. The desired object in the first oral phase is the maternal breast or its substitute, the bottle. Abraham called this phase "preambivalent," that is, free of the conflict between love and hate, because upon swallowing the milk the child does not yet experience hostility toward the breast that feeds her, nor does she realize that upon swallowing the milk she destroys it.

In the second, or cannibalistic, oral phase this situation is distinct. When the first teeth appear the nature of the search for pleasure changes profoundly. This search is still centered mainly in the mouth, although the mode is no longer sucking but biting and chewing. Now the infant wishes to use her teeth and to destroy all the objects with which she comes into contact. In her phantasies she treats the persons connected to her as food. She desires to eat them because she loves them. And because she hates and fears them, she wishes to destroy them, to chew them up. These phantasies, which are manifest in neurotic and psychotic patients, as well as in fairy tales and myths, have a cannibalistic character. We have only to recall as an example the story of "Little Red Riding Hood." In this period the child realizes that the breast forms part of her mother, whom she now wishes to consume completely. In the child's wish to eat her loved ones is contained the fear of being eaten by them. The desire to eat includes simultaneously loving feelings and aggressive urges and is thus connected to the conflict of ambivalence.

In infantile development the anal erotogenic zone comes to substitute for the oral zone. During infancy the child has had pleasant

---

*I have decided to approach the use of gender pronouns when referring to the infant or child in the following manner. So as to avoid the traditional bias inherent in the universal use of the masculine pronoun "he" I shall generally translate references to the child as "she". However, in paragraphs which contain references to both mother and child, I will use "he" to refer to the child for the sake of clarity.

sensations in this zone during evacuation and while being cleaned by her mother or treated by her physician, especially during the administration of enemas or suppositories. But only at the beginning of the third year does her principal erotic pleasure concentrate around this zone. Now she experiences the act of excretion with a pleasure that in a certain sense can be considered the precursor of intercourse, with the fecal material substituting for the penis and the anal mucosa substituting for the vagina.

This phase and its corresponding sensations can be subdivided into two stages. Psychologically, during the first anal stage the pleasure of expulsion predominates, and the expelled excrement is equivalent in the unconscious to a loved object. Again, an ambivalent situation toward the object exists. On the one hand, the child wants to retain the fecal material because it is esteemed and, on the other hand, to expel it with hostile and destructive motives because it is feared and hated. This explanation may seem highly theoretical, but we shall later see in detail how this process serves as a model and causes various psychosomatic disorders. Two brief examples will suffice here. In a miscarriage the woman may revive her tendencies of hostile expulsion, only now toward her unborn child, who in her unconscious has the significance of demeaned excrement; in some cases of difficult childbirth, the child is unconsciously treated as valuable intestinal contents from which the woman does not wish to separate. Perhaps at first glance it seems strange to claim that in the unconscious the child is identified with excrement. But this comparison, which appears absurd to an adult, is a common one made by children, who typically hold to certain theories about adult sexual life, conception, and birth. Adapting little-understood genital experiences to processes with which they are familiar, children imagine that a woman becomes pregnant by eating something or by being kissed on the mouth. These theories, which assume that the fetus grows in the stomach and is eliminated like excrement through the anus, reemerge in only slightly disguised form in fairy tales, mythology, and folklore.

In the second anal phase the principal pleasure is not expressed so much in the expulsion of the object as in its retention. In other words, the object is more appreciated and less hated than before. It is interesting to note that adults who suffer from diarrhea are fixated at the first anal stage while those who have their point of fixation in the second anal stage usually suffer from constipation. I mention *fixation*, which, along with a related term, *regression*, needs to be defined. These two concepts form an important part of libido theory and are useful in explaining how illness occurs.

There are two distinct types of fixations. The first refers to the fixation on an object. This concept helps us to understand that a child for whom a specific person has played a very important role in her development may, as an adult, always desire to reencounter that person and thus searches for her in many different objects. The other meaning of fixation refers to instinctual satisfaction. The child passes through different phases of pregenital satisfactions. If in a specific phase she experiences excessive satisfaction or is detained in this same phase because the gratification belonging to the following phase is forbidden and anxiety-provoking, she will remain fixated on the type of satisfaction permitted her. Let us take a practical example. The intensification of the development of muscular activity parallels the entry into the anal phases and is instinctually linked to them. Let us imagine a mother who satisfies the oral desires of her child excessively but imposes a severe toilet training and restricts her games and play. In order not to lose her mother's love, the child will renounce the pleasures corresponding to her development and will conform to oral satisfactions. Later, when she suffers some disillusionment or feels distressed—as with the fear of losing maternal love—she will regress to the oral stage with its permitted satisfactions and become perverse, psychotic, or, if her conflict is expressed psychosomatically, over-weight. She will regress, in other words, to the instinctual satisfaction from which she enjoyed so much pleasure in a specific period of her libidinal development and that has been unconsciously preserved in her memory. Regression, then, signifies a movement in the opposite direction from the normal development already achieved by the child.

I have spoken of fixation at a phase in which the child has obtained excessive instinctual gratification; although it seems to be paradoxical, fixation may also result from frustration. Often a child who has not obtained at least part of the desired satisfaction in a specific period of childhood will, as an adult, continually seek to fulfill the denied gratification and remain resentful throughout life. Abundant clinical material will be presented regarding this pattern in subsequent chapters. In close relation to fixation at the anal stage are various perversions, principally sadism and masochism, as well as different manifestations of homosexuality.[*]

---

[*]Langer later would come to define homosexuality in nonpathogenic terms. No longer considering it a perversion, she came to think that homosexuality could not necessarily be explained as the result of a particular oedipal constellation, excessive penis envy, or disturbance in gender identity. However, she never developed a theoretical approach that conceptualized homosexuality in light of her feminist and political principles, which endorsed gay rights. For recent psychoanalytic perspectives on homosexuality, see, for example, E. Person, "Sexuality as the Mainstay of Identity: Psychoanalytic

At the end of the fourth year, the child enters the phallic phase. During this period masturbation reappears and the male child highly esteems his penis. His pleasurable sensations are accompanied by more or less conscious phantasies directed toward his mother or substitute figures. Because he is attracted to his mother, he becomes jealous of his father, whom he wishes to replace or to castrate. In other words, he wishes to prevent his father's sexual life with his mother and to eliminate him. This triangular situation, which typifies all infantile development, Freud called the "Oedipal situation," based on the classic tragedy of Oedipus, who killed his father and married his mother without knowing who they were. A serious conflict emerges for the child because he also loves his father, depends on him, and fears his punishment. Following the biblical law of Talion ("an eye for an eye, a tooth for a tooth"), the child fears his father could do to him all that he himself wishes to inflict on his father. In other words, his father could castrate him for his masturbation and his forbidden phantasies, cutting off the sinful organ. It is this fear that motivates the child to renounce his mother and his infantile sexual activities and to develop his sexual conscience, his "superego." The male child's fear of castration is reinforced through his observation of female genitalia. Only at this stage does he actually comprehend the difference between the sexes. Verifying that the female has no penis, he imagines that she has been mutilated as a punishment for forbidden genital activity. He begins to fear for his own organ and to demean and avoid woman as a castrated and inferior being.

Up to this point I have referred only to the male's development. However, according to Freud, until the onset of the phallic phase, no difference whatsoever exists in the psychosexual development of children. As I said earlier, Freud was principally concerned with the investigation of male development. He found that it was more difficult to study the female. In "Three Essays on the Theory of Sexuality" he asserts that woman is more "mysterious and insincere." In 1923, after three decades of psychoanalytic research, he still maintains in "The Infantile Genital Organization," that we lack sufficient data to explain the psychosexual development of girls. One year later, in his fundamental work on this subject, "The Dissolution of the Oedipus Com-

Perspectives," *Signs: Journal of Women in Culture and Society* 5-4 (1980); S. Mitchell, "Psychodynamics, Homosexuality and the Question of Pathology," *Psychiatry* 41 (1978); J. McDougall, "The Dead Father: On Early Psychic Trauma and Its Relation to Disturbance in Sexual Identity and in Creative Activity," *International Journal of Psychoanalysis* 70 (1989); for an insightful critical contribution to the literature, see M. Magee and D. Miller, " 'She Foreswore Her Womanhood': Psychoanalytic Views of Female Homosexuality," *The Clinical Social Work Journal* (forthcoming).

plex," Freud continues to affirm that the female condition is mysterious. I shall summarize this essay's exposition of female sexuality and add some observations from works more recent than those of Freud.

In "The Dissolution of the Oedipus Complex" Freud postulates female development in the following manner: Like the boy, the girl passes through the oral and anal phases to enter the phallic phase. At first, like the boy with his penis, the girl derives pleasure through stimulation of the clitoris. All of her narcissism and her sexual excitation are centered in this zone, and she accompanies her masturbatory activities with phantasies about her father. In this way she necessarily enters into conflict with her mother. When she has occasion to observe the sexual organ of her brother or a playmate during this period, her first reaction is one of violent envy. She would like to have the identical organ, and she feels inferior because of the rudimentary form of her clitoris. She hopes that with time it will grow and be transformed into a penis. In this way she initiates her "masculinity complex." Or she imagines that she has once had a penis and has lost it as a punishment for her sexual play. She assumes that other women, especially the most important ones, like her mother, have a penis. Thus, while the boy fears castration and renounces his mother as well as masturbation in order not to lose this highly esteemed organ, the girl believes she has already suffered its loss. Therefore, she lacks an important motivation to renounce her incestuous link with her father and to form her moral conscience, the superego. Freud thus concludes that woman has fewer moral qualities than man. The girl remains tied to her father, waiting to receive the desired penis from him. Little by little this desire is transformed into another one: to receive a baby as a gift from her father. With time, she realizes that the father cannot satisfy her desires, and she becomes disillusioned with him and slowly distances herself. The way is now open for another object choice.

In 1925, in "Some Psychical Consequences of the Anatomical Distinction between the Sexes," Freud develops this theme. He says that for the girl the principal consequences of her discovery of the lack of a penis and of the inferiority of her clitoris in relation to the desired organ are the feminine propensity to suffer inferiority feelings and the greater inclination toward jealousy than the male. In addition, he notes that the girl withdraws from her mother, whom she blames for her genital inferiority. He goes on to explain why it is that women masturbate much less than men, a phenomenon frequently confirmed in psychoanalytic practice. Many women do not remember having masturbated as children. A deep analysis can bring about the discovery of childhood masturbation that had been repressed early on. The rejection and repression of masturbation occur as a consequence of the discovery of sexual difference: this activity, previously so pleasurable for the girl, becomes sinful and anxiety-provoking because it constantly reminds her of her inferiority in relation to the boy.

Another aspect of female development already mentioned in earlier works is elaborated by Freud in 1924, in "The Economic Problem of Masochism." He describes the content of the girl's erotic desires directed toward her father. These are manifested in the form of pleasurable phantasies of being castrated, enduring sexual assault, or giving birth—always accompanied by pain—phantasies interpreted by Freud as manifestations of female masochism, which he believes to be biologically based.

Only in 1931, in "Female Sexuality," does Freud dedicate all of his attention to the problem of feminine sexual development. In 1933 he elaborates his ideas in one of his conferences, "Femininity," which appears in "New Introductory Lectures on Psychoanalysis." Since the concepts of both works are complementary, I will summarize them together. Freud details the outcome of his investigations of the girl's development until she enters the oedipal phase, including the significance for her of her lack of a penis and the characterological consequences of this presumed "failure." First, he calls attention to the difficulty of clearly defining masculinity and femininity in the psychological sense. They cannot simply be equated with active and passive because of the great activity that the mother develops biologically toward her children. Besides, it would be difficult to discern the extent to which feminine passivity is innate or a product of our culture and gender socialization. Nor does masochism seem to be a feminine characteristic in and of itself, because while it is normally found in women it is also present in men. Freud leaves this problem in order to describe in detail the development of female sexuality in childhood. In the first work he offers very important new knowledge: the girl's libidinal fixation on her father, often so very intense, is now seen as the repetition of an earlier situation of equal intensity with the mother. Moreover, this primitive connection usually persists during the greater part of early childhood.

Referring to the girl's sexual evolution, Freud again affirms that she behaves and feels like a "little boy" until she enters the phallic phase and that clitoral masturbation corresponds directly to the boy's masturbation of the penis. In this period the girl is for all intents and purposes unaware of her vagina. Sexual behavior, then, is identical for the two sexes during the first years of life. In this essay Freud also calls attention for the first time to a fundamental fact: Both the boy and the girl at first direct their libidinal impulses toward the same object, the mother or mother substitute. For the boy, the sex of the first love object coincides with the sex that will normally attract him his entire life; or, in simpler terms, from the beginning the boy loves a woman, and it is a woman who will later be a heterosexual object choice. But the girl will have to disentangle herself from her mother in order to move toward her father and to thus create the childhood model for her later heterosexual object choice. The girl has to undergo three important changes in her libidinal structure to achieve normal development. She has to abandon her mother for her father, to displace the major part of sexual excitability from the clitoris to the vagina, and to transform her active sexual aims into passive ones. These changes are realized in part during the phallic phase and in part only in puberty. The experiences of the preoedipal phases are of central importance for the satisfactory achievement of these changes. Her first love relationship with her mother is fundamental for the girl's capacity to later identify with her. If the relationship with the mother has been good and the girl achieves this identification, she will be a good mother to her children and a good wife to her husband. If the relationship with her mother was conflictual, there is a danger that later she will repeat the same conflicts with her husband, substituting him in her unconscious for the maternal image. Moreover, during the first stages of development a desire exists that appears rather strange to the adult mind: that of making the mother pregnant and of being impregnated by her, of giving her a child or receiving one from her. The form in which this desire emerges, develops, and is finally abandoned is very important, precisely in relation to the problem with which this book is concerned, namely, the understanding of the causes of the various disorders of female reproductive functions.

Freud poses another important problem: What accounts for the girl's withdrawal from the mother, her first love object? Is biological heterosexual attraction sufficient as a cause, or must we suspect that important psychological processes exist obliging her to abandon her mother? Freud enumerates all the reproaches the girl usually makes of her mother, causing her primitive love to be transformed into rivalry and unconscious hatred. The girl interprets her mother's physical caretaking, which has produced pleasurable erotic sensations, as attempts to seduce her, and she reproaches her mother for having awakened her sexually only to then devalue her for masturbating. She has also felt rejected by her mother because of the birth of new siblings and reproaches her for having breast-fed her too little or having weaned her too early.

It is clear that the girl makes all these charges against her mother, but the boy suffers the same disillusionments with his mother without normally distancing himself from her. There must be, then, something specific that is the unique destiny of the girl. The structure of the girl's genitalia makes her reproach her mother because of the absence of a penis. At first when she realizes the existence of sexual difference, the girl believes that only she lacks a penis and that her mother has one. The beloved mother of the early period will always be a "phallic mother." Only slowly does the girl understand that her mother also lacks the highly esteemed organ. She perceives that there exists no possibility of satisfaction between herself and her mother, whom she begins to scorn. She turns toward her father, first in the hope that he will give her a penis and then that she will receive a child from him. If in her play with dolls she has assumed the roles of mother and daughter, now she plays the father's wife, who has children with him. Later, in the relations of homosexual women, two types of constellations are to be distinguished, both of which are consequences of fixation at different stages of development. Sometimes the homosexual couple parallels a married couple to some extent, with the woman who denies her lack of a penis playing the man and acting like the husband. But perhaps in the majority of homosexual couples, sexual regression leads back to the preoedipal stages, with the two partners appearing to play the roles of mother and daughter, characterized generally by the oral type of sexual satisfaction.

Let us pause for a moment in our exposition of Freud's ideas in order to include Ruth Mack Brunswick's commentary from a very interesting work that she wrote in collaboration with Freud, taking into account step-by-step his ideas and suggestions. Brunswick analyzes the problems of the preoedipal phases I just described, adding new and important research data. She suggests that children of both sexes are passive in relation to their mother and that they struggle continually to acquire some kind of active position, imposing the passive role on the mother. A very important aspect of their development is that they achieve a positive identification with the active mother. Later, the situation of boys and girls becomes differentiated. When the girl moves toward her father, she identifies with her passive, castrated mother and sublimates her active urges. Only much later, when she herself becomes a mother, will she have the opportunity of expressing her active attitude in relation to her children. Brunswick explains that in their attempt to identify with the mother children of both sexes desire to have a baby, just as she has, and, in their desire to make her passive, to give her a child. Once having entered the oedipal phase, the boy renounces the passive desire to give birth to a baby, while his phantasy to impregnate his mother persists. The girl renounces her active desire in relation to her mother, moves toward her father, and hopes to receive a baby from him.

Brunswick reviews the factors that may separate the girl from her mother. She mentions that penis envy and the inferiority feelings caused by her perceived inadequacy are already known and emphasizes another situation that Freud had not described. The girl reproaches her mother when she realizes that they both lack a penis and that she has inherited from her an inadequate genital organ that will never permit her to conquer her mother. It is as if she reproaches her for too little love and for not having cared enough to create her daughter in a way that would allow them to form a happy couple. While she cannot accept her castration in relation to her mother because it signifies separation from her, she accepts it in relation to her father, thus identifying with her castrated mother but loved by her father. That is, if she accepts her femininity she can reclaim her mother through identification with her and attain the father as a love object. She renounces her desire to have a penis, returning to the former and more "legitimate" wish to have a child. Resigned, she waits to receive (from her father or, later, from her sexual partner) the penis during intercourse.

Generally, the girl represses her childhood sexual activity much more than does the boy. Many women maintain in all good faith that they never masturbated. Why would female childhood masturbation be the object of a much more intense repression than that of the male? Freud believed that the girl abandons masturbation in disgust when she realizes the difference between the sexes and perceives her lack of a penis, preferring not to touch her genitals anymore and to forget in this way her presumed mutilation. According to Brunswick, another important reason is the fact that clitoral masturbation of the first phases is intimately connected to phantasies about the mother. When the disillusioned girl abandons the mother as a love object, she often simultaneously renounces the clitoris, the organ she believes is responsible for implementing her desires. She comes to scorn as useless her mother's genitalia as well as her own. Later, when I discuss problems related to puberty, other aspects of this fundamental study will be addressed.

We now return to our exposition of Freud's thought [in "Female Sexuality" and "Femininity"] regarding the girl's development during puberty and how she manages to change from a "castrated male" into a woman. Antedating puberty, there is a stage in the life of children of both sexes that Freud calls latency. Beginning at the end of the fifth year and ending in puberty, the notable characteristic during this period is that children have been able to repress the greater part of their infantile sexuality. They have identified with the parent of the same sex, have become easy to socialize, and use their instinctual forces for study and the acquisition of knowledge. In general, during this period they avoid having friendships with children of the opposite sex and repress masturbation, or else engage in an active struggle against it.

For the girl, puberty is initiated with the appearance of her first menstruation, or menarche. In this period an intense sexual excitement emerges, stemming from the changes occurring in her body, which provoke a powerful revival of infantile sexuality. During puberty unconscious objects are still the same as they were in early childhood. The clitoris also retains for some time its predominance as the central zone of sexual excitation. Only little by little, generally after the first intercourse, does the vagina succeed in becoming the focal point of sexual excitement. In vaginal pleasure old exciting sensations of an oral and anal origin are revived. But Freud points out once again that the woman arrives at her feminine position only after puberty and only through complicated processes of development. The fact that many fail in this protracted evolution causes Freud to believe that the mystery of woman resides in her bisexuality, which also explains the great frequency of female frigidity. There are three types of frigidity: a psychogenic frigidity accessible to psychoanalytic treatment and two other types, one of an anatomical and the other of a constitutional origin.

Brunswick takes up the discussion of this matter; in contrast to Freud's earlier contention, she maintains that a certain vaginal excitability probably exists during infancy, the origin of which is anal. The anus transfers a part of its passive sensitivity to the vagina. However, once again she insists that the role of this vaginal sensitivity is decidedly minor and secondary with respect to the clitoris, which is the young girl's sexual organ.

Freud offers his final judgment regarding feminine development in 1937 in his important technical work "Analysis: Terminable and Interminable." Here he suggests that the expression *rejection of femininity* is a better term than those previously used, such as *masculine protest* and *penis envy*. He asserts that the woman's rejection is a biological fact and a fragment of the "grand mystery of sexuality."

Freud's concept of femininity provoked a series of heated and somewhat personal scientific discussions. The subject of the sexes is difficult to deal with dispassionately and objectively, even among psychoanalysts. Freud himself says as much in his "New Introductory Lectures on Psychoanalysis," where he explains how the theory of bisexuality had functioned to avoid animosity. He describes how his female colleagues protested against the "masculine" approach, claiming that many analysts had not overcome their deeply rooted prejudices against femininity, which biased their investigations. The thesis of bisexuality made it easy for male psychoanalysts to avoid being completely discourteous by being able to say to their female antagonists, "This isn't true of you. You are an exception, because in this specific way you are more masculine than feminine."

In the same work Freud names three important collaborators who, without abandoning his basic concept about the girl's unawareness of her vagina and the sexual predominance of the clitoris in childhood, shed new and important light on our understanding of feminine development. He is referring to Ruth Mack Brunswick, whose research I have cited; Jeanne Lampl de Groot, whose contributions I do not mention because they are not directly related to my psychosomatic focus; and Helene Deutsch, a very prestigious psychoanalyst who belongs to the pioneering generation of psychoanalytic researchers.

Helene Deutsch's publications have appeared over a period of several decades, focusing on an investigation of feminine psychology, for which she adopts a psychosomatic criterion. The results of her many years of experience are expounded in *Psychology of Women*. Deutsch's concepts about feminine psychology shall be summarized here, with emphasis on the specific contributions made by her.

Like Ruth Mack Brunswick, Helene Deutsch points out that the boy, as well as the girl, struggles to acquire an active and independent posture in relation to the mother. In this struggle the father represents the outside world, or reality. At a certain point in her development the girl abandons the mother and turns toward the father in search of the external world. For both sexes, to abandon the mother of early childhood represents the development of an active and aggressive position. Such impulses are connected to erotic urges. In the boy they assume the character of aggressive desires to penetrate the mother and are experienced in the penis (phallic phase). What is the corresponding situation for the girl? She also becomes active, and the primitive object of this erotic activity is the mother, although for Deutsch, it is possible that from the beginning the girl is more biologically passive than the boy. Her organ of aggressive–erotic desires is the clitoris, anatomically and embryologically similar to a rudimentary penis. According to Freud, all the girl's infantile genitality is concentrated in this organ and her penis envy stems from the unfavorable comparison of the clitoris to the penis. In contrast, for Deutsch, phallic envy is important but not fundamental in female development and it would be a mistake to later interpret the majority of feminine neurotic difficulties as expressions of penis envy. While the girl does affirm that the clitoris is not adequate to be the central organ of her erotic tendencies, her reaction is not necessarily one of envy but one in which she converts her active-aggressive urges into passive-masochistic ones; or, as Deutsch puts it, the girl develops an inwardly directed activity. The sexual organ that corresponds to these tendencies is, obviously, the vagina. But Deutsch shares the opinion of Freud, Brunswick, and other authors to the effect that, normally, if the girl has not been violated or has not experienced other external stimuli, she is unaware of her vagina and has little vaginal sensation until puberty. What is the fate, then, of the girl's passive-feminine urges? Just as earlier she lacked the appropriate organ for the realization of her sexuality with its active aim, now she subjectively lacks the central organ to realize her passive sexuality. Thus the girl experiences the lack of an appropriate organ twice during her childhood sexual development.

Helene Deutsch calls this double deficit a "genital trauma," which, rather than penis envy, is mainly responsible for subsequent neurotic disorders in woman. This same double deficit obliges the girl to retain the excitement of the clitoris as the central, though inadequate, organ of her renewed active urges and to once again aggressively charge with libido the oral and anal zones as focal points of the receptive-erotic urges of a passive nature. Also, for Deutsch, only the biological and instinctual development of puberty awakens within the girl her vaginal sensitivity. The vagina now inherits the passive excitability of the mouth and the anus. To summarize in this regard, the girl's basic conflict does not originate from penis envy but from the definitive absence of an active sexual organ and the temporary or subjective lack of the receptive-passive organ, the vagina, which only later will be the center of her adult sexuality.

In the chapters that follow, I will refer to the rest of Deutsch's theories, especially with respect to the primordial importance of the early mother–daughter relationship, theories that will help us understand numerous manifestations of psychosomatic disorders in female reproductive life.

We turn now to a review of Karen Horney's theories pertinent to our subject, which she formulated while still part of the psychoanalytic movement. By 1923, in her study "On the Genesis of the Castration Complex in Women," Karen Horney expresses her doubts that penis envy constitutes the nucleus of feminine neurotic disorders. She acknowledges, however, the existence of envy, which originates from different sources. Freud insists on the narcissistic character of such envy, as if the girl suffers mainly from the absence of something libidinally valuable possessed by the boy. Horney discovers other causes, partially of an instinctual nature, partly connected to problems deriving from feelings of guilt and anxiety. The penis permits the boy a larger discharge of urethral sadism and facilitates the satisfaction of exhibitionist urges during the act of micturition. The girl is envious of these two types of childhood sexual satisfactions. Moreover, like the boy, the girl suffers from guilt feelings because of her masturbatory activities; she feels unjustly treated, being under the impression that the boy can touch and stimulate his genitals with impunity during micturition. She, on the other hand, is not permitted to touch herself or to look at herself and is punished and condemned if she does. Because of multiple guilt feelings, children of both sexes suffer castration fears. But while the boy can easily prove to himself that his genital organ has suffered no damage, the girl cannot ever eliminate her anxious doubts about this possibility because the major part of her genitalia, situated in the interior of her body, cannot be inspected. Obviously, this entire phenomenon of childhood envy is unconscious or becomes so through repression of all childhood sexuality. Later, it is expressed in a disguised form, when, for example, women complain of having less sexual liberty than men. In this way Karen Horney acknowledges penis envy but argues that it can easily be overcome by children and that its damaging effects appear only later, such as in the adult woman's masculinization or her aggressive or rejecting attitudes toward men. These developments might occur if the girl has failed in her childhood identification with her mother. Normally, the girl identifies with her mother and, like her, is amorously inclined toward the father, wishing to have a child with him. But if in her childish affection she becomes disillusioned with her father, the girl tries to identify with him in order to later adopt a virile attitude of rivalry with men, characterized by resentments and wishes for revenge. In addition, if the father has given a child to the mother while the girl anxiously seeks his love, she is filled with envy and unconsciously equates the father's child with his penis. She returns to her prior position of penis envy, which now substitutes for her envy of her mother, who possesses her father's baby. Like Deutsch, Horney emphasizes the fact that the hope of a future motherhood cannot compensate the young girl for her frustrations, because it is too far removed from immediate possibilities of gratification. Horney criticizes as antibiological the contemporary psychoanalytic position that takes penis envy as axiomatic. The conviction that all women are unconsciously dominated by penis envy would amount to an assertion that one half of the human race does not accept their sex and that this supposed discontent could only be overcome in certain individuals and only under especially favorable circumstances.

Horney returns to the subject with new scientific arguments in her second important work, "The Flight from Womanhood." She believes that in a primitive fashion psychoanalysis has always sought out the male as its object of research. She explains that Freud and all his initial collaborators were more interested in and more understanding of the psychology of their own sex, suspecting that when they finally came to investigate feminine psychological processes, they approached the problem from a masculine perspective—typical for our patriarchal society, which, without realizing it, has adapted all its criteria of value, morality, or ethics and the like to the masculine character. Women themselves have come to unconsciously accept this criteria and to consider everything positive they might possess as masculine and everything negative as feminine. Horney then criticizes Freud and especially Ferenczi, whose theories suggest that all of woman's femininity is something like a poor substitute for her masculine desires and that even motherhood and the desire to have a child are nothing but a substitute for the never-attained penis. Horney argues that if this were so, to be a woman would be a sad and unfortunate destiny, and she concludes:

> As women, then, we should ask ourselves in a perplexed fashion: And motherhood? And the blessed consciousness of carrying inside oneself a new life? And the immense happiness experienced in the ever more intense expectation of this new being? And the joy, when finally it is born? And when one has it for the first time in one's arms? And the complete and profound satisfaction during breast-feeding? And all the gratification of the care of the newborn?

Departing from this somewhat defiant and polemical aspect of her work, Horney explicates the scientific results of her psychoanalytic investigation. From the beginning, she says, the girl feels and behaves as a feminine being. But motivated by a variety of factors, she may come to identify with her father and adopt a masculine attitude. This identification is established in order to hide her incestuous and frustrated desires for her father and her guilt feelings toward her mother. Moreover, this identification serves the girl (just as, according to Freud, does all identification) by enabling her to better tolerate the abandonment of the object—the father—only to recover him through the attempt to be equal to him. Horney believes that prior to the phantasies of being castrated in the masculine sense described by Freud, Deutsch, and others, the girl fears suffering vaginal harm through relations with the father. In her identification with the father, the girl succeeds in substituting this profound fear for the less threatening one of suffering castration of her imaginary penis, the unreal nature of which she unconsciously perceives.

In "The Denial of the Vagina," Horney's last work dedicated to this subject, she again explains why she has arrived at the conclusion that the girl adopts a primarily feminine position in accord with her anatomy. She maintains that the girl has vaginal sensations during the apogee of her childhood sexuality and adopts a feminine attitude toward her father and in her behavior in general. Her early notion of the vagina, based on physical sensation, succumbs later to repression due to multiple anxieties connected to this early vaginal sexuality. Vaginal frigidity and the overevaluation of the clitoris do not represent penis envy and a denigration of femininity as much as an attempt to deny early anxieties. But why would the vagina be a source of anxiety for the girl, and why would she imagine that the possession of a penis could liberate her from her fears? Horney postulates that the girl's early vaginal sexuality is dedicated to her father. Either because of direct observation or through phantasy, the girl confirms that the father's penis is disproportionately big compared to her own genitals, and she fears being destroyed internally in her phantasied relationship with him. Moreover, if she has the opportunity to observe the remainder of menstrual blood in her mother's or other women's clothing, she becomes convinced of the vulnerability of the female body. This impression is even more pronounced when she has the opportunity to learn about miscarriages, difficult births, and female genital illnesses. As the idea of childbirth is linked intimately to the representation of coitus, an infantile fear of childbirth can easily cause frigidity later on. The girl desires to have a penis in place of an opening that goes to the inside of her body because she envies the boy his ability to continually confirm that he has not been damaged by his masturbatory activity. She, in contrast, has no possibility of calming her anxiety about having definitively injured herself through her masturbatory activities, her sinful incestuous phantasies, or her sexual play with other children. Therefore, if the girl seems to be unaware of her vagina and to demand a penis, concentrating her genital sensitivity in the clitoris, this functions for her as a denial of early vaginal experiences, which are loaded with guilt, incestuous phantasies, and anxieties.

In support of her thesis, Horney cites an important publication by Josine Müller, in which the author indicates how in analysis it can be demonstrated that masculine women dominated by penis envy pass through a clearly vaginal phase in childhood and repress their feminine sexuality because of guilt feelings provoked by their desires and incestuous phantasies about their fathers. This finding of the existence of early vaginal sensations is also documented in Fanny Hann-Kende's article, "Masturbation of the Clitoris and Penis Envy."

Horney argues, furthermore, that just as penis envy can be observed in the girl, a desire to have breasts is often noted in the boy. She interprets the two attitudes as a manifestation of innate human bisexuality.

In order not to tire the reader with this long theoretical exposition, I will now pose a concrete problem related to our subject. We saw that when speaking of genital trauma in the girl, Helene Deutsch insists that the girl does not perceive her vagina and does not emotionally comprehend the future function of her genitals, even when she has received an adequate education on the subject. This presumed lack of understanding of her future femininity makes it difficult for her to accept her sex. In a prior work Deutsch explains that because motherhood is only an expectation related to the distant future, the girl is fixated on her virile protest and resentful position. Karen Horney also postulates that for the girl the realization of her desire to have children is too far off for her to accept her feminine role.

The observation of this fact is in and of itself undoubtedly accurate. While the boy can see his genital organs and take pleasure in them, the girl suffers because she does not yet know about her vagina (according to Freud, Deutsch, and others) or has repressed her vaginal sensitivity (according to Horney and the "English school," about which I will speak later) and thus does not understand that as an adult she will have as much capacity to have pleasure as the male and will obtain a specifically feminine and extremely important gratification in motherhood.

I now direct our attention to whether or not a young girl who grows up in a culture totally different from our own is able to assess her future as a woman more accurately. We will attempt to determine if a clearer sense of her future adulthood permits the girl to automatically accept her femininity or if penis envy and the female feeling of inferiority are biological attributes and thus inevitable.

In her book _Coming of Age in Samoa_ Margaret Mead describes a society distinct from ours. Throughout the time she spent in Samoa, Mead dedicated herself mainly to observing the ways in which adolescent girls adapt socially. She went to Samoa in order to ascertain whether the difficulties experienced during puberty by girls in our own culture are due to biology, as is usually asserted, or are the consequence of cultural factors. Living intimately with girls and young women from three villages, she arrived at the conclusion that puberty did not present special problems for them and that, in general, women seemed very accepting of their female role, even though they lived in a patriarchal society that accorded more rights to men than to women. I agree with Mead, who notes that frigidity, which is totally unknown among the Samoans, is an index of women's acceptance of their sex. Indeed, full sexual enjoyment is a sign in women of this acceptance.

Now, how might we understand Samoan women's acceptance of their sex, in spite of their living in a society where men play a more important social role than they? Among the superficial determinants we should include the fact that women are very highly regarded, that they can come to play an important role in society, and that the birth of a female baby is celebrated with the same joy as the birth of a male. But there are more profound factors in the culture that allay the conflicts found so frequently in our own culture. Later, I will show how frigidity and other female disorders are rooted in conflicts belonging to the early relationship between mother and daughter, especially with respect to oral frustrations. The structure of Samoan society eliminates this source of conflicts. The child is breast-fed on demand and from the beginning is also fed other foods by all the women who live in the household. Therefore, if for one reason or another the mother is unavailable to feed her child or she withholds affection, another family member cares for and feeds the child, thus avoiding frustration.

I spoke earlier of the idea that the girl is incapable of appreciating her own genitals because she has little knowledge of them. The vagina appears to her as a sinister opening and she fears that sexual play could permanently harm her. Also, motherhood, the compensation for her sex, is too far away or unreal to her. This situation is distinct in Samoa. From very early on, girls observe adult sexual life and understand perfectly well the capacity and significance of the female genitals. They engage freely in sexual play and are present during intercourse and births. Interestingly enough, the only girl in whom Margaret Mead was able to observe manifestations of penis envy did not have parents and lived with two older couples who no longer had children present in the household.

Samoan girls understand early on, then, their future role as women. Moreover, the social structure of Samoa offers them maternal experiences. Earlier we cited Ruth Mack Brunswick, who believes that during their development girls have to abandon their active tendencies until finally, as women and mothers, they can experience their maternal functions toward a child. In Samoa this situation is different. The mother concerns herself with the child during the time she nurses her. Afterward, she leaves the child to the care of a "nursemaid," a girl in the house the same age as girls who in our society are still playing with dolls. Before puberty, when the girl is capable of carrying out more complicated tasks, she leaves her "doll" to the care and responsibility of another younger girl. In spite of the fact that Mead sees this early responsibility for other children as a burden for the girls, I think that in the instinctual domain it is a satisfactory activity for them because it permits them to acquire a sense of self-confidence, to conquer doubts and irrational feelings of guilt, and to express very early on the biological maternal urges of their own sex.

Another factor contributing to Samoan women's acceptance of their sex probably comes from the extensive sexual liberty enjoyed equally by both sexes. The only taboo is that of incest, which is tolerable because children are allowed to relate sexually to other permissible objects. Thus, the Samoan girl cannot develop the conflict between sexual satisfaction and the ego-ideal so rooted in our own society, especially among women.

Assuming that Mead's observations about the absence of penis envy among the Samoans are correct, I believe I do not err in interpreting this phenomenon as a result of the girl's satisfaction of her active and maternal impulses and the sense of security that she acquires at a young age regarding her future role as woman and mother. However, I do not wish to deny the inevitability of conflicts and profound frustrations during early childhood and their consequences for the future life of the individual. It would be tempting and very comforting to attribute the causes of all of our suffering to merely cultural factors, but that does not correspond to reality. The total helplessness into which the human infant, in contrast to animals, is born and the long period of almost absolute dependence until adulthood, when she is capable of taking care of herself, satisfying her sexual

---

*Over the years Langer came to doubt the existence of a maternal instinct and remained convinced that culture is the important determinant with respect to women's attitudes toward their psychobiological potential. During the last 14 years of her life, in her work as a therapist for Central American refugees exiled in Mexico and as a consultant and supervisor to the Nicaraguan Revolution's new national mental health system, she had the opportunity to study the Central American woman's views of motherhood, which she believed to be significantly different from the views of middle-class Argentine women. Through her contact with female political activists, who had developed a critique of patriarchal society, and with nonpoliticized women from all social classes, Langer concluded that the Central American woman links her capacity to have a child, which is central to her self-esteem and self-respect, to her capacity in other domains. The Central American woman is convinced, Langer believed, that she will be accepted by men as an equal on the basis of her childbearing capability. As an example, Langer referred to one of Nicaragua's famous female revolutionary leaders, Gladys Bias, who, after being captured by Somoza's National Guard, was so badly tortured that she underwent a complete nervous breakdown. Her comrades made sure that she would be well cared for, but were convinced that she would never recover to participate in the revolution. However, Gladys did recuperate, but she was certain that the only way to prove her renewed capacity for political activism was to give birth to another child. Doing so, she returned to the mountains with babe in arms and, as she had predicted, was immediately accepted by her comrades. As Langer put it, "This is the Third World woman whom the Western woman does not understand . . . we need to be careful; I don't know if this is maternal instinct unimpeded or simply another conception of femininity and womanhood, but it is the Third World woman's view, influenced by culture and the preindustrial emphasis on the value of labor. The Nicaraguan Women's Federation's political commitment to reproductive rights is a political strategy that needs to be carefully developed in light of this tradition."

needs, and simultaneously adapting to her community, makes the experience of anguishing and irrational states inevitable. Thus, I cannot agree with Mead in this and her other studies—for example, *Sex and Temperament in Three Primitive Societies*—in which she attempts to reduce the psychological differences between men and women to mere socialization or cultural factors. This point of view is unacceptable from my perspective. If we consider the human being as a psychosomatic unity, we cannot assume that the anatomical and functional differences between male and female do not simultaneously involve a profound psychological difference. We will study this issue when I review Melanie Klein's theories about female development. I do not believe that the influence of biological factors on psychology can ever be overestimated. However, this influence can be erroneously interpreted, which in fact occurs if women are considered to be biologically inferior to men or a priori unaccepting of their sex. Wherever this lack of acceptance is encountered, it is indicative of a developmental disorder.[*]

Karen Horney has the great merit of having been one of the first to call attention to this error with great perspicacity in her scientific argument. She later abandoned this direction in her research in order to attribute all causes of disorders to cultural factors quite removed from early childhood and instinctual life. Thus, she came to negate precisely what she had so correctly affirmed before: the need to interpret the human being in a holistic sense, as a psychobiological or psychosomatic unit.

So far I have mentioned the concepts of Freud and the Vienna school regarding feminine psychology. I have emphasized that in their fundamental approach with respect to the psychosexual domain, the male is considered the "standard" type and the young girl is believed to be unaware even in her unconscious of her female genital organs, thus

---

[*]Langer continued to believe that biology is an important determinant of psychology. While she admired the work of contemporary feminist psychoanalysts, in her opinion they tend to pay too little attention to the biological differences between the sexes and its potential impact on gendered differential experiences. "I am still a Kleinian in this regard; for me, we are biopsychosocial beings. I think that the psychological domain is a superstructural aspect of the biological and social infrastructures and that we remain in a very abstract mode to believe that we can erase all differences between the sexes through, for example, childrearing practices shared equally by men and women. Even with both father and mother participating equally in terms of their time commitment, the child will experience her time with each parent differently because of heterosexual attraction and complementarity. Physiology affects phantasy life: The man is always the one who will penetrate the woman—the little girl will have unconscious phantasies about the father and how he will penetrate her, and the little boy will have unconscious phantasies about penetrating the mother. This is a gender difference about which I will never change my mind."

considering herself to be physically and psychologically equal to the male. Afterward, at three or four years of age, she becomes aware of the anatomical difference between the sexes, reacting to this discovery with envy and inferiority feelings. Slowly, through complicated psychological processes and the physiological development of puberty and postpuberty, she comes to accept her femininity. This occurs only under very favorable circumstances. I referred to Horney's critique, which portrays as unlikely and unscientific the belief that half the human species does not *a priori* accept their sex, and I reviewed some of her more important findings in this regard.

Now I direct our attention to the ideas of Melanie Klein and her English school. As an example of their disagreement with Freud, I cite Ernest Jones: "Woman is not psychologically merely a castrated male; on the contrary, she has been born a female." I shall briefly summarize two articles by Jones, "The Early Development of Female Sexuality" and "Early Female Sexuality," because they are basic to the subject. The most interesting concept for us, discussed in the first of the two articles, is that of *aphanisis* (extinction of sexuality), which helps us understand multiple neurotic anxieties. In disagreement with Freud's contention that both sexes fear castration, Jones maintains that the fundamental fear is not one of suffering or having suffered the loss of the penis but of being denied all possibility of sexual pleasure. I want to expand on this assertion by reminding us that in this loss the most important consequence is the loss of the possibility of linking oneself libidinously to the love object. Depending on the sex and the level of sexual organization achieved, the fear of aphanisis can refer especially to the danger of the destruction of either the penis, the vagina, the anus, the mouth, and so on. Or when the satisfaction of a specific erotic zone, for example, the vagina, contains too much danger, the sexual sensitivity is displaced onto another zone, principally the clitoris, thus avoiding aphanisis.

In his second article on the subject, Jones sketches the principal differences between the Viennese and English schools. He recapitulates how the latter conceives of infantile psychosexual development in the boy and the girl, both of whom early on experience sensations corresponding to their genital organization (that is, in the boy urges to penetrate located in the penis and in the girl receptive desires in the vagina). I will refer here to the girl's evolution only. She will necessarily experience frustrations in the oral stage, caused by her mother whose breasts do not give the girl all she desires. As a consequence of these early frustrations, hate and "oral sadism" toward the mother will emerge. This idea will be more extensively treated when I explicate Melanie Klein's ideas. In part, because the girl imagines that the mother also feeds the father with her breasts, she develops a rivalrous attitude toward him. She also believes that her mother receives a breast-penis and much more generous milk from the father than she herself gives her daughter. The girl assumes, as well, that the inside of her mother's body is full of things (milk, penises, babies) received from the father, which the girl would like to have for herself. So she would like to penetrate the maternal body and rid it of its contents. She represses these sadistic phantasies for fear of suffering a corresponding punishment through her mother's destruction of her own body's insides. Besides, she cannot permit herself much aggression against her mother because she totally depends on her during early childhood (the boy more easily tolerates his hatred toward his father, the same-sex parent, because he is not the person upon whom the boy depends). Already in this early stage the girl feels the desire to have a penis. This desire stems from different sources. The girl forms two opposite ideas of the penis. One, already mentioned, is that the penis seems to be a more potent breast, something good that feeds and comforts. The girl wishes to have it in order to give it to her mother and reconcile herself with her own feelings of having damaged her mother in her phantasies. But the girl also sees in the penis an aggressive weapon that can serve her in her attacks against her mother. Moreover, a visible penis could neutralize the aggressive penis that she believes she has incorporated (swallowed), thus enabling her to return a penis to the father, whom she has castrated in her earlier phantasies. In summary, the girl desires to have a penis only in part for libidinal (erotic) reasons. More important is her need to dominate her sadism and to liberate herself in this way from the resulting anxiety and guilt feelings.

To put it another way, according to Jones and the English school, the girl's desire to have a penis is not primary but already a defensive neurotic attitude, a consequence of her distress from the early Oedipus complex, unleashed by oral frustrations with the mother. In addition, while for the Vienna school the young girl is unaware of her vagina and concentrates all of her infantile genital sexuality in the clitoris, for the English school she has an instinctual and *a priori* knowledge of her genital organs and their receptive functions. According to the Vienna school, her failure in the masculine position obliges the girl to accept the feminine role. The proponents of the English school believe the opposite: The girl temporarily or permanently adopts a virile position because of the frustrations suffered in her primarily feminine tendencies. She imagines that she has a penis so that the mother cannot destroy the inside of her body and so that she can alleviate her guilt feeling by offering her imaginary penis to her mother or father, whom she has robbed in previous phantasies.

I present this exposition of Ernest Jones's ideas, repeating some of the concepts already discussed, because I believe it is important to firmly establish the differences in the points of view of the Vienna school, represented here by Freud, Ruth Mack Brunswick, and Helene Deutsch; Karen Horney, with her intermediary ideas; and the English school, whose principal exponents are Melanie Klein and Ernest Jones. Familiarity with all these perspectives will be useful for understanding the female psychosomatic disorders discussed in subsequent chapters of this book.

I turn now to a summary of Melanie Klein's concepts of female development, with the warning that her theory is difficult for those who are unfamiliar with psychoanalysis. An understanding of Jones's ideas will help the reader to follow this exposition, which partly echoes and partly completes the previous discussion.

In *The Psychoanalysis of Children* Klein argues that small children of both sexes already try to imagine intercourse between their parents (the "primal scene" is the technical psychoanalytic term). Because children relate to the mother and the external world primarily through the mouth, all their ideas are expressed in oral terms. They believe that the mother feeds the father with her breasts and that, in turn, he feeds her with the penis. Now, how can the little girl, who has never seen a penis, develop this phantasy? Earlier, Freud had expressed his thinking in a personal letter to Jones: The first idea that the girl forms of the sexual relationship between her parents corresponds to an act of fellatio. According to Klein, the girl reacts to the frustrations suffered at the maternal breast—which in this early period directly represents her mother or, at least, the most important part of her—imagining that the father has a similar organ but better, something like a more generous breast than her mother's. She later identifies the father's penis with this phantasized organ. In her disillusionment with respect to the mother the girl believes that the mother gives her very little because she prefers to feed her father, provoking in the girl rivalry with her father and resentment toward her mother. On the other hand, as I have already indicated, the girl also imagines that the father feeds the mother with his penis, filling her with penises, babies, and milk. This phantasy stimulates the girl's envy and sense of rivalry with her mother. Contrary to Freud's idea, Klein postulates that in the first year of life the girl enters into a rivalrous situation with the mother and an amorous inclination toward the father. In contrast, for Freud, this Oedipal situation is only experienced by the girl at four years of age, when she searches out her father, simultaneously rejecting her mother.

According to Klein, this situation of early hatred toward her mother drives the girl to wish to destroy the inside of the maternal body and to take possession of its desired contents. As a consequence, the girl fears a corresponding attack by her mother and the destruction of the inside of her body (following the biblical law of Talion, which rules in the unconscious). This irrational fear, also posited by Horney and Jones, is seen as the basic female fear and represents another difference between the schools. According to Freud, the girl is afraid of suffering or of having suffered a castration of her imaginary penis; according to the English school, she fears the destruction of her internal female organs, which has already occurred or is about to occur.

We now arrive at the third fundamental difference. I have already stated that according to the Viennese school the girl does know about her vagina and so during the phallic stage (that is, at about four years of age, when she discovers her external genitalia) concentrates all excitability in the clitoris. According to the English school, the girl adopts a feminine receptive position toward her father from the beginning, aware of her vagina and desirous of having the paternal penis inside her. This process occurs simultaneously with the phantasies of fellatio that were mentioned earlier. Because the girl is frustrated in her desires for the father, she directs sadistic phantasies toward his penis. She then projects her own aggression onto this organ and in this way comes to fear its contact. Thus her early "masculine" position emerges as a defense against her fears. Frustrated by her father and envious of him, she identifies with him and tries to play the role she accords to him in her phantasy. Because she confuses phantasy and reality, she believes she has introjected[2] his penis and, since she now possesses it, can obtain all that she desires from her mother. Moreover, as we already witnessed in Jones's perspective, there is the belief in the English school that the idea of possessing a penis calms the girl's distress because it not only represents an offensive and defensive weapon but permits her to give to her parents what she has robbed from them.

Before examining another important concept of the English school, I shall first briefly summarize Karl Abraham's theories about early object relations. On the basis of Freud's investigations in "Mourning and Melancholia" as well as his own discoveries, Abraham arrives at the conclusion that the human being tries to overcome the loss of a loved being by introjecting her—or in the unconscious, by eating her—thus arriving at an identification with the lost object. Following this line of reasoning and studying the results obtained in the analysis of melancholic and paranoid patients, Abraham was able to more profoundly penetrate the nature of the first object relations of the child. Freud had maintained that the child primitively loves only herself—primary narcissism—and later slowly becomes interested in and connected to the principal persons in her environment. Abraham argues that it is necessary to include between this first narcissistic phase and the succeeding one, which contains interpersonal relations, another stage during which the child enters into a relationship with a single important part of the loved person. For example, she does not love her mother nor does she perceive her mother as a person but as breasts; that is, she loves a "part object." In her phantasies she defends against the possible loss of the maternal breasts by incorporating them in a cannibalistic fashion. Her bond with the part object is ambivalent; that is, she has loving and hateful feelings toward it. The hatred leads her to fear introjecting the object and so she tries to liberate herself by expelling it. This concept helps us to understand what it means to say, as was claimed earlier, for example, that the girl has already incorporated the paternal penis or the contents of the maternal body.

Following this line of reasoning, Melanie Klein and other colleagues came to the conclusion that the small child does not ambivalently seek out only one maternal breast and one paternal penis but instead has multiple objects. The child would have in her mind the representation of a good breast—one that gives milk—and another, bad, breast—one that denies her and causes her to suffer hunger—or of a good penis that feeds and another, bad, penis that has the characteristics of a dangerous weapon. I have already explained how the child confuses her phantasies with reality. She believes that she has really introjected a quantity of bad objects and she anxiously searches in the environment for good objects to incorporate in order to neutralize the damaging action of the bad ones. She also tries to expel all the bad objects she carries inside. This highly theoretical conceptualization can help us understand very concrete problems. For example, in this way Klein explains how in the sexual act many women experience a great calming of their anxieties, independent of their erotic enjoyment. They fear having introjected a bad penis, a fear that can become conscious in the most varied of ways. For instance, in women for whom the hypochondriacal idea of suffering from cancer emerges, each sexual act with a "good" partner calms their irrational and unconscious anxieties because they experience intercourse as the incorporation of a good penis, which cures and neutralizes the bad objects.

The English school has often been reproached for drawing too phantastic and pessimistic a picture of early infantile development. Because the first oral frustrations are practically inevitable, it might be feared that if already in the child's first year of life she passes through such terrifying and decisive anxieties and experiences, the role of the environment in avoiding serious neuroses later on might be almost null and void. However, this is not the case. Klein emphasizes the great importance of the actual supportive attitude of the environment in counteracting the damaging influence of this phantastic world of the infant by helping her to acquire little by little a growing sense of a reality distinct from her irrational anxieties. The same reality also offers the girl possibilities of ascertaining that she has not been destroyed and, in symbolic acts and through sublimation, of reconstituting the loved persons whom she has harmed in her phantasies.

We now return to our problem, that of the girl's psychosexual development. I indicated earlier that Klein speaks of an early masculine position. Often the girl returns to this resource to deal with her frustrations. But normally she enters a "postphallic" phase, in which she now fully accepts her feminine role and adopts the corresponding attitude toward her environment.

With regard to the psychological differences between the sexes, Melanie Klein attributes much importance to the fact that the girl is exposed to more frustration in her early development than the boy because of her inability to confirm the integrity of her genitals or to see the achievement of motherhood as anything other than a vague and future possibility. In contrast to Freud, Klein maintains that feminine receptive tendencies permit the girl a greater introjection of her parents, that is, the acquisition of a superego or moral conscience more intense than that of the boy. Moreover, the girl's insecurity about the inside of her body and the need to dominate its bad contents cause her to develop an acute power of psychological observation and vision together with a certain inclination toward trickery and intrigue. Her greater dependency on her superego obliges her to be altruistic and predisposed to sacrifices. Her fears of having damaged the interior of the maternal body and of having been punished in the same way cause her to try to give birth to and nurture beautiful children, either in reality or in the form of sublimations.[*]

---

[*]The case for primary feminine identity, to which Langer subscribed, has been strengthened by recent research on early awareness of the vagina and internal organs which is thought to influence body image in little girls; see J. Kestenberg, "Regression and Reintegration in Pregnancy," *Journal of the American Psychoanalytic Association* 24-Supp (1976): 213–250 and R. C. Friedman, R. M. Richart, and R. L. Van de Wiele, eds., *Sex Differences in Behavior* (New York: Wiley, 1974); for views on the early development of gender identity see, for example, J. Kleeman, "Freud's Views on Early Female Sexuality in the Light of Direct Child Observations," in *Female Psychology*, ed. H. Blum (New York: International Universities Press, 1977); J. Money and A. Ehrhardt, *Man and Woman, Boy and Girl* (Baltimore: Johns Hopkins University Press, 1972); and R. J. Stoller, "The Sense of Femaleness," in *Psychoanalysis and Women*, ed.

This theoretical explication has addressed only partially the scientific contributions of psychoanalysis with respect to our subject, an incompleteness justified, I believe, by the complexity of the material and by the fact that one cannot arrive at a profound understanding of psychoanalysis without having experienced firsthand the process of coming to know one's own unconscious. I wish now to conclude with my own conceptualization regarding the distinct theories of female psychosexual development. In this chapter I have emphasized Freud's "phallocentric errors," pointing out those specific aspects of his theory with which I disagree, based on his disciples' research as well as on my own observations. But in criticizing Freud for one aspect of his theory, using as a weapon the methodology elaborated exclusively by him and based on the scientific results of 50 years of psychoanalytic theory and practice, is in no way meant to imply that my vision is more clear than his. By being favorably disposed to new perspectives, Freud himself encouraged a critical attitude among his disciples, admonishing them never to respect anything that could not be considered to be beyond doubt and debate. In "Psychoanalysis and the Theory of the Libido" Freud referred to psychoanalysis as an empirical science, contrasting it to the objectives of philosophy. He wrote that philosophers begin with certain precisely defined fundamental concepts with which they apprehend the totality of the universe. Once concluded, the system is closed definitively to new discoveries and knowledge. In contrast, he contended, in psychoanalysis one stands by the facts of one's specialization and tries to resolve the most immediate problems of observation; one gropes, without setting aside the evidence offered by experience; and one always considers one's theories inconclusive and is always ready to rectify or to substitute them. Like the physicist or the chemist, the psychoanalyst also admits that certain concepts are obscure and some hypotheses provisional and hopes that future labor will yield a more precise determination of both.

Psychoanalytic treatment of women often reveals the fundamental significance of penis envy, castration feelings, and a masculine attitude. But this posture in women is already a defense against more profound fears of the destruction of their femininity. We shall see how our understanding of two different castration phantasies will be useful to us for an understanding of psychosomatic disorders in women and how both usually appear in a single reaction or in the same symptom. For example, the girl's response to menarche often represents a curious

J. B. Miller (New York: Penguin, 1973) and H. Blum, "Primary Female Identity," in *Female Psychology*, ed. H. Blum (New York: International Universities Press, 1977).

mixture of humiliation, rejection, and rebellious joy. The humiliation corresponds to the loss of her supposed virility, to her "castration." The joy is the consequence of the relief experienced at her intact femininity which exposes the unrealistic nature of her fears, as well as of the perception of the first menstruation as the promise of future motherhood.

In anthropological material as well, these factors can be observed. Generally, in patriarchal societies woman's phallic envy is of primary importance, although we saw how in Samoa, under cultural conditions very different from our own, such envy does not appear to exist or at least seems to occur only infrequently. In completely different societies, like that of the Marquesans, for example, where women enjoy social equality but their maternal role is devalued, genital fears take on a distinct form. In *The Individual and His Society*, Abram Kardiner reports finding no characteristics of penis envy among the women of the Marquesas islands because, he argues, the privileged role of women eliminates any reason to envy men. But the phenomenon of pseudocyesis (imaginary pregnancy), so frequently encountered among the women of the Marquesas islands, should be interpreted in my opinion as a manifestation of the fear of castration of female genitalia. That is, pseudocyesis appears as an attempt to deny the internal destruction and presumed loss of fertility associated with menstruation.

Finally, an explanation is in order as to why in a book with a clinical focus I have presented the entire evolution of psychoanalytic theory on the psychosexual development of woman in place of giving a brief summary of the current state of our science. First, those readers only interested in the practical aspect of the subject might wish to skip over the parts that seem irrelevant, although I do believe that a minimal amount of theory is necessary for adequate comprehension of clinical material. Second, I assume that a brief exposition of the historical context and development of this complex theory is of interest to the reader unfamiliar with psychoanalysis. And finally, for the experts and students of psychoanalysis, I hope I have offered a review that can be of use to them in their own research.[*]

---

[*]For reviews of the psychoanalytic literature on femininity published after *Motherhood and Sexuality*, see J. Chasseguet-Smirgel, C. J. Luguet-Parat, Bela Grunberger, Joyce McDougall, Maria Torok, & Christian David, *Female Sexuality: New Psychoanalytic Views* (Ann Arbor: University of Michigan Press, 1970); C. Zanardi, ed., *Essential Papers on the Psychology of Women* (New York: New York University Press, 1990). Zanardi includes North American and European psychoanalytic views on female sexuality, as well as a section on feminism and psychoanalysis.

The Image of the "Bad Mother"[1]

I have spoken of demeaning attitudes toward women and of how the belief in female inferiority is based on old infantile resentments. Both men and women unconsciously reject the mother. The human infant's total dependency on its mother and its great vulnerability make it fear, envy, and hate her. At the same time, this very dependency and deep intimacy between mother and infant causes the infant to love her. The fact that the child knows his mother better than any other human being and depends totally on her lends an insatiable character to his love and a desire for exclusivity, which leads him to suffer a variety of frustrations. The child loves his mother but reacts to frustrations with an impotent and desperate hatred. The projection of these feelings onto the mother makes the child fear her.

In the first chapter I reviewed the theories of the English school regarding the psychology of the very young girl. I described how in her phantasies she wishes to destroy the maternal body through all the means at her disposal and how she fears being destroyed in retaliation for her hatred. We saw that in her unconscious, beside images of the "good mother" who caresses her and has milk-filled breasts, the child develops the images and the representation of the retaliatory "bad mother."

In order not to leave the impression that these concepts are too complicated and difficult to understand, I wish to demonstrate through an analysis of a variety of sources that they are a psychological reality and that all of us carry within both the image of a good mother and that of a terrifying bad mother—one who kills, destroys, and devours the child. In succeeding chapters I shall examine how this phenomenon is manifested in clinical material. But for now I want to interpret a rumor that circulated a short time ago among the working people—servants, taxi drivers, and hairdressers—of Buenos Aires that will demonstrate the psychology of everyday life.

We are dealing with something that could be referred to as a "modern myth." This expression is taken from Marie Bonaparte's *Myths of War*, in which the author describes how the collective psychological conditions created by the Second World War produced persistent rumors that circulated at an astonishing rate from person to person. An analysis of their latent content demonstrated that, as with myths of the past, they facilitated in a disguised form the psychological assimilation of a situation of collective anxiety and profound conflict.

The rumor to which I refer (in a single week nine different versions came to my attention) was accepted as truth by persons quite capable of critical judgment, revealing the manner in which, in a disguised and elaborated form, rumors respond to repressed thoughts and feelings and to infantile anxieties that persist in the vast majority of people. The most complete version of the strange story that was reported throughout Buenos Aires in June of 1949 was as follows: A young married couple hire a servant as the wife approaches the end of her pregnancy. The baby is born. Several weeks later the husband and wife go out one evening to see a film, leaving the baby in their trusted servant's care. Returning home, they are received quite ceremoniously by the servant, who, according to one version, is dressed in the wife's bridal gown. She tells them that she has prepared an elaborate surprise for them and invites them to go to the dining room so that she can serve them a special meal. They enter and encounter a horrifying spectacle: In the middle of the table, arranged with a great deal of care, they see their small infant son in a large bowl, roasted and surrounded with potatoes. The distressed mother goes mad immediately. She loses the ability to speak, and no one has heard her say a single word since. The father, a military officer according to some versions, takes out his gun and kills the servant. Afterward, he flees and is never heard from again.

In some versions the tragedy was explained by the fact that, unbeknownst to the couple, the servant was a psychotic patient who had recently escaped from an asylum. Other versions of the same incident differ in details. In some, the husband is a physician, who does not flee after killing the assassin but instead commits suicide. According to others, the baby is not just a few weeks old but is exactly six months old.

This rumor has characteristics that agree with Marie Bonaparte's observations about modern myths. Everyone who tells the story says he has heard it from others who know the protagonists very well. I was told repeatedly that the entire drama had appeared in the newspapers, although nobody who told me this had personally read about it. Almost everyone was immediately willing to believe that the tragedy had actually occurred.[*]

The story seems very strange, perhaps too much so for us to be able to insist that its latent content corresponds to a psychological condition common to all people. Indeed, would the tale not therefore have had to appear in this or a similar form with much greater frequency? It would be important to see, then, if others stories exist in which a child is served as a meal to its parents. We will first turn to classic mythology. The existing material is abundant, and the most well known version that approximates our own modern "myth" is the story of Tantalus.

In order to prove his divinity, Tantalus, king of Lydia and nephew of Jupiter, made a meal of the different parts of the body of his own son, Pelops, to serve to the gods. Only his wife, Clytia, the goddess of fertility, overcome by the pain of the loss of her son, ate this horrendous dish. After restoring life to Pelops, Jupiter gave him an arm of marble to replace the arm that his mother had eaten. He exiled Tantalus and condemned him to be the victim of a devouring hunger and unquenchable thirst. In the myth, Tantalus is subsequently portrayed standing in the middle of a river whose water races by too rapidly as he tries to reach it with his lips and standing beneath fruit

---

[*]This translation is based on the 1964 edition of *Motherhood and Sexuality*, which contains a different version of this chapter from the original 1951 edition. In the original version Langer related the circulation of this rumor to contemporary social and political events in Argentina, specifically the political tensions provoked by its controversial president, Juan Peron, and his wife, Evita, and the mass-based political movement they led. Passions ran particularly high with respect to Evita Peron, who was the first woman in Argentine history to play such a prominent role in politics. She was scorned and resented not only for being a woman who penetrated the barriers of male-dominated politics but for being of humble and illegitimate origins. Langer argued that because open criticism of the Perons was assumed to be too compromising by those who opposed them, this rumor represented a compromise, allowing an indirect expression of class-based resentment. Evita's humble origins and rise to power were expressed indirectly in this "myth"; its symbolic meaning contains the idea that the child—Argentina—is victim of a resentful woman—Evita—who is capable of avenging herself. In her book *Fantasias Eternas: A La Luz del Psicoanalisis*, Langer offered a complex analysis of the meaning of the myth in relation to each social class, which held radically different views of Evita Peron. In the present version she was obliged to remove the political dimension of the discussion by the publisher, who was concerned about possible political repercussions.

trees whose branches rise up just as he tries to pick their fruit. Before interpreting this myth, we turn to two fairy tales that describe similar situations.

In *Snow White* the bad stepmother, envying Snow White for her beauty, asks a hunter to take the girl to the forest to kill her and return with the girl's heart. Moved by the beauty and kindness of the girl, the hunter kills a hare instead, whose heart he brings to the cruel queen. She has it cooked and eats it, believing that she will thus incorporate an integral part of her beautiful stepdaughter's body.

In *Hansel and Gretel* the children's father, hounded by the poverty that prevents him from continuing to feed them, lets himself be persuaded by his wife, the children's stepmother, to take them into the forest and leave them there. The children wander alone through the forest until they arrive at a witch's house made of gingerbread. They begin to eat parts of the roof and are caught by the witch, who imprisons them. She fattens up Hansel in order to kill and roast him. Gretel thinks up a scheme and saves her brother. Again we find the attempts of a wicked woman to kill a child in order to eat him. The circumstances of this story are very similar to our modern "myth."

We are reminded of our earlier description of the mythological material from the Marquesas islands, a culture distinct from both the classical world as well as our own, where pregnant women fear that the *vehini-hai*—spirits of wild women—may steal their expectant child in order to eat it.

Let us now describe part of the dream of Berta, a young homosexual woman: She sees a tree, in whose shade she observes some little pigs; she looks up and discovers an enormous "spider/crayfish" suspended from the top of the tree. Suddenly the spider begins to lower itself. The little pigs flee, except for one, which remains as if fascinated and paralyzed. The spider throws itself on top of the pig and begins to suck on it. The dreamer sees with horror that the poor little pig cannot defend itself and that the pink color of its skin turns pale and white because the spider has sucked out all of its blood. We can anticipate the interpretation of this dream by saying that the three little pigs—known as three little brothers through the comic books of Walt Disney—represent the dreamer and her two younger brothers, while the spider—as generally happens in dreams and folklore—symbolizes the mother.

An analysis of this material—myths, fairy tales, and the dream—will help us understand our modern "myth." As already indicated, a situation common to all of these cases is the possibility that a child may be eaten. Sometimes the crime is carried out, but at other times the protagonist is frustrated in her perverse intention. But who does the protagonist represent? Who achieves or attempts to implement the cannibalistic crime? In a word, who is the criminal?

In the myth of Tantalus it is the father who kills his son, but the only one who completes the crime and eats the horrendous meal is Clytia, the mother. In *Snow White* the stepmother orders the princess killed and wants to eat her heart. In *Hansel and Gretel* the situation is more disguised, because the stepmother uses her poverty and inability to feed the children in order to achieve her goal, which is to expose the children to the danger of being eaten by the witch. It is yet another image of the bad mother who refuses to feed her children. In the Marquesan myth, the *vehini-hai* either make the fetus disappear from the mother's uterus or eat her young children.

Freud demonstrated that in the unconscious, the cruel and inflexible law of Talion—"an eye for an eye and a tooth for a tooth"—rules. Thus, as a punishment for our bad deeds we always expect the other person to do the same to us as we have, in reality or phantasy, done to him. So the crime of the *vehini-hai* is exactly the same as that committed by children of both sexes when, driven by their jealousy, they experience unconscious hostile phantasies toward their pregnant mother or the wish to steal or kill her small children, their younger siblings. We can deduce from this phenomenon that when the little girl becomes an adult woman pregnant with her own child, she will fear her mother's retaliation and so will convert her into the savage woman of the myth who steals and eats her children.

I have already interpreted the dream of the spider and the three little pigs: The bad mother is symbolized by the spider, and the three little pigs represent the dreamer as a child and her two brothers. While she observes the tragic scene in the dream, the dreamer simultaneously identifies with the little pig, who is the spider's victim. She dreams, then, that her mother kills her by sucking the blood from her.

In all of the material we find almost identical situations. In the myth of Tantalus the father is responsible for the crime, but the mother executes it. In the two fairy tales mother substitutes (stepmother, witch) attempt to execute the crime. In the dream the mother is a vampire who kills her daughter.[2] In the myth of the *vehini-hai*, the terrifying aspect of the mother—the wild woman—kills and eats her daughter's children. In spite of the fact that the tragedy appears displaced onto the next generation, the psychological situation is the same as that of the other examples, because the young mother identifies with her infant and considers it to be a part of herself, flesh of her flesh.

We shall now examine the situation of our modern "myth." In it the servant is the one who kills her young employer's child. If we consider the servant to be a declassed representative of the bad mother, we find the same situation as that of the *vehini-hai*. Now, if this is so, what are the unconscious motives responsible for the servant coming to play the mother's role? They are various and can be discovered in the psychoanalytic treatment of many women. A great part of the difficulties and constant complaints by female employers about domestic servants originates in an unconscious projection. In the first place, the activities of the servants are very similar to those carried out by the mother for the child: The servant has the obligation of feeding, cleaning, and taking care of her charges. In contrast to this similarity, the servant's dependence and social inferiority in relation to her employer permit the latter to realize an old and infantile vengeful phantasy: to reverse the roles. This phantasy is often exposed when the small child says to her mother, "You will see when I am big and you are little." All the ways in which the small girl suffers because of her dependency on her mother and her duty to obey her she can now make the servant experience. All the criticisms of her mother that she had to repress during her childhood can now be expressed directly and clearly toward the servant. She can avenge herself on the servant for all the frustrations suffered in her childhood.[3] All the repressed hatred that even as an adult a woman does not dare to display toward her mother is discharged toward the servant. She fears her servant and because of her hatred she believes that her servant is capable of any atrocity. Many women continually believe that servants are guilty of a host of offenses—they steal from them and seduce their husbands or their sons. One of the reasons that the story of the stewed child was accepted as truth is due to this unconscious relationship between the mistress of the house and the servant.[*] In all that has been said we find ourselves with variations of the same situation, in which the son or the daughter is always the victim of the criminal mother.

The person who is deeply moved when hearing the sinister story identifies with the child, innocent victim of the crazed servant-mother. And she feels sympathy and compassion for the young mother onto whom is projected the conscious positive image of her own mother. I

---

[*]Langer was fascinated by the class dimension of this rumor that circulated in Buenos Aires. The class conflict to which the rumor refers symbolically is one in which the lower-class Evita was feared and despised by upper-class women, who scandalously refused her entry to their prestigious and elite Women's Charity Society, thus violating an Argentine tradition in which the president's wife always assumed the directorship of the organization. Their refusal was but one example of their fear and hatred of Evita, representative of the class that had always been exploited by the class to which these women belonged, and of their projection onto Evita of this hatred. These women and the men of their class feared retaliation in kind at the hands of Evita and the populist, anti-oligarchic movement she represented.

already described how, through repressed jealousy in childhood, one comes to attribute to a mother substitute the strange desire to eat one's child. Another more profound reason exists as well. Following the law of Talion, the person who believes in the mother's cannibalistic desires and identifies with the victim fears experiencing from the bad mother what she, in her childhood, wished to do to her mother. She attributes to her mother her own perverse desires in order to be able to condemn her mother for that for which she refuses to reproach herself. To demonstrate this phenomenon, I will be obliged to show that the primitive crime of our "myth" is actually one in which the child devours the mother and that the apparent victim is really the true criminal. For this I return to the sources whose content relates to our myth.

Tantalus's punishment consists of being condemned to eternal thirst and of being unable to reach the branches full of fruit when he extends his hand to reach for them. The fruit is symbolic of the female breast. The character of the punishment reveals that his primitive crime was the voracity of his hunger. In the myth the situation appears changed into its opposite: It is not the son who wishes to eat his mother, but the son—represented in his infancy—who is served up as the delicacy to Clytia. Snow White falls as if dead after eating the poison apple offered to her by her stepmother; that is to say, she is punished for her gluttony, for having desired to eat the breast of the hostile mother. In *Hansel and Gretel* the children are thrown out of their home because of their voracity (it is no longer possible to feed them) and the witch surprises and punishes them when the children eat a part of her house. In psychoanalysis the house is a well-known maternal symbol. In the myth of the *vehini-hai*, the punished child's hunger does not appear. But we know that mothers in the Marquesas islands deny the breast to their children and feed them in a rough and perfunctory manner. As a consequence, strong cannibalistic and vengeful desires are provoked in the children, which are later found in their cannibalistic practices toward their conquered enemies. During the psychoanalytic treatment of the young homosexual woman whose dream was cited previously, strong oral aggressive tendencies directed toward her mother were manifested. Given the similarity of these situations, we can conclude that in our modern "myth," as well, the primitive crime is the aggressive hunger of the child, a hunger that has been intensified by the mother's abandonment (the tragedy occurs when the mother has left with the father).

The criminal is always, then, the child himself, and his own guilt feelings result in his carrying within him the repressed image of the witch-mother with cannibalistic and wicked desires toward him. The persistence of this image in those who heard our modern "myth" is the cause of their ingenuous credulity; in a specific period of our infancy we have all felt cannibalistic desires toward our mother's breast. Karl Abraham was the first to discover that at about 6 months of age, simultaneous with the appearance of the child's first teeth, sadistic desires of biting and chewing the breast emerge, accompanied by loving tendencies. I call the reader's attention to the fact that in one version of our myth the child was exactly 6 months old. To the child, taking in food—the maternal milk as much as anything else—signifies eating his mother. This same act acquires two opposite meanings. The mother is incorporated because, through his love for her, the child wishes to take her inside himself. But he destroys her with his teeth because he hates and fears her, projecting onto her his own aggression. These aggressive tendencies are reinforced in the child with each painful experience and through all the frustrations caused by his mother. The small child projects his hunger onto the mother and experiences it as if she ate and destroyed him from within as a deliberate aggression and a punishment for his own greediness. Thus, the servant who cooks the infant to serve him as a meal to his parents represents the mother who wishes to calm her own hunger with the flesh of her child instead of offering him her breasts.

Until now we have been exclusively concerned with the oral aspect of the mother–child relationship in this myth. But the father also appears in the scene. The protagonists of the drama are the following: the father-physician according to one version, the father-military officer according to another; the mother; and the servant. I believe that the two professions assigned to the father are not accidental but correspond to the internal condition expressed by the myth. An officer is an important person, authoritative, rather like a president or a king; that is to say, he corresponds to the image that the small girl creates of her father. The physician is the man before whom no sexual secrets or prohibitions exist. He knows everything and is authorized to examine our most intimate physical selves. He has, then, a role similar to the one the father plays with the mother in sexual relations. Now let us see the situation of the young girl confronting her united parents. In a specific period she falls in love with her father and wants to take the place of her mother. She feels violent jealousy of her mother, hates her, and wishes to eliminate her. This is one more reason for the little girl to fear mother's retaliation and to see her as bad. Furthermore, if more siblings are born, she experiences this as a parental betrayal and directs all of her jealousy and hate toward the recently arrived brother or sister.[4] She becomes sensitive in the extreme, feeling overlooked and treated like Cinderella.

We have seen how, in the oral domain, the myth's servant represents the bad mother onto whom the child projects his own cannibalistic desires. In terms of the oedipal situation the role of the servant is different; it represents the resentful girl in love with her father. The rivalrous situation with the mother is expressed with more clarity in the version of the myth in which the servant puts on her mistress's bridal gown; that is, she puts herself directly in the place of the young mother at the father's side. The girl is jealous of her parents' sexual life. In the myth the disaster occurs when the couple leave the servant at home and go out together at night. Moreover, the servant has come to the house before the birth of the baby; that is, initially an only child, she becomes the older sister, seeing herself displaced by the birth of the little brother. She regresses to the oral phase and avenges herself, killing the baby and preparing him as a meal. Her vengeance is that the baby, instead of continuing to eat from his mother with the approval of the father, becomes a meal for the two of them. For that she must be punished. In one version of the myth the father beats the servant to death; in another he shoots and kills her. The two punishments represent, in the masochistic regressive position of the girl, her intercourse with the father. The prohibited and denied sexual satisfaction that is repressed erupts once more into consciousness, although in a disguised and painful form. It exists for only a brief time, though, because the father disappears or commits suicide and the mother becomes mute, which also symbolizes death. Thus, the girl-servant suffers the most serious punishment that a child can imagine: for her crime of jealousy she is abandoned by both parents.

Marie Bonaparte found that the modern myths she analyzed were reactions to an agonizing situation that was real—the Second World War—and that they coincided with a psychological constellation common to many people. I stressed an analysis of the unconscious and universal content of our myth in order to show that it corresponds to a psychological constellation common to all of us. It is accepted by people because their various identifications with the protagonists succeed in capturing that constellation and its psychological truth. The interpretation of the myth brings us to this point. We discovered that the one who is guilty of the crime is the little girl who hates her mother and who, because of this hatred, fears her and represses her frightening image. We use the term "guilty." But with what right? Is it his wickedness that moves the child to hate his mother and to want to destroy her, or is it because of the frustrations she imposes on him? Psychoanalysts postulate different hypotheses about this. Those who base themselves in Freud's theory of the death instinct maintain that the baby is born with the capacity to love, hate, and envy, experiencing the world and its bad mother in light of its own impulses. Others see in the baby's hatred the reaction to the mother's hostile attitude and the frustrations she imposes on it. Whether partial to one or the other of the two perspectives, all psychoanalysts interpret the behavior of the child as a result of the interaction between its constitution and the real experiences it has in its childhood. The *Weltanschauung* of each analyst determines which of these two factors is stressed.

In our discussion there has been no attempt to distinguish between the two perspectives. We will see further on in the clinical material that from a subjective point of view, one always experiences oneself first as the victim and only afterward as the persecutor. However, in psychoanalytic treatment one becomes capable of accepting responsibility for what one has done to oneself and to one's own objects. In the subsequent clinical chapters I will refer to psychoanalytic material of both "daughters" and "mothers." For example, I will discuss how the fear of her mother prevents the girl from menstruating at the appropriate age. I will also analyze the hatred that a pregnant woman can feel toward her fetus, a feeling that can possibly result in a miscarriage, and the young mother's rejection of her newborn, which can result in disorders in breast-feeding. But do we consider these patients with rejecting attitudes toward the child "bad"? Surely not. Through analysis of them we understand that they repeat with their own child—without realizing it or wishing to—what they suffered as children with their own mother. That is, everything that appears hostile and nonmaternal in them originates in their own infantile frustrations that fixated them to an immature attitude unsuitable to their role as mothers. In other words, the mother is moved to reject her child and to frustrate her, often cruelly, because of her unconscious identification with the image of her own "bad mother" as well as the infantile impulses connected to this image.

Clinical Section [1]

We shall now explore the stages of female life in both their normal and pathological manifestations. The latter are fundamentally the manifestation of the same conflict: the fear of identifying with the image of a destroyed bad mother or the fear of her retaliation. We will see how these fears, overcome in one stage, often reappear in different forms in a subsequent stage.

Before systematically examining the subject of menarche and menstruation, I shall briefly describe the case history of a young woman.

This patient was elegant and attractive, although when she became nervous she manifested a slight strabismus (involuntary winking or squinting). Details about her childhood emerged in her analysis with me. She had been an unattractive girl, short, "with no neck," as her mother would say, and a notable strabismus. The mother, a beautiful and very proud woman, would tell her adolescent daughter, whom she accompanied to her first dances, that although she was older she was still the more beautiful of the two. At other times the mother seemed very worried about her daughter's future, fearing that she would never marry. The girl devoted all of her energy to her studies and her friendships with other girls, apparently unperturbed about her physical appearance. But even at 16, she was still not developed; she was very short, had not begun to menstruate, and although her mother had already insisted on a number of operations to correct her strabismus, none had proven successful. During this period she was hospitalized in a sanatorium for yet one more corrective surgery, this time with positive results. Before her young physician knew the outcome of the surgery, he began to court her. She responded enthusiastically to his advances, feeling for the first time like an attractive woman. The day she left the sanatorium she had her first menstrual period.

Years later, when I met her, she was no longer the short, fat girl of her childhood. She was a pretty woman, tall and thin. However, what appears to have been a "cure by love" had not fundamentally changed her. She had married the physician for neurotic reasons. The marriage began to go bad when she herself became a mother. She separated from her husband, unconsciously doing all she could during the divorce proceedings to lose the custody of her little daughter, whom she adored. We shall see how her failure as a woman was directly related to her maternal incapacity. In her adolescence she had rejected her femininity because of her mother's attitude. She had believed that since nobody was going to love her as a woman, she had better remain a child and live as if she were a young boy. But her first love had been enough to make feminine destiny seem attractive. Menstruation had arrived, transforming her into a woman. However, her resentment toward her own mother prevented her from living happily with the man her mother had chosen for her and from fulfilling her maternal role with her daughter without anxiety. Consciously she feared treating her own daughter with the same malevolence that her mother had directed toward her. In order not to hurt her daughter, she preferred to abandon her and to begin her life anew.

To any girl the first menstruation represents a very important event. She has acquired biological maturity and is now a woman, physically capable of sexuality and motherhood. This day deserves to be celebrated, and it ought to be recorded along with the dates of her marriage and the births of her children. In fact, this very thing occurs among primitive peoples.* Menarche is surrounded by taboos and ceremonies, culminating in a grand celebration during which the girl is accepted by the society of adult women as one of them. At the same time, an analysis of initiation rites also demonstrates the primitive male's ambivalence toward puberty. The adult menstruating woman excites, tempts, and scares him, motivating him to protect himself with many taboos against the disastrous contact with her. Primitive man fears the menstruating woman and imposes restrictions on the young girl who menstruates for the first time. In some tribes she is even submitted to cruel operations. Many psychoanalysts have studied the male fear of menstruation, and Freud himself interprets it as a fear of the woman's castrated and bleeding genital. However, it is important to note that once the girl passes through the rituals to which she is submitted, she is always treated to the joyful communal celebration of

---

*I have retained Langer's term *primitive* in this translation, though she later criticized it for its ethnocentric and pejorative implications; she came to prefer terms such as *pre-state*, *pre-agricultural* or *indigenous*.

her sexual maturity. She sees herself as the center of attention and interest, accepted and esteemed for her recently acquired femininity.

In our society the opposite occurs. The first menstruation is seen as a shameful and unacknowledged event. Helene Deutsch points out that many mothers speak with their daughters about conception more easily than about menstruation and that young girls' guilty feelings and shame are reinforced by a similar attitude in their mothers. However, like their primitive sisters, many girls believe that menarche should be celebrated and feel betrayed by the prevailing attitude of indifference or rejection. Mary Chadwick describes a girl's reaction to her first menstruation: Her initial feeling was negative, but when it was explained to her that this disquieting symptom was an indication of her femininity, she felt very relieved. Rapidly she understood many mysteries that had previously tormented her and she began to feel very excited. The desire and hope that her entrance into womanhood would be acknowledged led her to believe that she would now have the right to be the center of a grand celebration. Yet everything seemed to her to be tainted. She understood that she had suddenly become an adult who could now marry and have a child. She wished that her mother would tell her father that he now had one more adult daughter. But since nothing she hoped for actually occurred, she returned to the monotony of school life.*

In *The Second Sex* Simone de Beauvoir also gives examples of girls' reactions to menarche, taken from *Jeunesse et Sexualite* by Dr. W. Liepmann, two of which I quote here. We once again see the girl's joyful reaction to her newly attained maturity, a feeling that often conflicts with her mother's lack of understanding: "My mother had told me about menstruation, and I was much disappointed when, being indisposed, I dashed radiant and joyful to my mother's room, awakening her with a triumphant cry: 'Mama, I have it!' 'And for that you woke me up?' was her only reply. In spite of it all, I considered it to be a pivotal event of my existence." Another girl relates the following: "I always had known what all of that meant. I even awaited it impatiently, thinking that finally my mother would explain to me how babies are made. The famous day arrived, but my mother remained

---

*These negative and fearful attitudes toward menstruation still abound; they reveal the continuation of ambivalence with respect to female sexuality and act as a hindrance to the joyful acceptance by young women of their newly acquired adult capacities and status; see, for example, F. Fromm-Reichmann and V. Gunst, "On the Denial of Women's Sexual Pleasure: Discussion of Dr. Thompson's Paper," in *Psychoanalysis and Women*, ed. J. B. Miller (New York: Penguin, 1973) and D. Dinnerstein, *The Mermaid and the Minotaur: Sexual Arrangements and the Human Malaise* (New York: Harper & Row, 1976).

silent. In spite of that I was very happy. 'Now,' I said to myself, 'You also will be able to have children. Now you are a woman.' "

In the past girls felt the same way. In *Diary of an Adolescent* (author anonymous), the protagonist anxiously awaits the sign of her maturity. She grieves, feeling inferior and abandoned because her best friend has developed sooner than she. Here are some of her notes:

> January 5: Very important! Hella got it last night! . . . Yesterday she didn't go to school because she already felt horribly under the weather. Her mother was afraid that she might have another appendicitis. In place of that! She has such a long-suffering and interesting demeanor that I stayed with her the entire afternoon.
>
> July 2nd: Dear God, it came today . . . No, I can't write it down. It was in the middle of my physics class. We were supposed to stand up because A. came in, and when I stood up I thought: But . . . what could that be? And instantly I realized: Ah! During recess Hella asked me why I had blushed so during class and if I had been eating candy. I didn't want to tell her the truth immediately, so I responded: "No, I almost fell asleep from boredom, so I got frightened when A. entered the classroom!" On the way home I didn't say a word and walked slowly (they say you're not supposed to walk fast if you have it . . .). Then Hella said: "But what is wrong with you today? Why are you so distant? Have you fallen in love without telling me or has it really finally come? . . . " I answered: "It's really come!" And she said: "Finally, now you deserve my friendship again," and she kissed me in the middle of the street. Two boys passed by and one said to us: "A kiss for me, too."

In these examples, two typical reactions to menarche can be observed: The girl feels happy and proud to be closer now to her mother or her schoolmates or the infamous "best friend." In other words, with the arrival of menstruation, she unconsciously satisfies homosexual tendencies. But, simultaneously, the hope for heterosexual gratification emerges; she now is "a woman" who can have children. Thus, while her best friend kisses the young diarist because now she is a woman, two boys go by and make a pass at her; together with her best friend, she has entered the adult world and awaits her first love.

A positive reaction to menstruation is an indication of the girl's normalcy and her acceptance of her sex. Rarely is a positive reaction ever mentioned in the psychological, psychoanalytic, pedagogical, and anthropological literature. More frequent are the descriptions of the great "menstrual trauma." But is trauma an inevitable part of woman's psychobiological destiny?

Let us now examine evidence that belies a biological basis of adolescent menstrual conflicts. I have already described Margaret Mead's studies of a primitive society in *Coming of Age in Samoa*. Examining a radically different cultural environment from our own, Mead tried to ascertain whether or not the difficulties and disorders so frequently found in our pubescent girls were caused by biological forces or social circumstances. She explored the attitude of Samoan girls toward menarche and menstruation and found that in general they reacted to the arrival of their female maturity with complete simplicity and with no display of shame. Moreover, in a detailed observation of 30 Samoan adolescent girls, only 6 of them complained of pain during the menstrual period, which never became intense enough to inhibit their participation in play or work. The vast majority appeared free of conflicts about their destiny as women. As Mead points out:

> With very few exceptions, adolescence does not represent a period of crisis or tension, but, on the contrary, the harmonious unfolding of an ensemble of interests and activities that slowly mature. The young women were not despondent as if suffering from some profound conflict, nor were they tormented by philosophical questions or hounded by abstract ambition. Instead, from their point of view, to have many lovers for the longest possible time, then to marry in the proper village near one's parents and have many children, such were the satisfying goals they shared.

Simone de Beauvoir (1953) insists that, in general, menarche causes the young girl to feel humiliated, ashamed, and inferior. She goes on to explain how the different reactions of the girl and boy toward puberty are a consequence of our social and cultural conditions. In this regard she asserts that even if the boy experiences the awakening of his instincts and the transformation of his body with a certain degree of anxiety, he experiences with pride what the girl often turns into a secret tragedy: "In his body hair, the boy admires his growing undefined promises; the girl remains confused in the face of the brutal and endless drama that defines her fate. The penis acquires its esteemed value from the social context, while social circumstances transform menstruation into a curse.[2] The one symbolizes virility, the other femininity; because femininity means a change for the worse and inferiority, it arrives as a shock." And, continues de Beauvoir: "Menstruation inspires horror in the adolescent girl because it places her in a category of inferiority and mutilation."

Thus, both anthropologist Margaret Mead and feminist Simone de Beauvoir see menarche's traumatic effect on the girl as a consequence of unfavorable social conditions that place obstacles in the path of her ability to accept her femininity. A similar perspective can be found among educators who, during the first decades of this century, argued that menstrual trauma stemmed from inadequate sexual education. They blamed mothers for not adequately preparing their daughters before the onset of menarche for their new condition of reproductive capability.

In 1913 an entire issue of the first journal of psychoanalytic pedagogy, *Zeitschrift für psychoanalytische pädagogik,* was dedicated to the problem of menstruation and the reaction it provokes in adolescent girls. The authors were adult and child psychoanalysts and psychoanalytically oriented teachers. The latter discussed the difficulties observed among grade school girls, the majority of whom had only a smattering of sexual knowledge, and pointed out how much the girls might benefit from a sex education program provided by teachers. Today there is debate among teachers about the relative importance for young people of sex education, some asserting that while helpful, it is of secondary significance. In this regard Dr. Heinrich Meng (1931) argues:

> The challenge of educating young girls about menstruation cannot be met through the teacher's explanation of the physiological, psychological and biological facts of maturity just before the onset of menarche. While this explanation can be somewhat valuable, what really determines the attitude of the pubescent girl is the fate her instinctual life has already undergone in early childhood. Protection from pubescent disorders consists principally in adequate psychic hygiene of the small child. A teacher who is uninhibited and free of guilt feelings will be able to save the young person from a number of conflicts in childhood, latency, and puberty, or at least to help resolve them.

Melitta Schmiedeberg believes that, in general, sex education by the mother or another person close to the girl is beneficial. The positive effect, however, would stem only in small part from the information itself. More important, she argues, is the adolescent girl's perception that her mother's explanation represents her permission for her daughter to be concerned with sexual matters. Moreover, the girl values her mother's efforts as proof of her confidence and love. For reasons I will examine later, the first menstruation often awakens in the girl a fear of her mother, which can be counteracted by her mother's open and understanding attitude. In some instances where infantile anxieties are too intense, clarification of sexual matters will be rejected. Schmiedeberg relates the case of a neurotic girl who at first reacted to this kind of information with increased anxiety and later repressed the knowledge she had acquired against her will. In such cases the root of the problem is, as Meng maintains, found in early childhood and is the consequence of the link to a neurotic mother. A mother who rejects her own femininity will unconsciously adopt a hostile attitude toward her daughter, who later will be unable to become a woman without feeling guilty and inadequate. She will experience menstruation as definitive evidence of her castration. This process could lead her to regress and to feel ashamed of her menstrual hemorrhage, equating the lack of control over the loss of blood with the shameful infantile lack of control over excrement and urine.

This regression to the anal or urethral stage occurs when there are difficulties of this type during childhood. Once again, a neurotic development prevents the girl from later accepting her femininity. Moreover, her primitive anal or urethral symptomatology is already an indication of states of conflict provoked in her by the attitude of her parents or parental substitutes. Later, when femininity presents itself unequivocally in the biological realm, the girl oscillates between a flight toward masculinity—the desire to possess a penis—and a return to childhood—menstruation experienced as anal and urethral incontinence.

In order to illustrate the different causes of a girl's rejection of menstruation, that is to say, her femininity, I offer fragments of the analysis of an adolescent girl treated by my colleague, Matilde Wencelblat de Rascovsky, who generously shared this material with me.

Teresita, the older of two sisters, was brought to analysis because of serious difficulties at home and at school. With the exception of her father, whom she adored, Teresita was disconnected from her environment and lived continually in a world of phantasies. Her mother, her sister, and her friends believed she was crazy and eccentric, and she herself felt like an "oddity." This term had been used in her presence by a physician whom her concerned mother had consulted when she began to menstruate at the age of 10. It is generally thought that girls react with anxiety to their menstruation because they see it as a punishment and a consequence of masturbation. Some girls are also afraid because they confuse menstruation with some kind of venereal disease. We will see in the fragments of Teresita's analysis how she associates menstruation, masturbation, and syphilis with one another. However, the main reason for Teresita's rejection of her femininity was the impossibility of identifying with her mother. It is always hatred, which then provokes fear and guilt feelings, that prevents this identification. Teresita hated her mother. Let us, therefore, first explore the analytic material related to this hatred.

When Teresita was 4 years old, in the midst of the oedipal struggle, loving her father and fearing her mother's jealousy and retaliation, her mother became pregnant. Teresita's conscious awareness of her reaction to the birth of her sister emerged only later during her analysis. She says in an analytic session:

> Now I understand: I believe that my mother abandoned me for my sister, and these aren't stupid ideas because I can see very well that she is more loved than I, and the damage they've done to me I can see in my jealousy of other girls and in the fact that I don't have any girlfriends. With Fulana [a teacher in her school], whom I adored so much, I would have liked to kill her because she favored another girl. Well, all this I understand now. And now I also see that when I was little, nothing bad would have occurred in reality and Mama

would not have wanted to have another child if I had not made her jealous of my father's preference for me. So she wanted to have a daughter who was exactly like her and she abandoned me . . . I'll never forget the year 1935. I closed myself away; my sister was born and I had to give up the presidency to her and go off to jail . . . for my parents, my sister's birth was a party, for me it was a funeral.

We see, then, that Teresita hates her mother, believing she became pregnant because she no longer loved her and in order to punish her for loving her father. This very hatred toward her mother and the jealousy she feels toward her sister are what fixate Teresita to her mother, preventing her from becoming an adult. She rejects femininity because she cannot separate from her mother owing to the frustrations she has suffered. Nor can she identify with her because she hates her. She says:

For me, when a woman has children she breaks with the world [Teresita's world continues to be her mother] and is left only with her children. So my crying yesterday was about not wanting to be a woman; I want to be single, with lots of lovers who court me. It must be because of this that I also wanted to kill myself. You yourself say that I walk around bent over with fear that they will see my breasts, that I don't want to be a woman. But now I can't be a baby anymore. So I was disgusted and afraid and wanted to die, but it's because I don't want to be a woman and have children, and mainly I'm afraid of repeating what Mama does, that I'll grumble at my kids like she does and be as insensitive as she is [impossibility of identifying with a good mother]. That's why I fell, in order to die. In that way I don't have to estrange myself from the world nor have sexual relations, and that's why I'm afraid of sex, afraid of men and of having to confront the situation that everybody has to. Sure, you'll say that I cry for other reasons. But I cry because I have to have breasts, children, sexual relations, to be a woman; and that's why I go through my crises and want to die.

Teresita phantasizes about love, but in reality she does not like to go out with boys. They scare her. She would like to remain at her mother's side: "And even though on the outside Mama says to me, 'Go out, get together with some of your friends,' inside she doesn't let me, she tells me, 'No, you're still my little girl.'" In reality it is Teresita who wishes to be told this by her mother and to be kept by her side. It would be a proof of love.

Let us see how she thinks about menstruation: "Although you tell me I'm not, inside I feel like a twisted foot. And I've felt that way ever since I was a child and got my period. That's why I've felt like a twisted foot inside and not because I didn't know about sex like the other girls."

For Teresita, masturbation is connected to menstruation:

Today I didn't want to come to my session. I didn't want to get up. I think it was because my bed was all warm and I masturbated so well that I didn't want to come here. I don't dare do it awake, and I have my hand underneath the pillow, as a defense, but when I do it in spite of everything, I suck my thumb and think of being a grown-up woman, married with lots of children, and that I'm making love with a man. And suddenly I stop and say; "Don't be foolish, Teresita, you aren't the right age for this."

In these associations it is easy to see Teresita's double situation. She phantasizes that she is an adult woman, that is to say, she identifies with her mother and loves a paternal substitute; but at the same time, she sucks her thumb, like a little girl who misses the maternal breast.

Teresita explains why she masturbates:

You know that I should have gotten my period on the 27th? Since it didn't come, I masturbated to get it out. I got it out like my grandmother gets flan out of the oven—she says that sugar calms the nerves. I think that only masturbation is calming. Before masturbating I feel really nervous. [Thus she compares masturbation to eating sugar and believes, moreover, that masturbation brings on menstruation. It is her birthday; because of that she says a little later:] That's what I want, to be a newborn baby and not be this awful age of sixteen. It's clear that inside I've always wanted to be a baby, without knowing it outside . . . I already said when I'm eighteen, I'll get engaged and when I'm twenty, I'll get married and afterward have lots of kids. [Thus she oscillates, once again, between the desire to be a young girl and the wish to be like her mother, with a husband and children.]

Teresita has a strange idea about syphilis:

I'd like to talk about syphilis today. Could it be that a girl gets sick because of having sexual relations? I looked up this illness in the dictionary and it said, "Disease due to heredity or intercourse." I'm afraid of getting this disease and now I don't want to have sexual relations. This morning I was gripped with such fear; does that mean that because parents have sexual relations with each other before getting married the daughter is going to have syphilis? If I go out with a boy and we make love without being married, will syphilis get me? If the mother has had sexual relations with many men, when the child comes out does she have this disease? I don't understand the part about heredity. How is it the child's fault that the mother has it because of what she did? It's an injustice from above. I think that the child isn't saved. Let's look at it from another point of view: if the mother goes out with fifty men before getting married, the husband will realize it and won't love her; it would embarrass him if they say about his children: "The mother of this one has had fifty men." Every time I talk to a man, it disgusts me to think that he might have syphilis. Afterward, a child who goes to the doctor is told: "It's not your fault, it's your mother's." [The analyst asks her why she believes she has syphilis.] It's because of the discharge. I have it before every menstruation. I change my underpants and Mama asks me why. I tell her that I have my period. Surely if I told her what I have she would know it's because of masturbation . . . How do underpants look from syphilis? I thought that a person who masturbates before her period has syphilis.

For Teresita, masturbation brings not only menstruation but syphilis. This is seen more clearly in the following session:

Sometimes I think that men are the cause of so many diseases. I blame them for syphilis. The woman lets herself be attracted to men and has sexual relations with twenty guys. The man shouldn't let himself get carried away by his impulses. And sure, men are to blame for my masturbation. For me, syphilis, masturbation, and menstruation are all connected. But a woman who has never had a sexual relationship, according to the dictionary, could inherit syphilis. [In this way, Teresita makes her parents completely guilty for her "syphilis," that is, her masturbation. Because they have had sexual relations without worrying about the damage it caused her, she masturbates and has syphilis-discharge and menstruation.] For me, syphilis always represents little drops, always dripping, and during each period a little flesh comes out. I blame masturbation for this because a person who masturbates a lot removes little bits of skin [possible meaning: is always losing the penis again.] I dirty lots of underpants, I have pools of blood. But the discharge is worse, it comes a week before the menstruation. This time it's been very strong. It didn't stain the bed, but it did stain my underpants. I put them on the chair and Mama criticizes me and tells me to clean myself better after going to the toilet. I get embarrassed with her, not with you, and I don't dare to tell her because I would have to talk about masturbation. When I was a little girl, I had pools and pools of discharge and I felt uncomfortable, like a little baby with a dirty diaper. I didn't tell my mother, but I did talk to my uncle who is a doctor. He said that it came because I was developing early. But for me it is the masturbation; to the point that I thought that even when I'm married, during my husband's trips away from home, I will masturbate. [Masturbation appears here like the consequence of feeling alone and abandoned.] I have always masturbated, it kept me company on trips. That's why I accuse it and hate it; it's like a person, it accompanies me, but I blame it for the menstruation, the discharge, for everything. You will tell me, "But, Teresita, how do you see masturbation as a person?" That's how it is, a person has his good and bad side. [Masturbation appears personified because basically it represents her mother who does not love her and her father who fondles and excites her but leaves her in order to have sexual relations with her mother. The good side represents the father-seducer; the bad side, the father united with the mother. Moreover, in actuality, neither of the two parents "accompanies" her. In order to deny this painful situation, she insists that masturbation always accompanies her.] The bad thing about masturbation is that when I finish I am wet: my hand, the bed, everything. When a woman is expecting a baby, she masturbates. Good-bye child! No wonder children are born all twisted and deformed. [We already saw that she considers herself "a twisted foot" and "an oddity," that is, deformed because of menstruating. Now she clarifies that she blames her mother for her deformation because of having masturbated, that is, for having had a sexual life. Children never tolerate their parents' sexual life, because they feel excluded and abandoned while the parents gratify themselves sexually.]

My uncle, the doctor, gave me some pills to make me urinate more and to regulate my period. I had so much discharge that sometimes months and months went by without my getting my period. Mama said that it was because I developed early, but my uncle told me that Mama tricked me, that it was because of the discharge. You said that the discharge will disappear when I am big and have sexual relations. I can't believe that. I believe I will have it till the end of my life. I see my grandmother has wet underpants, and she doesn't pee in them, so she must have discharge; when I was little I thought that she peed on herself. But why is it you say that with sexual relations the discharge goes away? My grandmother has it. Is it a phenomenon? I'm afraid of having it my entire life; when one is too old to masturbate, the discharge remains. The strange thing is that Mama doesn't have it. [The discharge also represents a consequence of loneliness, of abandonment. Mama doesn't have discharge because she has Papa. The grandmother is an "oddity" like her, because she is as alone as Teresita and has no sexual companion, in other words, no one who loves her.]

I would like to be syphilitic to see how it is, where it comes from. I think the dictionary is mistaken when it says that it is a consequence of intercourse or of heredity. There must be something else: the third cause of syphilis is masturbation.

At one time this belief of Teresita's was widespread among adolescents. It continued to appear at the turn of the century in the "scientific" books on sexology. But why does the adolescent see syphilis as a consequence of masturbation or, better said, as its punishment? Masturbation is a normal phenomenon during certain periods of development. It becomes excessive, as in Teresita's case, when the child feels abandoned by her parents and treated with indifference. She reacts to everything with hatred. It is this latent hatred, linked to excessive masturbation, that makes her feel her onanism as something very sinful, deserving of the worst punishments.

Teresita continues to elaborate the subject of abandonment, which she feels she has suffered from her parents. She experiences this real abandonment in sexual terms and she returns to the past once again, now to the period just before she was born:

My birth was a good one, but Mama masturbated too much. Papa traveled a lot and I was born when he was away. I think that Mama had sexual relations with other men when I was about to be born. And Papa traveled. So, no one is going to tell me that I formed myself alone, with what Mama fed me: Someone came to put more semen in. I'm not going to let my husband leave when I have a little girl. When I was small they told me that children develop from the food the mother eats; lies, they form from intercourse with men. [Teresita expresses a thought that we already encountered (in Chapter 1) in the primitive belief that, once conceived, children need, in addition to the food from the mother, the father's semen to grow. In Teresita this idea expresses an unconscious reproach. Since she feels rejected by her mother and cannot let go of her, she blames her father for having abandoned her and for not having assumed a maternal role with her.] When I was born, and even before that, my father was far away, so they had to put me in the incubator. Mama wanted a boy, and because she was disappointed, denied me love. [Penis envy appears very clearly, but as a consequence of the rejection suffered at the hands of her mother.] Papa was a factory owner and wanted a son, not a daughter who's no good for anything; I am still terrified of being a woman. I would like to be a man in order to control everything: women, children. To be a woman is to be defenseless, to need a man in order to function. Papa adapted, but Mama still wants revenge because I'm not a son. In those times sons were the rage and Mama safeguarded her love for the second child, and plaf! it was another girl. I accuse her of having had sexual relations with other men and of not loving me because I'm female. I don't want to be a woman, to have hair down below and protruding breasts. If I were a boy, Mama would be happy and would give me the love I have to search for in strangers. She kisses me but she accuses me of not being a male. When I was little, I believed that you could change dolls, and I said; "I don't want that one, I want a real one." Mama still does the same thing. You can see she wants to give me back, for that reason I don't trust her and I never tell her anything. But since you take the child as she is, I come to you; I am your daughter. You are my incubator and sometimes I think that I am your daughter, and would like it to be so, because you don't think about the boy who is yet to be born. Mama wanted me to be a boy and the beneficiary of Papa's factory, but a woman doesn't count for anything, only for washing dishes, cleaning house, and having children. That isn't worth anything. I want to be a man; it might be an inferior wish, but Mama would love me much more.

We now understand the meaning of Teresita's accusation that her mother has had 50 men and is syphilitic: "She doesn't love me; it must be because she loves others, men." Moreover, since Teresita imagines that her mother devalues her femininity and leaves her in order to dedicate herself to men, she wishes to be a man in order to keep her mother. Her hatred toward her mother motivates her to deprecate everything feminine. Her desire to conquer her mother leads her to a virile position and the wish to have a penis. She might have been able to separate from her mother if her father, with whom she had a good relationship, had been stronger. This is expressed in Teresita's re-proaches of him for his absences when she was "about to be born." But with a weak father and a rejecting mother, only two solutions remain: the desire to return to early childhood, when her mother treated her better, or the wish to be a man, in order to conquer and dominate the mother. In Teresita's phantasies about her mother's promiscuous life and her syphilis, the girl expresses her idea that while her mother is a cold person, she can be seduced and dominated by a man. Thus, if she were a man, she could satisfy her mother, who would then love her.

We have seen that through masturbation Teresita has tried to identify with her mother, phantasizing about a husband and children. But she cannot maintain these phantasies because she considers herself to be too young. We also saw that masturbation is like a person who accompanies her, that she connects it to thumb sucking or compares it to eating sugar, that is, to recovering her mother. With respect to this last point, additional material from Teresita's analysis proves to be illuminating. Teresita comes from B., a small foreign city. She says in a session:

I read a very sad book that made me remember my childhood. Not even masturbation did anything for me. I masturbate for pleasure, but immediately B. comes to me, the flower market and all the rest, and it seems that everything is saying to me, "Masturbate, we are not dead, in spite of the years gone by, we will always live within you and masturbation will always bring us to you." I saw it all so clearly that I became the little girl of those years, the queen and princess because of how pretty I was. In that moment I felt all of this, so I thought; In order to feel my early joy I need to masturbate, but I can't do it forever. For me, masturbation means being a little girl, and now that I am too weak to be able to live in the present, I return to the past. [She explains again why she rejects the present and the future:] Now, with sex and men, I am so afraid I wish I'd never been born, so that I wouldn't have to have either sex or children, because I can't get rid of the idea that all married women have syphilis, you, and Mama and all of them. I don't want to get married so I won't have to become a syphilitic. It's already enough with the discharge and the masturbation.

Some sessions later, Teresita explains what syphilis is for her:

I would like to be your daughter; you listen to me and analyze me, but all Mama cares about are her clothes and her hats. She resents it because I am not more vain and I don't look at myself in the mirror. I think I don't do it in order not to be like her or because looking at oneself in the mirror is to see inside and I don't want to see more repugnant and shameful things, the ugly witch with horns and long fingernails that I have inside me. So I dress very fast in front of the mirror and I leave. In contrast, my sister spends entire hours in front of the mirror. Besides, Mama is always giving me the example of others: "Look how the Gonzales girl walks so straight . . . " How does she expect me not to have an inferiority complex if she's always thinking other people's daughters are better than her own? It was the same when I was small. But Papa would say to me, "Don't worry, because you have the voice of a swallow." I acted like it didn't bother me, but inside I felt terrible. Tell her not to compare me to other people's daughters. How does she expect me not to feel inferior to the rest and not to feel like I have a big case of syphilis? And when I'm angry, I masturbate more, especially when they compare me to the other girls.

Therefore, to Teresita, "to have syphilis," like the need to masturbate, means that she does not feel loved by her mother, whc, she believes, prefers other girls to her.

Let us summarize what Teresita has shown us in order to assess the significance of her fears and preoccupations. In Teresita we find all that is typical for a girl of her age: rejection and desire for sexual life; guilt feelings because of masturbation, along with phantasies that partially anticipate her life as an adult woman; the experience of menstruation as a punishment for onanism; the fear of syphilis and of sexual life in general; penis envy and so forth. But her serious neurosis magnifies everything, permitting us to obtain more clarity about the underlying basis of such typical conflicts. We see what lies behind pubescent fears, which seem to have a single source. Teresita herself expresses this when she tells us, "Syphilis, masturbation, and menstruation are all connected." The three conditions are linked to the distressing discharge, which makes her reexperience her enuresis, and to her complaint about the lack of a penis. All her fears and symptoms express her rejection of femininity, the consequence of her persistent tie to a cold and frustrating mother who does not permit identification with her. Even though he deeply loves her, her father is too weak to detach her from her mother. Thus, to be an adult woman signifies, on the one hand, to lose her mother and, on the other, to be forced to identify with a hated object. To be a child who phantasizes about her past implies the retention of her mother. Teresita desires this, because although her mother is unloving, she has no other choice. She still needs a mother. Her conflict is clearly expressed in her masturbatory phantasies. Although they are sometimes composed of images about her future life as a married woman with children, Teresita avoids this adult condition by sucking her thumb, thereby regressing to her early childhood. At other times she consciously uses masturbation in order to return to a period when her mother still loved her. The birth of her sister was so traumatic for Teresita because she interpreted it as her mother's retaliation for her loving and being loved by her father. Frightened, she turned back to her mother and never again detached herself from her. However, in reality she remained in a vacuum. Her mother rejected her for her younger sister, and her guilt feelings separated her from her father. She wants to have a penis in order to reconquer her mother and be preferred to her sister. She equates syphilis with the sensation of being compared to other girls and being judged inferior and thus rejected, of losing her mother's love to her sister. Menstruation signifies something disastrous for Teresita, it means to be an "oddity" or "a twisted foot inside," deformed and destroyed. But basically, to be an "oddity" means not to be loved by her mother and to hate her in turn, for which she must suffer the consequences.

In Teresita we see how a woman's two preoccupations about sexuality can be superimposed: the more superficial is penis envy, expressed in her desire to be a man; the deeper preoccupation is the fear of being destroyed inside, in her female sexuality. Moreover, Teresita has a cold, dominating, and rejecting mother and a seductive but weak father. We shall encounter this family constellation in other cases of psychosomatic reproductive disorders. Teresita herself presents symptoms in this respect. Her discharge, her early menarche, and the disorders and irregularities of her menstruation are an expression of the conflicts produced by her family situation.*

In Teresita the appearance of menstruation, although traumatic, does not represent new problems for her. It is bound up with her phantasies about syphilis and masturbation. However, menarche intensifies preexisting conflicts and anxieties because with the advent of this profound biological change the girl realizes that her prior childish sexual phantasies and games are now converted into the potential reality of adult life. This condition is confirmed by the intensification of sexual longings which, related to biological changes, only serves to increase the girl's guilt feelings.

Helene Deutsch relates a case that clearly illustrates this situation. A young 14-year-old girl became ill with an acute psychosis on the second day of her menarche. Following her internment in a psychiatric clinic in Vienna, she would spend her time dancing and laughing uproariously. She would put makeup all over her face, curl her hair, lift up her skirts, and mutter obscene words, constantly repeating the word *politik*. When she was able to obtain treatment, it was discovered that this German word, which means politics, was composed for her of two other German words: *polizei* (police) and *dick* (fat). These two words symbolized her pubescent anxieties. *Polizei* referred to the forbidden and feared idea of prostitution, which in her country was under police surveillance; and the second word, *dick* (fat), referred to the danger of pregnancy. Her mother reported that the girl had always been rather strange but before reaching menarche had never manifested serious disturbances. So the first menstruation, intensifying prior conflicts,

---

*Langer continued to stress the unconscious significance of this and other biological processes in women, although as a physician she always proceeded in her evaluation by attempting to discount physiological causes of menstrual disorders. In the later years of her life, because her primary interests lay elsewhere, she may not have been aware of the research that has tended to shift from the symbolic meaning of menstruation to the impact of the cyclic hormonal changes of the menstrual cycle on the psychological experience of women. See, for example, T. Benedek, *Psychoanalytic Investigations* (New York: Quadrangle Press, 1973); J. Kestenberg, "Phases of Adolescence: Part I," *Journal of American Academy of Child Psychiatry* 6: (1967): 426–463 and "Phases of Adolescence: Part II," *Journal of American Academy of Child Psychiatry* 6 (1967): 577–611.

converted her sexual phantasies into something now possible to enact in reality and thus disrupted the neurotic equilibrium maintained until that point.

In another of Deutsch's cases, we see once again how the young girl is distressed by biological maturation, which is discrepant with her psychosexual development. Moreover, what clearly emerges in the case to be described is how the intensification of her sexuality moves the pubescent girl to erotically reinvest her first amorous objects and to reexperience her oedipal conflict. Consciously, she defends herself against her incestuous feelings, repressing as much as possible her sexual excitement and denying its manifestations, especially to her mother, toward whom she feels guilty. Since repression often does not manage to dominate sexual desires, they come forth in a disguised form and the girl is obliged to defend herself against them with phobias and conversion mechanisms.

Deutsch describes this phenomenon in the history of Molly, brought for psychiatric consultation by her mother because she presented multiple phobic symptoms. These had been present for a long time, but suddenly became so intense that the girl was forced to abandon school and all other social activities. Molly was constantly afraid of fainting. As a result, she avoided going out, fearing she would fall and remain sprawled unconscious on the sidewalk. In enclosed environments she felt calm but only with the assurance that she could escape at any moment. At home she alleviated her anxiety by eating apples or drinking milk. She had other fears as well, including dying, and did not like to go to sleep.

Molly's parents did not get along well and considered divorce, an idea the girl found difficult to contemplate. She could not decide which of the parents she would live with if they actually divorced one another. She believed her illness had helped to bring her parents closer again. Molly's mother suffered from fainting spells that sometimes occurred following turbulent exchanges with her father. Molly had developed a fear of death when her older sister had been pregnant and she had learned that women can die in childbirth. Important as well was a serious illness that had recently befallen a schoolmate.

Molly had begun to menstruate a few months earlier. She was very inhibited when she told her mother, and it was her sister whom she asked to accompany her to buy her first sanitary napkins. Her mother reported how strange it seemed that Molly tried to hide her period from her. On one occasion, when the mother saw a bloodstain on her daughter's sheet and asked if she was menstruating, the girl flatly denied it. In reaction to her first period, Molly told her married sister, who was living with her husband and baby in her parents' home, "From now on anything can happen to me. I can have a baby." Her sister replied, "But, no, darling, for that it's necessary to live with a man." "I know that," the girl responded, "but I live with two men, Papa and your husband."

This conversation with the sister gives us the key to understanding Molly's neurosis. Menstruation established the certainty that she would be able to have children. But that possibility made her anxious and filled her with guilt feelings toward her mother, because she phantasized having those children with her father or his substitute, his son-in-law. She expressed her desire and her fear in an ingenuous way, without consciously understanding the entire meaning of what she said. Unconsciously, the idea of being able to conquer her father and have his children, now that she was a woman, was a psychological reality, and we should interpret all her symptoms as derivative of this reality. She tried to hide her menstruation from her mother so as not to make her suspicious and jealous. She phantasized about uniting her parents through her illness in order to deny her desire to separate them. The illness was a self-imposed punishment for her forbidden desires. She experienced all of the oedipal conflict directly with her parents and simultaneously displaced it onto her brother-in-law and sister. She was less anxious with them because the situation was less forbidden.

Freud describes a psychological mechanism that he terms "identification through guilt." If one wants to take the place of another person in order to castigate oneself, one identifies with the other's specific ailments. It is as if one said to oneself, "You want to have what she has, and you really deserve it." We see how Molly identified with her mother's illnesses and also with the threat of death that her sister had to endure. She was afraid of fainting, like her mother, or dying, like her sister might have, because of having wished to take their places and having envied her father and brother-in-law's love for them. Moreover, she feared going to sleep because while asleep one's defenses are weakened and forbidden sexual desires emerge more freely.

Freud taught us that all symptoms are a compromise formation. They function as a defense against a forbidden desire as well as the satisfaction of that desire. Molly's fear of fainting was a warning against the forbidden identification with her mother. But at the same time, the hope of fainting, as well as the anxiety produced by enclosed places, signified an unconscious continual expectation of sexual attack. Yet she was not very sure of her innocence: Basically Molly feared losing her mother if she came to be sexually attacked, even if she had not provoked the situation. For that reason she was anxious in enclosed rooms from which she could not flee in case of a hypothetical attack. The only thing that could calm her anxiety was eating an apple— symbol of the breast—or drinking milk. That is to say, she calmed her fear of losing her mother—because of her genital desires—by regressing to an oral stage and relating to the good mother of her early childhood. We observed the same mechanism in Teresita, who sucked her thumb after masturbating and dreaming of a husband and children. Two factors made Molly anxious with regard to the intensity inherent in puberty: the fear of dying in childbirth, of being destroyed internally if she adopted the role of an adult woman like her mother or her sister, and the fear of losing her mother's love and of having to thus abandon her position as child and daughter. Furthermore, in Molly it is evident that her rejection of menstruation did not originate in a frustrated desire to be a male and possess a penis; rather, menstruation was traumatic for her because it made her relive her infantile oedipal conflicts. She hid her menstruation from her mother in order to calm her presumed hostility. She feared that her mother's hatred would be provoked by witnessing the rivalry of an adult daughter, whose femininity was expressed in menstruation.

Molly's history represents a typical conflict of the pubescent girl, which in her case gave rise to the creation of rather serious neurotic symptoms. At other times—later we will see an illustrative case—these conflicts are expressed psychosomatically, provoking amenorrheas and dysmenorrheas. These might present themselves as the only indication of conflict but generally are accompanied by psychoneurotic disorders.

While amenorrhea—the absence of menstruation—is always considered a pathological phenomenon, some degree of dysmenorrhea —menstrual disturbances—are generally considered to be normal.* The influence of the menstrual period on the personality was at one time a frequently discussed topic. An important argument among antifeminists was that inevitable menstrual pain and weakness made women inept for sustained physical work and sports. It was maintained, moreover, that women could not have professions or be engaged in

---

*The tendency within contemporary medical research has been to discount the psychosomatic origins of dysmenorrhea; moreover, contrary to psychoanalytic assumptions, successful treatment of dysmenorrhea has not appeared to result in symptom substitution. Many contemporary feminists have argued that in some ways sexist thinking on the part of the mental health profession has tended to attribute dysmenorrhea and other menstrual problems to psychogenic causes, which leads to ineffective treatment. See, for example J. Lennane and J. Lennane, "Alleged Psychogenic Disorders in Women—A Possible Manifestation of Sexual Prejudice," in E. Whitelegg, M. Arnot, E. Bartels, V. Beechey, L. Birke, S. Himmelwert, D. Leonard, S. Ruehl, & M. A. Speakman, The Changing Experience of Women (London: Martin Robertson, 1982). Although Langer continued to hold with her psychosomatic perspective, she herself warned against psychologizing the complex female experience, which has biological and social underpinnings.

socially important activities because they became clinically "irrespon-sible." Statistics were used to demonstrate that the majority of the crimes committed by women occurred during the premenstrual or menstrual time of month. Let us see, then, if women necessarily experience, either before or during their periods, a state of depression or irresponsibility and if the hemorrhage itself must normally be accompanied by pain.

Some women do present a clinically depressive premenstrual state. What happens in such cases is that each time they feel bad or anxious and cannot understand why, the first menstrual flow suddenly changes their state of mind, permitting them to understand the cause of their depression. Based on her analysis of such patients, Karen Horney arrives at the following conclusions in "Premenstrual Tension" (in *Feminine Psychology*): Women who suffer from such depressions can consciously desire to become pregnant, but are unable to because of an unconscious conflict. Their intense desire to be mothers is opposed by an equally intense rejection, rooted in anxieties and guilt feelings due to their strong destructive tendencies. Horney assumes that at the point during the cycle when the body biologically prepares for motherhood, the desire to have a baby, as well as the fear and the rejection of it, are reactivated. The result of this conflict is depression. The depressive state ends with the appearance of menstruation, which is an indication that a pregancy was not realized. I often observed the opposite cyclical picture: infertile women who consciously want to get pregnant experi-ence euphoria and optimism in the premenstrual state, thereby denying their intimate perceptions of failure; these feelings are followed by depression at the beginning of the menstrual period, which is experi-enced as a miscarriage and a frustration yet again of the longed-for motherhood.

Although the frequency of menstrual pain has declined in our society, it is still considered normal, especially in young girls. While cramps vary a good deal in intensity from woman to woman, they normally oscillate between the sensation of awareness of the uterus to light discomfort. Intense cramps are an indication of conflict, whose psychological genesis is demonstrated when they disappear in the course of adequate psychotherapeutic treatment.

Let us return to the description of a clinical case and assess the causes of a serious dysmenorrhea in an adolescent girl, Adela B, who was analyzed by my colleague, Arminda Aberastury (personal commu-nication). Adela's menarche arrived without complications when she was 13 years old. Some days later an apparently traumatic event occurred. The butler tried to rape her, but desisted when the girl vigorously rejected him. Her second menstruation was now accompanied by symptoms that occurred with each subsequent menstrual period. The girl was given every kind of nonprescription medicine, and finally, when she was 16 years old, her parents decided to seek psychoanalytic treatment. She was a humble, inhibited, and very religious girl who had the physical appearance of being much younger than her 16 years. Her breasts were not developed, and every feature of her body gave the impression of an accentuated immaturity. Menstruation always brought on a severe depression, with sensations of being dirty and devalued. Moreover, she had intense cramps that obliged her to stay in bed for several days and a marked seborrhea on her face and hairy body.

The family constellation was similar to the one cited in Teresita's case: a cold and dominating mother who preferred the younger sister and a weak and seductive father whom the girl loved very much. As a four-year-old child, Adela had suffered from a vulvovaginitis of unknown origin. The treatment was applied by her mother, and the child was simultaneously humiliated and excited.

In her analysis it became evident that Adela experienced her menstrual cramps as if they were the pains of childbirth. That is to say, she unconsciously considered herself to be pregnant as a consequence of her sexual phantasies, which had increased because of the intensification of sexuality inherent in puberty. The cramps also represented the punishment she felt she deserved because of her phantasies. She exhibited her suffering in order to calm her mother's presumed hostility and rage. She unconsciously repeated the situation she had experienced in her childhood, in which the treatments for the vulvovaginitis were perceived as a punishment her mother administered for her oedipal phantasies. In that period she had expressed the "filth" of her sexual desires through the discharge, which she thought of as a disgusting secretion. Now this "filth" was expressed through the seborrhea and menstrual blood. The causes of her depression appear to be those suggested by Horney. An unconscious desire for motherhood made her transform each menstruation into a birth, which conflicted with a deep feeling of guilt because of the incestuous character of her desires and her intense hostility toward her mother.

It might be said that such an interpretation is not applicable to a 16-year-old girl. Adela would be too young for motherhood. On a rational level this is obviously true. But we are not dealing with rational processes. We recall Molly, who declared after menarche: "Now anything can happen to me." Adela had had a normal menarche. Afterward came the butler's attack, an event to which Adela attributed much importance. Only later did the menstrual disorders begin. For Adela the rape attempt, quite easily frustrated, was unconsciously equivalent to actual intercourse and was followed by phantasies of pregnancy and childbirth. Moreover, only after a relatively long time in analysis did the girl dare to confess that she herself had done everything possible to provoke the butler, displaying herself to him in her underwear long before the "illegal act" occurred.

Apparently Adela, in response to the pubescent intensification of her sexuality and her unconscious phantasies, had recourse to drastic means. Her provocation of the butler—a humble working-class representative of her father—had a double objective: On the one hand, it satisfied her sexual desires and, on the other, the attack functioned for her as a warning. She demonstrated to herself that she was now a woman, an appropriate object for conquest, and that she should be careful and repress her dangerous sexuality. Psychoanalytic treatment profoundly transformed Adela. The dysmenorrhea disappeared, along with all of its symptoms. Moreover, from an immature and inhibited girl, both psychologically and physically, Adela developed into an attractive young woman.

Adela expressed her pubescent conflict by means of a dysmenorrhea. In another case we will see how a young woman, Mary, suffered from a prolonged amenorrhea, through which she sought a total negation of her femininity. She was analyzed by Dr. Eduardo Krapf, from whose published case I present a brief summary. Mary, a 21-year-old young woman, came to analysis because she had suffered from complete amenorrhea since the age of 20. This condition had appeared after a short period of dysmenorrhea. Mary also suffered from a marked depression and various conversion symptoms, such as vomiting, diarrhea, and constipation. Moreover, because of both her depression and her physical state, she had been obliged to abandon her university studies. Her family constellation was typical enough. Once again we encounter a seductive and affectionate father and a cold mother who rejects her child because she is female. Mary had an older brother, and her mother had accepted her second pregnancy in the hope that she would give birth to another boy. When Mary was born, her mother's disappointment was so intense that she refused to see the baby for 15 days, a fact that she later frequently spoke about with the family in front of Mary. Mary tried to conquer her mother and to defend herself against her inferiority feelings in comparison to her brother. She competed with him constantly, actually surpassing him intellectually. Furthermore, in order to avoid feeling too guilty toward her mother for her own close relationship to her father, she adopted a "virile" posture with him. She would comment in her analysis, especially when she referred to anecdotes of her life as a student, that she and her father treated one another "man to man."

Menarche was experienced by Mary in a traumatic way because it attacked the defenses with which she denied her femininity. She hid the fact of her first menstruation from her mother for an entire day. Her mother's reaction when Mary finally confessed reveals to us quite well the mother's neurotic attitude toward her female child. As an explanation of menstruation, she told her daughter, "It isn't anything special, but a disagreeable and dirty thing that all women have, which they have no choice but to endure." However, in spite of the traumatic effect of menstruation, Mary slowly dealt well with the situation. She tried to accept menstruation as "a concession made by her mother to her," that is, as permission for her to be a woman.

In my exposition of psychoanalytic theory, I spoke of the young child's unconscious phantasies of destroying the inside of the mother's body in order to steal from her the penises and babies she believes are stored there. These hostile phantasies provoke a fear of maternal retaliation, which, following the Talion law of "an eye for an eye and a tooth for a tooth," could dispossess the girl of her internal organs and of any possibility of her own future motherhood. Mary's analysis demonstrated that she suffered intensely from this fear of female castration. During an analytic session, this fear made itself conscious through a phantasy that Mary experienced with tremendous anxiety and a sense of reality. Before describing the phantasy, I should clarify that in the prior session the analyst had interpreted to Mary that for her he was dangerous because she unconsciously saw every man as her father or her brother and thus she feared her mother's punishment. Mary arrived in an anxious state to the following session, phantasizing that the analyst-father could abandon her. She said that without his support "from behind" she would fall and that ravens would come to eat her "from behind her back when she was defenseless." When asked what ravens ate, she replied: "The entire body . . . the intestines . . . the womb and the legs . . . the arms and not the face." When her attention was drawn to the fact that the genitals are between the womb and legs, she immediately associated to the fear of having an operation to take a baby out of her body.

Thus Mary hid her femininity from her mother in order to avoid this punishment. Earlier I described how she adopted a pseudo-virile posture in order to compete with her brother and to be close to her father. A deeper analysis demonstrated that this attitude also functioned as a defense against her mother's presumed hostility.

Mary's neurotic equilibrium disintegrated in the face of her first genital experience. When she was 21 years old, she fell in love with a young man, Pedro. Her first late menstrual period occurred just before a party, where she was expecting a decisive development to occur regarding her romance. Her analyst interpreted this first delay as the consequence of her anxieties. Not menstruating would signify closing herself up genitally and denying her femininity to her mother. Apparently, Mary achieved what she desired at the party, and when the young man kissed her, she felt vaginal excitement for the first time. Hours afterward, her period started. However, the relationship with Pedro ended in profound disillusionment. It was then that the serious menstrual irregularities began, followed by other reverses in the ensuing months. Mary failed an exam because "this time she did not know how to engage the sympathy of her examiners." Another problematic situation was inadvertently discovered by her father, whom she realized loved her much less than she had imagined. Only after this shock did she develop amenorrhea, which lasted for more than 3 years before finally responding to psychoanalytic treatment. She ultimately overcame the depression and conversion symptoms. The latter are fairly typical in hysterical girls after their first romantic kiss. Vomiting and intestinal difficulties are reminiscent of pregnancy and correspond to the unconscious phantasy of oral fertilization and pregnancy. The significance of the amenorrhea was more complicated because it was intimately linked to Mary's fear of her sexuality. Following the trauma caused by the intensification of her sexuality due to menarche, she completely repressed her sexual feelings and could then accept her menstruation without any difficulties. The first symptoms developed only when Mary fell in love and experienced sexual excitement, which intensified all her conflicts with her mother and, thus, her fear of her. But she was ready to fight for her femininity. Her delayed menstruation arrived after Pedro's kiss. Moreover, she always retained an important defense against her mother in her intellectual capacity, which to her represented the possibility of disguising herself as a man. Only when she failed as an adult woman—the young man and her father rejected her and the school examiners were not sympathetic enough—was she overcome by great anxiety. In response, she withdrew from her professional positions, which had been attained at one time through great effort but were now totally devalued. The adult woman, a brilliant although somewhat "masculine" student, had become a defenseless and asexual little girl, and her menstruation disappeared. Since menstruating meant to open herself up genitally—exposing herself to an amorous attack from the man-father and the hostility of her mother—and to be an adult woman, her amenorrhea represented becoming a little girl and closing herself off genitally, avoiding the castration of her femininity. Mary's psychoanalytic treatment succeeded in curing her of her amenorrhea and the concomitant symptoms. She matured psychologically and was able to successfully resolve her conflicts with her parents.

Let us summarize the clinical material presented thus far. Teresita's case directly demonstrates the thought and preoccupations of an adolescent girl with respect to menstruation and its related problems. While Teresita was a disturbed girl, as I pointed out, her condition permits us to see with more clarity the psychological processes that develop, though not as intensely, in less neurotic girls. Helene Deutsch demonstrates in Molly's case how menarche can unleash a serious neurosis, even when the girl does not appear to have been affected by the appearance of her menstrual period. In this case all the symptoms developed in the psychological realm only. With Adela, on the other hand, we saw how menstrual conflicts were the derivatives of a psychosomatic disorder, dysmenorrhea, accompanied by neurotic symptoms and skin problems. Mary's situation was similar. Her amenorrhea was produced on the basis of unresolved conflicts and accompanied by a depressive state.

If we compare the families of these girls, we observe that in every case, except for Molly—for whom sufficient data is lacking—there is a typical family constellation. The cold mother's rejecting attitude provokes the girl's hostility, which is then converted into hatred because of jealousy of a sibling preferred by the mother. The father's seductive attitude attracts the girl, but since the father is weak, the girl does not feel protected against her mother, whom she fears. This fear stems from the guilt feelings caused by her rivalry with her mother for her father's love and by her hatred because of her mother's rejection. This hatred and the ensuing guilt feelings do not permit her to identify well with her mother. On the contrary, they make her fear her mother's retaliation. For Teresita and Mary, the desire to be loved by their mothers and their fear of them provokes a wish to be a man. In this way, they also deny their more profound fear of not being able to be a woman because of having been destroyed inside. The fear is repressed, protecting them from having to admit that they might have definitively lost the possibility of identifying with their mothers and of thus having a husband and children.

In these four cases we discern something observed by Melitta Schmiedeberg, namely, that the instinctual understanding of the biological process of menarche can be especially traumatic for the girl because she fears that all her desires and sexual play, heretofore inoffensive, can from now on bring real consequences. The first case I describe in the next chapter contains the same dynamic. In subsequent cases I will demonstrate that the girl's awareness of having achieved sexual maturity can have the opposite effect, that of calming her irrational anxieties. Moreover, in all the cases I present we shall see that the same conflicts that make puberty difficult bring about psychosomatic disorders in the various stages of the adult woman's reproductive life.

Menarche and Related Disorders [1]

Menstruation has been studied more frequently by psychoanalysts than any other female function. Much has been said about the taboos related to menstruation, as well as its traumatic effect on both men and women. However, very few published clinical histories refer specifically to this subject. Perhaps the "phallocentric" focus in psychoanalysis, that is to say, the consideration of woman as a castrated man, has been responsible for the relative superficiality of existing research. At one time it was argued that for women menstruation often represents a castrated imaginary penis. However, no satisfactory explanation has been given of how this idea of castration occurs or of the nature of the more profound anxieties against which it is an unconscious defense. Our understanding of these questions could only emerge when analysis of patients was deepened and theoretical assumptions were discarded. In the process, the "phallocentric" perspectives in psychoanalytic theory about feminine development had to be completely revised. The progress made within the most recent endocrinological research provided a biological foundation for the shift in psychoanalytic perspectives regarding femininity. While it may seem paradoxical, only after this conceptual revision took place could menstruation come to be understood as an inherent and pleasurable manifestation of femininity. Certainly, each time it occurs, menstruation represents the loss of the hope of motherhood. But it simultaneously symbolizes youth and fertility, a woman's capacity of continuous regeneration, and the promise of a new motherhood.

I feel obliged to focus on the subject of menstruation because menarche marks an extraordinarily important moment in a woman's life. In puberty the girl relives all of her infantile conflicts as she simultaneously enters into others corresponding to her sexual maturity. When neither menarche nor the first menstrual periods have been an unconscious trauma for the girl, we can assume that she has had a satisfactory childhood. Moreover, such acceptance almost guarantees subsequent psychosomatic health. When, on the other hand, menarche presents conflicts, these may be reproduced in each stage of a woman's reproductive life. Sometimes they will be manifested in psychological problems or in physiological disorders or both. The case I shall describe will serve to illustrate this point and will demonstrate as well that even when menarche appears to have little impact on the girl, it is unconsciously experienced otherwise, unleashing symptoms that the patient does not relate to this physiological change.

Isabel, an intelligent young woman, has been married for some time and has recently moved to Buenos Aires. She sought psychoanalytic treatment because of conflict over professional goals. Aside from other symptoms, she presented a phobia of cockroaches. This fear had intensified in Buenos Aires, which she attributed to the fact that these insects are much more numerous here than in her own country. The phobia had first appeared when Isabel was 3 years old, after she had moved to a new house where cockroaches abounded. Before moving, she had sometimes seen them but without experiencing any response in particular. Consciously, she was perplexed by her phobia because as a young girl she had always liked insects. She remembered that her brother had given her a grasshopper when she was 4 years old. She grew very attached to it and kept it in the kitchen until one day her maternal grandmother intentionally killed it. The relationship between the girl and her grandmother was very tense. The grandmother adored her grandson, Isabel's brother, and she kept a watchful eye on his expressions of affection and dedication toward his sister. She always forbade Isabel from playing with her brother. Isabel associated her disgust for cockroaches to the grasshopper episode, especially because the grandmother had smashed it. The thing she could least tolerate later on was the sight of smashed cockroaches. However, she did not understand why she associated the experience of the grasshopper to the phobia, which had appeared only when she turned 13 and then in relation to another type of insect.

When she was a child, her parents would always tell her that she should not get married. Her mother did not consider her to be pretty or healthy enough to marry, and her father thought she was too intelligent to live an ordinary woman's life. In reality, she was very likable, although perhaps not as pretty as her older sister. Her father wanted her to pursue a university career without becoming distracted by an amorous involvement. Moreover, he would fly into a rage if he came upon her sewing or cooking, because these activities seemed to him to be a waste of her time. In spite of her parents' opposition, though, Isabel married, but never thought of having children in her country of origin where her parents still lived. In her analysis she began to worry about this problem and soon decided to have a child. She did not become pregnant immediately but suffered one of those transitory sterilities that occur with some frequency. This condition is often interpreted by gynecologists as non-ovulatory periods unrelated to psychological factors. Later, we shall see how I was able to deduce the cause of Isabel's difficulty. During the period described here, the phobia became worse. I interpreted to Isabel that possibly the grasshopper had unconsciously represented her and her brother's baby and that she had experienced her grandmother's prohibition against playing with her brother as a prohibition related to something sexual and the grasshopper's death as the corresponding punishment. Isabel rejected this interpretation. She alleged that she had never loved her grandmother and that, apart from the impotent rage she felt in response to the grasshopper's death, she was not accustomed to attributing much importance to her grandmother's attitudes.

Eventually, Isabel became pregnant. The phobia remained during the entire pregnancy. She give birth in autumn and proceeded to forget about cockroaches, facilitated by the fact that they had disappeared due to the cold weather. Some months following the birth of her baby, she suddenly analyzed the significance of her phobia. She agreed with my interpretation, which this time provoked the emergence of a forgotten memory. At 3 years of age, when her family had moved to their new house, Isabel observed her mother showing great disgust at the cockroaches she encountered, claiming that the filthy creatures lived off excrement. It was then that the phobia began. After remembering this, the patient thought that she would now experience no fear or disgust toward cockroaches. A few days later she confirmed that, in fact, the phobia had disappeared. She mentioned this development in her analysis without telling me more details. A few days later, she noted that her attitude toward cockroaches had altered once again. Now when she came upon one, she would closely examine it in order to prove to herself that it truly caused her no fear or disgust. She had a dream, a part of which I will relate. She saw two cockroaches, impaled on toothpicks. Then she remembered that as a child she used to like to collect chestnuts with her brother, who had shown her how to make pretty dolls, connecting the chestnuts to one another with little sticks. The impaled cockroaches in the dream represented the two children who played with chestnuts, as well as the little dolls—her and her brother's phantasized children. In the same dream another very strange cockroach appeared. It resembled a piece of excrement more than an insect. Isabel associated to this image the infantile sexual theory that the child is created inside the mother and then comes out like feces. Only then did she tell me about the conversation she had with her mother after the move to the house with the cockroaches, a conversation in which her mother, expressing a great deal of repugnance, identified the insects with excrement. In this way the origin of her phobia could be reconstructed. When the grandmother killed the grasshopper, the child was 4 years old and in the throes of the oedipal situation, rivalrous with her mother and competing for her father's love. But since her father was a severe man who mainly frustrated her, she sought and found a paternal substitute in her brother, 7 years her senior and very understanding and affectionate. In this way she replaced her father as an object of infantile love and admiration. When her grandmother, jealous of her preferred grandchild's love, protested against the relationship between the two children, Isabel was indignant. She felt even more so when her grandmother killed the grasshopper, tenderly loved as a present from her brother. But no neurotic symptom developed because she devalued her grandmother and did not need her love. During puberty the problem presented itself in a different form. I have already pointed out that infantile conflicts that culminate in the oedipal conflict abate and remain repressed for a time—the period of latency, so rich in sublimation—only to reappear in puberty. When Isabel menstruated for the first time, she reexperienced the time when she had been 4 years old. The love for her brother and the desire to have a child emerged in her unconscious. She apparently spared herself a serious conflict with her mother, because by loving her brother she did not enter into competition with her but, rather, with the despised grandmother. In this way she resolved the incestuous conflict of childhood. However, once in puberty, her love for her brother also became something dangerous. All of her desires were, of course, unconscious. They became anxiety-provoking because the biological fact of her menarche was accompanied by the conviction that now that she was a woman, these desires, previously only phantastic, had become realizable. When her mother reacted critically and with disgust to the cockroaches that fed on excrement, but that were also similar to her beloved grasshopper, Isabel felt as if her mother condemned her, as if she had said, "The child you wish to have is disgusting, rubbish." And this time it was not the despised grandmother who criticized her relationship with her brother but her mother, whom she needed and loved ambivalently. Distressed, she developed the phobia. To avoid the cockroaches signified not to have an incestuous baby. Unconsciously, the phobia represented a warning from her mother, as if she had said to her, "Remember that you should not have a child with your brother."

In the aforementioned dream, two impaled cockroaches appeared. The cockroaches symbolized Isabel and her brother in the dirt with their infantile sexual games that disgusted their mother. The third cockroach, made of excrement, corresponded to Isabel's idea about pregnancy and birth at the time when she was given the grasshopper by her brother. Moreover, the excrement was linked to her mother's rejection of the cockroaches and to dirty things in general. Later, when she married, her husband represented her beloved brother in her unconscious. The two figures became confused with one another in many of her dreams. In her country of origin, close to her mother, she did not even think of having children. But after moving to Buenos Aires, she began to struggle with the idea. Consequently, the phobia, an expression of the maternal prohibition, intensified. Her transitory infertility expressed her submission to the severe mother of her childhood, whom she was partially able to conquer by becoming pregnant. But the coexistence of her phobia with the pregnancy was an indication that her conflict with her mother had not been resolved. That is to say, the maternal prohibition that had produced a phobia in the psychological realm, caused first a transitory infertility and subsequently other disorders in the somatic realm, to which we turn our attention later. During the first months of her analysis we dealt primarily with the conflicts regarding her parents and parental representations brought on by the possibility, and later the realization, of her pregnancy. In her unconscious I represented her mother. Through interpretations that were tolerant of her infantile conflicts, I slowly became a mother who returned the grasshopper to her and permitted her in turn to become a mother. Because of this, when a healthy child was born—with my permission, one could say—the phobia disappeared without Isabel being aware of it. This is a frequently encountered phenomenon in which symptoms disappear without their having been completely interpreted and even, at times, without the patient clearly realizing the moment of their disappearance. As the conflict disappears in the transference relationship, the corresponding neurotic symptom loses its reason for existing. Only when she felt the desire to have another child did Isabel became preoccupied with the phobia again, analyzing it and rather compulsively attempting to verify whether or not it had really disappeared. She spoke to me for the first time of this desire in the same session in which she told me the dream of the cockroaches. The symptom of closely watching the cockroaches in order to assure herself that she no longer feared them signified, then, the confirmation that the desire to have another child was neither prohibited nor distressing.

To briefly summarize, Isabel had been raised by a strict father, who wanted at all cost to make a man of her, and a rejecting mother, who conceded femininity only to her older daughter, who in turn treated her younger sister with humiliating compassion. The grandmother rejected her completely. Her brother loved her, but this relationship succumbed to family prohibitions. She could win her father's affection only by renouncing her femininity. It is not strange, therefore, that Isabel preferred to be a man (penis envy) and that the appearance of menarche, indisputable proof of her femininity, produced anxiety and conflict. These were not conscious, but then the phobia appeared. Later, in almost each stage of her reproductive life, different symptoms appeared as derivatives of her unresolved conflict. She did not dare to be a woman, because as a girl she had been forbidden to dream of her future motherhood.

I have already described how the first menstruation can be joyfully accepted by the girl as a manifestation of her maturity and the promise of her future motherhood. However, frequently a contrary reaction occurs, and in almost all of the clinical material described here, one can observe the traumatic effect of menarche and menstruation on the girl. Let us explore the reasons why menstruation often seems so catastrophic.

Imagine what a small child might feel when it perceives its mother or another woman during menstruation by discovering, for example, bloodstained sheets or underpants. It is understood that this blood comes from the genital, in other words, from an organ capable of giving a great deal of pleasure but that is, because of the prohibitions associated with it, the center of many anxieties. Moreover, the child will clearly believe that the blood comes from a wound. The boy sees it as an external wound and will relate it to the absence of a penis in the feminine genitals and have the phantasy of a castration that has left a bleeding wound. The girl will realize that the blood comes from the inside of the body. So she will think of the wound as something internal to the body and will believe that something inside the woman's body is hurt. Children grow within the female body. So the hemorrhage would be an indication that these future children have been hurt and are slowly bleeding to death (a childhood phantasy postulated by both Helene Deutsch and Melanie Klein). There is always the idea of a wound, of the woman who has experienced some aggression. And since it is the genital organ that suffers the loss of blood, so the wound is understood to be the consequence of a genital act. Primitive peoples see in menarche the consequence of a sexual act between the pubescent girl and the ancestral spirit. The young girl has the same reaction unconsciously, that is, her menarche is the consequence of a sadistic intercourse with her father (according to Melitta Schmiedeberg). Moreover, if the hemorrhage is perceived as a punishment for the girl's forbidden sexual activities, it is immediately associated with masturbation, the blood being the proof of the damage inflicted during her masturbatory activity. Finally, in the unconscious, all that comes from the body is considered equal (Melanie Klein), and in this way menstruation can also take on the character of the loss of fecal material or urine.

Until recently, the value of menstruation as a manifestation of instinctual sexuality and sexual maturity, as well as a protection against anxieties, has been underestimated. Only Therese Benedek and Melanie Klein consider this dimension, although they always emphasize its negative consequences. I think we come closer to an objective understanding of the menstrual phenomenon in its totality if we analyze and elaborate its positive significance. With this in mind, I present additional clinical material.

First, the history of Ana. As a girl, she was very independent, the only daughter of rather irresponsible parents. She attended a coeducational school and was a very good student, competing successfully with her male counterparts. She allowed herself the kinds of sexual liberties permitted exclusively to boys in that era, claiming that because she worked as hard and as well as her male classmates, she had the right to their privileges as well. However, during the first years of her sexual life she was frigid, achieving orgasm only if she had masochistic phantasies. Her masturbatory phantasies were of the same nature.

The main phantasy had to do with a girl who was mistreated by a strict teacher for minimal transgressions. As a child, Ana had not played with dolls, preferring instead to read books. During latency she and her best friend indulged in play that almost exclusively involved creating dramatic scenes whose content was masochistic. It was Ana who invented most of the phantasies and took all of the initiative in directing their play. When she was 10 years old, Ana found out through newspaper reports about a scandalous trial involving a woman accused of mistreating and beating her daughter before a group of prestigious men who paid well for the spectacle. Suddenly, Ana became conscious of the fact that sadism was something "very bad and forbidden." In spite of having always consciously identified with the mistreated victim in her games, she reacted with intense guilt feelings.

She told her bewildered friend that she would never again play "those games." During the summer of the same year, she met some girls who explained to her in a very confusing way where babies come from. Her mother learned about these conversations and became very angry, forbidding Ana once and for all to keep such bad company. Hurt by her mother's behavior, and in an attempt to elaborate her new knowledge, in her phantasies Ana tried to do away with the woman's role in procreation. She guessed that the child grew inside the mother by feeding on the blood normally eliminated during menstruation. She imagined that sperm could be cultivated like bacteria in a receptive environment and, sprinkled with blood, could create babies without female participation. In this same period, a dramatic event involving a love triangle caused a huge sensation in her hometown. A famous singer's wife attacked his lover by throwing sulfuric acid in her face. Ana took advantage of this incident for her phantasies. Since women were no longer necessary, they could be eliminated by forcing them to drink sulfuric acid. In her phantasies, Ana got rid of all the women in the world, imagining each delicious detail of how the caustic liquid burned the mouth, esophagus, and stomach and of how miserably they died.

Ana was a tall and well-developed girl. When she was 13 years old, she began to anxiously await indications of her first period. She felt desperate when she reached 14 years of age without having menstruated, and she feared she would never be able to have children. She asked her mother to take her to a gynecologist. Her mother attempted to console her, minimizing the issue. In reply, Ana said that her mother would be the responsible one if she could not have children later on. When she got her first period at age 14, her relief was indescribable. At the same time, her behavior changed. She no longer cared about her studies and fell intensely in love with a boy some years her senior. She wanted to marry him as soon as possible in order to have children. She had ardently desired to menstruate, but always with the fear of not achieving it. Perhaps her guilt feelings had actually retarded the date of her first menstrual flow. She later reacted in a similar way to all aspects of her feminine experience. Still very young, she had her first sexual relations with a friend. It was she who persisted in the matter, since he was reticent to deflower her because of his scruples and fear of responsibility. Following her initiation into sexual life, she realized she was frigid. Later when she married and did not become pregnant within the first year, she felt desperate, convinced that she was infertile. Again she had the vague idea that her mother was guilty for her presumed infertility. Once she was able to conceive, she suffered several miscarriages. Desperate, she feared she would never be able to carry a full-term pregnancy. When she finally had a child, she could not breast-feed. Ana endured the discomforts associated with menstruation, loss of virginity, and labor with complete ease and without complaint. In fact, these various events typical of feminine sexual life brought her happiness, which for a time calmed her profound anxieties. Before analyzing them, however, I shall present Berta's case, because although her character is significantly different from Ana's, the roots of their neuroses have much in common. A dream of Berta's was described earlier when I spoke of the introjected image of the bad mother. Now her history will be summarized.

Berta was attractive, intelligent, and ambitious, but she felt inferior because of being a woman. She had an extraordinarily painful concept of love. For her, a woman who gives herself in love to her partner suffers abjectly and will ultimately be abandoned. Although she admired men and devalued women, she considered herself to be a homosexual. She had developed some platonic female friendships in which she had felt quite enamored and excited. In such situations she behaved like a gentleman courting the object of his infatuation, but she never attempted to consummate her love. In conversations she delighted in showing off her ostensible homosexuality. For that reason, she was shocked when in her analysis she realized that everything related to homosexuality, that is to say, intimate contact with another woman, horrified her. These feelings became evident in the transference, when she thought the analyst wished to seduce her. Her horror was manifested in a nightmare: She sees a tree and observes several little pigs in its shade. She looks up and views an enormous spider/crayfish hanging at the top of the tree, which suddenly begins to climb down. All of the pigs flee except one, which remains paralyzed and transfixed. The spider throws itself on top of the pig and begins to suck its blood. Horrified, the dreamer watches how the poor little pig cannot defend itself and how the rosy color of its skin turns pale and white because the spider is sucking out all of its blood. In this dream the three little pigs represent the dreamer and her two younger brothers while the spider symbolizes her mother or, in the existing transference relationship, her analyst.

Berta had always felt distressed at being a woman and had consciously experienced her penis envy. She had two younger brothers and was jealous of both because they were permitted many advantages that were prohibited to her. Her father was an important industrialist with an arrogant demeanor who adopted a seductive attitude toward his oldest daughter, all the while devaluing women in general. Her mother was a reserved and calm woman, given to feeling herself the victim in every family conflict. As a child, Berta adored boys' games:

weapons of all kinds, machines, and so forth. She hated and simultane-ously admired her father for his proud and exhibitionistic masculinity and scorned her mother for her hypocritical humility. Once her mother came upon Berta suddenly while she was furiously beating her statue of the Virgin Mary with a whip.

Berta began to menstruate when she was 12 years old, after which she changed radically. She later recalled that the next two years were the happiest years of her life. She became feminine, flirtatious and very keen on Tarzan. But when she was 14 years old, her psychological state once again changed due to a serious disillusionment suffered in relationship to a maternal substitute. Her depressed state began with fits of crying that little by little gave way to a depersonalization that lasted intensely for a number of years, never completely disappearing. She never recovered the happiness of her childhood. During her intense depersonalization she complained that everything had lost its relevance for her (which to her unconsciously signified that she no longer loved women) and that she did not like men anymore. Berta's depersonalization resulted from repression of both her heterosexual and homosexual feelings. Because of her hatred of her mother, which had been renewed in her recent disillusionment, she could no longer identify with her and continue to love Tarzan, a substitute for her virile father. Nor could she feel close to her mother or substitute figures in a homosexually amorous fashion.

When I met Berta, she was already married. It was a loveless relationship, and she felt constantly depressed and depersonalized. When she wanted to have children, she suffered a transient infertility. When she finally had a baby, she could not breast-feed for fear of losing her breasts to her infant.

In spite of the fact that both Berta and Ana undoubtedly suffered from intense penis envy, their initial reaction to menstruation was very different from what might be expected. They experienced neither shame nor depression, as if something beyond the experience of castration were occurring. Indeed, they experienced a kind of triumph, a great relief and a vague feeling of gratitude. They both changed in behavior and for a time became feminine. It might be said that they had not adopted their feminine role earlier because each doubted her capacity to be a woman and a mother. Now, how do we understand the fact that menarche did not distress them but instead brought visible relief of their neurotic states?

In "The Overvaluation of Love" Karen Horney observes that frequently women fear not being able to become pregnant because of having masturbated as children and having had sadistic phantasies about other women. Melanie Klein speaks of the girl's irrational anxieties originating in phantasied attacks on the mother's body and its contents and in her fear of having been victim to identical attacks in retaliation. It will be important, then, to see if in our two patients there are manifestations of hatred toward their mothers of such an extent that it moved each to doubt the intact quality of her own femininity.

A conscious elaboration of these attacks may be observed in Ana's sadistic phantasies of eliminating all the women in the world and in Berta's game of whipping her mother's statue of the Virgin Mary, the ultimate symbol of motherhood. But what is the origin of such hatred, and its special nature and consequences for both girls? Ana's retaliatory phantasies emerged when her mother forbade her to learn more about how children are conceived and born, which she interpreted as a prohibition against becoming a mother. She reacted by phantasizing about how she could eliminate mothers from the process of reproduction. However, there are indications that Ana already hated her mother, whom she considered to be a bad person. Although Ana had never been harshly punished, for years in her phantasies she tortured children for nonexistent crimes. She identified with the punished child, the nonexistent crime substituting for the real crime of her hatred and her unconscious attacks on her mother. When she read in a newspaper that the mother who punished her daughter in the presence of men was a criminal, she became frightened. She felt as if her own mother had been accused of treating her violently and without love in the presence of her indifferent father. However, she was unable to justify these accusations against her mother, since she felt guilty and deserving of every punishment due to her own hatred. Ana hated her mother and wanted to destroy her. But she loved and needed her. So she did not accuse her mother but, instead, became masochistic, repressing her hatred. Thus, she could forgive her mother, receiving pleasure from the punishment in place of fearing it. But her unconscious hatred of her mother—or mothers in general—persisted in spite of her masochism and love, making all identification impossible. The oral roots of her hatred can be seen in the way she attempted to eliminate women in her conscious phantasies.

We shall now examine Berta's situation. While Ana had phantasies of poisoning mothers, Berta dreamed that the spider-mother killed her by sucking her dry. In a very primitive stage of her life, Ana must have felt poisoned by her mother and avenged herself by poisoning her mother in her phantasies. Berta must have felt that her mother did not satisfy her or feed her well, that her hunger emptied her. So she must have wished to suck her mother completely dry and thus empty her. As a punishment, the mother sucked at her in her nightmares. In this way she came to feel empty inside. Consciously, she did not want to be a woman; unconsciously, she feared not being able to be one. So she could not identify with her mother, who was always full of children. Moreover, she feared the identification with her mother, a hated and scorned object. And so she found refuge in homosexuality, which also brought dangers. Berta could not assume a passive attitude toward women, repeating the mother–daughter relationship in the erotic realm, because she exposed herself to reliving her early experiences with her mother, all of which she feared. She risked being a victim once again of the mother-spider, just as she was in her dream. As a defense, she chose another form of homosexuality, masculinization. She wanted to be a man, to have a penis, and she behaved like a gentleman toward an adored woman. However, she feared and hated women too much to expose herself to the danger of intimate contact, which would only have demonstrated the illusory nature of her virile defense. For that reason, when facing in her analysis the danger of a homosexual love for the analyst, the primitive and distressing situation of her dream, in which she again became the defenseless little girl, emerged.

We see, then, that both Ana and Berta's failure at femininity is rooted in the failure to identify with the mother. This inability results from the persistence of their oral hatred and their fear of having been destroyed as a punishment. They remain in this state because of the absence, as well, of paternal assistance. Ana's father was too weak and passive for her to dare to confront her mother as a rival and turn toward him in a feminine attitude. Berta's father, on the other hand, was apparently too strong and virile, devaluing women and humiliating his wife. Berta fears reaching out to him in a feminine way because she does not wish to suffer her mother's fate. In both cases, when they are unable to conquer their fathers, the girls identify with them, adopting a masculine attitude and manifesting penis envy. That is to say, both girls might have perhaps overcome their difficulties with their mothers if their fathers had supported them. The lack of support exacerbated their conflict, leading them to perversion. But how do we explain the fact that menarche brought each girl to a much greater acceptance of her femininity, in contrast to all that has been generally said about the traumatic effect of menstruation precisely in women with masculine tendencies who experience penis envy?

We recall that Melanie Klein describes the girl's unconscious phantasies of destroying the inside of the maternal body in order to rid it of its contents of children and penises. As a consequence, the girl can also develop a fear of being destroyed internally. This is the mechanism found in our two patients. In each case the girl suffered an intense oral and ambivalent fixation on her mother. Her hostile desire to incorporate her mother totally or partially, thus destroying her, produced great anxiety. Because of her guilt, each girl projected her own oral hostility onto her mother. But this projection is equivalent to the fear of maternal aggression, as the dream of the spider demonstrates. The idea of not being physically intact through the fault of the mother is the consequence of this fear. This primitive idea is repressed. Later on, the discovery of sexual differences and of her own lack of a penis is experienced as a castration, because it provokes the resurgence of the old fear of having suffered an internal destruction, which is now related to a genital wound. Another patient, in response to my interpretation of her criticism of her mother for the castration of a presumed penis, replied: "I don't believe that I simply reproach Mama for my castration, but for having castrated me badly. She made me neither a woman nor a man." When during the analysis her fear of sexuality was discussed, an image from her childhood emerged. She saw her father beheading a chicken—which she associated with the loss of the penis—and afterward saw her mother put her hand inside the chicken, ripping out the intestines and the eggs and completely emptying it. She went on to associate this image with her incapacity to commit herself to serious studies, asserting as the reason that she herself was empty. The patient in this way expressed the two female fears of castration, the second of which is always linked to the fear of infertility.

Let us return to our central theme. What psychological significance as a sign of fertility could the first menstruation have for these patients when it arrived in spite of all of their doubts and fears? In the first place, menstruation was experienced as a reconciliation with the mother, who gave them their sexual reproductive capacity as an unexpected and undeserved present. It became equivalent to an absolution from the mother, thus permitting them to be like her and to have children in the future. This, and the fact of bleeding and feeling cramps, alleviated their guilt feelings. The bleeding also satisfied their masochistic phantasies in a form acceptable to the ego. Moreover, their feelings of triumph and relief came from no longer feeling like dependent girls but like women capable of renouncing their homosexual dependence on the mother.

This same phenomenon can be observed in the initiation rites enacted by primitive peoples after menarche to separate the girl from her parents, especially from the mother. In many tribes the girl has to abandon the mother when the first menstruation comes, after which she lives with an old woman—symbol of the asexual mother—until she is delivered to her husband. In some tribes the girls are enclosed in a small house, a cell, or a hammock during the first menstruation and ensuing months. Their departure after a determined period of time from this confinement, a symbol of the maternal breast, corresponds to a rebirth and signifies the definitive separation from the mother.

Moreover, just like every feminine somatic manifestation, menstruation can serve as a weapon against homosexuality itself. However, as we saw in Berta's case, homosexuality is not the deepest problem but, rather, serves to hide woman's most anxiety-provoking conviction, that of having been destroyed as a woman.

In one psychotic patient it became clear to me that the preoccupation with her menstruation, symbol of her intact or wounded femininity, was replaced by delirious homosexual ideation. She suffered from a hypochondriacal schizophrenia. For a long time her hypochondriacal preoccupation centered on her minor amenorrhea. She felt distressed if it seemed to her that her menstrual period did not last for enough days or that the flow was not heavy enough. She feared becoming seriously ill and felt that something inside her was not well. But this symptom persisted only while she struggled to maintain her femininity and refused to resign herself to homosexuality. She had a dream in which, as a man, she was having intercourse with her mother. When, a short time later, she believed she felt a penis growing within her genitals and that she was being transformed into a man, she lost all interest in her menstruation. Thus, her preoccupation with her period expressed her struggle against the perception that something within her, something related to her femininity, was in trouble. She renounced her destroyed femininity because she found in the delirious idea of her transformation into a man a psychotic escape from her anxieties. She could forgive her mother and retain her as an object because now she was not a destroyed woman but a man. In this patient we see a psychotic preoccupation. However, in general, the hypochondriacal preoccupation with menstruation, rooted in the fear of a damaged femininity, is very frequently observed in a less intense form in neurotic women,

Moreover, menstruation—the first as well as those that follow—can function to satisfy aggressive tendencies directed against the mother. In such cases the uterus itself, organ of motherhood, is identified with her, even more so because the uterus is the first feature we know about our mothers. (In Spanish a very clear philological relationship exists between the words madre [mother] and matriz [uterus]. In German this relationship is even more evident: *Mutter* = mother; *Gebaren* = to give birth; *Gebarmutter* = uterus.) I had occasion to observe this mechanism in a homosexual patient who had remained fixated on her mother due to an intense oral frustration. In her analysis she described the sadistic pleasure she felt when she saw her menstrual blood running down her thighs. She remembered having felt intensely excited when reading a novel in which there was a description of a peasant woman's menstrual blood running down her nude legs, staining the floor. For her, the uterus was her own mother who bled and suffered during menstruation. In primitive tribes the mothers perceive the aggression of the menstruating pubescent daughter. Winterstein explains that in many tribes the mother or her substitute carries out the most cruel of the initiation rites of pubescent girls, in revenge and unconscious defense against her daughter's incestuous and sadistic impulses.

In summary, the normal girl will accept menarche with pleasure and pride in spite of a certain feeling of strangeness and anxiety, because she sees in it the indication of her feminine maturity and the promise of her future motherhood.

On the other hand, upon becoming a woman the neurotic girl feels devalued. She will reject menarche, experiencing it as a castration or interpreting it as a punishment for the damage she has caused through her masturbatory activities. We have seen this latter response in Teresita, who rejected her femininity, believing it to be the cause of her mother's rejection of her. In Teresita we also saw how the loss of menstrual blood may provoke a reliving of old anxieties in relation to urinary incontinence. In other cases, menarche is also equated with the loss of fecal material.

Many girls reject or hide their menstruation because to be a woman signifies becoming rivalrous with the mother and provoking her hatred. Or through the identification with the mother the girl faces the danger of suffering all the ills she earlier wished upon her. We observed the first of these mechanisms in Mary and both of them in Molly. In Molly and Adela we also saw that menarche provokes anxiety because the girl is not yet ready to abandon her infantile position. Moreover, she fears the realization of her sexual phantasies, which were inoffensive as long as she was still a child and immature.

This mechanism was apparent in Isabel, whose condition also illustrated how a repressed menstrual conflict caused psychosomatic disorders later in life.

In contrast, Ana and Berta expressed an enthusiastic acceptance of menarche. As girls, they had apparently rejected their femininity because each felt incapable of being a woman and a mother. Menarche functioned to calm their profound feminine castration anxieties and their guilt feelings toward the mother. Even so, ultimately they continued to be convinced of their infertility, and thus their difficulties reappeared in the different stages of their reproductive life. These two cases reveal as well that menstruation can function in the service of other neurotic or perverse conditions.

Based on everything that has been said, we may conclude that while the violent rejection of menarche or menstruation generally indicates a conflict, its acceptance can either be an indication of normalcy or of repressed anxieties. Only a more profound analysis in each specific case permits an accurate diagnosis.

The Fear
of Defloration

In previous chapters I have discussed menstruation, a biological process of concern to women only. In contrast, the experience of defloration is shared by a woman and her partner. I have spoken of how phantasies and internal objects influence the functioning of a woman's body. Now our attention is turned to the couple relationship, which in contemporary society has usually been freely established through love. However, this choice has been motivated by many unconscious factors, including an unconscious perception of the character of the other, who all too soon will serve as a screen on which to project internal idealized and horrific objects. Moreover, for every woman an object choice already contains, although she might consciously discount it, the promise and threat of her future motherhood.

In primitive cultures sexual defloration is an event that, like menstruation, is surrounded by multiple taboos and ceremonies. According to Freud (*Totem and Taboo*) whenever primitive man fears a danger, he erects a taboo as a protective measure to embolden himself to face the threat. For example, defloration usually occurs in the midst of a celebration, with the consent of the entire tribe and the help of the priests. Even though we are fairly far removed from primitive societies, we follow identical rites. The virginity of the unmarried woman is taboo, and in order for defloration to represent a minimum of danger, it is necessary to provide a wedding ceremony attended by a benevolent public. Moreover, it is essential that certain symbolic rites be implemented, such as the bride's entrance into the church on her father's arm and her departure at her husband's side, the observing of established dress codes, and so on.*

But what kind of fear does the groom defend himself against through all of these rituals? According to Freud, man fears the hostility of his young wife, the deflowered virgin, for many reasons. During defloration, the husband sheds his partner's blood. The idea of blood is linked to violence, hostility, and crime. To have spilled it awakens feelings of guilt and fear of the victim's hostility. On the other hand, this fear is justified; the young wife will obviously feel resentment against her husband for his having inflicted on her a narcissistic injury through the destruction of an organ, the hymen. At the same time, since many women reject their feminine condition and envy man for possessing a penis, they hate him for obliging them to renounce their masculine phantasies and to recognize themselves as women. In this sense, defloration would represent the same thing as menarche, the castration of the illusory penis. We thus encounter once again the concept of woman's phallic castration as the cause of man's anxieties about her.

Moreover, the man who views intercourse as a humiliating and demeaning act for the woman, through which she is dominated by him, experiences defloration as a perversion and prostitution of his partner. He experiences it as a hostile act against her.

There are additional reasons why men fear defloration, which I analyzed in "The Trip to the Center of the Earth." The boy imagines the inside of the maternal body to be full of dangers. Such fear persists in the adult unconscious. This will not be as great when the man relates, even for the first time, to a woman who has already had sexual relations: Her body cannot be host to mortal dangers if her previous lovers escaped unharmed from the encounter. But to be the first to penetrate a woman is to explore a virgin jungle and to expose oneself to unknown dangers. We owe our understanding of these fears to the discoveries of Melanie Klein about the child's early fears of the maternal body.**

---

*It is interesting to note that while the wedding ceremony is no longer associated with the taboo of virginity and that even though approximately 50 percent of marriages in this country end in divorce, the formal wedding ceremony is still an important rite of passage in which the ritual features that Langer mentions continue to predominate.

**Langer understood that the psychological drama of defloration had diminished since she wrote this book. She believed that women, especially in the middle class, had undergone a kind of sexual revolution in the past several decades and that the exposure of young women to multiple sexual experiences and partners gave them the opportunity to know more about their sexual desire than did women of prior generations, the majority of whom lived their entire adult lives in a more generally repressive cultural environment with just one sexual partner who was often inept or ignorant of woman's needs. However, the change in sexual morality has taken place in

We see, then, that the man also has, with respect to the woman, two fears; his phantasy that she possesses an illusory penis, represented by the hymen in defloration, serves as an obstacle and protection against the fearful penetration of her body.

All of these unconscious fears have the effect of exaggerating the importance of the woman's first genital experience. One forgets that the consequences of this experience are already predetermined by a young woman's attitude toward men and sexuality. One woman will interpret her boyfriend's excitement as passion, while in the same circumstances another will feel afraid and bitter about man's brutality. Moreover, a woman who complains of her partner's brutality, awkwardness, or inexperience has unconsciously accepted him as a husband precisely for these characteristics. The same thing occurs in extramarital experiences. In *The Frigid Woman* Steckel insists on the importance of man's conduct with a woman during their first genital experience. He speaks of having seen serious disturbances in women who were "until then totally normal, because of the actions of neurotic men." Now, it appears ingenuous to suppose that a woman "until then totally normal" would choose as her first—and often only—partner a man of such inadequacy that she would be damaged for the rest of her life. Among the cases cited by Steckel is one in which a young woman had become ill with a psychosis. She consulted Steckel, who was able to discover the episode that unleashed the illness. MG, a 19-year-old girl from a very strict home, was raised with very high moral standards. She worked as an office employee. She fell madly in love with the head of her department, but following a girlfriend's bad advice, she slept with another man she did not love and then suffered a breakdown. Steckel maintains that this young woman would not have become sick if she had given herself to the man she loved within the context of marriage. Very well, but the factor inhibiting her from arriving at this successful resolution was precisely her neurosis, which predated the traumatic incident. Steckel blames the tragic undoing on his patient's girlfriend for having badly advised her. But it is naive to think that this advice would have been enough to make the young woman decide as she did, unless a situation of very neurotic dependency on this friend had existed.

However, the propaganda found in sexology books, such as Theodore van de Velde's *The Ideal Marriage*, is usually based on this type of case history. Here one finds the same issue that was mentioned

---

the realm of conscious experience; Langer was of the opinion that much of what she wrote in this chapter continues to address the unconscious symbolic meaning of aspects of sexuality for men and women today.

earlier with respect to the educational psychologists' concept about the importance of sex education for the prepubescent girl. Both menarche and defloration awaken profound anxieties and can, in certain cases, unleash pathological states. The causes of the anxiety are unconscious and unknown to laypeople, who try to explain them by blaming all the damage that is suffered on sexual ignorance. They attempt to prevent disturbances by giving suitable explanations to the pubescent girl and the bride and by teaching the groom, in a rather naive fashion, the techniques he should use. In saying this, I do not wish to imply that books such as *The Ideal Marriage* do not have a certain usefulness. Sexuality in our society is prohibited, and this repressive sexual morality causes inhibitions that are translated into clumsy and artificial sexual behavior. A serious book on the subject written by an authoritative figure not associated with the teaching of anatomy and sexology calms anxieties; to discuss as something natural what was at one time forbidden diminishes guilt feelings and encourages the couple to proceed with more freedom. But the very necessity of this education is another indication of the anti-instinctual nature of our culture. On the other hand, through these "amorous lessons" we run the risk of converting what was once the great event in the couple's life into an anxiety-laden test, especially for the man. While he is now charged with almost all the responsibility, the woman's conscious anxiety has diminished significantly, since virginity has come to be less valued and demanded by social norms. Conscious fears, unusually painful experiences, and stories of defloration involving serious hemorrhages have practically disappeared.

It appears, then, that the virgin is no longer afraid and that whatever possible conflicts she experiences with respect to sex are usually manifested only after sex has been initiated. However, many cases exist, known only to the gynecologist, psychiatrist, or psychoanalyst, in which the young wife or girlfriend—a partner in a couple who appear well suited to one another—demonstrates an apparently unconquerable fear that prevents defloration and initiation into adult sexual life. In these cases we observe the persistence in the woman's unconscious of an idea of sexual relations of much greater sadomasochistic intensity than ordinarily occurs in reality.

But where does this idea originate? For the woman, the sexual relationship implies passivity. If a girl has the opportunity to observe intercourse between her parents, or even between animals, she has the impression of a struggle in which the woman has the worst of it. The man is on top of the woman and penetrates her with rough movements. It is as if he were punishing her. This infantile representation of intercourse is very often never altered later but, instead, continues to operate unconsciously. Because of this, young girls have anxiety dreams in which they are persecuted by armed thieves. Also, in oneiric masturbatory symbolism the penis is represented as a knife or some other cutting instrument.

Does all this mean that the woman's pleasurable acceptance of coitus and later on of childbirth implies masochism or the love of pain? Freud ("The Economic Problem of Masochism") sees it this way in his equation of passivity with feminine masochism. Helene Deutsch writes that the woman considers her sexual goals as a danger to her ego because of the masochistic nature of her sexuality.

However, I believe that the problem is also open to a completely different interpretation. When I spoke of menstrual cramps, I suggested that they depend to a great extent on the norms of each society, as well as on the psychological disposition of each woman in relation to menstruation. We find the same "personal and social equation" concerning the pain of defloration and childbirth. It is true that something of fear and pain remain objectively inevitable, but this reality would not be sufficient for woman to have to be masochistic in order to accept her femininity. Another problem persists: intercourse. Does the man's penetration have to normally be experienced by the woman as an aggressive and hostile act? If so, in order to enjoy coitus she would have to become masochistic. Sandor Lorand, in an article about frigidity, maintains that woman's orgasmic incapacity stems basically from her fixation on the painful experiences of breast-feeding. This assertion is well taken. During the first months of life the human being forms the basis for her subsequent attitude toward people. The experience of coitus brings back the intimacy and union belonging to that long-lost period. The fetus inside the mother formed a single being with her. This union, which is rudely broken during birth, is reestablished in part through breast-feeding. If the first mother–daughter relationship was satisfactory, if the penetration of the breast in the mouth of the nursing infant represented a happy experience for the baby, an experience that was not negated during the course of her childhood by an accumulation of painful events, then as an adult she will have no cause to experience the penetration of her lover's penis as a sadistic and humiliating act. Her vagina would accept the sperm with as much pleasure as her mouth had accepted her mother's milk.

But precisely this analogy of situations and the revival of early feelings and sensations awaken infantile anxieties as well. If in her unconscious phantasies the girl violently attacked her mother's breasts, either because of frustration or envy, she would later fear the penetration of an organ that she unconsciously equates with the breast. (I described earlier the relationship between breast envy and penis envy.) If because of her violent jealousy the little girl in phantasy intensely attacked her parents' sexual union and the paternal penis, later she will feel that a penis, loaded with her own hostility, is a dangerous weapon. She will fear its counterattack in sexual relations and will defend herself against this and the implied surrender through the development of a masculine or masochistic attitude. And if she believes that her jealous attacks on the parental couple were successful, owing to the fact that she sees a wretched and destroyed mother who complains and suffers because of sex and her female destiny, she will fear having the same fate. It might be, then, as Helene Deutsch argues, that her erotic phantasies have such a self-destructive character that her ego, subject to the fear for her physical integrity, would have to avoid a sexual life and the entire feminine destiny with its presumed dangers. If her anxieties are less intense, in choosing a partner she will often seek out someone who is timid and not very potent in order to protect herself against the feared surrender. Even so, if it turns out to be very dangerous, she will defend herself against it in different ways, at times with a phobia of defloration.

This pattern occurs in cases in which the virgin loves her partner and is consciously ready to give herself to him. Even when unmarried, love conquers her moral doubts and her fear of society. She decides to be alone with her lover in a place where they can have intercourse without being bothered by anyone; she goes in order to surrender herself but draws back at the last moment. Later, I will describe Laura, an adolescent girl who suffered from a defloration phobia. After having visited her lover in his apartment, she describes her feelings and anxieties in her diary with all the drama appropriate to her age:

> Our last moment together and afterward—the ultimatum—yes or no! You have to decide! First it was a marvelous ecstasy, red and blue, a dance of fire before my eyes, he's going to kill me with his kisses. But, I can't. He says to me: "We make love or we separate, but I can't go on like this, halfway, it's driving me crazy." I would have liked to explain to him, but it's impossible, there's no explanation. I could tell him: "I don't know why, but I can't, I'm too young, I don't understand, I'm not attracted to you." There's no way out. There's a storm in my head. Suddenly there are two roads and I have to choose. Darling, I can't choose, because one road is closed for me [without realizing it, Laura speaks in symbolic terms of her virginity] and the other [that of the separation, the loneliness] is sad and black. Is there really no other solution?

Could it be argued that in Laura's case we cannot speak of a phobia of defloration? Is it not natural for a young girl, inexperienced and unmarried, to resist surrendering to her lover and to the dangers that sex represents under such conditions? Or that while consciously repressing them, she has moral scruples? All this is true. However, I believe that in spite of all these arguments, in Laura's case we are dealing with a phobic condition. I will elaborate this later. But in order to justify the term *phobia*, let us take a look at married women who reveal the same pattern.

Admittedly, this situation is relatively infrequently encountered. It does sometimes occur that defloration is not actualized during the weeks immediately following the wedding. There also exist marriages of convenience which are never consummated. But we refer here to a different situation, one in which, in spite of the fact that the couple consciously desire to initiate their mutual sexual life, the woman cannot surrender herself because of intense anxiety experienced when her husband approaches her to attempt penetration. Like it or not, the woman feels obliged to close her legs and, with a scream or even a struggle against him, to force her husband to desist for the moment. The next day she herself will ask him to try again. This situation can be prolonged for years, after which a drastic solution is sometimes sought. Generally deciding together, the couple resort to the gynecologist so that he can puncture the hymen. However, given the fact that such interventions do not modify the unconscious fears, the woman usually defends herself afterward against the feared penetration with vaginismus, a contraction of the involuntary muscles of the vagina, which, as Simone de Beauvoir correctly asserts, closes it much more securely than the hymen against intercourse. To force a woman with vaginismus to have intercourse or to oblige her to surrender in spite of her phobia of defloration is to convert the sexual act into a violation. A woman who suffers from such fear is generally able to provoke impotence in her partner, who in her presence and in the face of her uncontrolled anxiety feels a reaction similar to what is felt by the executioner before his victim. Thus, in order to secure psychotherapeutic success in cases of significant duration, it is necessary to simultaneously treat both members of the couple.

I obtained good therapeutic results in one particular case because I was able to convince my patient's husband to enter analysis at the same time with another analyst. In this way, as my patient became more feminine during the treatment, her husband became more virile. Thus, they were able to achieve a successful resolution. My analysand was named Gabriela. She was a 19-year-old girl, pretty, but masculine in appearance. She was tall, bony, and thin, with very pronounced features and lots of hair. When she sought out analysis she had already been married for 2 years without having allowed her husband to have intercourse with her because of feeling an uncontrollable fear when he attempted penetration. Moreover, she suffered from a profound depression and felt weary of living.

We know nothing about Gabriela's early childhood. But certain aspects of it can be deduced through her transference relationship to me and from the image she transmitted of her mother, whom she secretly and rebelliously feared and hated. In her analysis her desire and phantasy of having a penis became evident early on. She feared intercourse as a threat, in the sense of masculine castration. But in addition, she presented hypochondriacal fears that we now understand to be the fear of feminine castration. She was afraid for her femininity, for the inside of her body. She would say that a husband can shatter and destroy the woman during coitus and that she rejected her husband because of fearing she would become sick for the rest of her life if she surrendered to him. In a dream she equated defloration to surgical sterilization; the day's residue came from an anti-Nazi film she had seen in which a young woman was threatened with sterilization as a punishment for wanting to surrender herself to the enemy.

In order to understand how Gabriela came to fear such cruel punishments if she began her marriage relationship, we should know some details of her history. She came from a small town in the interior of Brazil and was the youngest child in a large family, wealthy but primitive and full of prejudices and superstitions. As a child she shared her parents' room and later slept in an adjacent room. Her mother was profoundly hypochondriacal, and would violently reject her husband if he approached her. Gabriela remembered perfectly well hearing arguments about this and the horror it stimulated in her. Nearing menopause, the mother developed a jealous paranoia. She denied herself completely to her husband while accusing him of infidelity and threatening his presumed sweethearts. When Gabriela was 10 years old, because of her mother's express wish she enrolled as a student in a religious school that was very strict, especially regarding sexual matters. At first she suffered because of the separation from her parents and siblings. She went home every weekend, but each Monday she repeatedly experienced an intense pain before the anticipated separation. At 12 years of age, in spite of the strict vigilance of the nuns and her mother, she managed to establish an innocent flirtation with a boy. When her mother found out, she violently criticized her daughter, as if she had committed a serious crime. I had the impression that Gabriela's physical masculinization began during this period. Since sexuality was so prohibited for the girl and since her mother became so enraged because she was blossoming into a woman, it was necessary to masculinize herself in order not to lose her mother's love.

When Gabriela was 14 years old, she left the religious school in order to return home. Meanwhile, the situation between her parents had worsened and they had separated. Gabriela stayed with her mother but missed her father very much. Her mother often reproached her because she secretly saw her father and continued to love him. When she was 15 years old, she became engaged. Although her mother was not in favor of the engagement, she did not openly oppose it because the boy was a good suitor. However, she advised Gabriela that it would be better not to marry so she would not have to experience all that she herself had suffered. She especially warned her against the misery of motherhood. Gabriela married when she was 16, but dominated by her mother and the prohibition against loving her father, she chose a man very different from him. Her fiancé was a passive, timid, very young, and almost impotent youth. Gabriela recounted that during the wedding night she did not put up a very big fight, but her husband proposed waiting a few days because he was nervous and felt impotent. When they next attempted intercourse, Gabriela then reacted phobically. In a certain sense, her phobia functioned to save her husband's dignity. Moreover, during her analysis when on one occasion she was ready to give herself to her husband, he was unable to perform.

Situations like these are frequently observed in couples incapable of consummating the sexual act. When either one of them is ready, the other assumes the role of avoiding the dangerous union. A verification of this pattern is the fact that the couple's mutual choice of one another in itself was directly connected to each one's fears.

But what was going on in Gabriela? Why did she repeatedly try to have sexual relations only to flee at the last moment from the possibility of their being realized? She feared suffering during intercourse like her mother, whose complaints had often been heard. Simultaneously, she desired that suffering because she loved her father and wanted to be united with her husband, just as her mother had been with her father, although always complaining and unappreciative. But she did not dare to take the place of her mother during intercourse, that is to say, to have a sexual life and children, because unconsciously it signified attracting her paranoid mother's violent jealousies and suffering all kinds of punishments. This fear was reflected in her dream about sterilization. Because she loved her father and feared living together with her mother, she searched for the opportunity to fall in love and marry at a very young age. But in order not to lose her mother's love, which she also needed, and in order to avoid her castigations, she chose a compromise that, in the long run, was unbearable: she married without having a sexual life and tried to live with her husband in total innocence, like a good little girl with her parents. We already saw in Teresita's masturbatory phantasies how in order not to have to confront her mother and risk losing her she decided to renounce genitality and to transform herself once again into a little girl. This mechanism, so frequently encountered, is what we also observe in Gabriela.

Psychoanalysis was able to modify this situation rather rapidly, since for Gabriela it was easy to substitute my image for that of her mother. I am a good deal older than she—I could have been her mother—but very different from her mother. She felt my sympathy and understanding with respect to her attempts to change her apparent marriage into a real one and her desire to live like other women, with a beloved husband and children. When she became more disengaged from her mother and less fearful of her, Gabriela's phobia began to disappear little by little, and she initiated her sexual life. But another type of defense against her unsatisfactory sexuality appeared. This occurred because she demanded that her husband be more virile than he could be at the time. Through unconscious phantasies in which she sought a man as strong as her father, Gabriela began to feel stimulated by the passes that men made at her in the street. She made gestures at becoming more independent and shedding her small-town girl lifestyle for that of a young sophisticated urban woman. After going alone for the first time one afternoon to the cinema, she suffered an attack of agoraphobia, which fortunately diminished rapidly in the analysis. Thus it could be established that her phobia of being deflowered was a kind of defense against the dangers of sexual life. No longer a virgin, she had recourse to another defense mechanism. Moreover, the agoraphobia served to avoid the analysis, because she would have been unable to attend the sessions if the symptom had intensified. This she desired, because to unconsciously make me a maternal substitute meant to simultaneously lose her real mother. However, at this point, she actually feared her mother much less. Because of that, she soon became pregnant. When dealing with the disorders of pregnancy, I will show that the persistence in Gabriela of a particular fear of her mother provoked difficulties that were resolved analytically.

To briefly recapitulate Gabriela's conflict: A girl, deeply attached to a mother predisposed to love her only if she renounces her sexuality, feels intensely attracted in her childhood to her father and later to young boys. She cannot pursue her desires for fear of losing her mother, of exposing herself to her cruel punishments, or of identifying with her unfortunate destiny. She masculinizes herself in order to avoid competing with her mother. But because she basically continues wishing to be a woman, she seeks a compromise between her desire and her fear in a marriage that cannot be consummated, defending herself from what is prohibited and simultaneously desired with a phobia of being deflowered.

In other cases involving a conflict between the desire to be a woman and the fear of realizing it, the young woman may seek the opposite solution. Both Ana and Berta, of whom I spoke in the previous chapter, would dominate their apprehension by repressing it and hastening the onset of the very thing that they unconsciously feared. In this way they were able to deny their deepest anxieties. Both actively sought their deflowering. This same mechanism can often be observed in women who are not morally repressed but frigid. Intellectually, they deny all fears of sexuality, in spite of the fact that it is by means of their frigidity that they successfully escape the much feared total surrender.

I will describe a psychoanalytic session with my patient Laura, the adolescent cited earlier. The session interests me for two reasons. First, because in Laura one sees how the phobia of being deflowered is directly followed by her frigidity and how both symptoms correspond to the same conflict. Secondly, I believe it is useful for the reader who has not been analyzed to experience an analytic session, even when, as in this instance, the intervention of the analyst is not described. Owing to the fact that Laura had recently begun her treatment and expounded on her thoughts quite fluidly, I had no reason to intervene. I want to give an idea of how the patient's free associations permit the psychoanalyst to arrive at an understanding of her conflicts. This session has been selected because it demonstrates with clarity, although in only one arena (the oedipal), the complete neurotic condition of the young girl. First, some details of her life known to me at that point are in order.

Laura, an intelligent 21-year-old young woman, was lively and agreeable. At 18 she had fallen in love with a boy who for quite a long while insisted on having sexual relations with her. They had arrived at a deep physical intimacy, and the girl, who had been raised in a fairly unprejudiced environment, consciously had no moral qualms of surrendering herself to her lover. But when the moment would arrive in which her deflowering seemed inevitable, she would always feel an unconquerable anxiety and violently reject her boyfriend. She suffered from a phobia of being deflowered. As a consequence of one of the violent scenes that usually occurred after his unsuccessful attempts to overwhelm her resistance, the sweethearts became mutually offended and broke off the relationship. In the beginning, the girl did not suffer much from the situation. Only when she discovered that he had another girlfriend did she begin to become desperate. Then she did everything to win him back, and with this as a goal she gave herself to him quite easily and free of anxiety. But she became frigid. A year later after the definitive breakup, she began her treatment, presenting various disturbances. She was frigid, often felt distressed and depressed, and suffered from various conversion symptoms.

Laura came into the session that I will describe displaying a timid and somewhat guilty smile and proceeded to speak:

1) Will you let me call you Maria? [I was a friend of her mother, who called me by my first name.]

2) Now I remember that one time when I was little, Mama hit me. It was only one time. I must have been five or six years old. I don't know why she hit me.

3) As a child I often had a distressing dream: My sister and I were in the clearing of a forest. There, on a branch, was my father's pullover. My sister disappeared and the pullover changed suddenly into a wolf. I got scared. And afterward, one of two things could happen: Sometimes in the dream I ran and ran, the wolf always behind me and I was scared that he would eat me. I would wake up screaming. Other times in the dream I didn't flee from the wolf. I pretended to be dead, lying down on the ground, immobile, and he lay down on top of me. Because it was as if I were dead, he couldn't do anything to me. Then I would wake up with pressure in my chest.

4) A short time ago I also dreamed about my father. I saw him seated at a desk and he was young. Almost younger than I've ever known him. My mother wasn't in the dream.

5) This summer a boy told me his problems. He has a relationship with a married woman. She would like to get a divorce for him, but he doesn't want that because she's married to a friend of his. He doesn't know what to do. When he finished telling me all of this, I went to my hotel. On the road that I was going up I got very tired, and when I arrived, I had a sharp pain in my heart. I've never felt anything like it. I got very scared. I thought I was going to die. A few days earlier I had attended a conference where hypochondriacal pains and madness were discussed, and I got more scared. I thought that what was happening to me was an indication of some mental disease.

6) Some days afterward I was invited to a ranch. My room was on the second floor. One night I was seated at the window, reading *The White Death*. Suddenly I heard a scream like from a dying animal. I got really scared. My heart raced. I went near the window and felt as if outside someone was breathing with much difficulty. But that was impossible, because it was the second floor and no one lived in the next room. Little by little I calmed down, and I think that I was only imagining the breathing.

7) This morning something very strange happened to me. Papa has a friend who often comes over in the morning because they work together on something. Today I went to the bathroom with only my bathrobe on. I didn't know that he was in the room I had to go through. I excused myself when I saw him, but without feeling particularly disturbed. To me he's an old man. It's true that he's no older than my father. He said to me, "Don't excuse yourself, the bathrobe looks very pretty on you." Afterward he asked me to get him something. When I gave it to him, he tried to kiss and embrace me. I

didn't feel anything and calmly defended myself without saying a word. He didn't speak either. So, afterward, it all seemed so unreal to me. And even now I know that it happened, but I have the sensation that everything was only a dream.

8) Now I know something is happening to me. Do you remember the married man I spoke about? I told you that he interests me so much . . . but that it's better if I don't see him anymore. I told that to my best friend today. She advised me to go on seeing him without worrying. I told her I didn't want to, that it was a shame that one always wants the impossible, but that he was for me a beautiful impossibility.

9) [The session ended and Laura left with an enthusiastic farewell:] Good-bye, Maria.

What is the significance of the subjects presented by Laura and how are they connected to one another? Let us look at the content of each association.

The "Will you let me call you Maria?" seems to function in light of her search for a friendly relationship with the analyst.

The second association, "Mama hit me," represents a screen memory. The patient remembers the punishment she received, repressing its cause. Because of her age when the incident occurred and the subsequent associations, it would appear that Laura interpreted her mother's attitude while hitting her for some childish misdeed to be a punishment for masturbating, which was stimulated by her erotic feelings for her father.

Already the next association (3), the childish nightmare, leads us to the relationship between Laura and her father. In the dream she is with her sister, a maternal substitute. They encounter the father, who is at first represented by his pullover, an inoffensive garment that is a protection against the cold. This calming aspect of the father, whom the dreamer searches for in order to calm her anxiety, does not endure. The pullover is changed into a wolf, and the sister disappears. That is to say, the child is left alone with the excited father. Freud demonstrated how in infantile animal phobias the animals always represent one of the parents, and the fear of being devoured expresses, in a regressive way, genital desire. It is the very sexual excitement, anxiety-provoking for the child, that is projected onto the father, making him appear like a dangerous animal. In her nightmare the little girl tries to avoid the attack of the father-wolf, employing two different defensive techniques. She utilizes a phobic technique—fleeing from the wolf—and a technique of depersonalization—playing dead. We shall see that later on, as an adolescent girl facing the real "danger" of surrendering herself to the wolf—to a man, a paternal substitute—she had recourse to the same techniques.

Laura continues to elaborate her situation with the father; she recounts a recent dream (4) about him. In the dream he appears rejuvenated, represented at the age he would have been when Laura was small and afraid of the wolf. This time it is a pleasant dream. Laura is not distressed, nor does she accord a terrifying quality to the father, because she has encountered another apparent solution to her conflict. She denies her oedipal rivalry with the mother—"Mama wasn't there"—and the presumed erotic aggression of the father—"He is calmly seated at his desk."

The attempted solution fails when Laura does not tolerate having distanced herself in her dream from her mother. Another anxiety-provoking memory (5) emerges; she speaks of the boy who loves a married woman, and whose guilt feeling toward his friend prevents the realization of his love. If we change the sexes, we encounter once again Laura's oedipal conflict. It is she who loves her father, a married man, and wishes to separate him from her mother. The story of the boy reactivated her guilt feelings. If her mother knew that she wanted to betray her, it would cause her great pain. Laura blames herself, feeling this pain in her own heart. The fear of going mad corresponds to the fear of her instincts.

Through the next association (6), she continues to elaborate her preoccupation with her parents. She confronts the "primal scene," their intercourse. As a child she would have been witness to her parents' sexual relations during the night through the sounds she heard, interpreting them in a sadomasochistic manner. Her nightly reading and loneliness revive this memory. The dying animal's cry corresponds to her mother's orgasm and the auditory hallucination of a painful breathing to the agitated breathing of both parents during coitus.

Another association in relation to the father (7) emerges. This time it deals with a recent episode in which the father's friend, who is his contemporary, substitutes for him. The patient, without any conscious anxiety, rejects the attempt to seduce him because she manages to repress her feelings. She says "I didn't feel anything"; that is, she has recourse once again to the defense of depersonalization.

The theme of the older married man continues (8); this time he now appears as the lover, the desired one. Laura no longer defends herself against recognizing her love, but she consciously renounces it. This love is "a beautiful impossibility."

Her renunciation permits her to say affectionately to me, a maternal substitute, "Good-bye, Maria" (9).

At this point we understand the unconscious content of each association. We have yet to see the underlying dynamic, the force that imposes a certain direction on Laura's thoughts in the analysis and in her life's activities. What moves her is her amorous desire to conquer the father or a paternal substitute, a desire that enters into conflict with infantile anxieties about sexual life and her fear of enraging and losing her mother, whom she needs and loves ambivalently. What, then, is the meaning of this session?

Laura comes in viewing me in an optimistic light. She wants to deny her conflict. I am her mother's friend, and her age as well. Most importantly, through the analytic situation itself, I become a maternal substitute. But Laura wishes we could be good friends and asks if she can call me Maria (1). Her attempt to deny her fears in this way fails. She remembers her mother's punishment for her incestuous desires toward her father (2). This association emerges because she unconsciously fears that the same punishment could be repeated with me in the analysis. Moreover, in order to better prevent the realization of her desires, she remembers the dangers she exposed herself to in phantasizing about her father. The wolf could devour her (3). Perhaps there is another way. Distancing herself from her mother and eliminating the erotic dimension from her relationship with her father, she could then love him without fear. The image of the young father, calmly and serenely seated before the desk—symbol of sublimated friendship, which in reality she always tried to establish with her father— represents this plan (4). The illusion of this possibility does not last. If Mama is absent, Laura is to blame. It is she who has separated her parents. She has betrayed her mother. So her heart hurts her, and the hypochondriacal fear of going mad appears (5). Furthermore, if she manages to occupy her mother's place, she is alone with her father and again in the dangerous situation already expressed in the nightmare. Unconsciously, Laura continues being a little girl, too young to have a sexual life. The memory of the panting and the dying animal's cry emerges (6). Her father is going to kill her during intercourse. But how can she defend herself? Perhaps if she adopted a cold attitude (frigidity), denying her anxiety and excitement. It is necessary to give the appearance of already being an adult woman who is not afraid and knows how to calmly reject the older man (7). But basically it is difficult to do this because she loves him. However, she will give up (8) and thus be able to keep her mother (9).

Laura's oedipal conflict entails a problem with no solution: how to win the father's love in spite of her infantile fears of sexual life and her need to be protected and loved by her mother. Laura's fixation on the oedipal situation causes a variety of disturbances that she, without realizing it, expresses during her session. Our analysis of the unconscious content of her associations leads us to an understanding of her dependency on her parents and the consequence, her symptoms. Laura is an intelligent girl with a great capacity to study, but she has not persevered in her intellectual work and has been unable to utilize her acquired knowledge effectively. Obviously, her capacity for sublimation is inhibited. To work intellectually signifies unconsciously to be with her father and to exclude her mother, as in the dream (4) about the father seated at a desk, ("Mama is absent"). She looks for other neurotic solutions to her conflict. I have already indicated that she suffered from a defloration phobia that, once overcome, was replaced by frigidity. The frigidity represents a compromise between the desire for and the fear of sexual activity. It means to surrender oneself physically and simultaneously to deny it. There is no danger or guilt because the mind does not participate in the surrender. Often during intercourse the frigid woman experiences a feeling of strangeness about what is happening to her body. This sensation has much in common with depersonalization, the state that Laura experienced in reaction to her father's friend's attempt to seduce her (7). She herself describes it with the characteristic words for such a state: "I didn't feel anything" and "everything seemed so unreal." On the other hand, frigidity consists of a physical insensitivity and therefore belongs to the symptoms of hysterical conversion. We find a hysterical conversion reaction, the pain in her heart, to her friend's story (5). When the stimulus is too intense, the neurotic mechanisms that function to dominate the anxiety fail and the anxiety emerges directly. This happened to Laura when she put herself in her mother's place in the primal scene (6).

It is interesting to note that in the nightmare she first had at the age of 5, Laura already demonstrated the same reaction in the face of the sexual danger that later reappeared during her adolescence. In her dream, when the encounter with the wolf was inevitable she alternatively sought two solutions: She fled from the wolf—that is, she adopted a phobic attitude, precursor to the phobia of being deflowered—or she pretended she was dead—likewise a precursor, to her subsequent frigidity. All of her symptoms are an expression of her failure to love the man and separate from the woman. She believes and acts as if she does not love her mother very much and is independent of her. However, she needs her mother and continually seeks her out. This she also demonstrates through her last association, that of the "Good-bye, Maria." In this way she returns to her mother after having struggled ineffectively to become detached from her.

Frigidity

Although frigidity has great clinical importance, I will treat the subject quite briefly owing to the fact that a great number of investigations already exist. Not only is it much beyond the scope of this present study to review the abundant literature within psychoanalysis, sexology, and gynecology on frigidity but its relationship to female reproductive disorders, which is our central theme, is indirect and controversial. However, frigidity is intimately connected to vaginismus and the phobia of defloration, since all three represent a rejection of intercourse. But while the latter two disorders often completely prevent a woman from biologically achieving motherhood, frigidity constitutes only a relative obstacle. There are many frigid women who achieve apparently normal pregnancies and childbirths and who competently nurse their infants. Some authors go so far as to maintain that frigidity does not cause infertility but that, on the contrary, a very passionate physical love can be an obstacle to pregnancy because it is exclusive and will not admit a third party—the child. Others, perhaps the majority, see frigidity as a precipitating factor in infertility.

In any case, a frigid woman is as afraid of femininity and of surrendering herself as is a woman who closes herself off to intercourse. The difference is that she accepts intercourse physically because she can achieve a mental absence. In this way she tolerates the feared penetration because by feeling nothing she is able to unconsciously deny the experience. If she fears orgasm as a loss of control, her inability to achieve it means that she has saved herself. If she fears depending on the other for sexual satisfaction and hates this dependency because of unconsciously equating her partner with hostile or frustrating objects, she inverts the situation by negating her own pleasure. Then coldly, often with a mixture of superficial affection and curiosity, she observes the man who becomes excited and suddenly disarmed by pleasure. It is she who controls the situation.

But how can one absent oneself in this way? What is frigidity, this unfortunately all too widespread disorder? Confusion about the subject abounds, as well as extraordinarily disparate statistics regarding its frequency, which oscillate from 40% to 90% of the female population. This discrepancy is due to a variety of factors, including the extent to which the subjects selected for the studies are in good health or have frequent recourse to gynecological care; the social and class standing of the participants; and the different techniques used by the questioners, as well as their different concepts and definitions of frigidity.

I believe that Edmund Bergler is accurate in his depiction of frigidity when he argues that the term applies to women who cannot achieve vaginal orgasm during intercourse.* His description of a woman's normal sensations during intercourse is as follows:

> The normal sexual act includes three phases for the woman. First, her genitalia become moist and an erection and pulsating of the clitoris is produced. Arousal due to the pleasure involved in the physical contact of kissing and embracing is followed by the desire for penetration by the penis.

---

*Langer subsequently discarded this concept of frigidity. In later years, she interpreted her exclusively Freudian focus in this chapter—an exception in her otherwise Kleinian analysis of female sexuality—as the result of her insecurity for having been so critical of Freud in the rest of her book. As she put it, "I left Freud the chapter on frigidity." Langer completely rejected the concept of the vaginal orgasm following the publication of Masters and Johnson's *Human Sexual Response* and the dialogue within academic and feminist circles sparked by these authors' reconceptualization of female sexuality and their demonstration that there is no vaginal orgasm separate from clitoral orgasm. She was also influenced by the debate within psychoanalysis that ensued after the publication of Mary Jane Sherfey's paper "The Evolution and Nature of Female Sexuality in Relation to Psychoanalytic Theory," *Journal of the American Psychoanalytic Association* 14(28): 28–128, in which the author argued on the basis of discoveries in modern embryology and other biological data that in the primates the marked development of the clitoral system, along with certain secondary sexual characteristics, produces an intense aggressive sexual drive and that this female sexuality had to be forcefully suppressed as a prerequisite for the establishment of culture. "Primitive woman's sexual drive was too strong," argued Sherfy, "too susceptible to the fluctuating extremes of an impelling, aggressive erotism to withstand the disciplined requirements of a settled family life—where many living children were necessary to a family's well-being and where paternity had become as important as maternity in maintaining family and property cohesion" (pp. 119-20). Langer's familiarity with feminist interpretations of the origins of patriarchy and its subordination of female sexuality led her to agree with Sherfy's ideas about an era prior to patriarchy in human history during which women's social power and sexual expression were extraordinary—the opposite of the repressive cultural patterns that framed modern woman's psychology. For a review of the scientific proceedings of the American Psychoanalytic Association in which there was a debate about these ideas, see W. J. Barker, "Female Sexuality," *Journal of the American Psychoanalytic Association* V. 16, 1968: 123–45.

Then comes the desire for movement and friction. The woman is conscious of the gradual increase of movement and wants it to continue. Simultaneously, or perhaps more often shortly after her partner's orgasm, the woman's orgasm is produced, accompanied by contractions of the involuntary muscles of the pelvic and genital region. Orgasm is followed by a sensation of relaxation of sexual tension. In contrast to the man's passion, which abates more rapidly, the woman's lasts for a longer period of time. Because of this, after orgasm she wants to remain close to the man, held in his arms with his penis inside of her.

Therefore, according to Bergler, any woman who does not experience intercourse in this way is frigid. He goes on to distinguish between "obligatory" and "occasional" frigidity. The first term refers to an absolute incapacity for orgasm, while those women who suffer from "occasional" frigidity can achieve the kind of orgasm described above with certain partners or in specific situations. Of course, to a certain extent every woman is situationally frigid, because she will not have an orgasm in unfavorable circumstances or with an inadequate partner.

Bergler's strict definition is not in accordance with lay opinion. Some women who are incapable of vaginal orgasm do not feel frigid, and in such cases their partners do not consider them frigid because they are not "cold." These women enjoy sex and in many cases seek it compulsively. Other women do not experience intense pleasure, but they enjoy intercourse because they love their partner and feel happy in giving him pleasure. However, the vast majority of frigid women, including the "passionate" ones, suffer consciously or unconsciously from their frigidity.

The same diversity of opinion that exists with regard to the appropriate definition of frigidity is also encountered in attempts to clarify its causes. Lay opinion generally has it that a woman is frigid because she has not yet found an adequate partner. Those who are avid followers of sex education books are convinced that the panacea for frigidity consists in discovering the adequate "technique" to awaken each individual woman. Analysts such as Bergler, however, argue that far from being an issue of technique, frigidity occurs in a woman who unconsciously perceives the nature of her potential partner's sexuality. If, as we already saw, in spite of her own perception of a man's sexual character, or often precisely because of it, she decides to become involved with him, it must be that she suffers from a neurosis that motivates her to make such an object choice.

If we agree that frigidity is caused by neurosis, how shall we classify it? Should we assume that frigidity has always been considered neurotic or that there have been historical periods and cultural circumstances in which frigidity was a normal pattern among women?

The first question is important because it brings us directly to the difficulty of diagnosis and prognosis that has clinically confronted us in each case of frigidity. From a somewhat oversimplified perspective, frigidity would represent a passing hysterical anesthesia of the vaginal mucous membrane. In this view frigidity would be considered a conversion symptom, that is to say, hysteria. If such were the case, the prognosis would be very good because hysteria is perfectly accessible to psychotherapeutic treatment. But if we accept a patient on the basis of this diagnosis, we may be faced with the disagreeable surprise that the cure of frigidity is difficult and of extraordinarily long duration, because what appeared to be a hysterical symptom is in actuality the expression of a profound conflict and personality disorder.

Let us now turn our attention to the second question. It is true that at the present time and within certain circles there is no opposition to our judgment that frigidity is a neurosis and that the healthy woman is capable of sexual pleasure. Moreover, as I indicated earlier, in certain quarters the woman's orgastic capacity is actually demanded; she herself expects it and feels guilty when she cannot achieve it. She often hides her incapacity as if it were a defect, pretending for her partner's sake to have an orgasm. But some decades ago it was still thought that a good and decent wife did not and should not experience orgasm. While she could feel warmth from affection, become excited from an ardent kiss, and experience a certain maternal pleasure during intercourse, orgasm was the sad privilege of the "crazy" ones, of the *Mesalinas* and hysterical women. And, interestingly enough, this was not a set of expectations held by men only; it was also shared by the majority of women. It seems, then, that in order to understand the entire problem, we should go beyond the specificity of each particular case in order to explore the anthropological data.

We return to Margaret Mead. In *Male and Female* she states that the female capacity to reach an orgasm is evaluated differently in each society. Her investigations lead her to the conclusion that orgasm constitutes a feminine potential and may or may not be developed in the individual or throughout an entire society. That is to say, just as there are frigid women, as in our own society, there are also frigid societies. In such societies some women have the capacity to enjoy sex, but they are the maladjusted ones who suffer and are considered to be "neurotic." On the other hand, there are societies in which women are expected to feel pleasure equal to that of the male, and in these cases the cold woman is the neurotic exception.

In *Sex and Temperament in Three Primitive Societies*, Mead describes how among the Arapesh both men and women behave in an extremely soft and maternal manner. The child is treated with extraordinary care and affection and is nursed frequently and over a long period of time. In this society it is assumed that the woman does not experience orgasm. While intercourse is pleasurable and leaves her with a warm, agreeable feeling, she does not highly esteem her husband's potency; nor does she insist on having an intense sexual life. Mead depicts the tragic history of Amitoa, a young woman who was very different from the rest of the women of her culture. She was strong and active, and openly reproached her sickly and impotent husband for not satisfying her sexual needs. She abandoned him in search of other men. Failing in her attempts, she was forced by her husband's family to return home. She became pregnant and tried to kill the newborn baby. Her efforts were prevented and she was then obliged to nurse her daughter. When she gave birth for the second time, no one was present. Taking advantage of the situation, she squashed the newborn's head with her foot. Obviously, Amitoa was maladjusted. But in her erotic demands, which were connected to her rejection of motherhood, she behaved similarly to many women in our own and other societies.

In yet another study, *Coming of Age in Samoa*, Mead shows how in this culture the child is raised among large family communities. In addition to the mother, many other women feed and care for the baby and educate the small child. Children are loved, but with a certain coolness. Sexuality is looked upon as a very agreeable diversion for both sexes. Adolescents have full sexual freedom. Tragedies of passion rarely occur. Frigidity and impotence do not exist, a phenomenon Mead attributes to the lack of individual love and the freedom with which any sexual play that might be considered perverse in our culture is accepted as normal and ordinary.

Mead notes that among the Mundugumor people both men and women are arrogant, irascible, and energetic. The women reject motherhood and do not love children. It is expected that women experience the same sexual pleasure as men. However, sexual acts appear more like a battle than amorous contact. A girl is advised the following in order to hide the fact that she now has a lover: "If your earrings have been pulled from your ears, if your skirt is torn or stained, if your face and arms are scratched and bloody, say that you heard a noise in the swamp, that you got scared and fell while running. Otherwise, people will say you have a lover." Mead says that "love in these rapid encounters takes the form of a violent embrace and a biting fight calculated to produce the maximum excitement in a minimum of time." I presume that the women of the Mundugumor experience much sexual satisfaction in this way, but not vaginal orgasm. There are also maladjusted individuals among this people. Mead relates the history of Kwenda, whose maladjustment consisted of her maternal character. She was tender and affectionate and was abandoned by her husband for another woman because she refused to kill her newborn son. While Kwenda was still nursing their child, her husband left her. Later she adopted a little girl whose natural mother did not feel capable of raising twins. Now she could not find a husband because she was devalued by everyone and her irascible former husband was greatly feared. She lived alone with two children, happy and loving and not the least bit embittered. The Mundugumor, then, are a society in which women experience violent sexual pleasure; Kwenda was considered neurotic because of her maternal character.

In *The Individual and His Society* Abram Kardiner analyzes the culture of the Marquesans, where, due to the scarcity of women, the male is very interested in satisfying his sexual partner. This is not easy to achieve. Kardiner says in this regard:

> It was the man's role to excite the woman through cunnilingus and by sucking her breasts until she reached an extreme state of excitement and gave the sign permitting intercourse. These preliminaries were carried out without any tenderness, including quite frequently bites and scratches on one or another part of the body. Apparently, sexual games were much more important than the actual orgastic experience. Everyone was sexually potent, but the woman's potency depended on these complicated preliminaries, without which it was impossible to have an orgasm.

In this society, devoid of maternal sentiments, the woman is capable of pleasure, but this enjoyment does not come from vaginal contact.

In spite of the profound obvious differences between our culture and that of the Marquesans, it is possible to compare the two. In both, woman has acquired sexual and social equality with man at the cost of a partial renunciation of her maternal capacities. It is true that in many respects the predominant situation in the Marquesan culture seems like a caricature of our own culture. On the other hand, Kardiner maintains that frigidity does not exist among the indigenous population, revealing a fundamental difference between the two cultures. In our society the statistics with respect to frequency of frigidity in women are extraordinarily high. But closely reading Kardiner's description, in the domain of sexuality the Marquesans appear to be similar to us. In her promiscuity, insatiability, and complicated sexual games, the Marquesan woman is reminiscent of a certain type of woman in our society. Frigid and uninterested in motherhood, she is driven by her frigidity and psychological dissatisfaction, continually going from one man to another in her demands for complicated sexual techniques from each in order to achieve satisfaction.

It is possible, then, that in the society of the Marquesans, which rejects motherhood, there exists as much frigidity as in our own society, in spite of the appearance of the women's great sexual appetite. Obviously, the same applies to the proud and savage society of Mundugumor. The situation in Samoa is somewhat different. There the child is well received and well treated. But besides his own mother, many other women take care of him with affectionate indifference. It is interesting to see how this situation is repeated in adolescence when sexual life begins. Both men and women treat each other affectionately, but they function as if they were unaware of individual love. The women feel sexual pleasure, but it cannot be deduced from Mead's exposition whether or not they experience vaginal orgasm. Finally, the prevailing situation among the Arapesh is similar to that which still existed at the beginning of the 20th century in our society. The highly esteemed woman is a good mother and wife. But she does not need a sexual life and during intercourse feels nothing more than an agreeable warmth and closeness toward her partner. The woman with intense erotic needs, like Amitoa, is for the Arapesh a mad woman who actively throws herself into the search for men and sexual pleasure, rejecting motherhood and ignoring her duties.

I fear we have arrived at a somewhat contradictory conclusion in the present anthropological exploration. It would appear that a girl raised by an affectionate mother would as an adult be a good wife in turn but with no interest in sex while the girl whose mother gives her very little love and care—or, more extreme even, the girl raised in an unloving and rejecting way—will later avidly search out sex and find satisfaction in it.

Before attempting a clarification of the apparently contradictory facts, we return to our former assertion that in our contemporary society frigidity is considered to be a neurosis. I think that the frigid woman suffers because of her frigidity, which is manifested as well in an inhibition in activities disconnected from the sexual domain. But if we consider frigidity to be a neurosis, we must examine its causes, after which we will also be able to better understand the anthropological data previously discussed.

In *Totem and Taboo* Freud interprets frigidity as hostility against the sexual partner, a hostility that can stem from penis envy and a rejection of femininity itself. This attitude is expressed most intensely toward the first sexual partner because the woman reproaches him for having deprived her of her hymen and having obliged her to accept a passive role. Freud's assertion can be illustrated with abundant clinical material. But the question as to why the woman wants to be a man and play an active role remains unanswered. In any case, if she feels such a desire, it is logical for her to be frigid and hostile to the man, who occupies the role to which she aspires. In these cases the woman's excitement is limited to the clitoris, which phylogenetically represents a rudimentary penis; she does not achieve the erotization of her vagina.* Freud explains this condition in terms of the sexual development of the girl, who, according to him, lacks vaginal sensations but quite early experiences the excitability of the clitoris. Only the man teaches her to discover her vagina. She learns to experience pleasure vaginally when she can displace part of the clitoral excitability to the vagina.

It is imperative to analyze, then, why a woman prefers to play the active role, values the penis, and, denying the existence of her vagina, remains fixated on the clitoris for her pleasure. We shall see this situation in Berta, a patient I described earlier. Repressing all of her anxiety at the thought of being deflowered, it was she who convinced her fiancé to deflower her the night before their wedding. In this way she took the initiative and could minimize the importance of the fact—so humiliating to her dignity—that a man deflowered and actively penetrated her. Moreover, she had a great deal of sensitivity in her clitoris, but she was frigid. Thus, she manifested her rejection of her feminine role through sexuality. Long before the analysis she was already fully conscious of her penis envy. However, we cannot arrive at an understanding of her frigidity if we wish to reduce it to envy, because her penis envy and her frigidity, as well as her rejection of any passive position whatsoever, originated in the same conflict. We saw, upon analyzing her fears, that her active masculine attitude was already a defensive posture. It came from her incapacity to identify with her very feminine mother, whom she hated, and from her horror of being passively at the mercy of anyone who would always basically represent her bad mother, who desired to suck at her and destroy her insides.

As another frequent cause of frigidity, Freud points to the unconscious persistence of the woman's incestuous fixation on her father. He has been the great love of her childhood. Later, she will see her father in every man she loves, but the moral prohibition and the fear of her mother's retaliation that weigh so heavily on this relationship will prevent her having any sexual pleasure. We saw this situation clearly in Laura's analytic session, described in the last chapter. Laura loves her father but imagines the relationship with him in a masochis-

---

*Langer later rejected this definition of the clitoris and instead believed it to be the focus of sexual excitability in the female. Although she no longer held that a woman had to transfer her erotization of the clitoris to the vagina in order to arrive at a mature sexuality, she did continue to understand a woman's fear of being penetrated as a rejection of her femininity.

tic manner, as if it were something very cruel and destructive (the nightmare of the wolf and the phantasy of the primal scene). We see here the girl's masochistic position with her father, which Helene Deutsch has underscored in many of her writings. Deutsch believes that when feminine masochism is too intense, it is a frequent cause of frigidity. Reflecting a bit, this seems clear enough. A woman who has her imagination filled with gory phantasies would not be able to abandon herself to orgasm because she fears that in the moment of abandon terrible damage might be inflicted on her. Such was the case with Berta, who hated her father but also felt a profound admiration for his aggressive virility. He appeared in her dreams as a bull. Berta had suffered from a phobia of bulls in her childhood. I indicated earlier that the fear of her mother's wickedness prevented her from giving herself to a man. However, if she had not also feared her father, if he had been more of her protector and more tender, later Berta would have been able to find in man a certain protection against woman. It was also very evident in Ana that her masochism prevented her from surrendering herself completely.

In his final writings on feminine psychology, Freud altered his ideas, arriving at the conclusion that the girl's early relationship with her mother is extraordinarily important because she will repeat this first experience later with her father. Freud argues that many marriages fail because the woman repeats with her husband the old conflictual situation with her mother. This idea appears amplified and expanded by Sandor Lorand, who sees the most profound cause of frigidity in the early oral frustrations with the mother.

Laura consciously experienced penis envy. She suffered from a defloration phobia. Later she became frigid. The causes of her frigidity are those already described from a psychoanalytic perspective. On a superficial level, Laura wanted to be a man, in this way defending herself against her desire and fear of entering into an amorous relationship with her father. The actualization of such a relationship meant to her the conversion of her masochistic phantasies into reality. If she, because of her jealousy, had in phantasy changed her parents' union into something extremely painful (remember her representation of the primal scene and her equation of her mother's orgasm with the cry of a dying animal), she could not risk accepting the feminine role in sexual relations. But she also changed her mother's pleasure into suffering because of her old rancor due to early oral frustrations and fear of her own oral aggression. Unconsciously, she equated milk with maternal warmth. She could not give love because she had not received enough. Moreover, if she lost control, she feared becoming the voracious and aggressive little animal she had been as an infant.

The following lines come from Laura's diary, written sometime before the analysis. In them she expresses clearly that to be frigid means to be starving. She says of herself:

> Emotionally I am a little girl, seizing at everything but never satisfied, always starving and incapable of giving. I'm even unable to receive what's due me, but in spite of that, I'm always grasping at the other person. He [she refers here to her fiancé] is right is saying that I am this way because I am emotionally hungry, and I always feel that he isn't giving me enough. That's why I flirt with others. But I feel lonely. I try to get physical satisfaction even while I know it won't result in anything and will hurt others. Then I feel nauseated by it all.

Laura establishes, then, a clear causal relationship between her frigidity and her oral dissatisfaction. Moreover, the nausea she feels about herself is a manifestation of her disgust toward her persistent infantile appetites. She still desires the breast, without being able to admit it to herself.

Laura also explains to us how woman's typical infidelity stems from her hunger and dissatisfaction. But there is one more cause, originating in her childhood. Not satisfied by her mother, the little girl believes that her mother frustrates her because she is unfaithful, having abandoned her daughter for her husband. She identifies with this image of the bad and unfaithful mother, and later on treats her lovers as she felt she herself was treated. She tempts them only to frustrate them afterward.

Laura is not resigned to her frigidity. On each occasion she attempts to achieve an orgasm. She describes in her diary the only sexual experience during which she almost reaches an orgasm, clearly perceiving the cause of her inability to completely surrender. She mistakenly calls it her "subconscience" and afterward, much more correctly, "the monster":

> Tonight it almost happened. I never had it so close to my subconscience as in that moment. I never confronted it that way. It came from the depths of the dark valleys like the invisible arm of a giant, like the wind that one only feels, without being able to see it, to oppress me and push me again toward incompleteness and unsatisfied desires. Rapidly, hysterically, I began to cry and told you to leave me. It was a very strange sensation; I might have almost vanquished the monster, but he defended himself and attacked me with teeth and nails.

The monster that her lover awakens in her has the characteristics of the frustrating mother of her childhood—the giant arm that grabs her and pushes her yet again toward incompleteness and dissatisfaction. Moreover, the monster struggles against her with teeth and nails; that is to say, it has the characteristics of her own oral dissatisfaction. For Laura, the vagina has been changed into a starving mouth, and the monster that separates her from her lover has as many features of the frustrated little girl as of the frustrating mother.

The vagina also has characteristics of the mouth for women capable of experiencing pleasure. During orgasm the vagina absorbs the "milk" [leche in Spanish], that is to say, the semen offered by her lover. But in many frigid women the vagina is no longer the mouth that sucks but the breast that is swallowed up. Heinrich Racker explains this somewhat odd-appearing phenomenon in the following way: The young girl experiences oral frustration as if something were eating her ("the hunger that devours"); with this she unconsciously changes herself into the breast. Each subsequent erotic link is essentially analogous to this original relationship and involves a corresponding danger. Confronting this situation, the girl tries to defend herself by identifying with the frustrating (devouring) object, thus denying her helplessness. Later on she cannot surrender herself to her lover because she projects her own infantile insatiability onto him. Then his penis becomes the mouth that sucks. To give herself completely would mean to give the vagina in the same way as the breast is given and risk being totally emptied out, just as she would have desired to destroy and empty her frustrating mother.

This idea seems strange because, obviously, during intercourse the penis is the organ that gives and the vagina the one that receives. However, it is said of the woman that she surrenders herself, that she offers her body. For the frigid woman's unconscious, the satisfied man becomes the well-fed breast-feeding infant and she, who has given him satisfaction without receiving anything in exchange, the victimized mother.

For example, Laura knew very well what it felt like to experience sensations of rage, envy, and exhaustion with her satisfied partner. From Berta's nightmare of the spider, we know her fear of being emptied out. Laura also suffered from this widespread spider phobia. Another frigid woman called the people who loved her "leeches." She would refer to the penis as if it were a syringe. But she would not describe feeling during intercourse as if this syringe injected her with something; on the contrary, it continually aspirated her until it left her destroyed and empty. In the dreams of another frigid patient, the penis was represented as an elephant's trunk or an animal's snout, that is, always an organ that sucks. Prostitutes are generally frigid. There was a prostitute famous for her custom of eating an apple during intercourse. That is to say, she always ate the apple—well-known symbol of the breast since biblical times—so as to be able to tolerate the experience that the man who drew pleasure from her body was consuming her. If questioned in detail about their thoughts during intercourse, some housewives who are frigid admit somewhat hesitantly that they think about what to cook for the following day's meals. In order to counteract the anguish of being eaten, consumed, during intercourse, they also have to reassure themselves that they will be able to retrieve in the next day's meals what they have lost.

In another patient I observed an additional possible cause of frigidity. She was a young woman who during her puberty had repeatedly engaged in sexual relations with her sister. Later, she married a man who in many respects unconsciously represented her sister. She was generally frigid with her husband. She devalued sexuality and was very accepting of her frigidity. But when she did have an orgasm, she felt furious, guilty, and humiliated because to achieve sexual pleasure had the unconscious meaning of returning to the humiliating vice of homosexual gratification. The difference between this case and the others being discussed is that this patient's early relationship with her mother—until the birth of her sister—had been very positive. It failed when she, resentful of her mother because of her sister's birth, wanted to be close to her father and he frustrated her. She identified with him and thus during puberty—the normal period for first falling in love—made a homosexual object choice. Later, she managed to repress her homosexuality and to make an apparently normal object choice. But in her unconscious, sexual pleasure remained tied to her infantile experiences. She did not tolerate satisfaction for herself because she rejected her homosexuality. She feared being emotionally bound and the possibility that she, having once felt the pleasure of the past, would be thus exposing herself again to the danger of suffering the same disappointment she had experienced with the primitive homosexual object, her mother.

We recapitulate briefly the various causes of frigidity we have discussed. The woman who is fixated on clitoral satisfaction and rejects her femininity is frigid and incapable of vaginal orgasm. The same occurs with the woman who is intensely tied to incestuous objects, because for her, pleasure acquires a prohibitive character. The masochistic woman cannot abandon herself during the sexual act because she fears the realization of her cruel phantasies. We recall Freud's belief that the most important cause of feminine sexual disorders lies in early conflicts between mother and daughter. The orally frustrated little girl repeats these first traumatic experiences later in her sexual life. Unconsciously, her vagina may represent her hungry mouth and the penis the frustrating breast; or she can fear that the penis, through her vagina, aspirates the inside of her body like a mouth.

I will not dwell on the superficial causes of a transient frigidity, such as the rejection by one's partner, guilt feelings because of a prohibited relationship, conscious fear for the consequences of intercourse, and so forth, because they are to some extent self-evident. But we have seen here the many factors that determine the symptom of frigidity, ranging from a relatively superficial conflict easily accessible to psychotherapeutic resolution to profound affective disorders stemming from early childhood.

Another important factor in frigidity among many women is the incompatibility of motherhood and sexual pleasure. It often happens that a women with complete orgastic capacity becomes frigid after having a baby. This occurs because she unconsciously maintains the concept of the pure mother, the asexual mother, the one she once wished for in order to be able to love her unambivalently.

It also may occur that a couple who have had a very satisfactory sexual relationship are disappointed to discover that shortly after their marriage, which has suddenly given them a right to a permissible sexual union, the woman becomes frigid. Perplexed, they ask themselves how the mere fact of having gone through a civil rite, where an unknown man authorized their union, could have had such disastrous consequences. There are two causes of this phenomenon. If for the woman sex remained tied to prohibited infantile play, she cannot experience pleasure when sex has lost this character. Moreover, to be married, to be a wife, now implies a future maternity that, as we mentioned before, for many women is incompatible with sex. When young, these girls unconsciously split the figure of the mother into a good and pure one, who feeds and protects, and another hidden, hated, and consequently bad mother, who abandons the child in order to seek pleasure with the father. The mere wickedness of this image often prevents identification with the mother.

We find this same rejection of the sexual mother among the Arapesh, a tribe exemplary for maternal feelings shared by both sexes. From the time a baby is born, the parents must abstain from sexual relations until the baby is capable of taking its first steps, which in this primitive environment means that the baby begins to become independent of the mother. They say that if this abstinence is not strictly observed, serious harm can come to the infant. Thus, in this culture the people identify with the small child and perceive quite well that while dependent on its parents, it feels hatred and impotent rage toward their sexual union, experiencing it as rejection and frustration.

Among the Mundugumor and the indigenous peoples of the Marquesas islands, the opposite situation prevails. No abstinence whatsoever is observed after a baby's birth, and the women reduce nursing to a minimum in order not to restrict themselves in their sexual freedom. They are not bad mothers but demanding lovers.

The Arapesh child is very gratified by her mother, who accustoms her to play with her breasts while she is being fed. The mother caresses her infant, hitting her affectionately on the genitals. They spend hours at a time in this way, playing and nursing. Because this culture endorses the expression of paternal affection, the figure of the father is confused with that of the mother. He is like her, but he has a great disadvantage for the infantile mind: he lacks breasts. Later, the girl cannot find pleasure with her partner because the gratification she received in her early childhood, plus the identification with a mother uninterested in genital sexuality, means that she feels pleasure only in motherhood. The figure of the father is too weak to break the extremely pleasurable union between mother and daughter.

Among the Mundugumor, the girl is weaned early. Her mother feeds her with little affection and her father rejects her. The two abandon her so that she does not disturb their sexual relations. The girl remains fixated in infancy because of the very frustrations she has experienced. Later on, she herself will be a rejecting mother but will appreciate sexuality, the cause of her parents' abandonment of her. She will aggressively vindicate herself with men for the gratification that she was denied in her infancy.

Within the frigid women of our society are feminine models typical of the Arapesh and of the Mundugumor. Currently, in an era in which women are in general considerably limiting their maternal functions, the women of the Mundugumor prevail within them, unsatisfied and avidly seeking sexuality. In their analyses it is clear that as children they had been frustrated by the mother and rejected by the father and that they are fixated to this situation in their erotic life. Basically, they continue to be hungry children, although they are mature women who often adopt an apparently independent and "virile" demeanor. Others, the old-fashioned women of yesteryear, follow the path of the Arapesh. They sublimate their eroticism into motherhood and are frigid without suffering, because genital love does not interest them. In this way they function in accord with the unconscious and infantile wish to deny and prevent—through identification—the sexuality of their own mothers. Moreover, they scorn genital sex because what it offers seems to them to be a pleasure inferior to the one they received in childhood, which they are offering to their own children. They are also basically fixated on the mother–daughter relationship. They do not continue to be little girls because they have identified with their ideal, the asexual mother, and because they enjoy infantile pleasures through the identification with their children. Lastly, there are women who do not attain motherhood because of having been excessively gratified in early childhood only to be subsequently frustrated; they search for the mother in the husband, maintaining themselves in an infantile position.

We may deduce from all of this the type of family constellation that guarantees a favorable sexual development for the girl. Both parents should give enough affection so that their daughter can accept their sexual relations without too much envy. A strong father, full of tenderness for his little girl, will help her abandon her mother as a love object and turn femininely toward him. A mother who is happy with her husband will be tempted neither to put all of her dissatisfied love in her daughter, thus overstimulating her, nor to reject her or devalue her for not being a boy, because she herself is content with her femininity. She will permit her daughter to identify with a mother who is affectionate with her children and loving with her husband.

These are the ideal conditions. But how can a woman who has not had a happy home life overcome her infantile frustrations? Evidently, motherhood exists without orgastic capacity. But according to a well-taken observation by Helene Deutsch, vaginal orgasm does not exist without the psychological acceptance of motherhood. In addition, through identification with the child and a good affective relationship with her, motherhood offers the woman the best possibility of overcoming infantile frustrations suffered in relation to her own mother. In our society the majority of women avidly seek orgasm without attaining it because many of our mothers were frustrated in their motherhood and frustrating to their daughters. Moreover, these women fail erotically because they feel restricted and threatened regarding the achievement of their maternal instincts, which makes them feel guilty for being bad mothers. In order to compensate for this frustration, they laboriously seek sexual satisfaction without understanding that they are locked in a vicious circle. Often the same type of search for sexual pleasure makes them feel guilty and incapable of motherhood, impeding the achievement of the desired orgastic pleasure.

In our present era, because of internal as well as social factors, woman's maternal desires collide more than ever with her personal needs, desires, and ambitions. However, the woman who renounces motherhood completely will not generally be happy or capable of full sexual pleasure.[*] Until society undergoes fundamental changes to be able to accommodate the needs of women in general, each individual woman is forced to find the most successful strategy for herself. The challenge to every woman is to develop a life that permits her to express her general interests and her erotic desires while realizing a part of her maternal instincts and satisfying her remaining reproductive capacity through adequate sublimation. In this way, she can recoup her infantile frustrations and feel that she has fully realized her psychobiological abilities as an individual and a woman.

---

[*]Langer discarded this view in preference for one that put the emphasis on woman as a biopsychosocial being who is able to find emotional and sexual fulfillment in life through the direct expression of some of her potential creative capacities and the sublimation of others, which might include motherhood.

Fertility Disorders

Fertility occurs when a healthy sperm penetrates the mature ovum. However, even when sexual relations are consummated without contraceptives it often happens that fertility does not result. Only in recent decades, as we have come to understand the precise time of ovulation, have we been able to clarify this problem. According to Knaus and Ogino, ovulation occurs in the middle of the menstrual cycle. A woman is normally fertile during the days just prior to and following ovulation.

Once this pattern was understood, it then seemed plausible to conclude that the sexual act often did not culminate in fertilization because it had occurred just before, during or after menstruation, a time which is usually referred to as "physiological infertility." However, despite this new scientific awareness, other apparently inexplicable situations were noted. For example, occasionally a woman became pregnant during intercourse that occurred a short time before or after her menstrual period. Or another woman, who had already proven her fertility because of past pregnancies, could not become pregnant, even though she had intercourse on the days corresponding to her ovulation.

The first phenomenon can be explained only by irregularities in ovulation, a subject to which I shall later return. The second phenomenon can be related to many factors. When speaking of infertility, I exclude all the disorders caused by serious anatomical anomalies, mutilating operations, acute infectious states, and so on. What interests us at the moment are transitory and chronic infertility due to hormonal factors or tubal spasm—in other words, psychogenic infertility.

My approach assumes that not only does this type of infertility exist but that, in fact, it occurs much more frequently than any other. This notion is not original. Human beings have always interpreted infertility as a punishment from God, one that could be neutralized with vows and pilgrimages. In other words, infertility has been treated as a psychological problem, one related to morality. Many primitive peoples have seen infertility as a consequence of promiscuity and the child as a prize of conjugal fidelity. There are women who attribute their failure to produce offspring to their frigidity, that is, to their incapacity to love and surrender themselves. But until recently the medical profession has been contemptuous of explanations corresponding to psychological reality because they are ostensibly naive and mistaken. However, of late this antagonistic point of view seems to be undergoing important changes. Increasing numbers of gynecologists recommend psychotherapy to their infertile patients owing to their realization that in spite of the growing perfection of gynecological technology in the domains of surgical intervention and hormonal medication, infertility is on the rise. Moreover, their deepening understanding of the influence of psychological factors on these disorders is due to the great diffusion of psychoanalysis and to the increasing influence of psychosomatic medicine.[*]

---

[*]Langer's conceptualization of infertility as a psychosomatic disorder and her emphasis on psychogenic factors in infertility would become the prevailing perspective in the psychoanalytic literature until the mid-1970s. However, as research and technology have improved, the medical profession has been able to more effectively detect structural causes of infertility. It is claimed that many cases previously diagnosed as psychogenic sterility are now, given increased technological sophistication, interpreted in the light of organic causes. For example, it is thought that of the current estimated 15 percent of the infertile population in the United States suffering from infertility of "unknown origin," 10 percent actually have undiagnosed obscure organic problems. Because of the increasing emphasis on technological intervention to cure infertility, the psychiatric and psychological research has tended recently to focus on the psychological consequences of infertility rather than on the psychological etiology of infertility. For an exploration of this shift, see S. A. Shapiro, "Psychological Consequences of Infertility," in Critical Psychophysical Passages in the Life of a Woman, ed. J. Offerman-Zuckerberg (New York: Plenum, 1988). Langer continued to hold with her psychosomatic view, arguing that familiarity with the psychological profile of an infertile woman or couple often demonstrates the psychogenesis of physiological complications in infertility and that psychotherapeutic intervention can help to resolve the basic conflict or anxiety about motherhood and fatherhood that inhibits conception. Langer also argued that in the many cases that do not respond to fertility treatment, psychological intervention should not only address the anxiety and pain of failed attempts to conceive but also take up the woman or couple's unconscious conflictual attitudes toward reproduction, which she considered to be a fundamental factor in the inability to respond to the new sophisticated fertility technology. For other sources that focus on psychogenic causes of infertility, see L. Hollander Blum, "Sterility and the Magic Power of the Maternal Figure," The Journal of Nervous and Mental Disease, 128-1,(1959): 401–408; B. Sandler, "Emotional Stress and Infertility," Journal of Psychosomatic Research , 12(1968): 51–59; H. Michel-Wolfromm, "The

The perfection of gynecological techniques related to artificial insemination has been an important achievement of the past several decades, a fact that helps us confirm the limitations of mechanistic therapies.

Therese Benedek and her collaborators (1953) studied this subject at length. They discovered that while in animals a single insemination yielded successful results in 90% of the cases, the success of inseminations in women oscillated between 4% and 30%, even though they were performed in optimal physical conditions and, of course, during the period of maximum fertility.

The authors observed that women who had perfectly normal ovulation began to present cycles without ovulation once they had begun artificial insemination. A detailed study was made of six women who had submitted themselves to artificial insemination because their husbands had problems of relative infertility. The women were considered to be normally fertile, but psychotherapy was advised in each case given the fact that without it, artificial insemination was unsuccessful.

The authors confirmed that the procedure of artificial insemination exercised an unfavorable influence on the husband's potency and fertility and on the couple's sexual life. It was also demonstrated that the favorable influence of psychotherapy on one of the women improved her husband's fertility to such a point that he could impregnate his wife normally. This occurred after they had interrupted the insemination procedures and decided to adopt a child.

Psychological Factor in Spontaneous Abortion," *Journal of Psychosomatic Research*, 12(1968): 67–71; for a contemporary analysis of the unconscious parameters of conception, pregnancy and infertility that parallel Langer's, see D. Pines, "Emotional Aspects of Infertility and its Remedies," *International Journal of Psychoanalysis*, 71(1990): 561–567. D. Gerson ("Infertility and the Construction of Desperation," *Socialist Review*, 19,(3), 45–64) argues that the issues of conception and infertility are socially constructed, in that there exists a discrepancy between the visible experience of infertility in white, middle-class women (made so by the medical and academic literature and the popular media) and the invisibility of the experience of working-class, black and under-educated women who are most affected by infertility. As Gerson puts it, "...the 'class specific nature' of infertility is manifest in the contrast between the epidemiology of the problem, which shows a greater prevalence among black, poor, and less educated families, and the literature of the problem, which presents the issue as one of white, middle-class couples. This contrast is partly explained by the greater use of infertility services by white couples." (p. 50) Clearly the high cost of infertility services is beyond the reach of lower income women and couples. Although Gerson does not deal with the causes of infertility among less advantaged groups in this country, one may surmise that multiple factors, such as inadequate nutrition, inferior medical care and the psychosocial aspects of class and gender-based discrimination may result, for women in particular, in physiological problems of conception as well as unconscious conflict about sexuality and motherhood.

In the five remaining cases, however, positive results were not obtained. Only one woman became pregnant as a result of artificial insemination, after which she entered into a state of panic and developed a fear of contracting cancer. She was visibly relieved when she suffered a miscarriage within a matter of weeks. The other women developed such anxiety that they interrupted their attempts to become pregnant through artificial insemination, two of them terminating their psychotherapy as well.

This study is suggestive in many ways, two of which I will briefly discuss. The first, already rather well known to us, has to do with the relationship between the two members of the couple. From the physical point of view, the six women were healthy but their husbands' limited fertility caused them to resort to artificial insemination. (In five of the six cases the husband's semen could be used.) Nonetheless, when the women were confronted with the possibility of actualizing their conscious desires to become mothers, they became so anxious that they lost, at least temporarily, their ability to become pregnant. Once again it can be deduced that their unconscious conflict about motherhood influenced their marital choice, just as it later affected their possibilities of conceiving or (in the second case) of carrying a pregnancy to term.

Secondly, the physical problem was provoked by the women's anxiety. It is possible, then, that intense or chronic anxieties (North Americans speak of "stress," a state of chronic anxious tension responsible for many psychosomatic disorders) seriously influence female fertility. I deliberately leave aside here the influence of stress on male fertility, because it does not pertain to our subject. Moreover, male fertility has not been widely investigated. But the studies cited here clearly demonstrate that psychological factors impact equally on men, a fact underscored by the participants as well. This is also confirmed by H. Stieve's experiments, herein briefly summarized only with respect to women.

The experiments occurred in Nazi Germany, where even though Freud's books had been publicly burned, authorities were preoccupied with the grandeur of the race and thus supportive of all studies of factors that might cause a decline in fertility. In the perverse conditions of the concentration camps, H. Stieve, a Nazi physician, used the disciplines of anatomy and histology to demonstrate the influence of psychological processes on the reproductive system.

A healthy person exposed over the course of weeks to a continuous death threat obviously suffers from anxiety. It occurred to Stieve to do autopsies on the cadavers of prisoners of both sexes who had been executed, in order to study the state of the genital organs. But first, while the subjects of his study were still alive, Stieve interrogated them about the normalcy of their sexual life. His findings indicated that 75% of the women who had previously menstruated normally stopped menstruating immediately after being detained. Evidently they were suffering profound anxiety, already assuming that they were condemned to death. In fact, they were executed within weeks. During their imprisonment, they were not mistreated and they received adequate food. Nonetheless, all of them suffered serious deterioration of their reproductive organs.

The mucus of the cervix of one of those executed, a 20-year-old woman who had been in prison for 68 days, had the thickness and appearance of the cervical mucus of a 70-year-old woman. The ovaries of another young prisoner, a 24-year-old who had last menstruated 62 days before her death, looked like the ovaries of a menopausal woman. During those 2 or 3 months of mortal anguish, all of these young women had undergone an aging process with respect to their reproductive capacity, and they died at the end of their suffering physically changed into old women. This, of course, implies that they had become infertile. From his investigations Stieve deduced that the damaging influence of anguishing emotions on the genital apparatus cannot be denied and asserted that much less intense fears can also be assumed to cause reproductive difficulties.*

The need to resort to such drastic experiments in order to demonstrate this influence is proof of the German National-Socialist physician's curiosity stimulated by the discovery of the psychosomatic process. However, once having become convinced of its existence, gynecologists in general became involved in systematically ascertaining the psychogenic causes of their patients' infertility. While they lacked the necessary scientific preparation to elaborate their findings, the abundance of clinical material they collected permitted them to arrive at empirically derived conclusions.

K. J. Anselmino, a physician on the staff of a well known Italian obstetrical clinic, inquired of each patient whether or not she had

---

*Under circumstances different from those of a concentration camp but nonetheless deleterious, Rene Spitz studied the impact of stress on the body in the case of children who were separated from their mothers while in the hospital or other public settings. In his observation of young children living in a foundling home, he determined that if a child in the first year of life is deprived of object relations, she undergoes serious deterioration that appears to be, at least in part, irreversible. Spitz also demonstrated that children who were adequately cared for physically but emotionally starved presented a new clinical picture after 3 months: motor retardation, including defective eye coordination, imbecilic facial expression, and progressive decline of the developmental quotient; by 4 years of age, such a child could not sit, stand, walk, or talk. See R. A. Spitz, *The First Year of Life* (New York: International Universities Press, 1965).

passed through long periods of infertility. In the affirmative cases, he did a detailed somatic and psychological profile in order to establish the causal factors of the infertility and the circumstances responsible for its ultimate disappearance.[1] In this way he brought together a great quantity of clinical histories, part of which he published in his article "Pregnancy Achieved After an Untreated and Lengthy Infertility." The author arrived at the following conclusions: The majority of the patients came from neurotic and conflictual family environments. Moreover, all of their marriages revealed causal factors of nervous tension and states of conflict, including marital problems, extraordinarily difficult economic situations, and the need for the woman to do exhausting work or work that contradicted her feminine role. When the tense state disappeared because of positive changes in their external situation, the patients became pregnant. Anselmino also included in his case histories his patients' experiences in childbirth because he was concerned about what he considered to be the extremely high percentage of surgical interventions during delivery. He interpreted this necessity as proof of the disposition of these formerly infertile patients toward functional disorders. While Anselmino is correct in his observation, there is another explanation as well. When psychosomatic disorders of reproduction are cured spontaneously, the basic conflict is not resolved. For this reason, very often when a woman has overcome a disorder in one period of her reproductive life, another obstacle presents itself in the following period. Anselmino's patients could not become pregnant because of certain conflicts, but when their psychological conditions altered, even superficially, they were able to conceive. However, difficulties during childbirth indicated the persistence of their essential ambivalence and the unresolved nature of their basic conflict about motherhood. The majority of the favorable changes in the patients' lives occurred in relation to World War II and its demands. Indeed, it is well known that neuroses usually diminish during emergencies. According to what has been discussed here, apparently the same holds true with certain psychosomatic disorders that result from the same conflicts.

Finally, Anselmino cites a group of patients for whom the war acted as a direct and immediate cure. He describes four of the many cases he observed in which infertile women had witnessed very serious bombings that had completely destroyed their homes. Their husbands were absent at the time. Following the catastrophe and during the first opportunity the women had to be together with their husbands upon their return from the front, they became pregnant. As we shall see later, a significant difficulty for the infertile woman relates to her fixation on her mother.[2] Another problem has to do with her guilt feelings. Having witnessed a serious bombing attack without suffering any bodily injury was most likely experienced by these women as an omen that God or fate had pardoned them or, in other words, as proof that they were not as guilty as they had previously believed. Moreover, the home is a maternal symbol and in the unconscious its loss may correspond to a destruction of the link with the mother. Thus, we have the conjuncture of the two events—their survival of the bombing and the destruction of their homes—that permitted these women to conceive.*

Let us now look more extensively at the type of conflicts that may perturb normal impregnation and the potential disorders that are consequently produced. First, there is a phenomenon that generally passes unnoticed because the patient herself thinks it too insignificant to consult a physician about. It is the transitory infertility of short duration that occurs extraordinarily frequently and whose physiological basis consists of menstrual cycles without ovulation. Even with normal ovulation, impregnation can also be impeded because of a spasm in the tubes produced by constant tension (stress) or an accident which prevents the union of the ovum with the sperm. (see Langer & Ochandorena, 1953) This condition can be observed during insufflation and yields readily to medication or suggestive methods.

It became clear to me in a number of analyses that the inability to become pregnant is the expression of psychological factors that have a negative impact on the pregnancy. I will first examine a 4-month episode of infertility in a young woman I will call Lina. She had been married for some years and wanted to have children, but her husband remained opposed to the idea. She finally persuaded him but then became infertile. Now he also wanted a child and reacted with great anguish related to his doubts about his virility.

Details about Lina's early history will help us to understand the couple's problem. Lina was an only child. Her father was a violent and

---

*In the late 1960s Langer had occasion to observe a similar reaction among women to conditions of war. At that time in Argentina, as elsewhere in Latin America, deteriorating economic circumstances and increasing class conflict motivated the emergence of a leftist strategy of armed struggle. University students and young professionals, along with their working-class counterparts, joined urban guerrilla groups that militarily confronted the repressive dictatorship. Langer knew young middle-class militants, women who under normal circumstances would have pursued careers and postponed motherhood, who as revolutionaries became pregnant and had babies in physically and emotionally difficult and often dangerous conditions; these women were consciously motivated by an ideology that encouraged the creation of new lives for the revolution and the society that was being fought for on behalf of future generations and, as Langer saw it, unconsciously motivated by the association of their female empowerment with fertility. Their pregnancies also had a reparative function; as Langer also noted, the birthrate always rises during wartime.

dominating man, and her parents did not get along well. She remembers her mother crying and asking her if she wanted to leave home with Mama or stay with Papa. When she was 6 years old, her mother fell ill with heart trouble. The little girl vaguely related this illness to the consequences of sexual activity. Within several months her mother died, and an aunt came to live with her father and her. In time, Lina began to worry about whether or not a romantic relationship existed between her father and her aunt. However, she loved her aunt very much and was inseparable from her. Her deep need and love for her aunt is explained in several ways. Lina had lost her mother and feared that her aunt could leave her as well if she did not do everything possible to keep her. Moreover, because at one point she had desired her mother's death in order to substitute for her at her father's side, her guilt feeling made her repress all hostility toward her aunt, compensating her with an exaggerated love. In order to eliminate conflict with her aunt, she also stayed away from her father. Besides, she reproached him for rejecting her because she was a female. Indeed, her father often said that he would have preferred to have a son, which made Lina hate him. But she also identified with him and was forced to masculinize herself in order to please him. She also sought out her aunt, for whom she competed with her father. Later she married a man who had many of her father's characteristics.

I would like now to present some analytic material from the period of Lina's treatment during which she experienced a 4-month infertility. When her first menstrual period arrived following sexual relations without contraceptives, Lina reacted ambivalently. She was distraught because of not having been able to get pregnant, but she was also pleased about being able to frustrate her husband, whom she unconsciously identified with her father. In the past her father had not wanted to accept her because she was a female, and similarly, her husband had not permitted her to become a mother. Now that he accepted her and asked for a child, she, resentful and distrustful, repressed her femininity and did not comply. In the following month they continued sexual relations without contraceptives, but Lina felt that she had not gotten pregnant.

The night before her period was due Lina had the following dream: She is lying beside a blond woman whose breasts are exposed. Sucking one of her nipples, she extracts milk, which runs into a glass. Lina says to her, "You see, you aren't married. But it doesn't matter now; since I've sucked out your milk, we can feed this child," indicating an infant who is in the bed next to them; Lina does not know to whom the child belongs. In the second part of the dream Lina discovers that an unmarried friend has had a baby. She is surprised that her friend's mother, who is generally very repressive, has allowed her to do this.

At this point I do not want to offer a complete analysis of these two dreams. I only wish to point out the most important aspects in relation to the patient's infertility. Resentful of her husband-father, Lena sought refuge once again in the infantile relationship. The image of the woman in the dream represents a condensation of the analyst and the aunt. In the dream Lina expresses her wish not to have a child with her husband but, rather, to be the child who still nurses. Moreover, the possibility of becoming pregnant stimulates an old phantasy, that of having a child with her mother (as was already mentioned, this phantasy is typical at a certain stage of infantile development). In the second part of the dream, in which she is represented by the friend and the analyst by the friend's mother, she tries to obtain her analyst's permission for the realization of this phantasy.

In the sessions following the dream, Lina remembered that before meeting her future husband she had always thought that as an adult she would never marry but would live alone with her aunt or a friend. Besides, during her entire adolescence she had imagined that there should be a way to have children without the intervention of a man. Because of her fear of pregnancy—her mother had died from an illness that, according to rumors Lina had heard from the time she was a child, resulted from various abortions insisted on by her father—and her resentment toward her husband, Lina returned to her infantile phantasies and a homosexual position. It was this situation that prevented her from becoming pregnant and also stimulated the dream.

During the following month, Lina went on to work through her conflict. She blamed her father for her homosexuality and often fought with her husband. Several days before the anticipated date of the onset of her menstruation—the third during her period of infertility—she told me, "This entire month, whenever I was angry with him, I thought that even though the little egg might have gotten fertilized, I must have killed it with my rage." Sure enough, her period came.

During the following month an enormous amount of material referring to her father came forth in the analysis. Lina became conscious of her repressed love for him and the intensity of her resentment for having felt rejected as a female child. She understood that this rejection was an important factor in her penis envy and her desires to be a man. She began to be concerned about her infertility and to seriously desire to become pregnant. This time she became depressed when she got her period. She had a dream in which she was concerned with finding out about the circumstances of her own birth and her mother's death and whether her mother had really been a woman of low morals, as her aunt had always maintained. She began to reconcile herself with her dead mother's memory, and her fear of identifying with her diminished. She had a long friendly conversation with her husband about her infertility. She felt relieved when he promised to have his sperm examined, which she took as an indication of his acknowledgment that he was possibly responsible for their failure. Lina then had sexual relations with her husband on the presumed date of ovulation. Afterward, she dreamed that she is walking along a narrow path. She feels like a man. She carries out a counterattack against an invisible adversary, called "the other," who, along with Indians shooting poison arrows, attacks her friends and her. If the arrows are quickly extracted, nothing happens. But if heed is not taken and they are left in the body, they can cause death. Lina feels that she is about to lose the battle. Later she meets "the other" in an apartment in order to make a truce (Lina, in fact, had gotten pregnant.)

This dream seems to be the psychological representation of her physiological defenses against impregnation and of her final surrender. Sometimes, when speaking of her husband, Lina would call him "the other." The narrow path on which "the other" attacks her is her vagina. The poison arrows represent the sperm. To be poisoned signifies to be pregnant and to die. To take out the arrows quickly signifies saving oneself from the danger of impregnation. In order to achieve the latter, one has to masculinize oneself. Lina is about to lose the battle; that is, she feels that this time she has become pregnant. But she no longer defends herself because she is reconciled with "the other," the enemy. At this point I do not wish to examine the extent to which "the other" represents another part of her ego and whether or not the hostility that she sees in her husband is her own hostility projected onto him. Lina associates the truce with the aforementioned friendly conversation. Because her husband already admits that perhaps she is not responsible for the failure to get pregnant, he is acknowledging as well that she is not "bad" and that he can love her. Then her own aggression against him diminishes, and she is less afraid about giving up her defenses, surrendering to him in a feminine way, and conceiving.

Lina was very happy when her pregnancy was confirmed. But within several days, she had another violent quarrel with her husband. Her reaction included the following dream: "I am with my husband and a woman of the sort he likes. He remains passive and makes no overtures to her. Then I come on to the girl and experience much pleasure in seducing her." Thus, in reaction to the first frustration suffered because of her husband, Lina returns to her previous mechanisms. She feels demeaned by her father (the husband), she robs him of his virility (he remains passive), and now identifying with him, she conquers the aunt. Lina was already pregnant, and her dream indicates her regret at having yielded. In fact, her persistent ambivalence about motherhood expressed itself during her entire pregnancy in different disorders, and during the final months it exposed her to a continuous danger of giving birth prematurely.

We have seen in this patient a very unfavorable family constellation for normal feminine development: a timid mother, repressed and submissive, who in her death abandons her daughter to a violent and seductive father. In order to defend himself against his incestuous feelings, the father cannot accept Lina as a female child. Lina was always consciously afraid of being pregnant because of the fear of dying in childbirth or of remaining deformed for the rest of her life, thus losing her husband's love. Moreover, unconsciously, she feared her mother's jealous rage if she had a child by her husband-father. She fears, then—if she becomes a mother—her internal destruction and the loss of both parents' love. She defends herself against these dangers by masculinizing herself. Thus, she becomes pleasing to her father and, as his rival, she can conquer her mother. She rejects her femininity, opposing it with her penis envy and her desire to be a man. Moreover, this virile position, which leaves her momentarily infertile, protects her against the greatest danger of castration of her feminine genitalia (deformation or death).

Through the analysis of her conflicts, the partial recovery of her mother in the person of the analyst, and the reconciliation with her father via the more understanding attitude of her husband, Lina is able to become pregnant. However, this victory of her feminine position is not yet firmly entrenched. After the first quarrel with her husband she returns to her prior defensive position.

We now turn to another case of transitory infertility that occurred during analysis. I refer to Isabel, already mentioned in prior pages, whose cockroach phobia I had interpreted as an expression of infantile conflicts reactivated and intensified by the appearance of menarche. Now I want to briefly remind the reader of some details of Isabel's childhood family constellation and to refer to others of her adult life that shed light on the factors affecting her infertility. Her father was a demanding man who pressured her to study and denied her access to all pleasures and activities considered merely feminine. Her mother was rejecting and arbitrary and had never forgiven Isabel for her existence, having experienced her as a bothersome infant who interrupted her comfortable life with her two older school-age children. Her sister, who was proud of her own beauty, demeaned Isabel. The only one who treated her affectionately was her brother. But her grandmother envied her and forbade this friendship. Isabel was of a passionate and violent temperament and as an infant had almost totally succumbed to the severity of her family environment. During puberty she came to feel so disgraced that she made two suicide attempts, once by taking poison and another time by attempting to drown herself. She met her future husband in medical school just as she began her university studies. When she became engaged, she dared not tell her parents. She had sexual relations with her fiancé in complete secrecy, became pregnant several times, and was forced to seek abortions under extraordinarily difficult circumstances. Finally she graduated and married. As I have already indicated, she did not dare to become pregnant in her country of origin. Only here in Argentina, far from her family and already in psychoanalytic treatment, did she decide to stop using any kind of contraception during sex in order to become pregnant.

Just as her great fertility before marriage had often made her feel desperate, now she was confused and soon also depressed and anxious to learn that she could not become pregnant. Through the analysis of several dreams from this period, we shall examine the fears that prevented her from realizing her strong conscious desire to have a child. Before her second menstruation she had a dream in two parts; in the first part she has given birth to twin girls. She does not breast-feed one of them, who remains a weak and silent baby. She feeds the other one well, and she becomes a fine, strong baby. In the second part of the dream she sees herself among her friends, frantically fleeing the city, persecuted by a demon, the "fire-daughter." She knows that it is the daughter she took such good care of. Now she laments not having concerned herself with the other, the "water-daughter," who was a better child. Following this dream, her menstruation began, but not on the normal date. After bleeding for 10 days, Isabel consulted a gynecologist, who diagnosed her condition as insufficiency of the menstrual corpus luteum and treated her with drugs to end the hemorrhage. It is not my intention to present all of Isabel's associations to the dream but to recount those interpretations directly related to her fears of becoming pregnant. For Isabel, to conceive represented the satisfaction of instinctual desires, a defiance of her mother—just like her strong and splendid sister, who has had children—and to allow herself to express what she has inside of her. Both the "fire-daughter" and the "water-daughter" represent herself. If she dares to allow herself to be seduced by the good treatment that I offer her—the analyst is like the mother who breast-feeds—and to become less repressed, her strong and violent personality would emerge, which she—identifying with her parents' judgment—sees as a demon. It would put her entire family in danger. Because of this, in the dream she feels bad about having abandoned her other personality, the "water-daughter," who had been treated without love and thus had attempted to drown herself (symbolized in the image of the "water-daughter") but who afterward had become calm, submissive, and inoffensive. Isabel, then, was afraid to conceive and give birth or develop her real personality because she had yielded to her mother, whom she considered to be very dangerous and hostile. In order to better defend herself against this temptation to abandon her repressions, she produced a prolongation of her menstrual bleeding, thus postponing the possibility of pregnancy.

Isabel very slowly began to realize that I, in contrast to the internal mother, wanted to help her actualize her desire to be a mother. She distrusted my "goodwill." She dreamed of someone who wishes to make another person ingest a dose of poison; this someone is known to have already assassinated another individual in this way. When the sinister character cannot realize his goals, he tries to poison himself. Isabel associated the poison in the ampules with the injections prescribed by her physician to stop the hemorrhage. While in the aforementioned dream she made an allusion to her second suicide attempt, this time, through the poison, she alluded to the first endeavor. Because I wanted to help her cure her infertility, she identified me with her physician. Moreover, she unconsciously confused me with her mother and so distrusted my ends. Because of a lack of understanding and love, her mother once led her to poison herself; I apparently wished to do something good for her, but surely I would reject her and make her suffer intensely once she was pregnant. Therefore, in her dream, the sinister person, who is a condensation of her mother and me, has already poisoned a person once and now tries to repeat the crime. In her unconscious I do not want to cure her, but to drive her to suicide. Thus, she defends herself, preventing the dangerous pregnancy, and phantasizes attacking me while using the same weapons with which I attack her (the criminal finally has to commit suicide).

Behind Isabel's conscious hatred for her mother, there appeared little by little a yearning for her. In another dream she expresses her nostalgic wish to return to the womb. This nostalgia also prevents conception because, to her, to become a mother means to definitively stop being a daughter. Because Isabel was frustrated so as a child, she still seeks to vindicate her infantile rights and is unable to accept their renunciation through becoming a mother herself. In the same dream in which she searches for her mother, Isabel can "maintain [her]self suspended in the air, a capacity [she] had known very well as a child and which [she] had forgotten." The patient offers no associations to this part of the dream. But, if one interprets symbolically, it appears to deal with the sensations experienced during her forgotten clitoral masturbation (the forgotten capacity that she knew as a child). Through the first part of the dream, which expresses her search for and loving return to her mother, it can be deduced that the erotic phantasies that accompanied her infantile clitoral masturbation are directed toward her mother. Exasperated by her mother's rejection and zealous to conquer her, Isabel adopted an erotic virile attitude (men's dreams of flying typically express an erection).

Now I present the last part of another dream related to our topic: Isabel is waiting for me. When I arrive, I indicate to her that I have to cut her hair. I cut one lock of her hair. She is very scared and thinks, "At least it was only a lock of hair from the front. But it would have been a disaster if she had cut it all off." Here Isabel returns to a theme of the prior dream, this time elaborating much more. She has understood that if she lets herself feel close to me, identifying with me in my maternal qualities, she can give up her imaginary penis (symbolized in "the lock of hair from the front") and her clitoral excitation, accompanied by unconscious phantasies of conquering her mother. She can renounce her virile defense as long as I do not "cut it all off" (that is, do not destroy her feminine genitalia, which her mother had earlier restricted) and permit her to become a mother. We see, then, in a single dream the two characteristically female castration fears: the more superficial one referring to the loss of the imaginary penis and the more profound one of the complete destruction of femininity.

Isabel did not become pregnant in spite of her renunciation of her virility in the dream. She reacted with profound depression at the onset of her period. She had a dream that explains to us her emotional state: She is supposed to pass along a narrow path, shrouded in spiderwebs. She is with other family members, including the hated grandmother, and they pass with some difficulty. She tries to get through, but when she feels the spiderwebs on her face she falls to the ground screaming in pain and anguish. The others rush to her aid and see that the spiderwebs have covered her with welts, which are burning her.

As I already indicated, Isabel feared losing her mother if she had a child. In her dream, she wants to be inside of the mother and wishes she had not been born (later I will explain the contents of these frequently encountered phantasies of the return to the womb). Unconsciously, for Isabel, to be born and to have a child are one and the same thing. But she was coming to understand that she would have to separate from her mother and assume her role as an adult woman, just as her own mother, her sister, and the rest of the women in her family had done in their respective eras. Her serious depression corresponded to the mourning for the anticipated separation from her mother. Let us return to the dream: To pass along a narrow road symbolizes to be born and to give birth. Many women in Isabel's family, even her hated grandmother, knew how to do this very well. Only she does not dare to. The spiderweb enclosing the road symbolizes her fixation on the bad mother. She feels like a baby, writhing on the ground, screaming at not being able to break away. Finally, the others —I—help her to pass through, that is, to be born, to separate from her mother. But if she passes through, she will be full of welts, that is, pregnant (welts=swelling of the skin; pregnancy=swelling of the belly). The welts burn her. Through this painful sensation Isabel expresses her suffering because of the separation from her mother and the fearfully anticipated pains of childbirth.

Following an elaborate interpretation of this dream and of her depressive state, the latter disappeared. I assume that Isabel became pregnant on one of the days between this dream and the next one, which occurred shortly afterward. In this dream, she is in the basement of her childhood home. She sees everything covered with dust, and dead cockroaches are hanging from the ceiling. One falls down. She is disgusted but does not feel terrified (as we commented earlier, she suffered from a cockroach phobia). She calmly begins to clean the basement.

In her depression caused by her ostensible infertility, Isabel often reproached herself for having been ruined by her abortions. Her mother gave birth to three children and had one abortion. She had already had three abortions and a miscarriage. Isabel was the youngest daughter and unconsciously believed that since her mother had no more children after she was born, this was proof that her imaginary attacks on her mother's body had been successful in robbing her of all reproductive capacity. Thus she feared, as the most appropriate punishment, that she, like her mother, had used up her reproductive capacity after four pregnancies. But basically this fear, as well as her infertility, was already a defense against the anxiety that her vengeful mother would destroy her ("she would cut it all off" in the dream) if she dared to abandon her. On the other hand, fixated on her frustrating mother, Isabel felt incapable of separating from her, even when she consciously denied this situation. I interpret her depression as an expression of this difficulty (Isabel's incapacity to pass through the narrow path in her earlier dream). When this situation became conscious for her and she experienced my understanding as supportive, she was able to disengage from her mother and from the past and to have the optimistic dream about the basement. The childhood home in the dream represents her mother (the house possessed by the father) and herself in identification with the mother because of her guilt feelings. The basement symbolizes her mother's uterus, as well as her own. It is empty and filled with dust, that is to say, in disuse. The dead cockroaches represent her siblings (assassinated by her in her unconscious infantile phantasies) and her own children, whom she killed by aborting them. (In previous pages we saw that the cockroaches came to take on the significance of children for Isabel.) In the dream Isabel is surprised because of not feeling horror at the sight of the cockroaches. This horror had been the expression of her guilt feelings and fear of punishment. Its disappearance permitted her to clean the basement, which was equivalent to preparing the uterus for a new pregnancy.

Isabel feared a pregnancy because of her own hostility toward her mother and her mother's hostility toward her. Her virile attitude provided two important functions: to defend her against a pregnancy, which for her would have signified her internal destruction, and to connect her to her mother, who rejected her as a female child. She was able to renounce her imaginary penis and become pregnant when she felt that her analyst-mother would neither abandon her for her past sins nor reject her for her femininity. While her abortions had represented a kind of defiance of her mother, in the long run they signified Isabel's submission to her. When she felt that her analyst did not blame her for such an attitude, but fully understood her, her guilt feeling and her own reactive and defensive hostility diminished, permitting her, by means of her pregnancy, to identify with her healthy (not destroyed) mother and to be capable of giving birth. However, her conflicts, though less intense, persisted and became aggravated at various times during the pregnancy and provoked different psychosomatic disorders, which will be described in subsequent chapters.

This exposition presents us with a variety of problems. What is the significance of the phantasies of returning to the womb? Are they mere phantasies or do they perhaps correspond to forgotten memories that return from the repressed? As we saw, Isabel often expressed such phantasies in a disguised form in her dreams. Now, the explanation of the appearance of such phantasies in Isabel is obvious. From the time she was a child, she felt mistreated by an extraordinarily nervous and irritable mother, whose attitude she interpreted as rejection and an indication that she was unloved. But it is intolerable for a small child to be convinced that the mother on whom she depends so much does not love her. So she constantly phantasizes about her brief life in order to find a period during which her mother has loved her and to locate an explanation for the change. Individuals who have fallen into disgrace usually become religious, blaming themselves for their sins and phantasizing about the joy of Paradise. In order to avoid accusing God of wickedness for having expelled them—that is, for no longer loving them—they blame Adam and Eve for their fall from Paradise. In the same way, the abandoned child cannot accept her mother's wicked-ness. She prefers to believe that her mother stopped loving her because of her sins and that she was once loved when she was still innocent and part of her mother. Thus, she will later be fixated on her mother because of the very frustrations she suffered, and in moments of feeling threatened with losing her she will return in her phantasies to the intrauterine period, happy and free from dangers.

There is a second problem in Isabel's history that demands attention. In a certain period of her life, during which becoming pregnant was really catastrophic for her, Isabel was extraordinarily fertile. Later, when she consciously wished to become pregnant and there no longer were external obstacles to the realization of her desires, she became infertile. Helene Deutsch offers us the explanation of this apparently contradictory phenomenon. She speaks of a "conception compulsion" in cases where the woman easily conceives precisely when the psychological and external circumstances are unfavorable. The author demonstrates through abundant clinical material that the same psychological factors causing infertility in one woman can, in another woman, cause a compulsion to conceive. This in itself explains, to my way of thinking, how a woman can alternate between both symptoms.

Let us return to Isabel. Her mother forbade her to be a woman. Consciously, Isabel hated her mother and wished to deny her fixation by defying her. Unconsciously, she needed her and was fixated on her. Her illegitimate pregnancies had various psychological functions. They were an expression of her defiance; they confirmed to her that her parents' prohibitions did not matter to her and that, in spite of it all, she was a woman and could have children. But she defied them during a period in which she knew perfectly well that she would have to eliminate her pregnancies by aborting them. In those abortions she subordinated herself to her mother, once again turning toward her. By depriving herself of the desired child, she punished herself for having prevented her mother—in her phantasies—from having other children after she was born. Moreover, she feared that if she defied her mother by having a baby, her mother would destroy her internally. The abortion signified a compromise between this fear and its negation. Isabel confirmed her fertility without risking the punishment of her enraged mother by carrying the pregnancy to term. We will see this situation more clearly later when we examine the disorders she suffered during the pregnancy she was finally able to achieve.

Upon marrying, the external situation in Isabel's life radically changed. Still, to have a child continued to mean for her a defiance of her mother, accompanied by the unconscious fear of losing her or of suffering a cruel punishment. Moreover, now she could not permit herself to get pregnant as a way of affirming her independence because, since there was no longer any pretext to terminate the pregnancy, she would have to carry it to term. Now she defended herself with her infertility, simultaneously expiating her sins through her suffering.

It was also clear that Isabel had actually been traumatized by her abortions, to which she consciously attributed her infertility. Besides the psychological reasons already mentioned, this trauma was related to the fact that when she had her abortions, it was considered a serious crime in her country, whose punishment was rigorously enforced by the law. Such circumstances had made abortion difficult and represented very real dangers to her health and freedom. Without delving into the controversial issue of a woman's right to freely decide for herself whether or not to continue with a pregnancy, I wish at this point to call attention to the fact that a pregnant woman forced against her conscious will to have a child is in serious conflict. She unconsciously seeks punishment for herself and retaliation against society. To oblige her to have her child under such circumstances is to satisfy these destructive tendencies and to make her responsible for the existence of an infant who, because of its mother's attitude and not infrequent economic difficulties, will be doomed to live life as a resentful and neurotic individual. Sooner or later, these unfavorable circumstances will make him a burden to society.

On the other hand, it is important for the gynecologist and the psychotherapist to know that a curettage or induced abortion always signifies a serious trauma for a woman. I do not refer to the merely somatic damage that it can cause, because a curettage performed by a specialist and in adequate conditions is, clearly, less dangerous for a woman's physical health than carrying a fetus to term. But I wish to stress that she suffers a psychological trauma. Even the woman for whom a curettage has no apparent importance beyond a visit to her dentist basically feels like an assassin. Apparently, even the woman who is an atheist unconsciously accepts the Catholic idea that the fertilized egg has a soul and is a child. This occurs because, consciously or unconsciously, during her entire life she has phantasized about the child she will one day have. It is enough for her to find out that she is pregnant for these phantasies to reemerge and to be connected to the fetus she carries inside of her. She thinks of herself as a criminal because, unconsciously, it is not that she destroys the fertilized egg several days after a curettage but that she assassinates the child, the focus of all her maternal phantasies. She will always seek and find a way to punish herself and often her partner as well, whom she experiences as complicit in a crime for which he wishes to remain unpunished. And if the woman is already a mother, her children will consciously or unconsciously perceive her curettage with horror. They will experience her as a witch and a dangerous assassin, asking themselves to what strange luck they owe their own salvation and birth. And they will feel guilty, because upon eliminating the resented sibling, she executes her children's criminal phantasies.

In terms of all that has been discussed, an undesired conception should generally be considered a neurotic symptom, aside from the significance of the partner's attitude, the woman's ignorance, or other factors that influence the situation that may not be connected to her neurosis. It could be said that a woman somatizes her conflict by means of the pregnancy. Certain menstrual delays, whose psychological causes have never been denied by the medical profession, constitute a more minor somatization. It is well known that in her fear of becoming pregnant, in her need to be punished, and, ultimately, in her rejection of motherhood the single woman very frequently suffers from delayed menstrual periods. She believes she is pregnant, becomes desperate, and anxiously seeks any kind of solution until, with the appearance of her period, she is instantly calmed, only to suffer the same tragedy the following month.

In the infertile woman desirous of having a child, the same menstrual delays due to apparently opposite motives may be observed. She, like the single woman, begins to observe herself and to feel pregnancy signs before the menstrual date. When her period is only several days late, she is sure this time of having achieved the desired goal. She continually observes herself and takes great pains to be careful. She phantasizes about her child until the flow begins, generally between the 8th and 15th day of her late period, immediately destroying all of her illusions. Both women express in the same somatic symptom, menstrual delay, but through an apparently reverse psychological state, the same conflict: their ambivalence about motherhood and their desire for a child, to which, for one reason or another, they feel they have no right. Menstrual delays are a somatic expression of their frustrated phantasy of motherhood.

In rare cases, this phantasy assumes apparently more real contours. We refer to the condition of pseudocyesis, or false pregnancy, in which menstruation disappears and the woman takes on the appearance of being pregnant, manifesting certain apparently unequivocal symptoms, like abdominal movements that seem to be those of a fetus. In this way a woman makes an imaginary compromise between her desire to have a child and her incapacity to achieve motherhood, which stems from real psychological or physiological factors. In her attempt to deny such incapacity she plays a trick on herself and others; she is apparently certain of expecting a child and transforms her body to the point of convincing everyone, often even her physician. In order to analyze this disorder, I summarize a published clinical case treated by Ruth Moulton.

Winifred N, a 16-year-old unmarried daughter from a large and very Catholic family, is a member of the working class. She came to the hospital in order to give birth. However, in spite of her large and prominent abdomen in which certain spastic movements were observed, the attending physician immediately diagnosed a false pregnancy. Moulton makes the interesting observation that only those women who have already had children or are very familiar with the biological processes of maternity are capable of realistically producing all of the external symptoms of pregnancy, including the pigmentation of the nipples, the swelling of the breasts, and so forth. Winifred had no personal experience in this regard, but she had seen her mother and her older sisters pregnant. She saw them with their unwieldy abdomens and was used to hearing their complaints about nausea and back pains. While she copied those symptoms in her imitation of motherhood, she could not, of course, copy those unknown to her. Two days after her admission to the hospital, Winifred felt intense abdominal pains, interpreting them as the onset of labor. They lasted for hours, followed by a vaginal hemorrhage. Several days later, Moulton began psychotherapeutic treatment with the young woman, bringing together data that will now be summarized.

Winifred had had a difficult childhood. Nonetheless, she seemed well adapted to her environment. From early on she helped her mother in household tasks, taking pleasure in caring for her younger siblings as if they were her own children. She had never let her mother explain to her how babies are made or how they are born, so when she was hospitalized "in order to have a baby," she did not even know "where children come from." Although she seemed to be closer to her mother, she was on good terms with her father. However, she was troubled by the fact that her mother slept with her father, and during the night she would try to convince her mother to stay with her. She was resentful toward her family when they sent her out to work immediately after she graduated from high school. Shortly afterward, she fell in love with an 18-year-old boy, whose marriage proposal she rejected because she considered herself too young to marry. She twice allowed herself to be persuaded by him to have sexual relations, with little conscious awareness of what was happening. After the second experience the boy told her, "Now you're going to have a baby and you will have to marry me." Following that episode, she considered herself to be pregnant and ceased to menstruate during the next 9 months. When her mother found out what had happened, she denounced the youth, influencing the judge to decide that the boy would have to marry Winifred within 1 year or be subjected to a prison sentence. Winifred's father never spoke one word to her after learning of her ostensible pregnancy. The girl spent the 9 months making a complicated layette, phantasizing about the marriage and exhibiting her pregnancy to the women of her family in order to quell certain doubts with respect to her state. Upon beginning psychotherapeutic treatment, she was still convinced of her pregnancy. She wanted to have a daughter, insisting that her child would be the only thing her mother could never steal from her because she would not permit it. When she finally had to admit that she was not going to have a child, she became very depressed. She said that her mother had won because through her prayers she had successfully prevented her from having a child and bemoaned the fact that now she would not be able to marry or leave her parents' home.

Moulton sees the psychological causes of Winifred's pseudocyesis principally in her fixation to the oedipal situation. Although consciously repressed, a strong amorous inclination toward her father existed, as well as a great resentment and envy toward her mother because of her sexual relations with the father and the many children she received from him. Winifred experienced the same conflicts with her married sisters, who were maternal substitutes for her. Because of her rivalry with them, she wanted to have a child, marry, and create her own home. This is a correct but incomplete interpretation. In my opinion, Winifred's major conflict consisted of her preoedipal fixation on her mother and the persistence of her infantile desires for love and affection. The birth in close succession of her younger siblings robbed her of an adequate period of time in which she could have remained the youngest child, the adored smallest one of the household. She still sought out and demanded this affection but in the only way available to her, through an identification with the maternal role, in which she treated her younger siblings and cousins with the love and affection she had lacked. She seemed content with this way of life, even more so because her mother appreciated her, referring to her as the one child capable of taking her place at any moment. She lost this possibility of sublimating her infantile desires when she was sent out to work, an indirect way of devaluing her maternal qualities and denying her right to identify with her mother. To this was added the intensification of her homosexual tendencies. In despair, she decided to fall in love as soon as possible in order to be able to marry and leave her ungrateful family. At the last minute she balked, feeling too young, that is to say, tied to her mother. But her conflict persisted. She tried to have children of her own but was prevented by her guilt feeling and resentment toward her own mother. When Winifred states, "I will never let my mother steal my child," it represents in the oedipal domain her refusal to allow her mother—who has already taken away her father—to steal her husband, who is tied to her by the expected child. But more profoundly, Winifred tries to deny her greatest fear; just as she would have liked to have magically taken away her mother's children, her rivals, from her, her mother will do the same to her by stealing her child. When she says, "My mother arranged through prayers [that is, with magic] for me not to have my child," she admits with impotent fury and pain that her mother achieved with her "pregnancy" what she herself could not achieve in her childhood, namely, to magically destroy the fetus. Therefore, it is her mother who made her little daughter disappear. Winifred gives the same explanation for the disappearance of her pregnancy that is found among the Marquesan women when they accuse the *vehini-hai* of the loss of their imaginary children.

In summary, Winifred despairs over feeling expelled from her home; in conflict between an emerging desire to have an adult heterosexual life, including authentic motherhood, and her link with a mother toward whom she feels an infantile fear, she chooses a false pregnancy as a temporary compromise. In this way she satisfies her desires for motherhood without exposing herself to the danger of destructive maternal punishment and she avenges herself on her mother with the illegitimate "pregnancy," which, moreover, permits her ultimately to remain at home at her mother's side. Finally, she punishes herself and expiates her guilt for her destructive wishes toward her pregnant mother by accepting the final dissolution of her phantasy of motherhood with the magical disappearance of her hopes centered in her daughter.

Winifred could not be a mother. Possibly, she protected her physical integrity by resigning herself to play at motherhood. But there exist much more self-destructive compromises of similar psychological conflicts. I refer to the extrauterine pregnancy, which exposes the pregnant woman to mortal danger. Also in these cases there is a conflict between the desire for motherhood and a strict prohibition against it, maintained through guilt feelings and the need for punishment. The desire, as well as the prohibition, find their somatic manifestation. The former leads to impregnation, while the internal prohibition of continuing the sinful pregnancy is manifested through the partial spasm of the tubes. The spermatozoa are allowed to pass but the fertilized egg is not, thus causing it to be sheltered in an inappropriate organ. Each day that the egg grows it brings the pregnant woman closer to danger and exposes her to the alternative of death or renunciation of her child by means of a dangerous operation. I was able to observe in a number of cases that the product of a tubal pregnancy unconsciously represented the child of an incestuous and extraordinarily forbidden relationship, even though in reality it resulted from the woman's sexual relationship with her own husband. Sufficient material is not available to give a detailed and profound analysis of this situation, and I lament the fact that there does not yet exist, as far as I know, psychoanalytic literature on the subject. However, as of the present, even meticulous analyses have failed to yield information regarding the question of why the same conflict leads one woman to infertility, another to a compulsion to become pregnant, another to pseudocyesis, and yet another to extrauterine pregnancy. We know about the conflicts, but we do not yet understand why one woman has recourse to a specific type of somatization while another expresses conflict through mechanisms of hysterical conversion or elaborates her conflictual situation in a merely psychological manner.

It is to the latter situation that I now wish to turn. There are women who when facing the impossibility of realizing their intense desires to be mothers resort to stealing or lying. Helene Deutsch has analyzed the psychological factors that lead some women to steal small children. Some time ago, an event occurred in Buenos Aires that shocked the public, and although I have access only to the information gathered by the media, I would like to offer an analysis of this event, which had to do with the following situation. A wealthy, single, middle-aged landowner denounced his lover for having forced him to recognize his paternity regarding their ostensible son upon discovering that she had simulated the pregnancy. Pastora de Verissimo (as the false mother was called) had bought the child some time before from the owner of a birthing clinic, where she had interned herself in order to create the impression that she had given birth to the baby. The motives of the woman, who had a long history of involvement with corruption and scandal, seemed obvious. Having arrived at 44 years of age, she saw her last opportunity; if she had a child by Mr. X, he would be forced to support her. In addition, following his death, she would become "the mother" of the only heir to a huge fortune. However, close attention to the police story gives the impression that Pastora had different motives.

In fact, some of the reporters must have held this opinion because they sought to avail themselves of the significant details of her life in order to clarify her motives. Pastora had never had a child but had always lived obsessed with the idea of motherhood. She left her home and country at an early age. From abroad she announced to her mother that she had married, and 10 months later she sent her a photograph of her presumed son. Until her mother's death, which occurred some years later, Pastora never returned home but continued each and every year to announce the happy event of the birth of another grandchild. She returned to her country of origin, and there she provoked a scandal, accusing a married man of great prestige of having made her pregnant. She refused the medical examination demanded in order to verify the supposed pregnancy, and nothing more resulted from the situation. There were other similar episodes. She married a physician but was widowed the following year. She wrote a book called *Nobody's Child*, which was very successful. The book is an exultation of free love and illegitimate children belonging only to the mother. Now close to menopause, she had a brief intimate affair with Mr. X. She immediately withdrew from him, but a short time later advised him that she was pregnant. Later, she asked him to come to see her at her friend's obstetrical clinic—the friend who had arranged her purchase of the child—in order to meet his son, who had just been born. Mr. X did not suspect anything at first and acknowledged his paternity. He only began to doubt things when he found written on the back of his son's birth certificate the following note: "My son, the final and only time that I was with your father was the last Saturday of April, and on the following day the pregnancy test was positive." His "son" had been born at the beginning of November. But according to what was written, Pastora had conceived him at the end of April. When Mr. X had first seen his newborn son in the clinic, he had been impressed by his extraordinary health and strength (in reality, the infant was already 1 month old). Only when reading the note did he learn that the child would have to have been born prematurely. He began to doubt, to reconstruct the past, and little by little the fabrication unraveled. The midwife and the nurses confessed. Only Pastora insisted until the end, against all logic, that the infant was her son and that she was the only one with rights to him.

Pastora was infertile, the cause of which is unknown. But her condition must have been very significant in her mind because she spent a lifetime trying to imagine and convince everyone that she had children. She had finally achieved her goal. What, then, led Pastora to write on the back of the birth certificate such a thoughtless inscription, which ultimately caused her to lose what she had finally acquired and, moreover, to suffer legal punishment? I cannot be certain, but we may presume that it might be the same psychological factor that provoked her physical infertility. In her novel *Nobody's Child*, the plot reveals an infantile phantasy already known to us and frequently found among single mothers. They try to have a child without a father in order to live with the child alone, as in their own childhood they would have desired to live with their mother, alone and without the interference of another. If Pastora had not been infertile, she would have been able to realize her ideal. But, she had to be satisfied with only expressing it in the thesis of her book. In my review of psychoanalytic theory, I spoke of another phantastic desire described by Freud. It is the girl's preoedipal wish to either receive a baby from her mother or to give her one. Pastora sent pictures of her supposed children to her mother, who probably responded by congratulating her, offering advice about childrearing, asking for more news of the children, and so on. Those children, then, existed only for her and her mother. No one else knew about them. This would be a way of realizing, although in the domain of illusion and deception, the old phantasy of the child received from the mother or given to her, but which, in either case, belonged only to the two of them.

Pastora came one step closer to the realization of that phantasy when she asked the midwife-owner of the clinic to obtain a baby for her. Thus, she would actually receive her child from another woman. But the two were poor; they needed money. For that reason, they had to look for a wealthy father. I believe that what Pastora essentially expressed when she searched for a rich father for her child was not her greed for money but her resigned recognition that women cannot have a child between them. They are poor because they lack what is necessary to create the child, namely, the penis. So, finally and reluctantly, they had to resort to a man. The message that Pastora wrote on the back of the birth certificate had various meanings. She tried to please her son and herself by reducing to a minimum—one single intercourse—the intervention of the unfortunately necessary penis. Thus, she attempted to assure her "son" that he was her only love and to reduce as much as possible the jealous feelings of hatred toward the sexually united parents that she as a child must have violently felt to fear so intensely their emergence in her son. She must have demanded that her mother renounce men completely because when she confessed her sexual union with a man to her son on the birth certificate, she did it in such as way as to surrender herself to the law, losing her own right to pure motherhood. She expressed this with the words that I earlier referred to as "her resigned recognition," through which she confessed the failure of her infantile phantasy of giving a child to her mother. When she had to admit to her son that he had a father, that he was not her product with another woman, already her beloved phantasy was dashed. It no longer mattered that she denounced herself and—through the message to her son—doomed the entire project to failure.

There is probably one more cause of Pastora's bizarre behavior. The woman led an unfortunate life. She had been infertile, a pathological liar, an adventuress. All this leads one to assume that her childhood had not been a happy one. From her actions it appears that her father had been absent or too weak or rejecting to woo her from her mother. Her very situation of dependency on her mother must have been the result of frustrations, as well as a source of hatred. Probably her guilt feeling because of this hatred did not permit her to realize the fraudulent motherhood and led her, through the clumsy message to her son, to indirectly turn herself in to the law in search of punishment.

Five Psychoanalytic Cases of Infertile Women

In the previous chapter I described how anxiety prevents impregnation and referred to popular beliefs that interpret infertility as a punishment for our sins. Even though this belief now lacks rational validity, it retains authenticity in the infertile woman's unconscious mind. Why is she guilty and what is the nature of her guilt?

In order to reveal a cause of infertility that is rather typical, I will present the beginning phase of the psychoanalysis of a young woman who was infertile. In the first consultation she told her analyst the following:

> When we married, I didn't want to have children. Luckily, my husband agreed. The idea of being pregnant made me extremely anxious. I was very young. We wanted to enjoy life a little before becoming parents. Years later we changed our minds. But although we did everything possible for four years, I didn't get pregnant.

The patient details all of the treatments she and her husband underwent to cure her infertility, all to no avail. Then she says:

> I am the oldest of many siblings. As a child I was obsessed with the fear that Mama would have another child. When I was young, I used to hit her in the abdomen, either in play or due to thoughtlessness. If she didn't react, I was relieved, thinking, "Very well, if she doesn't take care of her stomach, that means that she's not pregnant. I was seven years old when Mama returned from a trip. I hadn't seen her for months. But in the port, in fact, already from the jetty when I recognized her on the ship, I realized that she was expecting

another child. I was right; Mama was in the fourth month of her last pregnancy."

When the patient began her analysis, her period was a month late, and she was in doubt as to whether or not she was pregnant. Her first dream during the treatment was the following: "I am in the bathtub, which is more enclosed with higher walls than normal. I feel very good. The water is pleasant, greenish-blue. My mother takes the plug out of the bathtub. At that moment, a stream of blood appears in the water and I know that my period has come." She awakens, goes to the bathroom, and sees that, in fact, it is true.

We see how the patient spontaneously relates her infertility to her infantile fear that her mother would have more children. She is completely conscious of this relationship. However, she told me, as if they were amusing anecdotes, about her attempts as a child to find out if her mother was pregnant or not by hitting her in the stomach. She did not consciously perceive this activity as an indication that she had hated her pregnant mother and had wished to destroy the siblings she carried inside her. In this hatred and her subsequent fear of punishment appears a basic factor in her infertility. I mentioned earlier the utilization of the term *guilt* in relation to the problem of infertility. Hatred is the earliest guilt of the infertile individual. So in the first dream related by the patient, her mother's act, which represents a just punishment for her guilt, magically makes her menstruation appear. That is to say, the mother, like the *vehini-hai* of the Marquesans, undoes her pregnancy.[1]

Another dream the patient had some months into the treatment reveals to us additional causes of her infertility, for which she unconsciously feels guilty. In the dream she tries to dilute some very compact dough with milk in order to make pancakes with a special filling. Each time she adds milk, the dough appears to be diluting. But afterward it absorbs the liquid and remains the same. In another part of the dream she sees a woman having a difficult delivery, and a midwife is kneading a mass on the lower abdomen of the woman in labor. This procedure appears very dangerous to her.

In the first part of the dream the dough represents the patient herself, to which she fruitlessly adds milk. The "milk" signifies "semen" in common [Spanish] language and represents her husband's sperm. He would have to function well in order to make her pregnant, in order for the dough to be changed into the pancakes with their special filling. But she does not become soft. She absorbs all the milk and remains the same; that is, she is insatiable. She wants to enjoy sex without the consequences; she wants all her husband's love for herself, just as when she was a little girl she had wished to be an only child and take all of her mother's milk for herself. She wants to continue being a loved and attractive little girl instead of becoming a mother and being deformed. The second guilt of which the infertile woman unconsciously accuses herself is, then, her insatiability and her infantile selfishness, both of which are feelings that stem from early frustrations.

In the second part of the dream a woman appears who is involved in a dangerous childbirth and another, the midwife, who kneads her. As has been seen with reference to previous dreams, in the unconscious, the midwife represents simultaneously the patient's analyst and her mother. The midwife kneads in order to make tortillas. In the popular dialect of Buenos Aires, homosexual women are called "tortilleras." The patient's third "guilt" motivating her to avoid childbirth, by transforming it into something too dangerous for her, is her unconscious homosexual and infantile fixation on her mother. The three causes cited—hatred for the pregnant mother, the desire to continue to remain a loved little girl, and the unconscious erotic fixation on the mother—make her feel guilty and prevent her from maturing and becoming a woman in her own right.

Different authors, such as Lewis Robbins in "Suggestions for the Psychological Study of Sterility in Women," now stress the need to investigate the psychological causes of infertility in order to distinguish two types of infertile women in the psychological and psychosomatic domains: the infantile woman and the masculine woman with a dominating character. Both types of women suffer from ovarian insufficiency; the first has a primary hypoplasia of the pituitary gland and the second a hyperfunction of the endocrine glands, which leads to a process of luteinization of the ovary. My patient suffered from a slight ovarian insufficiency, manifested in her physical appearance and in frequent menstrual delays. I believe, however, that these factors were the consequence of her psychological problems. In any case, she belonged to the infantile type of infertile woman. But among women who appear masculinized as well, we observe that this masculinization is but a defense against the basic situation of the infertile woman, her infantile fixation on a frustrating and, therefore, hated mother. This fixation obliges her to retain her mother at her side, and she seeks the best method of doing so. If her mother loves her and still treats her as a defenseless little girl, she will remain infantile. If she hopes to be able to get more from her mother by pretending to be a man and dominating her, she will become masculinized and have phantasies of having a penis. As we have already seen, masculinization also permits the woman to elude all the presumed dangers concomitant with her femininity.

In order for the girl to maintain an intense fixation on her mother, another important factor generally intervenes, one that existed in my patient's childhood. It is the lack of a father capable of conquering his daughter's love and strong enough to defend her against her unconscious fears of her mother. My patient's father was a cold man, totally absorbed in his profession. If he had instead permitted his little daughter to be amorously drawn to him, she would have broken the frustrating and infantile link that tied her to her mother and would have later been able to become a normal woman.

We will now see if we encounter the same determinants in some clinical cases of infertile women. First I summarize a case of Edith Jacobson's, a patient who suffered from serious hormonal disorders, which were evident in her physical appearance. Silvia, 35 years old and married, looked much younger in appearance and was extremely thin and undeveloped. She sought psychoanalytic treatment for an acute depression, which she identified with her infertility, the cause of which seemed obvious. Since 16 years of age, Silvia had not menstruated, except during some months when she was undergoing intense hormonal treatment. By the time she began analysis, she had long since terminated these treatments and therefore suffered from complete amenorrhea. Her depression was unleashed by an event closely related to her infertility. Some months prior, in agreement with her husband, Silvia had adopted a baby. But when the baby arrived it was clear that just as Silvia was not able to become pregnant, she was also too immature to be a mother. She began to be anxious with the child, to doubt if she could care for him adequately, and to fear for his health. Finally, she became ill and had to return the baby to the adoption agency. As a consequence of this failure, she fell into an acute depression.

Silvia had been on hormonal treatment for years. Because of her obvious glandular disorder, her chronic lack of appetite, and her physical weakness, her condition had been diagnosed—fortunately incorrectly—as emaciation. When she began psychoanalytic treatment, her analyst requested that she be reexamined. The examination results are as follows: blood pressure, 90/70; pulse, 64; a small and atrophied uterus. The biopsy of the endometrium revealed small and atrophied cells. The gynecologist advised against any future treatment of her infertility as he saw no possibility of success. However, Silvia began to physically change from the beginning of her analysis. She gained weight and her breasts developed. She became pregnant in the 8th month of her psychoanalytic treatment, without ever having menstruated.

Edith Jacobson presents her patient's history in order to clarify the determinants of her infertility and her glandular disorder. Silvia was the fourth daughter of eight children. She came from a very poor family of Jewish immigrants. Her mother had a demanding and rigid character, and her father, though more understanding, was a man quite over-whelmed by life's difficulties. Moreover, his work took him away from the family. Silvia was insufficiently nursed by her mother, who, besides not having enough milk, was forced to wean her early because of becoming pregnant again. Silvia was 15 months old when her fourth sister, Mary, was born. It seems that she reacted to her sister's arrival with intense jealousy and oral envy. Later, her mother would relate the following story as an ostensibly entertaining anecdote: At night she would always leave a full bottle of milk for Mary beside her bed. Each night, Silvia would crawl to the bed and take the bottle, completely unaware that her mother would later refill it for her little sister. Silvia refused to give up her own bottle until she was 5 years old. The family's impoverished conditions caused each sibling to fight continually with the others in order to get enough food. Such conditions were obviously not propitious for Silvia to be able to overcome the oral frustrations of her infancy. She suffered from enuresis until she was 5 and from night terrors, during which she dirtied the furniture with excrement. In fact, until the very day of her wedding, Silvia needed to suck her thumb like a baby in order to fall asleep. Evidently, her rivalry with Mary led her to enact the wish to prolong being a baby.

Mary was the ugliest and weakest of the five sisters. She suffered from strabismus [involuntary squinting], for which Silvia felt guilty because she unconsciously feared having caused her sister's condition by stealing her food (the bottle). When Silvia was 5 1/2 years old, a brother—the family's first male child—was born. This event coincided with Silvia's entrance into preschool, where she was introduced to an environment full of clean, well-dressed, and well-fed children. In her house she saw her mother feeding her little brother. She imagined that if a mother feeds her baby well, a penis grows and it becomes a boy. Her envy of the breast and the bottle became penis envy. But she did not permit herself these bad thoughts. In order to deny them, she took very good care of her little brother. She experienced his circumcision with guilt feelings, as if a little piece of his penis had been cut off in order to satisfy her hostility and envy. Later, she expressed her penis envy through phantasies focusing on ambition. She imagined achieving great successes that would attract the profound admiration of a good and noble woman who would adopt her. That is to say, Silvia believed that her mother could love her if only she were a boy. But for that to happen, she needed a penis and successes, which, according to her, were only accessible to men. Embittered by her mother's love for her first son, Silvia phantasized about male deeds and an ideal mother who belonged only to her. She also expressed her penis envy in a direct way: In her analysis she remembered with guilt having treated her brother roughly when she had to change his diapers or touch his penis.

When she was 10 years old, Sylvia overheard her mother tell a neighbor, "I don't know why they say that children are gifts from heaven. For me they are a curse." During that same period Silvia began to consciously worry about sex. Since she shared the bedroom with her parents, she frequently had the opportunity to observe their sexual relations. She developed a cruel and anxiety-provoking impression of intercourse, pregnancy, and childbirth. Her oral fixation led her to imagine that the woman becomes pregnant by eating some of the man's penis. When her mother became pregnant, Silvia oscillated between two opposing positions. Sometimes she wanted to be a boy; her envy of the penis—the organ that, according to her infantile theories, was an indication of having been fed by the mother and a guarantee of continuing to be fed in the future—fomented this desire. At other times she envied her mother the pregnancy, a consequence, she believed, of her father having fed her mother something. In other words, her envy of both the penis and the pregnancy was essentially the consequence of her oral frustrations. Silvia had hostile phantasies against her pregnant mother. She hoped that her swollen abdomen would explode, that her mother would die, and that she herself would wind up with the baby.

Another boy was born. Because of her guilt feelings and her rivalry with her mother, Silvia took care of him very well. Unfortunately, the child died in an accident at the age of 1 1/2. The mother reacted with an acute depression, which she only overcame with another pregnancy. Once again, Silvia felt guilty. In her analysis she remembered with anguish having felt relieved as well as saddened by her brother's death, which meant that now there was one less mouth at home to feed. She repressed those sinful thoughts and became a good little girl, compliantly sad.

During puberty her menstruation was normal. But her recently awakened instincts struggled with her submission to the moral rigidity and sadness of her family environment. She fell in love with a Christian boy and argued with her family that she be allowed to pursue her university studies in an attempt to escape from her poor and depressed home life. Moreover, she wished to realize her phantasies of masculine success through her studies so as to win the love of an ideal mother. Her family was opposed. Her sisters, who had had to go to work immediately after finishing high school, reproached her for her selfishness. But Silvia continued to struggle, finally overcoming her family's resistance. However, she punished herself, internally submitting to her family's judgment, and reduced her eating to a minimum. Her thinness and lack of appetite date from that period. In addition, she tried to repress her prohibited passion for her Christian boyfriend. She began to menstruate irregularly until, just 2 years following menarche, she suffered a complete amenorrhea. But she could not completely conquer her instincts. Only when she gave herself to her boyfriend was her remorse so great that she could renounce her desires. She broke off the relationship and during the following years dedicated herself exclusively to schoolwork, refusing completely to relate to men.

Later Silvia married a man whom her parents accepted. At first, she continued with her professional work. But little by little she became weaker and more sickly, unconsciously converting her husband into a loving mother who took care of her and fed her as if she were a little girl. In this way she achieved what she had not had in her childhood. But her old desires of having a penis or a profession—in order to win her mother's love—or of being a mother—in order to conquer her mother through an identification with her—remained alive within her. She managed to convince her husband to adopt a baby. He agreed, but unfortunately Silvia failed in her attempt at motherhood. It was this failure that finally led her to analysis.

Before attempting to understand Silvia's infertility, we should analyze the two symptoms that provoked it organically: the chronic loss of appetite and the glandular disorder. In her patient's loss of appetite, Jacobson saw a self-punishment for her oral envy. This syndrome of not eating emerged for the first time when Silvia wanted to study and, in so doing, imagined herself to be stealing the food from her family by not contributing to their maintenance with a paying job. The practice of not eating served, moreover, to repress her sexual desires, which unconsciously signified the desire to eat something forbidden. On the other hand, Silvia's lack of appetite also satisfied her: She did not dare accuse her mother of having fed her badly, but her lamentable physical appearance was a visible accusation for everyone to see. Finally, her adolescent-like, shapeless, and painfully thin body corresponded to a partial realization of her desire to be a boy. This same desire was expressed through her other symptom, amenorrhea, the psychological causes of which were multiple. Silvia had envied and hated her pregnant mother and had wished her dead. She grew up and became a woman. When she herself was in love and anxious to have a child, she feared being punished for those death wishes. The ingenious solution that she found to this anguishing conflict was her amenorrhea, which signified both an escape from her femininity and the realization in phantasy of her wish to be pregnant. Moreover, not to menstruate was to be like a man. Later, during her marriage, more regressive desires emerged and Silvia renounced her pseudo-virility. She then utilized amenorrhea, lack of appetite, and her entire precarious physical state in order to be able to be a little girl, loved by her husband-mother.

Silvia became pregnant 8 months into her analysis, which she continued until shortly before her baby was born. According to Jacobson, she had changed enough to be able to become pregnant and, in general, to attain improvement in her psychological and physical condition. But she was far from achieving a complete cure of her neurosis. However, she was so happy with her daughter that she did not wish to resume treatment.

The persistence of her basic conflicts soon became manifest again through organic symptoms. The birth experience was easy, but nursing had to be interrupted early on because of a mastitis. Her menstruation—the first in many years—appeared at the normal date following the birth of her child. In spite of the fact that now both Silvia and her husband used contraceptives, she quickly became pregnant again. She submitted to a curettage and became even more vigilant with respect to the use of contraceptives afterward, but she once again became pregnant. After another curettage, she wanted to have a surgical sterilization performed in order to definitively avoid future pregnancies, but she gave up the idea after discussing it with her analyst.

Jacobson calls attention to this surprising development in her patient's endocrinological picture, which is a clear demonstration of the great influence of psychogenic factors on hormonal processes. The patient's analysis had transformed her infertility into hyperfertility owing to the fact that her basic conflicts had not been resolved. Her envy of her mother, who had many children, and her tendency to punish herself for this envy, led her to what Helene Deutsch calls "compulsive conception," which in this case manifested itself in the tendency to become pregnant and to punish herself each time with a curettage, torturing herself until she decided to definitively renounce her femininity by means of an artificial sterilization. Apparently, the conversation with her analyst, who advised her against this extreme measure, was unconsciously experienced as her mother's forgiveness. Silvia then found a less painful means of avoiding future conflicts and anguish: Her amenorrhea returned, and in this way she achieved infertility without a drastic intervention. At the same time, she began to work again, no longer, however, in her previous profession, which for her signified masculinity. She chose something that satisfied her very much, achieving success as an author of articles on child psychology published in mass circulation magazines. So, from an abandoned child with many siblings who were preferred by the mother,

Silvia eventually became an ideal and understanding mother, whom she herself had desired her entire life and had to some extent found in her analyst. Moreover, she had only one child, to whom she gave everything that she herself had fervently desired. This double identification with a good mother and a happy child—her own daughter—permitted her to abandon her rivalry with the frustrating mother who had many children and to also give up her masculine desires, whose aim had been to change this frustrating mother into the good and understanding mother she had been with her male child.

We turn now to the clinical history of a patient treated by Dr. Celes Carcamo, a more detailed version of which appears along with two other case histories in an article coauthored by Dr. Carcamo and myself (Langer & Carcamo, 1948).

The patient, 34-year-old Mrs. Z, suffered from insecurity, depressive states, sadness, and suicidal impulses. In the somatic domain, she presented an irregular and painful constipation, which increased during her menstrual periods. Various clinical examinations confirmed the diagnosis of ovarian dysfunction and progesterone deficiency.

Mrs. Z had an unhappy childhood with a very neurotic mother. Her childhood home was a theatre of frequent conjugal quarrels. The father, virile, affectionate, and tolerant, more out of indifference than kindness, was a somewhat shadowy figure in the family, exercising roles of secondary importance. Family life was ruled by the mother, a capricious, extravagant, and tyrannical woman who was the personification of masculine protest and ambivalence. She admired and hated men, who, according to her, did terrible things to women to cause them heartache, among the most intolerable of which was making them pregnant. She attempted to inculcate these sentiments in her daughters, presenting love exclusively as a game of deception and revenge. The mother was disappointed at the birth of this daughter, our Mrs. Z, because she wanted a son. She never forgave her for being a female, nor for the discomfort of the pregnancy or the abnormally long and painful labor. To make matters worse, Mrs. Z grew up a bit ungainly and less beautiful than the other daughters, which only increased the maternal resentment of any blunder resulting from her childish behavior. The little girl intuited the means of ingratiating herself with her mother, who she was convinced hated her because she did not have a penis. She then repressed her femininity and exaggerated her masculine characteristics, expressed in her independent demeanor and masculine tastes. She became audacious in her actions and stoic in her suffering. She unconsciously phantasized about returning to the maternal womb. The content of these phantasies aimed at the recovery of her mother or her violent and sadistic possession of her. But turning the aggression against herself, she suffered masochistically, attaining in one and the same act satisfaction and the cancellation of the destructive impulse, that is, the destruction and the salvation of the maternal object. This mechanism remained as the subsequent model of her masochistic character. Each attempt toward genital achievement and distance from her mother was followed by a series of failures and punitive conflicts. She felt quite happy far away from her mother but simultaneously missed her. Her failures and moral tortures represented the complex road back to mother.

To her mother's lack of understanding and rejection— equivalent to weaning—were added in childhood the trauma of the lack of a penis (castration) and her attempts to recover it. This was expressed in screen memories, one of which is the following: Sucking through a straw, she makes soap bubbles, which, when breaking, land on her face as voluptuous drops, making her eyes close. The memory is an allusion to Mrs. Z's castration phantasies and masturbatory activities. The soap bubbles are a symbol of the lost penis and of the masculine ideas that had to be renounced. The patient hoped to compensate for what had been by a heterosexual relationship, represented by the rain of revitalizing drops. But the soap bubbles also represent the maternal breast or womb, which she destroys and desires to recover by returning to the mother. The patient associated the refreshed sensation produced by the drops on her face with the memory of fountains and lakes, that is, with maternal symbols. She expressed, then, through her phantasy, the belief of having lost her mother because of her lack of a penis and the hope of being able, in her genital heterosexual life, to recover the desired gratifications. However, in her sexual partner she essentially searched for her mother. This is confirmed by the content of her unconscious phantasies during intercourse, which were of oral aggression and stealing the paternal penis. In fact, her sexuality was entirely dominated by intense destructive pulsatings. But through her analysis she discovered that hidden behind her external masculine and dominating demeanor was a delicate and tender affect.

Mrs. Z came to marriage sexually immature. Her masculine protest and unconscious fixation on her mother prevented her passive-feminine surrender to her husband. The maternal image continued to frustrate and forbid all personal legitimate desires. The patient's analysis confirmed that her depression was the result of internal conflicts, experienced earlier with the mother and then linked to the husband and the external world. These conflicts were manifested each time her instinctive longings committed her to a gesture of independence, thus exposing her to the threat of punishment and abandonment by the internal image of a frustrating mother. The submission to her mother was achieved at the cost of renouncing her instincts through the infantile mechanism of stifling rebellion and obliging her liberating aggression to turn against herself. So, for example, she had depressive crises and suicidal ideation when her marriage date was proposed, symptoms which were repeated in response to many different conflicts. The analysis was able to help the patient discover this pattern, and as she abandoned her reactive masculinity, she began to develop her femininity and to modify her character. As her femininity awakened, she also discovered her maternal desires, which at first were expressed anxiously and timidly through a fear of becoming pregnant and obsessive vigilance of her menstruation and later through nightmares in which she saw herself as an idiot, terrorized by the threats of her analyst, who symbolized her mother (her mother used to denounce as idiots women who became pregnant). Her frigidity disappeared, as did the constipation and the pain and irregularity of her period. Then there were unexpected menstrual delays, from which we can deduce the repercussion on menstrual function of her desires to be a mother. When her period was 2 months late, a pregnancy was confirmed and continued without complications. Meanwhile, the analysis moved ahead, slowly resolving her maternal fixation and guilt feelings.

We will now examine another case. Mrs. L, a 32-year-old woman, came to analysis exclusively to cure her infertility. Married 2 years previously, she had resorted to all the latest gynecological and hormonal treatments in order to become pregnant, each of which had failed. Her husband was perfectly healthy.

Mrs. L was a sensible, agreeable, and intelligent woman, well adjusted and without sexual disorders. Her childhood had been difficult. When she was very young, she became ill with an acute case of polyarthritis, which caused a cardiac lesion. Although as a child she suffered from restrictions imposed by her delicate health, by the time she entered analysis, her heart problem had been under control for some time. She had an older sister and two younger brothers. At a very young age she fell in love with an adolescent boy, whom she later married. She was happily married, her only anguish being her infertility, which made her feel inferior to other women and overwhelmed with guilt feelings toward her husband, who wanted to have a child.

Mrs. L became pregnant after 9 months of an analytic treatment that focused exclusively on her relationship with her mother. It seems reasonable, therefore, to look for the principal cause of her infertility in her preoedipal relationship. In the initial months of the analysis, the patient began to understand the intensity of her fixation on her mother, her penis envy, and her rivalry and jealousy toward her younger siblings. In fact, these three themes were intimately related. Then the analysis proceeded with a kind of monotony almost until conception. After each menstruation the same complaint emerged, to the effect that her mother did not want her to have children and that therefore she was not to blame for her infertility. In part this was true because, in fact, her family had taken her heart condition as a reason to advise her against getting pregnant. Sometimes Mrs. L also blamed her father or her husband. However, her dreams demonstrated an intense guilt feeling and wish to punish herself in relation to her pregnant mother. She fell into a grievous state when she came to understand that her reproaches of her mother were basically reproaches against herself. The mother who had forbidden her to become pregnant was she herself, who as a child had tried to magically prevent her mother from becoming pregnant again, feeling that she had achieved her goal when her mother suffered miscarriages. Mrs. L felt guilty because of her fear of abandoning her protective masculinity and the gratification of her resentments against her mother. Before consciously realizing she was pregnant, her dreams revealed that she had something valuable she wished to guard and hide from her analyst. Her fear of exposing her pregnancy was a fear of the retaliation of her mother, upon whom she projected the aggression she had felt toward her during her pregnancies.

To sum up, the patient could not become pregnant because of an intense oral fixation on her mother, probably a consequence of weaning and her mother's sudden withdrawal of affection each time she was pregnant and a baby was born. This fixation was never completely overcome. The birth of the second brother reawakened the same trauma. Moreover, her mother often became pregnant, only to seek abortions. The little girl must have felt an intense hatred toward her in these circumstances. This hatred prevented her from identifying with her pregnant mother and from thus achieving motherhood herself as an adult. In addition, she wished, through her infertility, to magically prevent her parents' sexual relationship, which was repeatedly confirmed by her mother's pregnancies. She satisfied this phantasy, identifying with an asexual mother who cannot have children. In order to liberate herself from her guilt feelings, she was denying and projecting her rejection of the pregnant woman: It is not she who wants to forbid her mother the pregnancy but her mother, and later her analyst, who does not permit her to have a child. The father hardly appeared in her infantile conflicts, as he played no important role in the family. Her mother was forced to do everything: take care of the children, the house, and the business. Thus, little time was available for the children, who grew up in an affectively deprived environment. The father gave little and even robbed the children of maternal affection by sleeping with their mother and making her pregnant. Because of this, the patient was deeply rivalrous with her father. Both with him as well as with her brothers, she experienced penis envy, which was often symbolized in her dreams as oral envy. This envy also prevented her from becoming pregnant. She could not have a child without renouncing definitively the hope of one day having a penis and of conquering her mother.

From the moment she was pregnant, Mrs. L's psychological condition changed. At first, she experienced the pregnancy with guilt feelings toward her father, as if she had stolen his penis (a phantasy in which she equated the penis with the fetus and then accused herself of thus having deprived her mother of sex with the father). She tried this time, then, to satisfy her infantile desires, now with her pregnancy rather than with her infertility. Later on, she relived in her analysis the pain it caused her to leave her mother. In spite of her heart condition, she did well during the pregnancy and gave birth without complications and in a good psychological state. Afterward she interrupted her analysis, to which she returned when she suffered a serious setback in her cardiac condition upon weaning her infant. I will describe this situation and its causes later.

I now present the case of Mrs. B, a healthy 35-year-old woman with a very masculine appearance who has been married for 12 years. She came to psychoanalytic treatment because she suffered from a serious depression with anxiety states, suicidal ideation, and obsessive impulses. She had experienced a strong compulsion to murder her entire family, especially two nieces who lived with her. She had never been pregnant, in spite of having been treated several times some years before beginning her analytic treatment with me.

The patient was the 7th of 11 siblings. In the analysis she revealed that she had twice suffered a series of almost identical traumas. In early childhood, when she was 6 years old, her mother, whom she adored, died in childbirth. Abandoned by her mother, she—her father's favorite child—gave all of her love to him, only to feel betrayed when he remarried a year later. Because of having lost her father, she tried to identify with him. Moreover, she displaced a significant part of her affection onto her brother, Juan. Later, the same traumatic situation of her childhood was repeated. Juan married a short time before she did. Once again it was not she who had children but her sister-in-law Alicia, who had two children and a number of miscarriages. Alicia died under terrible circumstances related to an abortion. Mrs. B then decided to take charge of her brother and two nieces, whose upbringing she took on with great dedication and sacrifice. When she later found out that her brother had a lover, she tried to shun her as she had her stepmother years earlier. Moreover, Mrs. B was the man of the house in that she managed everything and dominated her husband and brother. Some years later, when Maria, her younger brother's wife, became pregnant, Mrs. B suffered a brief amenorrhea. Shortly afterward her melancholia began, reaching its most intense point when Maria had her baby.

In the first phase of the analysis, the patient's most evident feeling was hatred, conscious hatred toward Alicia, her dead sister-in-law, and hatred just barely repressed toward her mother. She transferred this hatred onto me. Moreover, in her nieces, whom she had adopted, as well as my own children, she continued to hate her younger siblings. She had phantasies of killing her nieces or me or stealing my children and torturing them. Simultaneously, she could not forgive herself for this hatred. So she tormented herself with melancholic self-reproaches and suicidal thoughts, the latter representing aggressive desires directed against the introjected mother. As a child she had been very attached to her mother. However, when her mother died in childbirth, the little girl showed no emotional reaction. During the first phase of her analysis, she reproached herself for this apparent indifference, which was the result of a melancholic conflict of ambivalence.

Later in the analysis, Mrs. B consciously admired her mother's kindness, her ability to enjoy the father, her modesty and capacity for suffering and sacrifice. Unconsciously, she rejected all these qualities as indications of feminine weakness. She would have preferred to have been a man. As a child she suffered an inguinal hernia that bothered her when she played games and participated in sports. However, she decided not to separate from her hernia, which she described in the following words: "I was ashamed to undress in front of other women because I felt different from them. I had a bulge near my genitals." The bulge unconsciously represented a hidden penis, which perhaps some day would be able to come out, changing her into a man. Only when she was engaged, shortly before marrying, did she renounce the hernia and decide in favor of an operation.

Mrs. B had always had a masculine demeanor. Very active, capable, and energetic, she was the "man" of the house. In her sexual life she was frigid, her pleasure increasing when she adopted the masculine position. However, during her depression, it seems that she abandoned her masculine role. She could not understand how she could have been so independent before. Consciously, she was anxious to become pregnant. She often spoke of undergoing another gynecological treatment, insisting that a child of her own would be her salvation. But she always associated childbirth with death. During a significant slip she confused the Nativity with Good Friday, maintaining that Jesus died on the 24th of December and associated the death of the child to the possible death of the mother. She often asked me with great insistence if psychoanalytic treatment might cure her infertility. She feared that I, representative of her maternal superego, would demand that she become pregnant. But while she spoke of the future and of her possible pregnancy, her depression continually increased, together with her aggressive ideas and suicidal thoughts. One day she phantasized: "I am going to get pregnant with the help of this treatment, but in spite of that I am going to commit suicide." When I understood that to be pregnant represented to her to introject her mother and to die—killing her mother again—I explained that there was no need whatsoever for her to have a child, that she could cure herself quite well regardless and be a useful and productive person. The patient became visibly calmed. I interpreted, in addition, her guilt feelings for her mother's death, her aggression toward her, and her unconscious fear of dying in childbirth.

From that moment Mrs. B's analysis entered a new phase. The melancholia disappeared completely from one day to the next. In the analysis the patient now began to work through her fixation on her brother Juan. Devalued by her father who had remarried, she had displaced onto her brother her infantile heterosexual feelings, continuing her positive oedipal complex with him. Her guilt feelings, originating in this fixation, were not the direct cause of her depression but one of the reasons for her infertility. Sometimes she would say in the analysis, "If Juan left home, then I could have children." This idea also appeared in her dreams, as well as in her great disillusionment with Juan, who had become involved in another relationship following his wife's death. The patient repeated the experience of disillusionment suffered as a child when her father married for the second time. And she repeated as well her rejection of femininity. In her adolescence Juan had appeared to her to be more virile than her husband. Now she saw that he was not a true man either, that she was much more active and did better in life than he. She remembered having once read in a newspaper that a woman had changed her sex through an operation. She observed that in her family the daughters resembled the father more than the sons did and that they also were more worthy. During her depression she would identify sometimes with a relative who, in a psychotic break, went outside undressed, exhibiting her menstruation-stained underpants; following this display, the relative killed herself. The patient once again demonstrated through these associations the intimate nature for her of the relationship between femininity, insanity, and death. Moreover, she had always experienced her menstruation in a traumatic way, the flow being abundant and painful.

There now emerged other dreams and memories related to menstruation and, in part, directly to Juan. As mentioned earlier, Juan's wife had died following an abortion. For that reason, Mrs. B feared that Juan, if he played an active role in their relationship, would make her, like her sister-in-law, menstruate, abort, and die. Her fixation on Juan thus represented two dangers: one of surrendering herself to him and the other of provoking her mother's wrath for wishing to steal Juan—who represents the father— from her. The first conflict was temporarily resolved by adopting an active posture toward Juan. She protected and dominated him, and in her dreams she castrated him. The other problem caused a tenacious resistance in her analysis. In the transference she lived out her desire to steal her father or his penis from her mother by seeming to wish to steal something from me. Or she defended herself by inverting the situation and suspecting that I wished to deprive her of something valuable. She wanted to interrupt the analysis because it seemed very expensive. She associated money with feces and her brother's penis. She dreamed that she communicated to me that she had obtained a good job. Afterward, she quit, and only when she was already far from my house did she realize that she had taken my oldest child with her. She returned, met me in the vestibule of an old house, and gave my child back to me.

The interpretation of the dream is as follows: I, in the vestibule, represent her mother; the child, my oldest son, represents Juan as well as another of her mother's children, or her father's penis, which is larger than her husband's. She wishes to leave her analysis, afraid that I will discover her wish to steal from me and fearful of the conse-quences. She would like to have a good job in order to be powerful (have money) and to have a more masculine activity, just as in her childhood she wished to usurp her father's place with her mother. In order to be able to realize this, she robs from her mother or me the penis of Juan, her father, or my child. She is compelled toward this masculine attitude because she is not a woman like her mother or me, that is to say, she does not have children. Then she tries to steal them; this solution fails because upon stealing them she destroys her mother and herself (she attributes her illness to her having taken in her deceased sister-in-law's daughters). No other solution remains but to renounce her femininity completely, returning what she has stolen and trying to adopt a masculine attitude.

When Mrs. B understood that I did not demand that she separate from Juan, her attitude toward me changed. I now appeared to her to be good but very weak and submissive, like her mother. Slowly, she entered into a slightly manic phase: She felt very good and full of activity, but she was very aggressive. For example, she created conflict with the neighbors of the apartment above because they watered the flowers on their balcony without being concerned about whether or not they got the sidewalk wet. The interpretation of her symptomatic protest is that she did not want them to get her wet because she did not want to be treated like a woman. She wished to dominate the family and to occupy the place that her father once had. However, unconsciously she doubted her capacity, and as we saw in the interpretation of a biographical dream, she understood that she had become sick because she had wished to play the roles consecutively of her mother, her father, and her brother's two women, while now she preferred to occupy the sister-in-law's place, which was a little like being the dictator of the family.

Besides being enmeshed in all of the family's affairs and generating a kind of hypomanic activity, she had yet another symptom: a great deal of aggression toward the two nieces who lived with her. Upon adopting a masculine attitude, Mrs. B's homosexuality was reinforced. Now she did not insist so much that Juan continue to live with them; she instead wished to be with her two nieces. Simultaneously, in order to defend herself against the reemergence of her homosexuality, she was very aggressive with the girls, who unconsciously represented her mother and sister-in-law. In a dream she saw the older of the girls sleeping in a provocative manner on her mother's bed. She associated that the girl now seems like her dead sister-in-law. Then she had phantasies of having seen me sleeping in the same provocative position as her niece in the dream. During the same period, aggressive ideas against pregnant women began to emerge. She thought she remembered my grotesque appearance while I was pregnant, in spite of not having ever actually seen me in that state. It seemed to her that her nieces were too romantic in spite of the good upbringing she had given them, that children have to suffer for their parents' sins, and that the girls would turn out bad. Relying on material from her actions and dreams, I interpreted that she had been very jealous of her pregnant sister-in-law and that in order to avenge herself for the latter's infidelity, she had adopted the nieces in order to pervert them. The patient slowly assimilated this interpretation, and when she had accepted it, changed her attitude toward the girls. Now she was no longer aggressive and treated them cordially. She once again adopted a more passive attitude. She felt very well and wanted to leave the analysis, believing herself to be cured.

Mrs. B had her period on the 1st of June. The following day she learned that her father had become very ill with a prostatic hypertrophy. She had not been in her father's home for 12 years because her father had opposed her marriage. Now she reconciled with him and her stepmother. For her, the prostatic tumor was equivalent to her father's castration. She behaved very well with her parents and also permitted herself for the first time to be affectionate with her nieces. One of them commented, "Auntie has changed, I don't know what's going on with her, but she is like silk." At the very time that her father became ill, she learned that her sister-in-law Maria was pregnant again. She was not very concerned when she did not get her period at the end of June because her illness began with an amenorrhea when this same sister-in-law became pregnant for the first time. However, slowly she began to think about being pregnant, but rejected the possibility. Self-reproaches and a certain ambivalence reappeared in her dreams, but the patient, anxious to leave analysis, resisted any deep interpretation.

Some days following my suggestion that she have a pregnancy test, she reported the following dream: She is hurriedly descending a tall stairway and sees some women doing gymnastics in the patio; she furtively passes behind the gym instructor. To rapidly descend the stairs was interpreted as the patient's rapid termination of her analysis. The building made her think of motherhood. The exercising women are women in childbirth, and the gym professor is the analyst. Thus, Mrs. B wished to enter motherhood without being seen by me. She finally decided to have a pregnancy test, and in her last session she told me that the result was positive. She departed with a friendly good-bye. Fifteen days later she suffered a miscarriage. Once recovered, she came to see me, and we conversed face-to-face (she did not lie on the couch). She confessed to a realization that she had unconsciously provoked the miscarriage. Serene, she said that she hoped to become pregnant again soon, admitting that she did not want to have a child that would have been for her "a triumph of the analysis."

At this point I do not wish to go more deeply, but a study of her later dreams indicated that her pregnancy, conceived during the analysis, which was paid for by her deceased mother's sister, signified for her a child stolen from her mother. Moreover, because of her ambivalence, she did not want to give me the satisfaction of "a triumph of the analysis." During the following months we had conversations from time to time, talking about the cause of her miscarriage. One year after leaving the analysis and, as she herself observed, precisely on the day of my birthday, she once again became pregnant. This pregnancy, like another one 4 years later, she carried to full term without complications.

To briefly summarize this patient's case: In childhood, she is orally fixated on her mother and hates her for her infidelity, confirmed by the birth of a number of children. When her mother dies, she is afraid she is responsible for the tragedy, for having magically killed her mother with the force of her hatred. Since that time, motherhood and death are unconsciously linked. However, she needs love and develops a feminine attitude toward her father. He rejects her when he remarries. She feels scorned and identifies with him, adopting in this way a masculine attitude. With this defense she manages to save herself from the dangerous identification with her mother, protecting herself from her punishment—internal destruction and death—and overcomes the disillusionment suffered because of her father. But her position is not yet definitive. She maintains an attitude of feminine affection toward her favorite brother. Later, through her pregnancies and her sister-in-law's death due to an abortion, she repeats her infantile experiences in an exaggerated manner. She has the courage to realize her sinful phantasies by bringing her brother and his daughters into her home, which has the unconscious meaning of committing a new crime: Besides once again having killed her mother—in the person of her sister-in-law—she has stolen her husband—the brother—and her children. At the price of another woman's death, she has been able to have children without running the risk of death represented by childbirth. After so much guilt, the only protection against punishment would be infertility. In the face of the threatening loss of Maria, her pregnant sister-in-law, who is another maternal representative and thus loved ambivalently, the patient introjects her, falling ill with melancholia.

I now briefly relate one more case, for which I am indebted to Dr. Simón Wencelblat. N, a 23-year-old woman married for 3 years, came to analysis because of infertility. Although previously treated gynecologically with no success, the patient was able to become pregnant during her psychoanalysis, which permitted her to understand the causes of her infertility. She was the second of five siblings. Her weaning had been sudden and early owing to her mother's subsequent pregnancy. When she was 3 years old, another sibling was born. N began her period when she was 10 1/2 years old. A short time later, her mother became pregnant again and after an attempted abortion had to be interned in serious condition in a sanatorium. She recovered and, in fear, abandoned her attempts to abort. The pregnancy ended in a difficult labor, which required a cesarean section. N was alone with her mother when the labor pains began. At her mother's request, she got her a bedpan and was shocked to see that it rapidly filled with her mother's blood. After her mother gave birth, N fell ill with peritonitis, which required surgical intervention.

In her analysis, N remembered how she had envied her father his place at her mother's side in the marriage bed. Her father occupied a secondary role in the life of the family, and she did not love him very much. She had displaced her affection onto her older brother and liked to play with him and his friends at boys' games. She had never felt really feminine. The analysis was able to clarify how N unconsciously experienced and elaborated the events of her childhood. She came to see how her sudden weaning had intensely frustrated her, exaggerating her oral envy. She reacted with hostility toward her pregnant mother. On the occasion of her mother's next pregnancy and the birth of a sibling a year later, she relived the same situation. In Dr. Jacobson's case, described earlier, the birth of male siblings had caused Silvia to transform her primitive oral envy, that is to say, envy because her mother breast-fed them, into penis envy. The same phenomenon was true of N. While her mother was pregnant, she hated her, phantasizing about destroying the fetus inside of her. When her brother was born and her mother nursed him, she hated and envied him because her mother gave him the breast. Later, she displaced that envy onto his penis. Afterward, she oscillated between attempts to identify with her brothers, envying their sex, and attempts to repress her rivalry, expressing love for them. When she felt abandoned by her mother, who dedicated herself to her younger siblings, N tried to abandon her as well and to affectively move toward her father but was subverted by his indifference. Then she began to repress her feelings for him, scorning both him and her parents' sexual life. She turned back to her frustrating and aggressive mother, to whom she would submit, humiliated, in the future. Unable to achieve an identification with her mother, N doubted that she could still be a woman; she could not be certain that her mother had not punished her, destroying her femininity because of her own hostile desires toward her mother when she was pregnant. Because of doubts about her intact femininity and her fear of her mother's retaliation, N became entrenched in her masculine position, thus reinforcing her penis envy. Her reaction toward menarche, however, demonstrated that her penis envy was secondary and that she basically wished to be a woman, a reaction that we have already recognized in other patients (Ana and Berta). N told her analyst that menarche did not scare her because her mother had already explained to her that it was going to happen. Moreover, the appearance of her menstruation made her feel happy, because it meant that she was now equal to her mother, to the family's housekeeper, and to all other women. That is to say, when she understood that her mother had pardoned her, authorizing her to be a woman, and that her reproductive capacity was intact, she accepted her femininity with relief and joy. But this situation changed fundamentally when her mother became ill in response to unsuccessful attempts to abort herself. Now N was filled with anxiety and guilt feelings, unconsciously equating her mother's illness with her earlier hostile thoughts. It was as if her mother had sought an abortion, thereby damaging herself, because it was what N wished as a child when she hated her mother because of her pregnancies. Her mother's hemorrhage when the labor pains started, her hospitalization and the news that the baby had been born by cesarean section intensified N's guilt feelings and her fear of being a woman. She punished herself with peritonitis in order to have to suffer an abdominal operation, too, and in this way ameliorate her guilt. She had felt responsible for her mother's cesarean section, and now the same thing happened to her because she also had had to have her abdomen opened. In the postoperative period N suffered intense pain in response to the hot enemas her mother was required to apply, and her reaction was such that her mother would tell her, "With such pain, you would already have been able to have your children." Her punishment, then, applied by her mother, consisted in suffering like her mother had in childbirth, in running the same risks but without the joy of having a child and being a woman in compensation for her suffering.

N accepted the arrival of menarche as a sign of her having atoned for her infantile aggression against her mother. She might have been able to renounce her masculine defense then, feeling equal to her mother and all other women and able to abandon her envy of her father and brothers for having a penis. She knew that she would later on enjoy the gratifications of her sex. But her mother's accidental pregnancy stimulated the emergence once again of guilt feelings with their accompanying fears. She punished herself with peritonitis and sought refuge again in her masculine defense. She doubted her capacity to be a woman, which she also feared, because in phantasy it was tantamount to suffering just as her mother had in reality, and being destroyed. So she became infertile. Furthermore, as long as she lived with her mother and did not have children, she could deny to herself that she had a sexual life while at the same time engaging in the same sexual activities that in her parents' case had seemed so despicable. If N had had a strong and affectionate father, capable of defending her against the unconscious image of her bad and destroyed mother, the outcome probably would have been different. The fact that she found such a paternal figure in her analyst permitted her to become pregnant.

Now let us explore in general terms what can be inferred from this clinical material. To do so, we return to the case of Mary to analyze two dreams and the rather typical material that emerges in the first session of her treatment. During our first conversation, I am quite impressed with her intuitive notion that the cause of her infertility lay in her conflict with her mother. Moreover, she associates her "obsession with [her] mother's pregnancies" to her infantile attempt to determine her mother's physical condition by hitting her abdomen. She talks about it without realizing that she thus reveals the principle source of her conflict to be her resentment of her mother's pregnancies and her intense aggression toward her mother in that state.

In her first dream Mary blames her mother for her infertility. This apparently irrational accusation stems from the unconscious and can be translated into our logical language in the following manner: "I hit my pregnant mother's abdomen in order to hurt her and destroy the fetus; she understood my bad wishes and so prohibits me from becoming pregnant now that I am an adult." This is one of the reasons why her mother appears responsible for her infertility. The patient's second dream unveils other typical causes. The first part demonstrates the patient's oral insatiability (the dough that eternally absorbs the milk), an insatiability that can be as much the consequence of a real lack of nourishment as of internal greed or the lack of affectionate mothering necessary for the baby, and perceived by it in oral terms. Later on, this insatiability is often displaced onto genital life, being manifested in an apparent sexual insatiability. The second part of the dream (in which a midwife kneads a mass on the abdomen of a woman in labor) shows the consequence of frustrations experienced with the mother and the absence of a good father. The affective insecurity in which the child finds herself obliges her to erotically seek out her mother in the hope of keeping her and, in so doing, appeasing her.

There is one detail in the history of this infertile woman, somewhat typical of infertile women in general, that has attracted the attention of many researchers who have found no satisfactory explanation. At first, Mary tells me that she and her husband did not want children and that her infertility was discovered only later on when they wanted to be parents. In fact, one finds in the histories of many infertile women that at the beginning of their sexual lives they used various types of contraceptives and that subsequently upon consulting a gynecologist for their infertility, they were usually told, "This is what happens when you attempt to go against nature, which now wreaks her vengeance on you." In general, the woman submissively accepts this explanation. We can also accept it after disabusing her of her apparent mysticism with an interpretation. If we substitute the word *mother* for that of *nature*—an equation quite universally made—we understand that both the gynecologist and the woman have intuitively perceived the problem. The infertile woman understands that she cannot have children because of having rebelled against her mother. She did not want her mother to conceive and have children; now her mother retaliates and does not allow her daughter to have motherhood.

Often it is learned that the woman who will later do everything possible to cure her infertility, becoming seriously depressed with each menstruation, spent the first years of her sexual life obsessed with a fear of getting pregnant and anxiously awaited the punctual arrival of her period. It would appear that for her both her potential fertility and her infertility have unleashed the same degree of anxiety. The reproductive capacity of such women was problematic for them long before they were diagnosed as infertile. Moreover, the fact that a pregnancy, apparently so desired in later life, has been feared in a previous period essentially clarifies that, although the woman finally consciously wishes to become pregnant, unconsciously she continues to try to avoid it with all psychosomatic means at her disposal. We may conclude that for these patients the pregnancy is no longer a biological process destined to end in a birth but an exposure to serious suffering and dangers that might contain the destruction of their femininity or even their death. If, in spite of this, they decide to become pregnant, they fail, deeply anxious about their infertility because they interpret it as proof of their having already been internally destroyed. They anguish about this destruction, a just punishment for infantile hostility, because it is experienced as proof of their guilt. The infertile woman who wishes to become pregnant usually oscillates between two equally painful positions: She fears menstruation as a proof of her infertility and guilt and she fears the lack of her period as an indication of pregnancy, that is to say, of the possibility of having to suffer her punishment. This is why we observe her lack of joy when she finally becomes pregnant.

There is a frequently occurring factor in the history of infertile women that does not appear in our "typical history," but that has been alluded to in previous pages. I refer to the tragic childhood event of one sort or another that can make the little girl believe in the effectiveness and omnipotence of her hatred. This has occurred with various of the patients cited. Silvia hated her siblings and envied them for the feeding their mother gave them. Her little brother died because of a tragic accident. He cut a finger when his bottle broke, and because he bled a lot, her mother took him to the doctor. The doctor anesthetized the child in order to suture the cut, and the child died as a result of the anesthesia. In other words, he died because he had the bottle for which Silvia envied him. When she was a little girl, Mrs. L fell ill with polyarthritis and suffered from a heart condition. When she later heard her parents say that because of her weakened heart she should never marry or have children, she felt that her hostility toward her mother, who had a sexual life and children, must have been very intense and dangerous for God (representative of her parents) to punish her in such a way. As a child, Mrs. B unconsciously hated her mother because of her pregnancies; her mother died giving birth to her 11th child, who because of being deprived of his mother, also died a few months later. As a child, N had wished that her mother would miscarry or die instead of having more babies. Later on, when she was in puberty, her mother almost died from attempting to abort a pregnancy that later resulted in a very difficult labor and cesarean section, and the little girl felt responsible.

We have observed, then, in the cases of infertile women whose histories we have at our disposal, the existence of certain typical factors.[2] Although it may seem a bit risky to generalize with such little clinical material, we see, in fact, a great concordance of factors in these patients. All have a particular family constellation in that the mother is the central figure for them, the father less important. However, this same constellation is also found in the great majority of neurotics and psychotics, a fact easy to understand because the small child depends totally on her mother, who is the sole object of her love. But this very dependency and the frustrations it engenders also guarantee that the daughter will concentrate all of her hatred and its consequent anxiety on her mother. If in early childhood the child has a father capable of becoming an equally important object, it will be much easier for her to become independent of her mother and to manage her feelings and anxieties. If she lacks such a father or other substitute object, she will not be able to liberate herself from such dependency and later on will become neurotic.*

Secondly, all of our patients experienced significant frustration during the oral stage, that is, during the first year of life. This factor is more specific to the profile of infertility, although it is also frequently

---

*Much has been written in the psychoanalytic literature about the importance the father has for both boys and girls as an object capable of freeing them from dependency on the omnipotent mother; feminist psychoanalysts have stressed the need for fathers and mothers to share the childrearing role in order to prevent what Nancy Chodorow has called "the reproduction of mothering," a gendered division of labor that institutionalizes inequality of status, power, and opportunity in the social sphere. Langer agreed with this perspective, but in the anticipation that a revolution in gender roles would not occur in the foreseeable future, she advocated the participation of the young child in professional or collectively shared child care situations at an early age, before she develops an exclusively dependent relationship with the mother; this situation enables the child to have intimate connections to other adults, which helps to diffuse the psychological struggles related to separation–individuation that are usually expressed intensely within the mother–child dyad.

found in other disorders. In four of our patients this frustration stemmed from a sudden weaning determined by the mother's subsequent pregnancy. But when I speak of frustration in the oral stage, I do not refer to inadequate feeding; from a biological point of view, the feeding can be very adequate even if the child still feels frustrated. The infant may feel, as well, the complete lack of caring from her mother plus the various discomforts in the oral domain like hunger, all of which provoke her hatred against the frustrating mother and her desire to suck her, empty her out, and forcibly take away the denied contents of her body. These unconscious phantasies can later lead the girl to believe that her mother, in justified retaliation, has emptied her out and thus deprived her of her capacity to have children. On the other hand, a fear of pregnancy can develop in the adult woman. Unconsciously, she fears that now her mother will be able to deprive her of the valuable contents of her own body, represented by the child. In reference to our patients, the oral frustration and consequent hatred were tied directly to the idea of the pregnant mother because of the dramatically sudden weaning. Their hatred toward the mother had been reinforced and had caused them to envy their siblings, whom they saw fed by the mother. In one of our patients, Mrs. Z, this factor was not present since she was the youngest child. However, Helene Deutsch maintains that it is often precisely the youngest child who lives in continuous fear and obsession that the mother could become pregnant and if another sibling is not born, believes that she has magically prevented it because of the violence of her bad wishes. This concept is valid for Mrs. Z, whose mother, moreover, devalued her own sex and was obsessed by the fear of getting pregnant. Tragic events in relation to the mother's reproductive life intervened as a fundamental obstacle to the child's identification with her precisely in her maternal functions. Mrs. Z came to believe in the effectiveness of her envy, her jealousy, and her hatred and in the weakness and uselessness of her love and wish to repair. Thus, maternity became extremely dangerous for her, making her fear that if she exposed herself her punishment would be to suffer a fate equal to or worse than her mother's.

With regard to what could be called the patients' infantilism or masculinization, we refer basically to their characterological attitudes. In this sense, we would exclude the case of Silvia, who presented an obvious hormonal infantilism. I only mention this aspect of the problem because it is emphasized in the literature on the subject, which erroneously assumes it to be a cause of infertility. The pubescent girl does not remain infantile or become masculine as a result of the desire to be infertile but, rather, to protect herself against the dangers that fertility represents to her. She also becomes masculine if she fears being unable to be a woman. Finally, I have spoken of the difficulty of identifying with the mother. In this case, the girl chooses another form of getting close to her by remaining a little girl or by trying to partially change herself into a male, thus creating the possibility of being able to keep her or more effectively conquer her.

The factors that may have provoked infertility in these patients are, indeed, also found in fertile women. However, I believe that they will always cause psychosomatic or psychological difficulties with regard to women's maternal capabilities. I present three short illustrative case histories to demonstrate this point.

Mrs. M, whose history was included in the study I coauthored with Dr. Celes Carcamo, was one of the eldest of many female children. Her mother was psychotic and suffered a melancholic episode giving birth to the patient. Because of this, the child was taken from her home and given first to a wet nurse and then to friends, a married couple without children who treated her very well. She returned home when she was 4 years old. Her mother did not want her; she became irritated and punished her when the girl cried for her beloved adopted mother. Three more sisters were born. The father was a loving and soft man who adored his wife and suffered because of her psychosis. Although he was disappointed at not having had a son, and even though he had a great predilection for only one of them, he nonetheless treated his daughters well. The patient loved her father but felt that he was neither supportive of her nor particularly concerned about her. I will leave the rest of Mrs. M's childhood aside in order to summarize the details of her reproductive life, which were, in fact, the psychosomatic consequence of her childhood conflicts. Mrs. M fell in love and married, and in the beginning it seemed that all was going to go well. She became pregnant soon afterward and gave birth to a daughter. One year later, she had another girl and was very disappointed that her second child was not a boy. Some years later, Mrs. M became pregnant again, suffering a miscarriage in the 4th month. This time it would have been the son desired by both her and her husband. (It seems that her guilt feeling toward her mother could not be overcome, permitting her to give birth to a male child.)[3] Then she had an extrauterine pregnancy, after which she suffered a complete amenorrhea. When she was 34 years old, an early menopause was diagnosed. However, the analysis managed to provoke a menstrual period again, permitting her to work through her infantile conflicts and to improve her psychophysical state in general. But after this menstrual period, diagnosed as late ovulation, the patient became, at 41 years of age, definitively menopausal.

We find in this patient all the traumatic factors described earlier. Furthermore, there is no lack in her history of external events that she could have experienced with guilt as indications of punishment. Her mother abandoned her immediately. She lost her wet nurse and later her beloved adoptive mother, only to find herself with a cold and psychotic mother who rejected her. Moreover, she found out that her birth had been the cause of one of her mother's episodes of melancholia.

The patient whose case history I now summarize was treated by Dr. León Grinberg, to whom I am grateful for sharing with me the relevant information. Olga, as I shall call her, was from a poor family. Her father, deaf and irritable, was a difficult man who, fortunately, did not intervene much in rearing her. Her mother, a bitter and long-suffering woman, loved her but, because of having to work in a factory, gave her just the minimum attention needed in order to make sure she survived. Two older brothers had died very young before she was born. Her mother became pregnant often and obtained abortions. When the girl had already entered puberty, her mother questioned her one day about whether she wanted to have a little brother, indirectly asking her daughter's permission to continue with a pregnancy. Olga violently protested. The mother submitted to her wishes, dying shortly afterward at 37 years of age as the consequence of an abortion. Olga came to analysis because of depression along with compulsions and anxieties. She was married and loved her husband; after having a daughter, she miscarried a pregnancy that would have been a son. The month following the miscarriage, she almost died from a serious genital hemorrhage. Her depression and her fears began at that time. But even earlier she had lived obsessed with the idea that she would repeat the exact fate of her mother: She would have a live daughter, would give birth to two sons who could not survive, and would die at 37 from an abortion. She interpreted her miscarriage as equivalent to the birth of her older brother who died very young. Now she was even more certain that her mother's destiny would also be her own. So she protected herself against the dangers of her fertility with a transient infertility. She became pregnant again when she was about to begin her analysis and hoped that the treatment would provide a magical and immediate protection against the dangers of the pregnancy. But as it progressed— with the patient not yet capable of liberating herself from her infantile guilt feelings—she became convinced that she was going to miscarry again before the fourth month. She consulted her gynecologist, and he found nothing abnormal. In fact, as the date approached, she began to spot. She was given complete bed rest and appropriate medication, but she miscarried precisely on the day she had foreseen, which corresponded to the fourth month since she had menstruated.

And now I briefly turn to the case of Frida.[4] When Frida was born, her mother suffered a postpartum psychosis. She had to be interned in a hospital, which she never left. Her daughter was raised by the grandparents. She had a difficult and sad childhood. When she married, she wanted to have children, at least consciously. She became pregnant very easily, only to enter into a state of anxiety and desperation a few days later. The physicians, having reason to fear for her life, advised the interruption of the pregnancy. This situation occurred four times until finally, supported by her recently initiated psychoanalytic treatment, she could carry a pregnancy to term. After the birth of the baby, she rapidly decompensated. She began to suffer extreme anxiety and depression and to fill the house with used menstrual pads and excrement-stained underpants. She returned to analysis, which had been prematurely interrupted by the birth of her child.

Frida's particular symptom of madness had a double meaning. On the one hand, she demonstrated through the exhibition of her menstrual blood that she was not in her mother's pregnant condition and thus did not need to go mad. On the other hand, to some extent she simulated madness and internal destruction through the exhibition of blood and excrement. In other words, she lost her femininity and her sanity in order not to have to lose them as her mother had. It was as if in that way she said to the world and to fate: "I already know that because of my birth I destroyed my mother. But don't punish me any more for that, now that I am also a mother. I've already punished myself enough; I am already destroyed and mad, like her."

In Frida, envy toward younger siblings and hatred toward a pregnant mother do not exist. She had lost her mother at birth. Because of that, for her to become a mother meant to lose herself, that is, to lose her sanity. Her case allows us to understand that in spite of the importance of all the factors already mentioned, the most significant obstacle to a daughter's motherhood resides in the difficulty of identifying with her own mother in her maternal role.

However, in no way must we conclude that any woman who has experienced dramatic episodes in her childhood or has simply felt betrayed in her connection with her mother because of the birth of a younger sibling will be incapable of being a good mother. To affirm this would be to interpret the material erroneously and with excessive pessimism. Although early childhood notably influences future development, the later years also count. Loving and well-intentioned caregiving by those who surround the child can mitigate the impact of early infantile experiences and damaging events of childhood. Moreover, the extent to which childhood experiences become traumatic relates directly to the parents' behavior. For example, an expectant mother who does not deprive her little girl of affection and attention will not provoke the desperate jealousy easily stimulated by a preoccupied and bitter mother who, facing another pregnancy, rejects her young daughter, often in complete ignorance of her hostile attitude. Even tragic events need not be disastrous as long as they do not lead parents to subordinate the well-being of their healthy living children to a preoccupation for a sick child or to sacrifice them to the insuperable mourning for a dead child. The mothers of the patients whose histories have been described here were extraordinarily neurotic and frustrating, and there was no one strong enough in the child's environment to effectively counteract their damaging influence. However, children who have attentive and conscientious parents will be able to overcome many tragedies, such as those experienced by these patients, because they will not be burdened by having to unconsciously carry the weight of all the responsibility and guilt for what has happened.[*]

---

[*]The British psychoanalyst Dinora Pines has written recently that "there is as yet no literature regarding spontaneous abortion or miscarriage." Clearly unaware of Langer's work, Pines's approach to this subject in many ways echoes Langer. For example, Pines points out that analysis of patients who miscarry "reveals an early relationship with the mother which is suffused with frustration, rage, disappointment and guilt. Loss of the foetus either by miscarriage or abortion is experienced as a relief, rather than a loss, as if the continuing internal bad mother had not given permission for the child to become a mother herself. It is possible that the pregnant woman's unconscious anxieties connected with the fantasy of the foetus representing a bad and dangerous aspect of the self or of her partner may be a contributing factor to the stimulation of uterine expulsive movements, which end in miscarriage. The analyst is experienced as this malign internal mother in the transference. Analysis of these aspects of psychic life may enable a woman to maintain her pregnancy and become a mother herself." See D. Pines, "Pregnancy, Miscarriage and Abortion: A Psychoanalytic Perspective," *International Journal of Psychoanalysis*, 71(1990): 301–307.

Pregnancy and Childbirth [1]

According to observations of the healthy woman, pregnancy and childbirth represent a normal episode in feminine reproductive life. Until recently, however, this was not the case in our society. On the contrary, disorders of pregnancy, as well as pain, anxiety, and complications related to childbirth, occurred so frequently that they were considered to be normal, in other words, almost inevitable. However, a more profound exploration reveals that these disorders stem from psychological conflicts and from an identification with women who are already troubled with respect to their femininity.

In her anthropological studies of different cultures, Margaret Mead (in *Male and Female*) arrived at the conclusion that each society has preconceptions about female reproductive functions that are accepted by the majority of women. In societies in which it is assumed that nausea will be experienced during pregnancy and that labor will be accompanied by pain and danger, the majority of pregnant women do, in fact, suffer from nauseous states and have difficult deliveries. In other societies, where the pregnant woman is not surrounded with dangers and taboos, pregnancy and childbirth usually occur easily and without complications. How can this rather perplexing phenomenon be explained? Quite simply, if we keep in mind what was said earlier about a woman's identification with her mother's maternal functions. In *Childbirth Without Fear*, Grantly Dick-Read shares his observation that women raised by mothers who described the birth experience as very anxiety- provoking and painful also had difficult deliveries, while the exact opposite was typical of the history of those women who had easy childbirths. The Pavlovian school, dedicated to childbirth without pain, maintains the same perspective. The phenomenon that Margaret Mead observed with respect to different societies occurs, then, within much smaller groups as well. There are families in which the daughters, following upon their mother's ideas, have little fear of pregnancy and childbirth and, in fact, suffer less as a result than girls raised in families in which they are taught to be afraid of their femininity because of their mother's complaints and fears. Although these differences exist, it is important to note that we are all members of a society in which something painful and dangerous is associated with all feminine functions. Because of this, for example, the first theory Freud had of the psychological processes accompanying menarche was that the young girl experiences it as a castration. However, although each woman's attitude regarding her femininity depends to a certain extent on environmental attitudes surrounding her in childhood, more personal factors also intervene to condition her subsequent behavior. This explains why, in the same society, and even within the same small family, each woman develops her own unique anxieties and disorders related to pregnancy and childbirth.

I stated that our society accepts difficulties in pregnancy and childbirth as normal. Recently, however, a growing number of investigations among psychoanalysts and others have shown that these difficulties are the consequences of psychological conflicts and are, therefore, accessible to psychotherapeutic intervention.

Later, I will speak about Dick-Read and the Pavlovians, but for the moment I will share some observations from a strictly psychotherapeutic perspective. Flanders Dunbar and Raymond Squier recommend that the pregnant woman be attended not only by an obstetrician but by a specialist in psychosomatic medicine as well. They demonstrate the utility of this approach with the exposition of clinical material in which Enrique Salerno presents his successful experience carrying out two professional roles. The latter treated his patients simultaneously as a gynecologist and a psychotherapist and in one case was able to ensure that a patient who had previously miscarried or dilated prematurely was able to carry a pregnancy to term. In the hospital, it was my experience that brief (30 minutes) psychotherapeutic conversations maintained once a week throughout a pregnancy were sufficient for a satisfactory outcome in women who had experienced difficulties, especially miscarriages, during previous pregnancies.

Multiple causes of disorders in pregnancy may be illuminated in a psychological evaluation. But the appearance of the disorder always signifies a rejection of the child, often provoked by adverse economic or social circumstances, indifference on the part of the husband, and so forth. For example, three North American authors (Klein, Potter, &

Dyk, 1950) did a statistical analysis during the Second World War, researching the anxieties provoked by pregnancy and childbirth in 27 women pregnant for the first time in extremely impoverished social and economic conditions. Some of the women were single, others had been abandoned by their husbands, and still others were separated from their husbands who were away at war. Almost none had her own home or could look forward to any degree of basic economic security for herself and her future child. Such circumstances visibly influenced the problems and anxieties experienced by these women during pregnancy. However, even under adverse conditions, some women accepted their situations and were able to tolerate being pregnant quite well. The authors label the latter women as more mature personalities and point out that they came from families who, although poor, were emotionally well adjusted. In the majority of cases, however, difficult economic circumstances had already troubled the patients during their own childhoods, robbing them of the emotional security so essential to every young child. Consequently, as adults they were incapable of finding a partner who could guarantee the minimum external stability needed to enable them to easily accept being pregnant. We see, then, the interaction between economic and emotional factors and, once again, the adult woman's repetition of her childhood situation. During pregnancy and childbirth especially, she repeats her primitive relationship to her own mother. This fact has been observed repeatedly in psychoanalytic treatment, and Helene Deutsch interprets it as a consequence of a double identification. The pregnant woman identifies with the fetus, thus reliving her own intrauterine life. Moreover, in the pregnant woman's unconscious, the fetus represents her own mother and especially her maternal superego. Thus, her ambivalent relationship with the mother is reexperienced with her future child. But we have also observed that the fetus can acquire other representations for the woman, the most frequent of which is that it is something stolen from the mother. This something can be the child who belongs to the mother or the father's penis that the mother carries inside her. So, once again we encounter the girl's early and unconscious phantasies of having emptied her mother of the valuable contents of her body (Melanie Klein). The intensification of these phantasies during pregnancy and childbirth causes multiple anxieties and somatic disorders.

In order to illustrate, we return to the patient material already presented in previous chapters and speak again of Gabriela, the young Brazilian girl who feared defloration; of Ana, who needed to fail in each reproductive stage in order to be able to move ahead; of Isabel, who felt a phobic fear of cockroaches; and of Lina, who lost her mother. In addition, I will summarize the case of Erica, who became pregnant after a brief psychoanalytic treatment.

When Gabriela had overcome her fear of defloration and initiated her sex life, her menstruation was late. She did not want to interpret this as an indication that she was pregnant or to find out through a medical examination. She spoke of leaving her analysis and returning to her country of origin, at which point she had the following dream: She is in a hotel, busy packing to return home. She is very hurriedly packing some things that do not fit into the suitcase. She feels nervous because the maid is outside, and she wants to leave the hotel without the maid seeing her so that she does not have to tip her. The dream may be understood in the following way: The suitcase represents her uterus, the things that do not fit well represent the fetus and penis, and the maid represents her analyst. Unconsciously, Gabriela is still a young girl, too young to be able to become pregnant with the right to be a mother. So her uterus appears as a suitcase too small to contain so many things—the husband's penis and the fetus. In her treatment I had promised to cure only her fear of defloration, that is, to give her her husband's penis. Her pregnancy was something that I did not owe her, which she felt compelled to hide from me so I would not ask her to return it to me in the form of a tip. A complete interpretation of the dream would be, then, that she anxiously wished to return to her country without my realizing that she was pregnant, so that she would not have to give me the tip, that is, something to which I had a right, the child she had stolen from me. This dream, which expresses the young pregnant woman's fear of the analyst-mother because she feels she has stolen the fetus from her, reminds us of another dream described earlier about a gym teacher. The patient was Mrs. B, who when she had been cured of her sterility, reacted in the same way as Gabriela. She did not want to confirm her pregnancy and even terminated her analysis the day she discovered the positive results of her pregnancy test.

The appearance of the fear of the mother in the dreams of these two women who are possibly pregnant—even before their condition is clinically confirmed—turned out to be symptomatic for the development of both their pregnancies. I was alerted to the probability of somatic difficulties but could not help Mrs. B. at all because she left her analysis when she received the positive confirmation of her pregnancy. She miscarried some weeks later. Gabriela continued her analysis, and her disorders and anxieties were able to be resolved analytically without major organic repercussions.

Isabel suffered from the same fear, which also endangered her pregnancy. She lived far from her family and did not want to communicate the news of her pregnancy to her mother in a letter. She also hid her state for the longest possible time from her compatriots, so that they would not divulge the news that might thus reach her family. In one of her dreams her best friend (maternal representative) finds out she is pregnant through an indiscretion of her husband's. Then the patient furiously tells her friend: "Since you know that I am expecting a child, I prefer to abort it," and she rushes out of the apartment where she had met her friend; the friend pursues her down the stairs. This was the first of an entire series of persecutory dreams. In the dream she apparently defies her friend-mother and threatens her with an abortion. But then she escapes, pursued by the other. That is, her defiance is only apparent. She fears that her mother, once finding out, might take her baby from her, and her first resentful reaction is to renounce it by aborting. Her second reaction is then to flee in order to keep it. Some weeks after this dream a compatriot friend of hers, through whom her family could indirectly learn of her pregnancy, made it clear that he observed her weight gain. His observation enraged her. That same night she dreamed that her sister was pitifully dying from a miscarriage in front of their indifferent brother and mother; she sees with terror how her sister is losing her internal organs along with the blood. The following morning uterine pains began, which were fortunately stopped before they could cause a miscarriage. This episode occurred in the third month of her pregnancy. Two months later she told her parents she was pregnant, and the following day she suffered a slight hemorrhage.

In Isabel's first dream, in which her friend finds out her secret through her husband's indiscretion only to pursue her later, her infantile and present situations are conflated; the importance of this can be seen in the appearance of difficulties in the pregnancy. In her childhood her father often defended Isabel against her nervous and irritable mother. But later he always sided with his wife, abandoning his young daughter to her mother's rage. Because of her childhood situation, Isabel was already predisposed to certain difficulties during pregnancy, but their actual occurrence depended on the influence of her contemporary situation as well. Her husband was not very concerned with her while she was pregnant, which is precisely the circumstance in which women generally need more support than usual. This made her relive her father's lack of protection during her childhood, intensifying her already irrational fear of her mother. Because of this condensation of infantile and current conditions, Isabel's parents appear represented in her dream by her husband and her best friend, the latter embodying a relationship filled with highly ambivalent feelings.

In the second dream, the traumatic childhood situation appears with even more clarity, but it once again emerges in connection with the current conflict related to her husband's indifference toward the dangers of pregnancy. As a child Isabel had displaced her oedipal love for her father onto her brother; later, her husband. In the dream her sister represents Isabel, and her brother represents her husband and father. Her husband's indifference makes her relive early masochistic phantasies in which her united father and mother, cruelly indifferent, see how she suffers the punishment for her hatred and rivalry toward her mother. The punishment itself consists in the destruction of her femininity.

In another example demonstrating how the fetus can symbolize something valuable stolen from the mother, for which the pregnant woman fears her retaliation, I describe an anxiety attack Lina suffered when she was already far along in her pregnancy. It was during an evening when she was home alone. She had money in a safe that had been given to her by her father to keep for him. Suddenly, she was gripped with a terrible anxiety. She thought she heard footsteps and strange noises, and she saw strange shadows. She believed something terrible had happened. Perhaps the servant had poisoned her husband and was now coming with her accomplices to force open the safe and steal the money her father had entrusted to her. Lina did not perceive herself to be phantasizing but believed she was experiencing a frightening reality. The content of her anxiety attack is easy to interpret because its principal elements are already known to us from previously analyzed material. Once again we find the young husband's indifference to his pregnant wife, which unleashes a state of anxiety and causes the resurgence of old infantile phantasies. We already recognize the maid as a representative of the devalued mother. In her phantasy Lina attempts to let her husband off the hook: he does not take care of her because the bad and envious mother has poisoned him. But why and to what end? The carefully closed safe simultaneously represents Lina's pregnant stomach; its valuable content, the fetus; the father's money; and the father's penis. Lina's father is absent, abandoning her to her anxieties. In Lina's unconscious the figures of her father and husband are condensed into one. For her, the pregnancy signifies that she has stolen her father's penis from her mother. If he is close by, she feels secure. But the moment she feels unprotected by her husband and father, her fear of her dead mother's retaliation emerges.

Until now I have spoken of the pregnant woman who attempts to defend the fetus against her mother—the *vehini-hai*—who wishes to take it from her. But in the pregnant woman there is frequently a rejection of the fetus as well. Earlier I cited Helene Deutsch's concept of the double identification experienced by the pregnant woman with her pregnancy. If she identifies with the fetus, she projects onto it her own infantile voraciousness, her desires of early infancy to eat her mother. When the fetus represents her mother, whose oral retaliation she fears, it is experienced as something anxiety-provoking and destructive that she carries inside herself. The fear many pregnant women feel of giving birth to a monster, an abnormal being, expresses a judgment that their own infantile feelings were monstrous and that in their demanding phantasies toward their mothers they behaved as monsters. In dreams the fetus sometimes takes the form of a crab (the fetus destroys the pregnant woman with the same cruelty with which she wished to destroy her mother) or of a spider (another representation of the young girl who wishes to suck the mother dry) or of the child (who in her infancy sucked her mother dry because of the hunger she was made to feel). For example, during her pregnancy Lina dreamed that she was at her aunt's side in the dining room of her paternal home and both of them were covered with little spiders. The fear of giving birth to a monster also stems from the fear of one's own destructive feelings toward the child, who represents the husband, one of the parents, or a sibling (in other words, something that unconsciously belongs to one's mother).

When I spoke of infertility, I commented that a woman can also interpret the fetus as a punishment imposed by her mother. In contrast to this, the pregnant woman who fears being destroyed by her mother often experiences the pregnancy as a dangerous trap her mother has set, in which case the pregnancy itself becomes a punishment as well. The pregnant woman usually reacts to this fear with semiconscious attempts to miscarry, followed by intense guilt. At the beginning of her pregnancy Isabel decided to go horseback riding. She argued that her condition was normal and saw no reason to take extra precautions. This attitude functioned to throw her mother off the track and to hide her pregnancy from her. At the same time, to go horseback riding signified for Isabel an attempt to miscarry and to liberate herself from the dangerous pregnancy that just a short time earlier she had desired so much. She actually took part in a trip by horseback but was extremely anxious because she became obsessed with the idea that the horse was going to throw her and that she would die. In other words, driven by her anxiety, Isabel tried to miscarry. But now there was no escape for her because if she attempted to do so, fate would punish her with something worse, with death.

The very oral frustration that leads to the rejection of the fetus is usually also expressed in a defiant refusal to feed it, signifying a belated dialogue with the mother. It is as if the pregnant woman said to her mother, "How can you ask me to give sufficiently to my child if you have not given me what I needed?" Isabel expressed this feeling during her pregnancy in a series of dreams in which she felt continually troubled and anxious because of having to offer food to people whom she had not invited or because of not being able to take good care of loved and important visitors for lack of the necessary resources.

If it were only a matter of feelings of rejection toward the child or if this rejection were very intense, the pregnancy would not occur. In order for a woman to become pregnant and for the pregnancy to continue, albeit racked with difficulties, two opposite and conflictual tendencies have to exist. The fundamental reason a woman desires to have a child is biological. Her maternal instinct demands this direct gratification. I already indicated why I believe it is justified to speak of such an instinct.* The sexual instinct leads to falling in love and the establishment of a union that satisfies the couple's sexual appetite as well as a number of psychological needs. The woman's maternal instinct, which is an integral part of feminine sexuality, is simultaneously gratified. The woman's multiple desires are thus fulfilled. She wishes to have a child because it signifies the reclaiming of her own mother and it permits her to identify with her. She also desires a child to confirm her own fertility. The wish for a child can correspond to her infantile desire to give a child to her father. The fetus can unconsciously represent the desired penis. Of course, a woman's desire for motherhood is also influenced by more conscious or rational factors. She can want a child in order to relive her own childhood through it or to give to it precisely what she did not have. She can desire a child because of rivalry with other women, in order to keep her husband, to gain the status it accords her, or because of any other contemporary issue. But, basically, a woman's desire to give birth to a child stems from the psychobiological need to develop all of her latent capacities.

There are women who achieve this end with few difficulties. Others, those described in this book, are in conflict with their femininity. This conflict might also be formulated as something provoked by two different currents of unconscious phantasies: The first belongs to the paranoid-schizoid position and the second to the depressive position, both of which are described by Melanie Klein in "Notes on Some Schizoid Mechanisms." To shelter the penis, the semen, or the fetus within a woman signifies for her that she has stolen something that belongs to her mother, winning and triumphing over

---

* As I have indicated elsewhere, Langer came to reject the idea of a maternal instinct. However, she continued to hold the view expressed here with respect to the unconscious aspects of a woman's desire and need to have a child.

her. Because of this, pregnancy implies the danger of punishment and of destruction. Thus, salvation is sought in its total denial—frigidity—or in hiding from the mother (the dreams of Gabriela, Mrs. B, Isabel, and so on) or even in detaching herself from a stolen pregnancy (Mrs. B and, as we shall see later, Ana). But these paranoid fears enter into conflict with the woman's desire toward reparation (depressive position) of the destroyed mother through her own pregnancy and joyful childbirth, and with the wish to return to her mother, through a healthy baby, what was stolen. In this way she can demonstrate faith in her generosity and tolerance and in the goodness and integrity of her own body.

In the infertile woman paranoid fears prevail. In line with her personal character, certain barriers are erected in the infertile woman against the incorporation of the penis and the semen or the sheltering of the fetus within her. The most superficial barrier utilized by the woman who fears getting pregnant is the phobia of defloration, and when this has been overcome, vaginismus. Frigidity is another attempted defense, although in the realm of phantasy; by not feeling the sexual act, the frigid woman hopes to elude its dangerous consequences. Other women have recourse to hormonal disorders, and in this way fleetingly negate their femininity, which has become so dangerous. The spasm of the tubes is a more intimate and primitive defense against impregnation. Behind its hysterical disguise can be perceived the autistic attitude of cutting off all communication with a hostile world.

The infertile woman eventually becomes pregnant, motivated by her need for reparation. But while the child grows inside her, she feels that her persecutor, who will from inside attack all the good she contains, also grows (recall the dream of the fire-daughter). It is often quite striking to see some women who consciously wished to have a child become so intensely anxious at the beginning of a pregnancy. If the anxiety becomes intolerable, they will attempt to free themselves from the persecutory fetus by all means at their disposal. I saw two women achieve the interruption of their pregnancies through psychiatrically recommended abortion, a third through uncontrollable vomiting, and two who practically destroyed the embryo because of the force of their anxiety. But the most frequently encountered defense against the anxiety provoked by the growing fetus is miscarriage, the premature expulsion of the persecutor, which often occurs without being able to be halted by any preventative means or medication.

However, if the conflict toward the pregnancy is less intense and awakens less anxiety, its manifestations will be less offensive. The most frequent is of an oral character and consists of nausea, vomiting, and specific food yearnings. Another frequent symptom, in this case of an anal character, is constipation. The great occurrence of these two types of symptoms gives rise to the question whether they can be explained by the physiological changes that the woman undergoes during pregnancy or whether the psychological tensions provoked by the pregnancy tend to be discharged through some kind of conversion symptom.

Freud called attention to the theories that children invent to explain the mystery of conception, pregnancy, and childbirth. These theories correspond to the libidinal stages through which the child passes. They later succumb to repression but are manifested unchanged in the unconscious. The most frequent theory, also found in many myths and beliefs of primitive peoples, is that the woman becomes pregnant by eating something; this something generally symbolizes the pregnancy. Or the child represses his knowledge of the existence of the vagina, confusing it with the anus. Because of this and his own sensations and experiences during defecation, he believes that the baby is expelled through the anus and equates it with excrement. It is likely that the most frequent disorders of gestation—vomiting and constipation—are produced by the persistence of this infantile phantasy in the unconscious.

The influence of psychogenic factors in serious and repeated vomiting attacks has been recognized for some time. It has been observed that through environmental changes, directive therapies, mock curettages and so on, therapeutic successes were obtained, underscoring the psychic origin of this disorder. As early as 1921 Max Schwab considered unchecked vomiting[2] associated with the beginning of pregnancy to be a hunger strike against the pregnancy and, when it results in death, a form of suicide. In 1932 Susanna Hupfer pointed out the relationship between the pregnant woman's vomiting and eating binges, and the infantile theory of conception. She maintained that while vomiting signifies a rejection of the fetus, an eating binge expresses a desire to affirm the pregnancy and is a symbolic repetition of the conception. According to Helene Deutsch, during the first months of pregnancy the woman reacts with oral ambivalence toward the fetus and attempts to expel it by vomiting and to reincorporate it with eating binges.

I would like to add another perspective to these authors' theories. Indeed, vomiting (or nausea, which is the beginning of vomiting), like eating binges, is an expression of the conflict of ambivalence provoked by a pregnancy. Although eating binges are sometimes interpreted as a positive attitude toward the fetus because they express the need to affirm the pregnancy, this same need already indicates the existence of the opposite desire, that of expelling the fetus (or whatever it represents in the unconscious). This imaginary expulsion, carried out through the mouth, collides with the desire to continue with the pregnancy. If this were not so, the unconscious would not be allied with the vomiting as an attempt to interrupt the pregnancy, which (with the exception of uncontrollable vomiting attacks obliging the physician to perform an abortion) has no meaning other than a symbolic protest and a discharge of negative feelings. Moreover, as the different authors have indicated, the unconscious chooses the alimentary tract for its protest because of the persistence of old infantile theories with respect to conception. Another reason, in my judgment, the imaginary expulsion is through the mouth is that the pregnant woman's anxieties stem in great part from her oral frustrations and her distrust and oral resentment toward her mother. In her identification with the fetus, the pregnant woman experiences a profound regression to early infancy and thus in her difficulties has recourse to the mechanisms with which the infant rejects anything disagreeable or toxic, that is, through vomiting and diarrhea. We will take up the latter issue shortly. Also, the eating binge, which is an uncontainable hunger, expresses extremely infantile behavior.

The pregnant woman's oral rejection is sometimes displaced onto other organs, for example, the respiratory tract. I once observed a pregnant woman who, in a conflictual situation, had an expulsive cough stemming from an inflammation of the pharynx. An analysis of this symptom demonstrated her attempt to expel the fetus by means of the cough. During the first months of her pregnancy, Isabel went through a period in her analysis in which she fell into a deep silence. Arriving punctually to each session, she spent the entire hour without uttering a word. Her attitude changed when we understood that she could not speak because unconsciously her analyst represented her bad mother, from whom she wished to keep her pregnancy a secret. To retain her words was equivalent to retaining the fetus, while speaking— that is, allowing her words to escape—meant she might lose her child. When Lina was already far along in her pregnancy, she passed through a period in which there was a danger she might deliver prematurely. She had a dream in which she coughed until she spit up pieces of her lung. During the dream she felt very guilty, because she symbolically eliminated the fetus. It must be remembered, however, that although the rejection of the pregnancy can be expressed in these ways through respiratory symptoms, the digestive symptoms are the most frequently encountered.

If the rejection of the fetus is so intense that the oral symptom is insufficient to calm the pregnant woman's anxiety, the struggle is often expressed in the terminal part of the intestine, with much greater danger for the continuation of the pregnancy. The uterus is intimately linked to the rest of the visceral plexus so that the tonal variations of the autonomic nervous system is transmitted to it through its neuromuscular connections. A significant number of the popular medicines used to provoke an abortion work on the intestine, stimulating intense colic and diarrhea, thus unleashing a state of neuromuscular superexcitability and contractions of the uterus that can cause a miscarriage. Even a woman lacking in any theoretical knowledge whatsoever of this interrelationship perceives it through her own experience, in which any abnormal state of her intestine has repercussions in her uterus. Moreover, as I have already said, in the woman's unconscious the theory persists that the child is born as excrement through the anus. We believe this to be the reason that diarrhea is a less frequently occurring disorder of pregnancy than constipation. In the oral domain the danger of expelling the fetus is minor. The ego perceives this situation and thus permits the unconscious tendencies to express themselves through this symptom, just as in sleeping it permits them to be externalized in dreams. In none of these cases is there danger that this externalization will have serious consequences in reality. But if the defense mechanisms are such that they lead a woman to express her conflicts in the intestinal realm, the continuation of the pregnancy is endangered and she will have to engage in a struggle to maintain it, defending herself from her hostile tendencies toward expulsion by means of constipation.

Consciously, Gabriela fervently desired a child. But her constant fear of miscarrying betrayed the existence of intense unconscious sentiments to the contrary. During the initial weeks of her pregnancy, she suffered from extreme constipation until she was made conscious of the fact that her constipation stemmed from her desire to retain the fetus in the face of an irrational fear of expelling it when defecating. Thus, unconsciously the fetus was treated like excrement. Her obsession about miscarrying came from her fear that her enraged and jealous mother would take her baby from her. When she analyzed her constipation it disappeared, leaving in place another merely psychological symptom: She suddenly felt incapable of dealing with older women, especially her housekeeper, who reminded her of her mother and toward whom she developed an unconquerable aversion. In other words, her fear of her mother was no longer expressed psychosomatically through the provocation of constipation as a defense against diarrhea but now appeared in the form of a phobia of women who represented her mother.

Erica manifested even more clearly than Gabriela how constipation functioned as a defense against her impulse to expel the fetus.

Erica had come to see me to clarify through a series of informal conversations whether or not she still wanted to have a child. She was then 35 years old. She was in a deeply conflictual relationship with a man whom she loved very much. In the course of our conversations, she described the following masturbatory phantasy, which had begun in her childhood and continued to recur in periods of genital frustration. In her dream a young girl is given castor oil to drink. When she wants to go to the bathroom, she finds it locked. Feeling anxious, she tries to hold her bowel movement for some time, until the need is greater than her ability to control it and she defecates in her pants. The patient has an orgasm at the moment of imagining the defecation. This is a phantasy of masochistic rebellion directed against her mother, who had been a cold woman with exaggerated demands regarding cleanliness. As a youngster, the girl avenged herself in response to her mother's demands to give her a good bowel movement at the hour she determined by retaining the fecal material or by eliminating excrement in pieces or in diarrhea outside the expected routine. This behavior can be deduced from the aforementioned phantasy, in which the castor oil signifies the indifference and the bad food that the mother obliged her to accept and against which she is rebelling.

Erica came to see me to treat a number of personal problems, the fundamental one having to do with her doubts, because of her extremely complicated family and economic situation, about whether to have a child. I had the impression that, in spite of everything, basically she had already decided to have the child and that she only needed my approbation. My impression was confirmed when after just a few conversations she resolved to become pregnant. However, once pregnant, Erica developed new conflicts. She fell in love with her best friend's husband, and after beginning a sexual relationship with him, the fetus changed from something desired into an obstacle to the realization of her love and definitive union with her lover.

We will be able to understand Erica's change of attitude toward her own husband, her friend's husband, and motherhood during the pregnancy only if we follow the complex unconscious identifications Erica had with these objects. Her difficulties with her husband basically came from the fact that he was a maternal representative for her. The history of her pregnancy and childbirth seem like an updated edition of her infantile masturbatory phantasy. Her husband made her pregnant; that is, he gave her the castor oil to drink. Afterward, he decided to go away before the baby's due date on an important but dangerous political mission, leaving her and the baby about to be born completely unprotected. In the domain of her masturbatory phantasy, her husband's behavior is equivalent to the action of a sadistic mother who, after having given the castor oil, forgets about the child and locks the bathroom door, depriving her of a place adequate to her needs. As we shall see later, Erica retaliated, once again pursuing her phantasy. She gave birth in a hurried and uninvolved fashion, devaluing the child her husband gave her just as in her phantasy she eliminated her diarrheic excrement. On the other hand, the fetus also signified a maternal substitute for her, but a more anguishing substitute even than the husband, because her relationship and coexistence with the fetus was much more intimate than with her husband. In this situation she turned to her friend's husband, just as in her childhood she had attempted unsuccessfully to clutch onto her father. Erica was 4 years old when the First World War broke out; her father had to leave for the front, abandoning her to her bad mother. She loved him very much and in her childish mind it was not the war that separated them but her jealous mother, who had interposed herself as an obstacle to Erica's infantile love for her father. She must have thought that if her mother had not existed, her father would not have abandoned her. Her friend's husband, then, was a paternal representative, and the fetus the mother who separated her from the complete realization of her love. Finally she herself, in her pregnant state, was also identified with her mother, who had been left unprotected and abandoned by her husband when Erica was only 5 and her sister a newborn. Thus, when separating from her husband, Erica left the father of the child she was going to have, repeating the family situation, blaming the part of her personality that was identified with her mother and simultaneously suffering her maternal destiny as a punishment for her hatred against her mother.

Both Erica's childhood and her present situation offer painfully inadequate objects for a favorable identification with motherhood. Her fixation on a certain infantile and pregenital sexual gratification determined the form in which she attempted to free herself. I saw her during her pregnancy, which, except for a tenacious constipation, presented no difficulties. On the contrary, she gave the impression of denying her condition. She carried on her life exactly as before. Her pregnancy was not even noticeable until the sixth month, and she was not concerned with preparing a layette. At one point in her sixth month, after having taken a weak laxative to treat her constipation, she was trying to defecate when subtle uterine contractions began. Complete bed rest and medication were prescribed. From that time on, her desperate struggle against a premature birth began, a struggle she sustained for several weeks until, regrettably, her labor began with such force that she could not wait for the midwife to arrive and gave birth in less than half an hour to a barely viable infant. I was struck by the similarity between her masturbation phantasy and the progression of her pregnancy. It can be deduced from her apparent indifference toward the pregnancy—equivalent to a denial of her condition—that she doubted her ability to carry it to a positive conclusion. Unconsciously, she tried to save her child by defending it through an unrelenting constipation in the face of the repetition of her infantile attitude, which corresponded in the present to a miscarriage. We have seen that in Erica's unconscious when her husband made her pregnant, he was giving her castor oil. However, while she was in treatment with me, her positive transference with a tolerant maternal figure counteracted this idea of the pregnancy, especially because she experienced my permission to become a mother. But once alone with her husband, she became anxious and sought escape in a lover. In the long run, her anxiety and rejection of the pregnancy increased. When it intensified and came to approximate her infantile phantasy, a light laxative (here the phantasy of castor oil returned undisguised) provoked the threat of a premature labor. She began to fight against such an outcome, a struggle comparable to the little girl's situation in her phantasy in which she desperately defends herself against the catastrophe of dirtying herself. And, finally, in the same way that the young girl defecates, without being able to open the bathroom door, she expels the child like feces, without being able to await either the due date, the arrival of the midwife, or her transfer to the clinic. In Erica it was clear from the beginning that, because of her childhood experiences, she was inclined to undo her pregnancy and that she tried, through her chronic constipation, to protect her child from her tendencies toward expulsion. When she could no longer maintain the defense of her constipation, she was in continual danger of a premature labor, which, in fact, finally occurred. The same rapidity with which she went through labor for the first time at 35 years of age calls attention to the explosive defecation of the girl in her phantasy.

I now present Ana's history, in which the relationship between diarrhea and miscarriage is quite obvious. My approach will be to take up her earliest childhood memories, which may be interpreted in the same manner as dreams; their latent content is revealed in a condensed fashion, expressing important but repressed experiences and phantasies.

One of Ana's first memories was the following: When she was 4 years old, she went to visit her aunt, who lived in the same building, and felt an intense desire to defecate. She wanted to return to her apartment, which was on the same floor, but before she could get out of the foyer, she felt the feces, like a hard walking stick, come out and fall on the red rug. Frightened, she fled and tried to ring the doorbell of her apartment but was too small to reach it. Just at that moment, her uncle returned home and, addressing her very affectionately, rang the doorbell for her. Many years later, she recalled with a sense of humiliation the details of the episode: the sensation experienced when the feces slid out of her underpants and the shame she felt when she met her uncle and thought, "Oh, if he knew what I've done and how I left his home!" Another unforgettable incident occurred when she was 6. She had beautiful brown curls; her mother explained to her that the hairdresser was going to trim them a little so they could grow better. But it was a trick. Before she could protest, her curls were completely cut off. As an adult she still remembered the rage she had felt toward her mother and the desperate feeling that something irreparable had happened to her. She had felt the same anger when her mother had given her enemas. She also recalled that when she was 8, she caused much laughter among her family when she disdainfully responded to someone's request of her father for a penknife, "What would Papa be doing with a penknife! He never carries men's things on him."

Before analyzing these memories, it should be pointed out that for a young girl, excrement can have the significance of excrement or a penis. Ana's first memory, that of having dirtied her uncle's home, would thus represent the disguised expression of a phantasy in which she has stolen her father's penis (represented by her uncle) in order to have a sexual relationship with her mother (whose genital organ is represented by her uncle's foyer with the red rug). She remembers her guilt feelings for having committed an aggressive act—a robbery—against her uncle and a dirty sexual act with her aunt. In the second memory she expresses her reproaches toward her mother for having forcibly taken away the excrement and the penis (the brown curls). This same situation is relived during the application of the enemas.

The first fragment of Ana's history reveals her phantasies of being emptied by her mother and deprived of feces, the paternal penis, and children, which she believed she had stolen from her mother; these phantasies were the result of her oral hatred toward her mother, her own desire to empty her mother, and her fear of the corresponding punishment. Through her scornful words, indicating that her father was not virile, Ana expressed her reproach for his not knowing how to defend her against her mother, indicating that as a result of this and of her own hostility she considered him to be a castrated being. In fact, her father was a generous but weak and masochistic man, dominated by his wife, who controlled the family. When Ana was an adolescent, her father fell ill with diarrhea, which became the basis for multiple phobic symptoms; he could not even go to the barber shop or the theatre or travel in certain vehicles for fear that he would have an uncontrollable desire to defecate. He was the youngest of three siblings, the only one who was not university-educated. Because he had no male child, he always hoped that his daughter would become a professional. Therefore, for Ana to pursue her studies signified also to acquire a penis. Her father's phobias had not affected her until she enrolled at the university. On one occasion during her freshman year, she was seated in the last row of the classroom listening to the most feared professor in the course, who had a reputation for being a staunch opponent of female students. Unexpectedly, Ana felt an intense anxiety and a need to defecate. She had to get up and leave the classroom under the surprised gaze of the professor and the other students. From that moment on, she, just like her father, suffered from diarrhea, which occurred every time she was about to learn something she wanted to know about but simultaneously feared. For example, she would react in this way when she met a desirable man or was about to meet with important people or authorities of one sort or another.

The content of this symptom can be interpreted in the following way: In her phantasy Ana had stolen her father's penis. When she found herself before a man whom she considered to be strong and capable of conquering her mother, the same desire to steal from him emerged. She needed a penis in order to be able to get close to her father, to defend herself from her mother, or to be a male (now that she believed she could not be a woman); but most importantly, she needed a penis in order to unite herself with her mother, whom she simultaneously loved and hated. Because of her wish to steal the penis—to castrate men with whom she came into contact—she feared retaliation. She felt guilty, and wishing to win their benevolence, she repentantly expelled what she had stolen in the form of feces. To obtain a university degree without being a male or to conquer an interesting man meant, then, to steal the penis from the professor or the lover. Projecting her aggression onto the object, she became anxious and defecated. Not only did the defecation represent the reparative act of returning that which was stolen, but it also had a vengeful quality because Ana returned the stolen object in a devalued form. It was no longer the hard excrement in the form of a walking stick from her infantile memory but a destroyed and diarrheic excrement. Moreover, Ana's psychological disorder expressed her identification through guilt with her castrated and diarrheic father.

Ana always wished to have children, a desire she shared with her mother. But she also doubted her fertility. In fact, she was infertile when she first married. Afterward, she became pregnant but miscarried in the second month. The miscarriage was initiated by a violent diarrhea. In the sixth month of her second pregnancy, she found herself in the difficult situation of having to look forward to a separation from her future child, leaving it in her mother's care for a year. Consciously, she was in agreement with her family that the separation was the best solution. But a short time after making the decision, uterine contractions and diarrhea began, which, in spite of all medical intervention, led to a premature labor and the death of her infant. Some months later, she became pregnant again. Since the same situation prevailed, she wanted to have an abortion. Her mother insisted that she continue with the pregnancy. Ana had the thought, "After all, it's not so important. In any case, I am going to miscarry again." She did miscarry in the fourth month. She was only able to carry a pregnancy to term when the external situation fundamentally changed and she lived alone with her husband, independent of her parents and in a position that permitted her to experience her future child not as something stolen from her mother but acquired through sacrifices and her own effort.

The mechanism of habitual miscarriages was the same as that of diarrhea. Ana's infantile reproach that her mother emptied her body of its contents—of the penis, the excrement, and the children—stemmed in part from her mother's aggressive attitude toward her and in part from the projection of her own desire to do the same to her mother. This was the reason the fetus came to symbolize both the stolen child and her mother. When her mother advised her to leave her infant with her, Ana interpreted this suggestion as though she were reclaiming her stolen child. She became anxious and immediately returned the stolen goods. Simultaneously, she avenged herself upon her mother, giving back children destroyed through miscarriage.

Before going further with our theme, a summary of what has been said so far is in order. We saw that the pregnant woman needs help and protection because she suffers a partial regression. Her state awakens early anxieties, especially those linked to her relationship with her mother. She often fears her mother because she experiences the child as something stolen from her. In other cases the opposite behavior prevails, one in which the pregnant woman is tied closely and submissively to her mother. This is another way to elaborate the same problem. The favorable and adverse tendencies of pregnancy enter into conflict and are manifested in both the psychological and somatic domains, provoking typical anxieties and disorders. The most frequently encountered disorders are of an oral or anal type. Vomiting and food binges signify an unconscious and irrational attempt to miscarry through oral means and the defense against this desire. In diarrhea and constipation, the intent to miscarry and the defense are developed in the anal domain and are more serious for the continuation of the pregnancy. In actual miscarriage, the unconscious hostile tendencies toward the fetus are so strong that they are victorious and effectively impact on the relevant organs to terminate the pregnancy.

The difficult pregnancy is, then, an indication of the existence of conflicts. But the absence of problems in and of itself is no proof of a pleasurable and free acceptance of the pregnancy. I remind the reader about what was said with respect to the woman's attitude toward menstruation. The normal woman does not suffer because of her menstrual period, nor does she feel inferior because of her condition. However, the woman who becomes masculinized for fear of her femininity often does not resent menstruation either, owing to the fact that she can ignore it and accept it because it calms her anxieties and doubts. I analyzed the serious conflicts that pregnancy awakened in Erica, leading to a premature labor and threatening the loss of her infant. However, apart from the constipation, this was a very easy pregnancy. Erica did not feel restricted whatsoever in her activities, and physically she began to pay attention to her state only when she was almost at the end of her pregnancy. That is to say, basically Erica was very anxious about her pregnancy, which she tried to deny by displacing her fears and doubts onto apparently erotic and romantic problems. The rapidity of her labor, which might seem to be an ideal development of a complicated physiological process, was the consequence of a neurotic condition.[*]

But even while there exists no pregnancy exempt from anxiety and conflict precisely because of the great change and achievement it implies, normally it is accompanied by an intense feeling of joy. The pregnant woman feels serene and calm, identified with her maternal ideal and with her child, whom she protects. In this state, she experiences the most intimate union that can exist between two people. For the first time since the moment she was born, she is not alone.[3] It is difficult to translate into words this sensation of giving and

---

[*]It is important to note that current perspectives tend to attach as much importance to the biochemical changes occurring in a pregnant woman's body as to unconscious anxiety or conflict as causes of the symptoms Langer describes. For feminist concerns about overemphasizing the psychogenic source of physical symptoms in pregnancy, such as vomiting and diarrhea, see J. Lenname and J. Lenname, "Alleged Psychogenic Disorders in Women: A Possible Manifestation of Sexual Prejudice" in E. Whitelegg, M. Arnot, E. Bartels, V. Beechey, L. Birke, S. Himmelwert, D. Leonard, S. Ruehl, & M. A. Speakman, *The Changing Experience of Women* (London: Basil Blackwell, 1984). For contemporary psychoanalytic analyses of the unconscious meaning of pregnancy for the expectant mother that are similar to Langer's perspective, see J. O. Zuckerberg, "Psychological and Physical Warning Signals regarding Pregnancy," in *Psychological Aspects of Pregnancy, Birthing and Bonding*, ed. B. Blum (New York: Human Sciences Press, 1980) and J. Raphael-Leff, *The Psychological Processes of Childbearing* (New York: Routledge, 1991).

receiving protection and love, so we turn to poets who have been capable of expressing what they felt. Cecile Sauvage addresses the child she is expecting in the following way:

> Tu m'appartiens ainsi que l'aurore à la plaine
> autour de toi ma vie est une chaude laine
> Ou tes membres frileus poussent dans le secret.
> (As the dawn belongs to the prairie, you belong to me
> Around you my life is like warm wool
> Where your delicate limbs secretly grow.)
> [Cited in de Beauvoir, 1953, p. 503]

In a letter to her husband, she describes the sensations awakened by the pregnancy: "Je n'ai jamais été si près de la vie. Je n'ai jamais si bien senti que je suis soeur de la terre avec les végétations et les sèves. Mes pieds marchent sur la terre comme sur une bête vivante." ("Never have I been so close to life. Never have I felt so much that I am sister to the earth, with her vegetation and sap. My feet walk upon the ground as upon a living beast.")

It is interesting that when speaking of her pregnancy the French novelist Colette describes the same intimacy with the earth, a maternal symbol. She says, "J'étais reprise, comme dans mon enfance, par le besoin de dormir sur la terre, sur l'herbe, sur la terre échauffée. Unique 'envie', saine envie." ("I was compelled, as in my childhood, by the need to sleep on the ground, on the grass, on the overheated ground. The only 'craving', such a healthy craving.") When Colette speaks of her pregnancy, she does so in these words: "Sixième, septième mois . . . . Premières fraises, premières roses. Puis-je appeler ma grossesse autrement, qu'une longue fête On oublie les affres du terme, on n'oublie pas une longue fête unique: je n'en ai rien oublié." ("Sixth, seventh month . . . . The first strawberries, the first roses. Can I call my pregnancy anything but an endless celebration? One forgets the fears of the end, but one does not forget the long unique celebration; I have forgotten nothing.") [Cited in de Beauvoir, 1953, pp. 501–502].

*   *   *

But what about childbirth, the termination of pregnancy? For women in our society, does it have to be so difficult and the pain so unbearable without anesthesia? Each culture considers the birth experience in a different light—on the one hand, as something dangerous and painful or, on the other, as something interesting, satisfying, and important, accompanied by certain risks. In *Male and Female*, Margaret Mead maintains that these differences have little to do with the pregnant woman's real degree of danger or safety (as in our society, for example, where, statistically, the dangers of childbirth are minimal). As Mead asserts:

> That childbirth is considered to be a situation in which the woman risks her life or in which she acquires a child or a new social status or rights to heaven has nothing to do with maternal mortality rates but is related to the attitude toward childbirth. The argument that the biological basis of the process of childbirth influences woman's instinctual behavior much more than the attitude and experiences in her environment is contradicted by the great variety of concepts about childbirth. It cannot be argued simultaneously that to give birth involves intolerable pain and pain that is tolerable; that it is a situation woman naturally fears with all her soul and a situation woman approaches naturally ready and joyful; that it is a danger which has to be avoided and a fulfillment intensely desired. It has to be acknowledged that a part of these attitudes is acquired; and taking into account our current knowledge, it seems more justified to assume that both sexes' attitudes toward childbirth contain complex and contradictory elements and that each society takes as a model one or the other view, which sometimes even contains a series of mutually opposing attitudes.

What is our society's attitude toward childbirth? One dominant current, which has been questioned only lately, considers labor to be a terribly painful process and the mission of the obstetrician one of avoiding the pain at almost any cost if he does not want to risk being considered inhumane. We expect the pregnant woman to calmly and confidently enter a maternity clinic when she feels the first contractions and to relinquish all responsibility and activity to her obstetrician, who has promised her that she will not suffer at all. In more "progressive" environments, the situation is further exaggerated: The obstetrician determines when the birth should take place, choosing a date based on mutual convenience. He reserves a place for the woman at the clinic on a predetermined date and then induces labor. Induced labor evolves in this way: First an enema is administered to the patient, after which a series of injections stimulate the beginning of labor. Then the woman is anesthetized. Some hours later, she awakens slightly confused, indifferent, and in pain and is presented her unknown child, well washed and dressed in its fancy clothing.[4]

This procedure is rationalized in terms of the protection it provides the woman from the pain and danger of labor. The unconscious aspect of this development in modern obstetrics seems to be the robbery in every possible way of the woman's conscious and active participation in the unique experience of giving birth to a new being and the conversion of this process into something totally directed by the obstetrician. When Helene Deutsch discusses this phenomenon, she offers an interesting interpretation: She mentions the man's infantile and repressed desires to give birth. She defines modern obstetrics as a masterful piece of masculine efficiency that robs the woman of her active participation in labor and thus, on an unconscious level, also of her monopoly in this field. Deutsch suspects that in this way, without realizing the connection, man induces woman, in turn, to increasingly penetrate the fields of activity that he claims are genuinely masculine, thereby contributing to the progressive decline in the psychosexual and social differences between human beings.

The new obstetrics would, then, have a psychological kinship with the *couvade* or certain initiation rites of the young that are practiced in many primitive tribes. These rites and customs represent the males' expression of their envy of woman for her capacity to create new human beings and an attempt to substitute for her in this function. But why does the woman complacently submit herself to this goal? The woman who apprehensively approaches childbirth unconsciously fears her irate and retaliatory mother. More superficially, the physician who does everything is her father who protects her against her mother's rage. But on a deeper level, to surrender without consciousness to the physician's hands signifies an infantile submission to the bad mother and an attempt to win her benevolence by demonstrating weakness and lack of aggression. Women leave even the decision of the date they will give birth to the physician and allow him to induce labor with an enema. This is because unconsciously the child is equated with feces, and such women are like the young girl who obediently gives her intestinal contents how and when the mother demands. However, lengthy conversations with patients who are grateful to modern obstetricians reveal their rebellion against such treatment. Lina's physician had decided on a specific day and hour for her hospitalization with the aim of inducing labor some 10 days before the estimated due date. The night before the hospital appointment he communicated to Lina through his nurse that he was very busy with a seriously ill patient and thus would not be able to induce labor at 8:00 A.M. the following day as planned. Very indignant, the young woman went to sleep, only to awaken at 5:00 A.M. in the morning with labor pains that rapidly intensified. She had to be hospitalized at exactly 8:00 A.M., thus obliging the physician to be present at the birth at precisely the hour he had previously set but had later postponed because of its inconvenience to him.

I believe there is yet another cause of the "mechanization" of childbirth. This transformation of a biological process with tremendous individual psychological significance into an operation is rooted in the anti-instinctual attitude so characteristic of our era. Its parallel exists in the new regimens that recommend vitamin pills in place of vegetables or that regularize the hours of sleep and wakefulness with drugs. Now the newborn has to adapt to this tendency when after awaking from the drowsiness often provoked by its mother's general anesthesia it is offered the bottle instead of the breast. The latest scientific innovation in this regard, although undoubtedly necessary in some cases, has already acquired a grotesque character: artificial insemination of the woman in place of normal and pleasurable impregnation.

Our contemporary society betrays, then, a mechanistic and antipsychological attitude toward childbirth. However, the opposite attitude which emphasizes the extent to which certain psychological processes influence the normal or apparently normal course of childbirth, also exists.

In *Anxiety in Pregnancy and Childbirth* to which I have already referred, Henriette Klein, Howard Potter and Ruth Dyk analyzed the most frequently occurring disorders and anxieties of pregnancy and childbirth. They studied a group of 27 women, pregnant for the first time, who lived in extraordinarily difficult economic and social circumstances aggravated by the war and lack of housing. The research was carried out through extensive conversations held sporadically during and after the pregnancy and delivery. The hospital personnel were appropriately trained and collaborated in the research by observing the attitudes and vicissitudes of the patients during and following labor. The authors published all of the clinical material, which reveals the extent to which woman's psychological structure and attitude toward pregnancy affects the development of both the pregnancy and the delivery. However, due to the method through which the data were obtained, the study adequately captures the women's conscious attitude but is weak with respect to their unconscious feelings. This limitation is particularly important with respect to all that relates to woman's acceptance or rejection of pregnancy.

Before reproducing the authors' findings, I will clarify their use of certain terms. The expressions "good work of childbirth" and "an easy labor" are used if the delivery was relatively rapid, if the uterine contractions were regular in intensity and time, if the child was born without presenting serious obstetrical difficulties, and if the physical condition of mother and child was satisfactory. The authors consider the mother's "psychological reaction" during labor "good" if her emotional tension and anxiety were not excessive, if the patient did not complain exorbitantly, and if she cooperated effectively and utilized her contractions well. They speak of a "bad work of childbirth" when it did not evolve normally, and a "poor psychological reaction" when the mother's attitude during labor was difficult for those who assisted her. In addition, the authors use the terms "positive" or "negative" ambivalent attitude to refer to whether the woman's ambivalent attitude toward her state was dominated by acceptance or rejection.

The study's results are what we might have expected. The average emotionally stable or mature woman had a relatively easy labor, though it is unclear whether or not these women were among those who consciously accepted motherhood. Interestingly enough, the two women who totally rejected their pregnancies until the end had an easy labor, a fact I shall address below.

The mothers who were freer of psychological or psychosomatic disorders during pregnancy were those who belong to the group of "stable women," that is to say, those who were psychologically mature. Others in the same group had certain difficulties, the causes of which would undoubtedly be uncovered in a detailed investigation. For example, one patient is included among the mature women desirous of having a child, but she had a difficult labor and gave birth to a dead infant. This is not surprising given the fact that her mother had died in labor and that she herself was a single woman who had her first sexual relationship at the age of 36, the immediate result of which had been this pregnancy. Difficulties abound in the group of "unstable" women. The two patients who rejected their pregnancies from beginning to end belong to this group. They had difficult pregnancies but easy deliveries. Possibly through the rapidity and ease of labor they expressed their rejection of their child and their desire not to be pregnant, a mechanism already observed in the case of Erica.

Let us look at the problem of normalcy proposed by this study. In designating the aforementioned patient as a mature personality, in other words, well adapted to reality, the authors do not use this term in the customary way. The patient became pregnant outside the bonds of marriage by a man she hardly knew who then abandoned her, leaving her emotionally and economically helpless. Moreover, the patient was very anxious toward the end of her pregnancy, convinced that she was going to die in labor. When she learned she had given birth to a dead infant, she compulsively reproached herself for being responsible for the child's death because she had not taken care of herself during her pregnancy. This outcome and her reaction are indications of neurotic problems, undoubtedly in relation to her mother's death. However, the authors classified the patients correctly. They themselves state that the women came from very poor and unstable homes and that, owing in part to the war, the vast majority were living in extraordinarily precarious conditions. In other words, given this information about their patients, the authors included as "stable" those who reacted on the whole positively toward motherhood and its multiple internal and external difficulties. It is necessary to judge the terms "pregnancy" and "easy labor" in the same manner. Among the women who had "easy" pregnancies, many vomited, almost all experienced nausea, and, as their due dates approached, many suffered from nightmares, swollen ankles, and so forth. All feared for their own health and that of their child. The deliveries were "easy" if they did not exceed many hours and the women appeared to be "well disposed" by not complaining too much. Analgesics were given to all the women. Obviously, the pregnancies and labors were "normal" in relation to the authors' experience in general and especially to what was observed in these 27 patients. But if we take into account those pregnancies practically exempt from difficulties as well as deliveries free of pain—though until recently an exception in our society—we confirm that the concept of normalcy expounded in this study is relative and dependent on multiple complex factors.

The authors found that the combination of unfavorable economic factors and an unhappy marital life always acted counter to the positive urges toward motherhood. Generally, women who desired a child were emotionally mature and of a stable psychological structure while unstable individuals manifested an ambivalent attitude toward pregnancy or they totally rejected it. In cases where the mother, sisters, or friends described pregnancy and labor as happy and satisfying experiences, the woman expected the same for herself, which often, in fact, occurred. Finally, in all the women, fears and anxieties related to both pregnancy and labor were found. The anxiety was centered on the fetus or on the woman herself, often being displaced from one to the other.

We have already seen that the anxiety at the beginning of the pregnancy is based on guilt feelings for having stolen the child from the mother and on the fear of her retaliation. These feelings are reinforced by the persistence in the unconscious of the phantasy of forbidding the mother to become pregnant because of one's envy of her creative capacity and of having hated her if she succeeded. So it becomes dangerous to take her place and expose oneself to her hatred. Moreover, when the girl is transformed into the mother, the fetus takes on her role and becomes dangerous because it acquires her own voraciousness and her instinctual "monstrous" demands. All these psychological situations persist during the pregnancy, but mother and fetus arrive at a positive adaptation so long as it proceeds and the union is intensified. The woman who, because of her fears and the experience of the failure of her childhood maternal phantasies, doubted at the beginning of her pregnancy that she would ever be able to have a child begins to experience it not as a possibility in the far-off future but as a reality, now that she feels the movements of the fetus. Many women maintain that they have never felt so happy and serene as during the second phase of their pregnancy.

But this peace becomes disturbed when the pregnancy is nearing its end. Certainly, the part of the feminine personality most mature and adapted to reality wishes her child to arrive soon. The mother-to-be will begin to hurry the preparations, to enjoy the fact that her child will soon be changed from something that she does not know into something she can really feel, from a phantasy to an individual with a tangible reality. But there is always a part of her that flees childbirth. This fear of childbirth seems not to have diminished at all in spite of the developments in modern obstetrics that first reduced the physical danger of labor to a minimum and is now eliminating the much feared pain of the experience. The anxiety about childbirth has much more unconscious roots. It is at this moment that all the irrational fears that accompanied especially the first weeks of the pregnancy return because the woman feels she is facing a final examination. Only now, when she has given birth to what she created and carried inside, will she know if her insides were intact, if her mother has not punished her, or if she, due to her badness, did not hurt her child. This is the negative aspect of the fears. But the joy of the second half of the pregnancy now also becomes an important source of anxiety and an obstacle to the birth. According to Helene Deutsch, labor is the most exact revival that we can experience of our own birth trauma. Identified with her child, the woman experiences through it all the fear of separation from her own mother. She identifies with its helplessness and feels that she cannot continue to protect it against life. She feels that it loses its mother and she experiences the labor as the loss of it. This fear of separation is the most profound anxiety of labor and should be taken into account if we wish to achieve easy deliveries. Later, we shall see how this goal is possible and why it is so important.

But first, I will illustrate with two dreams how a woman near the end of her pregnancy experiences the approaching labor. On the night after discovering that the child's head was dropping, Isabel had a dream from which she awoke in anguish: She sees her small daughter as if she had already been born, sleeping calmly in the cradle. Her husband shakes the cradle and she angrily protests. She does not want her baby bothered. Afterward, she is bathing the infant. She sees her at the bottom of the bathtub, underneath the water, with a radiantly smiling face. Isabel thinks, "She seems very happy, but I'll have to take her out because otherwise she could drown." And she removes her from the water, slapping her on the back so she can spit out the water and breathe. The baby is fine but begins to become smaller. Isabel is very anxious. She thinks the little shirts she has made for her will now be too big. The small infant becomes even smaller, soon disappearing completely.

Isabel awakened in a desperate state. The interpretation of the dream is fairly easy: Isabel is depressed because she is going to lose her little girl. In giving birth she will have to separate from her daughter and, identifying with her, she fears exposing her to a childhood as unhappy as her own. The small child who calmly sleeps in her cradle is the fetus and Isabel herself, happy inside of her mother. Her husband who shakes the cradle is the father who interposes himself between mother and daughter, unable to further tolerate their relationship from which he feels excluded. The image of the little girl under the water, happy and smiling, is the representation that Isabel has of the fetal state and reminds us of children's stories that depict the prenatal state as one in which children live happily in the waters of a pond. But Isabel knows that she can no longer prolong the happy experience of the pregnancy without exposing her future child to danger. In spite of her fears, she knows that she should take the infant out of the water, she should give birth. When she removes her, the child rapidly becomes smaller and the shirts, lovingly sewn by Isabel as a symbol of her protective love for her daughter, are no longer of any value. She continues getting smaller, soon to disappear. In this way Isabel expresses her fear of losing her daughter, losing her to life—she will grow, she will grow and now she will not be able to protect her—or losing her to death, if she does not survive the separation of the labor. In any case, her ecstatic union with the child will have ended. Isabel's conflictual relationship to labor was expressed in a prolongation of the pregnancy for more than three weeks beyond her due date.[*]

---

[*]J. Raphael-Leff, in *The Psychological Processes of Childbearing* (New York: Routledge, 1991) explores the unconscious meaning of the experience of pregnancy and elaborates the phantasies of the pregnant woman toward the fetus, which the author suggests functions as a transitional object. With respect to this idea, Mirta Videla, Argentine psychologist who treats infertile couples and author of *Maternidad: Realidad y Mitos* (prologo: Marie Langer; Buenos Aires: A. Pena Lillo, 1974), reports that during the Argentine military dictatorship's "Dirty War", some female political prisoners who were pregnant during captivity managed to maintain emotional stability in the face of horrendous conditions because they were able to utilize the child in their wombs as a transitional object; they maintained sanity by means of communicating and sharing everything with the fetus; they had the strength to remain calm because they felt they must provide a holding environment for the fetus; and they felt accompanied in their pain rather than abandoned to go it alone with their torturers. Some suffered psychotic breaks or profound depressive episodes after they gave birth and their babies were taken from them. In another instance, during the Malvinas War, there was a rise in infertility and delayed labors, as if, according to Videla, women did not want to bring children

Another dream of separation and the end of a pregnancy will show an even more intense identification of the mother with the fetus. Several days before giving birth, Ana had a dream in which it was as if she were a girl again: She finds herself in the vestibule of her childhood home. It is nighttime, so the front door is closed and locked. Someone calls. Without undoing the lock, Ana opens the door slightly. Terrified, she sees a witch outside who puts her claw-like hand in through the crack to forcibly yank her from the house. She wakes up screaming.

Here the woman feels like a young girl in her childhood home or like a fetus inside her mother. She would like to stay, but the witch comes to remove her, signifying that she reproaches her mother for having given birth to her, for having separated them. Simultaneously, she is now going to be the mother-witch and will have to forcibly throw out the infant she carries inside her.

The anxiety of labor is, then, the revival of the oldest and most archaic anxiety we know, that of the separation from the mother. However, although it is such a primitive anxiety, it can be managed with a degree of ease. This fact is important if we want to understand what "normal labor" might be, in order to avoid numerous anxieties and difficulties. Many pharmacologists, anesthesiologists, and gynecologists enthusiastically attempt to acquire the best means by which they can prevent the pain of labor. However, the methods they have perfected always involve a certain danger, especially for the child. In his study "Prevention of Fetal Anoxia," Nicholson J. Eastman maintains that the most frequent cause of fetal death during labor or of newborns or young infants several days old is the application of anesthesias during labor that reduce the amount of oxygen in the mother's blood. This condition may occur if the anesthesia is given for more than 3 minutes or as a result of the application of a spinal or a block anesthesia. The danger is greater for premature infants. With the practice of inducing labor, which eliminates spontaneous labor in favor of an arbitrarily established delivery date, an error in the calculation of the duration of the pregnancy considerably increases the number of premature births. Induced labor almost always takes place with anesthesia. Offering another gynecological opinion regarding anesthesia in "Fetal Anoxia at Birth and Cyanosis of the Newborn," Stewart H. Clifford indicates that anoxia is the cause of 60% of newborn mortality and represents a big factor in morbidity. Anoxia stems from damage to the respiratory centers due to traumatic injuries or anesthe-

---

into a world going up in the flames of war (interview with Marta Videla, Buenos Aires, August, 1990).

sia during labor. Before anesthesia was commonly used in labor, 90%–95% of newborns cried and breathed spontaneously. Now, a normal condition is found in only 75% of newborns. The difference in these two statistics is accounted for by the somatic damage to the infant due to the application of anesthesia to the mother.

There is also psychological damage. The mother who is not conscious at the moment her child is born, who cannot hear its first cry, is deprived of an extraordinarily gratifying experience. I have already analyzed the woman's fear of losing her child during childbirth. She does not really know her infant until this moment. She experiences it partly as something real, partly as a product of her phantasies. In order for her to be able to conquer her irrational fears and recuperate from the trauma of the separation from her child, it is important that she be able to confront these fears with the help of a positive and calming reality and that she be awake and conscious when the birth occurs. The depression that often follows labor is short-lived and much less intense in these women, and they bond more rapidly with their real child than women who were unconscious during labor owing to either a general anesthesia or hypnosis. Among the latter, a sensation of confusion, indifference, and disappointment toward the child is almost always observed. It is impossible to judge the degree to which this rejection in the first moment of its real existence can be perceived by the child or the degree to which the mother's future reaction toward the child might be impeded so as to have an enduring influence on the mother–child relationship.

In contrast to researchers who wish to avoid the perception of pain among women in labor by means of increasingly effective anesthesia, Grantly Dick-Read, whose research was at first ridiculed or ignored but who is currently reaching an ever-wider distribution and acceptance, attempted to deal with the problem from a different perspective. Dick-Read asked himself if pain is really inherent and inevitable in childbirth. Better said, it was not he who asked the basic question but, many years earlier, a woman in labor whom he attended. Hers was an easy delivery that occurred without complaints or complications. When Dick-Read offered her chloroform, she firmly refused it. Puzzled, after the delivery he inquired as to why she had refused the aid of the anesthesia designed to alleviate her suffering. She answered him simply, "It didn't hurt; there was no reason for it to hurt me, was there, Doctor?" Following that experience, Dick-Read attempted to ascertain whether or not labor actually had to be painful. He studied the problem from every angle, observed his patients to discover when and under what circumstances they began to suffer during labor, and finally arrived at the conclusion that the aforementioned patient had been correct—it did not have to hurt. However, it generally did. But due to what? According to Dick-Read, the woman enters the experience expecting it to be painful because during her entire childhood she has been inculcated with the idea that labor is something extraordinarily painful and full of danger. The exposure to such an attitude creates a kind of conditioned reflex between the perception of the beginning of the work of the delivery and the appearance of the pain. But what would be the physiological basis of such a reflex? There are various muscles that govern the movements of the uterus. Some, with their spontaneous and inevitable contractions, warn the woman that the birth process has begun, and they gradually expel the fetus. The second group protect the fetus as it leaves the uterus and must remain soft and relaxed during a normal birth process so as not to hinder the work of expulsion. When a woman who is giving birth to her first child perceives these completely new sensations stemming from the uterine contractions and she is in a psychologically unfavorable environment, she believes she feels in these first and necessary contractions a "pain," and then this imaginary "pain," of a purely subjective nature, stimulates fear. This, in turn, provokes muscular tension that then impedes the work of expulsion, causing true pain, prolonging the duration of labor, and making the use of anesthesia necessary. The moment the woman, anxious and feeling herself at the mercy of an unknown and painful process, loses psychic control over herself she also loses, although it seems paradoxical, control over the complex mechanism of labor, which involves involuntary musculature. One part of the musculature obstructs the work of the other part, and the birth process becomes extraordinarily painful and often dangerous to mother and child. Dick-Read cites various examples of detailed observations of how an exaggeratedly protective attitude toward the woman in labor—which actually amounts to suggesting the existence of pain to her—as well as indifference and the lack of protection, intensifies first her fear and later intense pain. On the other hand, if the woman is pushed to the limit of her psychological tolerance, the delivery itself can be inhibited.

Let us illustrate with Isabel's labor. We are already aware of her difficulties during pregnancy. However, when she felt the first contractions, Isabel went to the hospital in a good mental state. Indeed, at first everything went well, but at a certain point her physician, whom she completely trusted, had to leave her to attend to another delivery in a different clinic. The midwife paid no attention to Isabel, who was ultimately left alone. Then she began to feel unbearable pain and to become quite anxious, screaming and crying and finally losing control and exhausting herself. After many hours the midwife reappeared and found Isabel in a desperate state without any uterine contractions. The midwife's absence and the abandonment that Isabel suffered resulted in a labor that, in spite of its completely normal beginning, had to be reactivated with injections to stimulate contractions, which were followed by surgical intervention requiring anesthesia.

In *Sex and Temperament* Mead recalls that among the Tchambuli labor is considered to be a rather easy affair if it is carried out with regard to specific rules. Although he is in a room far away from his laboring wife, the husband has to await the birth of his child in a serious mood, accompanied by the witch doctor and his friends. The laboring woman is surrounded by women and set firmly between the knees of her paternal aunt. In the case described by Mead, the husband, an irresponsible youth, was not affected by the seriousness of the moment. Upon hearing the laughter of her husband and his friends, his wife, Tchubukeima, suddenly interrupted her rhythmic lament—an indication of the progress of the labor—and fell deeply asleep. Advised of this complication, the men became frightened and very serious. Tchubukeima awakened and the labor continued normally until once again she could hear the men's irresponsible laughter in the next room. At first, she intensified her screams, and when this did not yield results, she fell into a deep stupor again. This scene was repeated many times from the early morning on. By noon the men were scared. They sought out magic rituals to end the labor, but they were ineffective. Then the women came to the conclusion that Tchubukeima's house was bewitched and that she would give birth more easily in a house on the other side of the village, as far away as possible from her husband and his prejudicial laughter. So they moved her, and once again enclosed, Tchubukeima anchored herself between the knees of her father's sister. But now another complication developed: The women had also lost their patience. Her aunt happily chatted with the rest of the women. At intervals she turned to the furious kneeling girl and said, "Have your child already." Again Tchubukeima got angry and went to sleep. Only at two o'clock in the morning, when her husband, now genuinely worried, paid his *kina* to the representative of the satanic spirits, did Tchubukeima have her baby. This labor, which took place in an environment so different from our own, nonetheless appears quite similar to our deliveries. The Tchambuli woman, as well as the European or American woman, needs emotional support in order to have the valor to give birth, because each feels alone and anxious in this state. It does not matter whether the environmental support is expressed by the witch doctor or through the presence of an important childbirth specialist. The essential thing is that the woman not feel abandoned and misunderstood in her anxiety. Mead interprets the interruption of the young Tchambuli's labor as an aggression against her husband and her aunt and as an attempt to make herself important. However, the young woman was anxious and felt alone. Perhaps she did not dare to continue with the labor in those circumstances and had to interrupt it until she could arouse, by means of the interruption, enough concern to result in a collaboration with her, rather than have to face abandonment during her difficult state, in which she was at the mercy of terrifying internal objects.

But let us return to Dick-Read's theory. He maintains, then, that fear causes muscular tension, which causes pain by making the work of expelling the infant from the uterus difficult. He attempts to eliminate the fear by explaining to the woman about the process that takes place in her body during pregnancy and childbirth. Or, speaking in psychoanalytic terms, he attempts to oppose the psychological reality based on irrational anxieties and infantile sexual representations about conception, pregnancy, and childbirth with an external reality that is good, calming, and rational. The exponents of this reality are the physician and the midwife, who from the first moment help the woman in labor, giving her adequate instructions so that she knows how to collaborate during childbirth.

In the past 15 years the Pavlovian school of psychological preparation for childbirth has become enormously popular, not only in the Socialist countries but also in France, Argentina, and elsewhere. The theory of the Pavlovians is distinct from that of Dick-Read. For them, the pain of childbirth is an objective fact that can be inhibited by psychological means. They differ also in terms of their practice. They substitute, for example, the relaxation of the final phase of dilation with the woman's panting breathing. However, both methods have much in common. They use prior clarification of the physiological processes, whose utility, while relative, is already known to us through other topics in this book. They insist on the need to modify the pregnant woman's ideas, so typical in this society, that labor "should" hurt. During the pregnancy they teach exercises that will permit the woman to competently collaborate during labor, and prior to labor they establish through regular classes a firm connection between the woman and the person who will accompany her. Both schools have excellent results as long as their representatives do not convert the system into a new routine that no longer permits the woman to express her individual feelings and even the pain that accompanies her labor.

How can the results obtained through such simple methods be explained? I believe that the greatest part of their success is already shown in the new focus expressed by Dick-Read's patient when she asked, "There was no reason for it to hurt, isn't that true, Doctor?" According to the Bible, labor pains are the punishment woman must suffer for having committed original sin. In this way the Bible expresses something that is a psychic reality, as much for the religious woman as for the atheist: the phantasy that her child is the fruit of a sin and to give birth to it means that she deserves to be punished. The midwife who assists her, admitting the "inevitable" fact of pain while attempting to mitigate it through analgesics and anesthesia, represents in the laboring woman's unconscious an accomplice who helps her to escape the just punishment. The physician who maintains that labor pain does not correspond to nature's intentions but is, rather, a consequence of environmental deficits, absolves the woman from original sin. But how is this achieved? In the first place, the anxiety generally experienced during the birth process that unleashes the vicious circle of fear, tension, and pain stems from an identification with the mother through guilt feelings. It is as if the mother said to her daughter in labor, "You wanted to usurp my place and rob me of my children. Now you have succeeded, but you will suffer as I suffered giving birth to you or you will die as you wished me to die giving birth to your siblings." The physician who assists her, denying the necessity of the pain, represents the father allied with her in order to protect her and a good mother who counters the threats and the curses of the internal bad mother. The latter terrifies the laboring woman through cruel and infantile representations of labor. The contractions are experienced as an indication that something horrible is happening within her body. The physician's rational explanations are like the voice of the good mother who says to her anxious child, "Don't be afraid of this shadow! It isn't a ghost. It's nothing but a piece of clothing." Just as the mother who says this to her small child does not succeed in curing him of his fear of ghosts but in calming him for the moment, so too the physician's tranquilizing explanations can calm the woman, anxious because of the incomprehensible and untamable nature of the process developing within her. Finally, the physician gives her instructions that are extraordinarily useful and appropriate with regard to her collaboration in labor. These instructions, I should note, are not new but in times past used to be given by good midwives to their patients. They have been lost through the rush and impersonal tone of the modern operating room, with its injections, induced labor, anesthesia, and forceps. These instructions are useful for a variety of reasons. The woman who collaborates intelligently actually facilitates the delivery. Moreover, when she follows her physician's instructions and experiences the resulting relief and progress, she feels understood by him. To feel understood signifies to feel pardoned. Upon recovering her active stance, the woman overcomes the most profound anxiety of labor caused by the separation from her child, which she approaches through this apparently so inevitable and uncontrollable a process. When she perceives it in this way, she feels as undefended and unprotected as the child. She feels she is the victim of uncontrollable forces and pains, just as when she herself was a small child at the mercy of her terrifying internal objects. Identified with her child, she sees herself flung into a cold and indifferent world. When she follows her physician's instructions and changes the labor into work that, while difficult, is within her capabilities, she recovers confidence in herself, breaks the identification with the undefended child, and becomes an active and effective mother who no longer fears the separation from her child. She feels she will know how to protect it afterward as she protects it in this moment, saving it from a difficult birth. By dominating the experience she gives herself the means to more easily overcome the trauma of the separation from her child and to carry out with all her power, but without fear and punishment—that is to say, without pain—the mysterious process of labor. Indeed, the procedure fails in very neurotic women, the so-called "nervous women," in whom the image of the bad mother is too deeply rooted to be modified, even temporarily, by favorable external influences. On the other hand, the mother's intense fear can be the stimulus that provokes a very rapid and thus almost painless labor, as we saw in Erica's case.[*]

This discussion leads us to the following conclusions: Pregnancy and labor are accompanied by discomfort, anxiety, and pain due to psychogenic factors. If we successfully educate healthy daughters, who have a minimum of anxiety and guilt feelings and can pleasurably

---

[*]The concerns Langer expressed about the technological approach to childbirth were the same that became the cornerstone of the alternative birth movements in the U.S. from the 1970s on. For an overview of the issues raised by Langer in this chapter as they apply to the United States, including conditions that produced the natural childbirth movement, see D. Kliot, "Emotional Aspects of Pregnancy and Childbirth," in *Critical Psychophysical Passages in the Life of a Woman*, ed. J. Offerman-Zuckerberg (New York: Plenum, 1988). For a contemporary feminist critique of antifemale biases in the medical profession as expressed in attitudes toward pregnant women, see H. Graham and A. Oakley, "Competing Ideologies of Reproduction: Medical and Maternal Perspectives on Pregnancy," in E. Whitelegg, M. Arnot, E. Bartels, V. Beechey, L. Birke, S. Himmelwert, D. Leonard, S. Ruehl, & M. A. Speakman, *The Changing Experience of Women* (London: Basil Blackwell, 1984).

accept their femininity, we can expect that pregnancy and labor will be once again what they still are in some societies or for some lucky women in our society: the maximum achievement of their biological capacities, accompanied by the complete awareness of participating in the greatest experience possible: creating and nurturing a new being within oneself and bringing it into the world.

Psychological Problems of Breast-Feeding [1]

Among female reproductive functions, breast-feeding plays such a secondary role that many women refrain from it. In the well-known work by Beaumarchais, Figaro says resentfully that the only inconvenience in life to which powerful men are submitted is being born. If one were to paraphrase certain aristocratic women, an identical comment could be made to the effect that the only irksome thing to which they are submitted is giving birth to their children and abandoning them to be raised by women they do not know. For a long time it was considered uncouth to raise one's own children, and even at the beginning of the century in many European countries it was considered good taste to hire a wet nurse, with the assumption that in this way the infant would be dutifully taken care of and the mother's health would be assured. However, the mother suffered the indirect injury of losing the affective bond that caregiving would have established between her and her child. In the unconscious mind of the child raised by a hired wet nurse, two distinct objects are easily established: the good mother of his infancy—the wet nurse—contrasted to the bad and frustrating woman—his biological mother.

But in the present period artificial feeding [bottle-feeding] is commonly used in all social classes. Among the 27 women of the poll that served as the basis for the book *Anxiety in Pregnancy and Childbirth* [H. Klein, Potter, & Dyk], none nursed her child for more than 3 months. Thanks to our technical progress, this hardly damages the infant physically. If, however, artificial feeding is so frequently preferred to maternal milk, there must exist psychological motives as well as social influences. The social reasons are obvious: The woman who works outside the home often cannot dedicate the necessary time to her child to take care of her over a period of months and thus stops nursing if she cannot or does not wish to give up her career. At first glance, the economic and social problem of the mother who works seems insoluble. But if modern legislators paid as much attention and attributed as much importance to woman's biological needs as to her participation in the wage-labor force during periods of emergency or prosperity, they could resolve this issue. Several of the more progressive governments in the world have now alleviated the problem through social legislation. For example, solutions that are readily available for the working mother include the installation of a nursery in the factory or a subsidy provided to a working mother by the government so that she may stay at home during the period of time she wishes to nurse her infant.

Apart from the social factors inhibiting such solutions, which are beyond the scope of the present study, others, psychological in nature, are no less important. I have already spoken of the tendency, inherent in our mechanistic era, to desexualize female reproductive functions or convert them from an instinctual and spontaneous process into something mechanized and controlled. Painless defloration by the gynecologist; induced labor that takes place under anesthesia; and the elimination of breast milk, through medication, and its substitution by artificial feeding of the infant are all manifestations of this tendency.

We know the psychological consequences of artificial feeding through numerous psychoanalyses. But analysis is not necessary to prove the lack of oral satisfaction in an experience that frustrates the child's first desires. It is surely not mere coincidence that in the United States, where artificial feeding is more widely used than in other countries, there has emerged the custom of chewing gum to satisfy frustrated oral desires, as well as the preoccupation with the burning question of drug addiction.* The mother, as well as the infant, is damaged by giving up the experience of breast-feeding. We are used to unilaterally interpreting the trauma of birth, judging all of its effects

---

*Langer came to disagree with the implication here that bottle-feeding necessarily had deleterious effects on the infant and that habits such as gum chewing and drug addiction could be traced to the practice of bottle-feeding. She felt that such assertions represented a glib misuse of psychoanalytic theorizing. She also rejected the idea that the mother's relationship to the infant would be impaired by bottle-feeding instead of nursing. Basically, she came to believe that such views functioned as harsh superego demands that pressured women to adhere to narrow definitions of femininity that were too rigid and guilt-inducing.

on the child, but, as we saw in the last chapter, the mother also suffers the trauma.

Helene Deutsch sees in labor an opportunity for the woman to elaborate her own birth trauma. She finds that there is a close relationship between the work of labor and nursing, pointing out that the baby's sucking stimulates the final contractions of the uterus. Thus, with the beginning of nursing the dynamic function of the uterus ends and it cedes its supremacy to the breasts. But Deutsch believes that besides helping the mother to overcome the trauma caused by the sudden separation from her child, nursing also serves the child by mitigating the effect of her own birth trauma. Nursing also reestablishes the infant's intimate connection to her mother, who weans her gradually, in contrast to the rapid separation represented by the birth experience. The analyses of adults who were not nursed or who underwent an abrupt weaning experience often reveal that the birth trauma later acquired an excessive importance for them. The absence of nursing, which involves an intimate relationship with the mother, can later in adult life bring about disturbances in relation to women. With characteristic artistic intuition, George Santayana poses this problem in *The Last Puritan*. I cite the passage that so clearly expresses this idea, which begins with Mario, a happy and optimistic young man, asking Oliver, the temperate protagonist of the novel:

"Tell me something, Oliver, were you raised with a bottle or a wet nurse?" Oliver began to laugh at the idea of a wet nurse. . . . Wet nurses did not exist in the United States. Naturally, he had been given the bottle. "That's what I thought," exclaimed Mario triumphantly. "You don't know what a woman is. You're not comfortable with them. And all because you never loved your mother, and she never loved you. There's a world of difference. My own mother raised me. . ."

We have here a conversation between men. But we have seen throughout this book that the young girl's first experiences with her mother are of fundamental importance for the rest of her life and especially for her future capacity to love and give of herself in a relationship.

It is also the case that there is a direct relationship between the love of life and the first oral experiences. We saw that among the Arapesh, who highly esteem a happy childhood and generously feed children how and when they wish, suicide is unknown; and among the inhabitants of the Marquesas islands, whose women feed their children sparingly and without significant demonstration of affect, suicide is extraordinarily frequent. The Mundugumor people demonstrate to us something that we have already discussed: the importance to the child not of nursing in and of itself but of the manner in which she is fed and the amount of love she receives. Although among the Mundugumor the women nurse their children, they treat them with such a rejecting attitude that as adults they, in turn, reject their own children. Among the Mundugumor suicide is very frequent and love is almost unknown. Sexuality is reduced to a struggle between the sexes just as nursing is reduced to a struggle between an ill-humored mother who attempts to nurse for the least amount of time possible—precisely long enough to stop the baby's crying—and an infant who latches onto the breast with rage and avidity, swallowing hurriedly as he tries to get a maximum of milk in a minimum of time. In *Male and Female* Margaret Mead describes the consequences of these early experiences of the Mundugumor people in the following way:

> In their adult life, making love is the first 'round' of a "catch-as-catch-can" fight, and biting and scratching form the most important part of the foreplay. When the Mundugumor capture an enemy, they devour him and later ridicule him as they speak of it amongst one another. When a Mundugumor becomes so angry that his own rage is turned against himself, he takes his canoe and goes down river to be eaten by the next tribe. This is the most common form of suicide among the Mundugumor.

Oral frustrations, which are equivalent to frustrations occurring during the oral stage, cannot necessarily be attributed to the fact that a child was not nursed or that the quantity of milk was insufficient. A bottle given by a mother who lovingly and leisurely embraces the child and encourages closeness when the infant needs it—even during intervals between feedings—will represent less oral frustration than the breast given coldly. But it will be easier for the child to feel the mother's proximity and love if she is attached to her, sucking at the nipple, than if she is taking her food through a bottle. And perhaps even more important for the positive development of the mother–child relationship, which is now being initiated in external reality, is the fact that an instinctual and spontaneous love for her infant is awakened more easily in the mother when she nurses, rather than when she is fulfilling all the medical injunctions about the most adequate manufactured food as if she were carrying out a complicated laboratory experiment. The importance of physical closeness for the baby has been demonstrated in many ways since René Spitz discovered the phenomenon of hospitalism, in which infants who were attended to "correctly" but without love during a prolonged period in a hospital or asylum suffered from serious disorders in their psychophysical development.

But the most convincing and spectacular experiment in this domain is perhaps that carried out by Professor H. F. Harlow in Wisconsin. He separated some newborn rhesus monkeys from their mothers. One group was put in a pen with a "wire-meshed mother" and another group with a wire-meshed mother and a "rag doll mother." The mother made of wire mesh was an artifact that had feeding bottles constantly filled with milk within the monkeys' reach. The rag doll mother was another artifact covered by a soft material that, because of the contact with the little monkeys, quickly acquired a monkey odor, in other words, a mother's odor. When the monkeys learned to rear themselves more or less well, a mechanical toy was introduced into each pen to stimulate the fear response. It was demonstrated that the monkeys that did not have the rag doll mother did not run to the feeding bottles but withdrew in a frightened way and became paralyzed within a short time. In the long run they developed behavior relatively similar to the precocious autism of the child lacking in contact and communication with the world. The monkeys that had the rag doll mother available to them sought refuge in her. Once they felt calmed in this way, they developed toward the feared toy all of the intelligent curiosity inherent to their species. However, it was later demonstrated[2] that these monkeys that were well fed and in contact with a kind of affectionate robot instead of a real mother suffered from a serious deficiency as adults: Although they developed normally in terms of all the physical signs of sexual maturity, they did not know how to behave toward a sexual partner and were incapable of taking the "amorous" initiative, if one can speak in such terms.

We observe once again, then, the importance of physical contact as well as nursing for subsequent development. However, in many places and environments, especially in the United States and other industrialized countries, the custom of nursing is disappearing. This change is accompanied by problems whose impact has only recently being glimpsed. Spitz has dedicated himself especially to the study of the nursing infant's first attempts to communicate and the development of the process of thinking. Noting the fact that both emerge within the mother–child relationship, he argues that when the modern Western infant no longer makes her first contact with the mother through a part of her, her breast, but rather through an artifact, the feeding bottle, such a shift influences her way of communicating, her subsequent relationships, her verbal and nonverbal symbols, and perhaps even her thinking processes as well.

In our Latin culture it is still expected that a woman will nurse her infant. But many women fail at this endeavor. They claim that they did not have enough milk or that the milk was not nutritious enough or that they had to wean the child because of painful sores on the breasts caused by its sucking. From the purely physiological point of view, the production of maternal milk depends on the adequate interaction of several hormones. But whenever a biological process is affected by recurring hormonal difficulties, the intervention of psychological factors is indicated. Indeed, for some time physicians and laymen, together with psychoanalysts, have recognized the great influence of psychological factors on nursing. Popular beliefs have always affirmed that the psychological state of the mother has a great impact on the production of milk. Physicians in general have the same dualistic attitude toward this problem that they adopt in regard to other hormonal disorders, maintaining that the cause of the dysfunction can be rooted as much in physiology as in psychology. But they fail to emphasize that, in fact, hormones and psychology are two aspects of the same process. Recently, it has been demonstrated in experiments with nursing mothers the degree to which emotions influence the amount of milk flowing into the infant's mouth (Newton & Newton, 1948). But perhaps these types of somewhat naive experiments are not required in order to demonstrate the obvious. Any mother who is conscious of being an object of an experiment no longer reacts naturally and without self-consciousness about her daily internal experiences, a fact that is possibly more important than the external stimuli to which the experiment exposes her. Breast-feeding usually develops without any difficulty among primitive women who have not yet had the opportunity to acquire certain inhibitions typical of our culture. We can see that among the peasantry nursing difficulties are rare. Indeed, women are still permitted the libidinal pleasure that is a part of nursing their infants, so that they frequently continue nursing the smallest child for 2 or 3 years. But women from other cultures also recover this ability if and when nursing is the only option. Spitz offers us the recollection of a physician who was a prisoner in a Nazi concentration camp. He claimed that none of the interned women who had babies in the camp lacked breast milk, a phenomenon he attributed to the mothers' knowledge that if they did not nurse their infants, the authorities would let them die of starvation.

What are the unconscious reasons impeding the normal development of nursing? The most frequently encountered are easily divided into two groups: (1) disorders caused by the woman's rejection of motherhood and her desire to permanently remain in a receptive and infantile attitude; (2) difficulties that have their origin in the persistence of aggressive infantile tendencies directed toward the woman's own mother. In both cases there is a basic oral dissatisfaction.

If a woman has suffered such oral frustrations and later cannot come to consider the child as a part of her self, she unconsciously denies to her what she herself has not received. In this way she avenges herself upon the child, identifying her with her own bad mother who made her suffer. Or she identifies with her frustrating mother, treating the child as she felt treated in her infancy. During nursing, then, the two types of identification we found when analyzing the psychology of pregnancy persist. The unconscious notion that it is the woman's own appetite as an infant who could not be satisfied by her mother that now constitutes the cause of her incapacity to breast-feed is expressed in the different kinds of advice offered by the young mother's relatives; for example, they encourage her to eat baby food, to drink lots of milk, and so on, so that she can better feed her infant.

The desire to satisfy her own oral desires rather than those of her child could be observed quite well in Berta, whose intense fixation on her mother we have already explored. During Berta's first pregnancy she had the following dream: She was in a room with a woman who she knew was going to make her laugh. Afterward, she nursed at the woman's breasts or the woman nursed at her breasts, she was not completely sure. She felt her stomach become hard and sharp. During the dream she thought that finally she would understand the meaning of the hardening of the uterus. She told herself, "The baby has an erection." It became clear through Berta's associations that to make her laugh was equivalent to producing a great oral satisfaction and an orgasm. Her doubt regarding who was nursing whom expresses her desire to drink from her mother's breast instead of breast-feeding her future child. The hardening of the uterus, a contraction, she had already noted before, during sexual arousal. For her the uterus and the fetus have the meaning of her own penis, and the oral satisfaction of breast-feeding excites her sexually. She expresses in this way, through the dream, her belief that if she had had a penis her mother would have fed her well; she would have loved her and made her happy. She rejected her own femininity because unconsciously she blamed it for her mother's rejection of her. In fact, she had been bottle-fed. Berta's dream reminds us of Silvia's infantile belief that a nursing infant develops a penis and becomes a male when his mother loves him enough to give him a lot of milk. Both patients thus demonstrate the oral origins of their penis envy and their rejection of femininity.

A short time after Berta gave birth, serious difficulties in breast-feeding developed. During that period she had the following dream: She is in the pasture with her two sisters. They move away through a meadow where there are bulls, and they are not afraid. The patient remains in the pasture with the cows. At the time of this dream

Berta's sisters were engaged and very happy. When she was a child Berta had suffered from a phobia of bulls, which symbolized her father. In the dream her sisters separated themselves from their mother—the cow—and dared to approach the man, the bull. She did not dare to, because to approach the bull signifies to fall in love with a man, to have children, and, in the last instance, to raise them. But because of her fear of the bull and of being an adult, she still wishes to be satisfied by her mother, remaining with the cows, unable to competently feed her child.

In another case, a married patient fell ill with a melancholia after her mother left on a long trip. When her mother returned, the depressive state improved and was slowly cured, only to be succeeded by an agoraphobia. The woman could only go out accompanied by her mother or her husband, but she could not be alone in the house with either one of them. When she became pregnant, she already knew ahead of time that she would not be able to nurse her child. Indeed, she had very little milk, and the physician recommended a special diet for her. She began to gorge herself. Later, she explained to me in her analysis: "It was very strange; I ate a lot, but all the food became fat instead of becoming milk for my baby." When she later wanted to lose the weight, she was unable to because each diet became the stimulus for a relapse into a state of anxiety and depression. To briefly recapitulate this case: In order to counteract the real loss of her mother, the patient introjects her and becomes melancholic. The mother returns and the patient, not wanting to expose herself again to the risk of losing her, develops a phobia that obliges her mother to remain constantly at her side. When she has her baby, she fears she has definitively become an adult and has thus lost maternal protection. Then she incorporates her mother in the form of food and refuses to eliminate her in the form of milk. Later, becoming thin signifies the demand to let go of her mother.

It would appear that the desire to remain dependent and receive maternal milk is so widespread that it is encountered as well in domestic animals. One of my patients told me that she has two cats, a mother and a daughter, both of whom became pregnant, the daughter for the first time. When the mother gave birth, the young cat—still pregnant—became very interested in her little sisters, attached herself to her mother, and several times even succeeded in securing for herself the primary spot to nurse. Some days later when she gave birth, she showed no interest at all in her own kittens and completely abandoned them, refusing to feed or warm them. When the mother was not around, the young cat pranced coquettishly and without a care around the garden. In spite of her owners' efforts, her litter died.

Simultaneous with the passive desire to be fed, there may coexist the active desire of feeding, a situation that is manifested in Ana's infantile phantasy. She was 7 or 8 years old when she observed an aunt breast-feed her baby and was very affected by what she saw. She developed several phantasies, one of which she remembered in her analysis: A mother and her daughter have gotten lost in the Sahara; they are on the point of dying of thirst and pray for a miracle; it occurs, in fact, when the breasts of both women fill up with milk and they can nurse one another and thus save their lives. In this phantasy Ana tries to overcome her own weaning trauma, which is symbolized by the Sahara, a place devoid of all liquids. Ana experienced her helplessness in the face of her weaning as if she had been on the point of dying of thirst. She phantasizes that her mother will continue to give her milk if she will offer in compensation her own milk to her mother. Even as an adult, the unconscious desire to receive this compensation persisted. Fixated on her own weaning, she found it difficult to nurse her own children. She had little milk, that is to say, in the language of her infantile compensatory phantasy, she left her children "to die of thirst."

However, the persistence of the mother's own oral desires can also facilitate lactation if she can identify with the baby and thus overcome her own frustrations. She fails in this identification if nursing assumes or acquires for her an openly erotic—that is to say, homosexual and incestuous—character, as happened unconsciously in Ana's case or consciously in Berta's. The concepts of "homosexual", "dirty," and "animal" are often identical in the unconscious, and it is precisely those women who believe they cannot nurse who usually reject this function because it is considered by them to be indelicate and animal-like. They deny to the child a satisfaction that they themselves still desire but cannot tolerate because of its erotic content. If the oral desire in a woman remains fixated completely on her mother and is accepted by the ego, it leads her to a certain kind of homosexual object choice in which all sexual activity is reduced to mutual sucking of the breasts and sometimes to cunnilingus, thus satisfying active and passive desires stemming from the early relationship between mother and daughter. Ana's phantasy about the miracle in the Sahara is based on the same desires.

I have shown how the unsatisfied wish to be a small girl who nurses and the rejection of this desire—interpreted by the young woman as homosexual—can lead to difficulties in nursing. But the inability to nurse also stems from the fear of one's own oral-sadistic tendencies, which are intimately linked to the aforementioned oral dissatisfaction. Women who during their infancy reacted to maternal frustration with intense desires of biting mother and destroying her breasts later often punish themselves when they nurse their children, inflicting on themselves what they wished to inflict on their mothers. They achieve this through the development of fissures on their nipples, which make nursing impossible and ultimately require weaning. However, these fissures signify not only punishment but at the same time a protection, because they permit the woman to avoid contact with the infant's mouth, which for her is unconsciously so dangerous. A baby reacts to the breast that frustrates her with wishes to bite and destroy, because she herself feels bitten and destroyed by the hunger her mother provokes. For the baby it is as if her mother were biting her. Later, her own child represents, in the double identification spoken of by Helene Deutsch, the voracious child the young mother herself once was as well as her own cruel mother. Nursing her, then, means exposing the breast to her cruel voracity. Because of this, the fissures on the nipples signify a lesser evil, a compromise. The sores represent the woman's bribe to her superego in that by accepting a small part of the feared destruction she can permit herself to stop nursing. One has the impression from observing women with fissures on their nipples that they are caused by an unconscious intentional failure to take care of herself. Such women follow all the physician's instructions to the letter of the law, but they ingeniously provoke these fissures by letting the baby suck for long periods of time or by not putting the nipple in the baby's mouth well or by not immediately treating a lesion when it first appears.

A patient who suffered from very painful fissures throughout nursing and subsequently developed mastitis recalled her very earliest infantile memory: She and her younger brother are seated in the hallway, each one drinking a large bottle full of milk. This is a screen memory, emerging in order to reject a contrary and traumatic experience. The patient was 11 months older than her brother and was precociously weaned because of her mother's new pregnancy. Later, she often enviously observed her brother nursing. Her mother excessively prolonged the nursing of this child. The memory—or phantasy—expresses the exact opposite of her actual experience; that is, she and her brother both appear happily drinking lots of milk from large bottles. Her brother's birth had deprived this patient not only of milk but also of maternal love, because her mother soon preferred her little brother. The patient avenged herself with a strong hatred that almost completely hid her love for her mother. Her temporary depressions revealed the oral-sadistic component of this hatred, as did the chronic periodontosis that began to manifest itself during her adolescence a short time after her mother fell ill with a manic-depressive psychosis.

During her psychotic attacks the mother would blame her daughter for all the ills that had befallen her, accusing her of wanting to seduce the father. When the patient married, she still consciously repudiated her mother. She was happy during the early period of her marriage, which was ruined by the birth of a child. When the patient was about to give birth, her character suddenly changed. She began to "understand" her mother and to reproach herself for her hostile attitude toward her. That is to say, now that she feared her mother by having usurped her place as mother, she felt that she was exposing her breasts to the attack of her infant's mouth, representative of her own oral aggression and her mother's as well; she then protected herself against direct contact with her baby through fissures on her nipples, thus trying to bribe her mother and reconcile with her. So that her mother would no longer have anything to envy and reproach her for, the patient transformed herself into as wretched a woman as her mother had been.

Lina spent a very bad second night after the birth of her daughter. She had continuous nightmares in which huge nasty dogs chased her puppy, Sugar, in order to bite and devour him. Two days later very painful fissures appeared on her nipples. Because of this, she weaned her daughter when she was only 10 days old. A short time later, Lina was overcome by a phobic idea. When she walked the baby in the pram, she took care to avoid dogs for fear that they could attack the pram and eat her child. How do we interpret Lina's sudden preoccupation? The appearance of the fissures indicate that her puppy, Sugar, represented her breasts. In his name itself there was already the association to something sweet that stimulates children's gluttony. The dangerous dogs who wanted to bite and eat Sugar represented her infant daughter wishing to bite and eat her breasts. Lina was obliged to expose herself to her daughter's aggression, and she was afraid. But this fear did not emerge at the conscious level; instead, it was represented by the fissures, wounds caused, in fact, by her daughter's hungry mouth. With the appearance of the fissures, Lina anticipated what her daughter could do to her, and her anxiety diminished, because the wounds in reality were much less dangerous than the bites to which the puppy, Sugar, was exposed in her dreams. Simultaneously, she bribed her superego, represented in the external world by her husband, by demonstrating to him her suffering caused by the fissures, achieving in this way his agreement for her to desist from the dangerous breast-feeding. But once saved from this danger, guilt feelings emerged because of what she had done. Then Lina identified with her baby, who was exposed to the suffering of a precocious weaning. The child who is threatened with being eaten by the dogs is she herself as a young girl at the mercy of the devouring hunger of her early oral frustration.

(In the phobic fear that her breasts or the baby could be eaten by the dogs, there exist the same psychological constellation and the same kind of identifications that we have studied in depth in the analysis of the modern "myth" of the roasted child, presented in Chapter 2.)

Both patients, afraid of the oral aggression that stemmed from frustrations suffered in their own nursing experiences, avoided the feared contact with their infants by means of the production of fissures. Berta, exposed through her experiences to the same fears, had recourse to another mechanism. Her dreams also revealed that she feared her infant's oral hostility. One time her baby appeared in a dream, represented by a crayfish, which was the maternal symbol for her (recall her dream of the spider-crayfish described in Chapter 2). In another dream he was a tiger cub, to which Berta associated a toy tiger that her mother had given her when she was a child and with which she had identified in her infantile games. Once again there appears, then, the adult's fear of the child resulting from a double identification. For Berta, the child represents both the crayfish (the mother) and the tiger (the dreamer as a child); both animals are feared for their oral aggression. In spite of her fear and aversion to breast-feeding, Berta did not wish to renounce her nursing function. She suffered from an intense penis envy, and having milk signified being potent. Moreover, her mother was a failure at nursing. She wanted to prove to her mother that she was worth more than she and that she knew better how to feed a child. But, basically, she dedicated herself to feeding him so her child would not hate her as she had hated her mother. However, she could not do it for fear of the aggression of the crayfish-tiger, fear of intimate contact that for her was incestuous and homosexual. She then resorted to a small compromise: Alleging that the child was lazy in its sucking, she extracted milk artificially over a period of several months and gave it to the baby in a bottle.

The unconscious perception of one's own aggression, a response to the former oral frustrations that were experienced as aggressions from the mother, can also disturb nursing in another way: through the mother's wickedness being projected onto the milk. Reliving one's own breast-feeding experience, the milk is then considered to be a destructive and dangerous substance, and because of this, the young mother believes the baby should not drink it. This explains the attitude among many women who find their milk to be insufficient and damaging to their baby.[3] But if a woman is able to overcome her fears and successfully feed her child, she destroys her old hypochondriacal fears tainted with the guilt feeling that she and everything that she could produce would be hurtful and dangerous to everyone.

We have seen how different neurotic mechanisms come to make nursing problematic. But the opposite can occur. In the normal nursing experience, the mother's identification with her nursing child always exists. A strong oral fixation on the mother should not necessarily cause difficulties in breast-feeding if the passive desire to nurse is satisfied in an identification with the baby and an active desire to breast-feed is achieved through a simultaneous identification with an ideal mother who nurses well. The woman thus can satisfy frustrated infantile desires and give to the child that which she did not have herself. In such women an intense aversion to weaning is found, representing the only superficial indication of a neurotic component.

Isabel breast-fed her infant very satisfactorily for 6 months. An acute illness obliged her to wean him suddenly. She anxiously observed the child to see how he reacted to what she considered to be a serious frustration. However, the child, surrounded by affection and already capable of finding other gratifications besides the breast, did not manifest any alarming signs. Then Isabel became very sad. She felt offended that her child needed her so little, and she acted so strange that her husband, an intuitive psychological observer, told her, "You're behaving as if the child had weaned you instead of the other way around."

Mrs. L could not accept weaning her daughter, either. In the first days after giving birth, she had very little milk. She was still in the sanatorium, an environment generally unfavorable for the development of normal nursing. The nurse (a maternal representative for her), after seeing Mrs. L's efforts and her initial inhibition to offer the breast to her newborn, became impatient and instead of helping her, offered to give her a bottle. Because of her heart condition, Mrs. L was accustomed to being considered less able than other women—especially her mother and her older sister—and she felt once again defeated by the capability of a maternal figure. She reacted to this failure with a depression that was alleviated only when, after returning home where she received compassionate support from her immediate family, she was able to nurse her daughter quite adequately. When the infant was several months old, Mrs. L took her on a summer vacation. Her cardiac condition worsened, provoked by an unimportant but bothersome illness suffered by her child, resulting in her physician's recommendation that Mrs. L immediately cease breast-feeding. She responded with a serious cardiac decompensation and a confused and regressed psychological state. When the decompensation did not improve with medication, she returned to analysis. It became clear that the provocation of her condition had been the weaning of her daughter. Mrs. L had been happy and free from physical problems while she breast-fed her child; in addition, identifying with her, she was able to realize something she had never experienced before: the feeling of being the only daughter, loved and well fed by a good mother totally dedicated to her. The weaning changed everything, because it destroyed this positive identification. The child, a younger version of herself, became in Mrs. L's unconscious a rival for her husband's and mother's love. That is to say, she changed into a mother united with the father or into an older sibling. On the other hand, Mrs. L oscillated between two equally unsatisfactory psychological positions: she felt again like a young girl who had been excluded or an older sister abandoned because of the arrival of a new sibling and—because of having frustrated her daughter by weaning her—she felt like a bad mother, just as she had felt her own mother to be when she weaned her prematurely due to a new pregnancy.

The identification with the good mother who feeds well is, then, as much for normal as for neurotic women the very basis of a positive nursing and weaning experience. But owing to the persistence of infantile desires in the unconscious, the good mother who feeds well should be asexual. Because of guilt feelings for having attacked the parents' sexual union in former phantasies and because of identification with the child's jealousy, there are women who surrender themselves quite well to nursing but afterward lose a part of their sexual desire and their orgastic capacity. Others may deny their breasts to the child because they consider them to be exclusively a sexual attribute. Both disassociate motherhood and sexuality, and for both the mother is an asexual saint. The same need is the basis of the cult of the Virgin, whose image, with the child at her breast, has been for many centuries the maximum symbol of motherhood for Western man. The same conflict leads the protagonist of Tolstoy's *Kreutzer Sonata* to demand that married couples abstain from sex during the period of breast-feeding. Some gynecologists demand this abstention as well. In many primitive societies there exists a taboo against sex during nursing. The belief that women are unable to become pregnant during this period is not only based on the observation that their capacity to conceive is diminished biologically but corresponds to the unconscious desire for the woman to be asexual. This desire stems from our most remote infancy, when we belonged exclusively to our mother and we believed that she also belonged to us—when we had not yet recognized our father as a love object or a rival. Slowly, our knowledge of reality cast us out of this paradise. But in all of us, as adults, the desire to maintain the old illusion of our infancy continues to persist.

To sum up our discussion, then, the woman who nurses her child is unconsciously reliving her own breast-feeding experience. If it was positive, she will enjoy repeating the same satisfactory experience with her own infant. If it was very conflictual and anxiety-provoking, it may occur that old memories reemerge in her unconscious and become an obstacle to nursing, sometimes even completely preventing it, causing the milk to disappear. But the opposite can also happen, in which the woman can master her old conflicts and in nursing find, through an identification with her satisfied child and an ideal mother, an acceptable means for overcoming past frustrations and forgetting old resentments and claims.

Menopause:
Final Considerations

In this book we have accompanied woman from the initiation of sexual maturity to the weaning of her infant, that is to say, to the point at which she fulfills her reproductive responsibility toward the child. We shall proceed now to an exploration of the passing of woman's biological capacity for childbearing, when motherhood and sexuality definitively lose all physiological interdependence. This stage in the female life cycle, menopause, appears to be as sharply defined as menarche in that it is assumed to follow upon the woman's final menstruation. However, the appearance of psychosomatic symptoms, which often accompany menopause and are responsible for its negative image as "the critical age" for women, are not produced exactly at that moment. It used to be that a 40-year-old woman was considered "old" and was expected to renounce much of her activity in the service of leading a resigned and dignified life. It was precisely at this age that women began to suffer from sadness and waves of heat or sweat—from anxiety attacks, as we would now put it. Some decades earlier, Freud would advise his colleagues against accepting a woman of this age into analysis, because, as he argued, her psychological rigidity did not lend itself to a successful therapeutic outcome. Now we consider a woman of 40 to be young, and of course we accept her in analysis. A 50-or 60-year-old woman in our society also has the possibility of actualizing herself in many domains. Indeed, the crises of age now appear, when they present themselves, at a much older age than in the past.

Flanders Dunbar postulates that the interpretation of senile psychosis as a direct consequence of menopausal hormonal changes will in the near future begin to seem as irrational as the belief at the turn of the century that masturbation or sexual excesses were the cause of psychosis. His thesis is supported by the fact that the senile psychoses cannot be altered through hormonal treatment. Moreover, careful studies demonstrate that women who present menopausal disorders already suffer from prior psychological disturbances. Such women whose confrontation with the aging process puts them at risk are characterized by poor sexual adjustment, a rigid personality unable to adapt to change, and a limited range of interests. This is easy to understand. A woman who has experienced sexual pleasure until the climacteric will rapidly come to understand that she has not lost this capacity, which is long since firmly established and independent of hormonal processes. On the other hand, a woman with a rigid character will find it difficult to tolerate the changes she experiences in her body and will suffer profoundly with the aging process. Since she sees the range of her activities deteriorate (housework often loses importance when the children leave home), a woman of limited interests will easily feel useless and become vulnerable to focusing all of her attention, once directed toward her family, hypochondriacally on her own body. In contrast, a woman who has always had multiple interests will more easily, and even without conscious awareness, renounce her capacity to biologically create, since she is creative in other domains.

Although growing old is always painful, even more so if one loves life, this process will become "critical" only owing to an interplay of personal, environmental, and social factors. But the concrete biological change that woman in this period of her life experiences will always revive in her unconscious the psychological experiences and conflicts of change in early life. Helene Deutsch sees in menopause and its psychic and somatic reactions as much a repetition of menarche as its complement. Woman passes through a psychological state of doubts, vacillations, fear of the future, intensification and rejection of her sexuality, oscillation between desires to isolate herself and become involved in more social activity, and so on, most of which appear in the reactions of the pubescent girl. Moreover, even some of the physical reactions, for example, the frequent vasomotor discomforts such as blushing and hot flashes, are similar. Deutsch remarks that in studying the conflicts of a woman facing menarche, one can predict her future difficulties in menopause. But this similarity contrasts with a fundamental difference: All that the girl acquires in menarche is lost by the mature woman in menopause. This loss means for her a partial death and a negation with respect to her functions dedicated to the species. Because of this, while the tone of her pubescent phantasies, desires, and conflicts is one of a resigned "too early," the menopausal woman encounters difficulties in her attempts to actualize herself with a sad "too late." The similarities and the character of psychological crisis associated with both stages stem from this impossibility of actualization imposed by age, too soon for the young girl, too advanced for the aging woman.

The psychological conflicts that affect the pubescent girl represent the reappearance of her oedipal struggles. According to Deutsch, the menopausal woman also repeats these conflicts. But while for the girl her forbidden love for her father was the source of her struggles, rebellions, and humiliations, the mature woman suffers because she must repress her incestuous love for her son or substitute object. In her unconscious, the son has taken the place of the father and the daughter-in-law is the mother who excludes her. But while the pubescent girl actively attempts to separate herself from her incestuous objects—the parents—the aging woman passively suffers the loss of her children who try to emancipate themselves from her.

Deutsch views the psychological crisis that accompanies menopause as inevitable. But she explains how its characteristics and intensity are determined by the woman's psychological structure, by her infantile conflicts, and by all her achievements and failures during her reproductive years.

Within the vast array of studies about menopause, Therese Benedek offers a dissident point of view in a book with the suggestive and controversial title *Climacterium: A Developmental Phase*. She explains that the biological changes inherent in menopause, in spite of their regressive character, stimulate psychological processes in woman that, under favorable conditions, are capable of leading her to a better control of life's difficulties and to a progressive adaptation. Like Deutsch, Benedek compares the girl's reaction to menarche to the aging woman's reaction to menopause. But she disagrees with Deutsch in her assertion that menopause deprives woman of all that she attained at puberty. Benedek became well known for her investigations of woman's psychological reactions provoked by hormonal changes during her menstrual cycle. In a comparison between the menopausal hormonal situation and the premenstrual condition, she argues that the adult woman who has achieved adequate sexual gratification and a satisfying, fulfilling motherhood no longer suffers from regressive symptoms during the premenstrual period and thus arrives at menopause (during which time the same hormones whose temporary disappearance has characterized the premenstrual period disappear definitively) without experiencing psychological or physical problems. She opposes Deutsch's perspective because in her view menopause cannot deprive woman of everything she has acquired with respect to psychological maturity and her emotional ties with her partner, children, and the entire social world. On the contrary, she maintains that the desexualization of the menopausal woman's emotions can serve her in lending a more serene character to her affective relations, freed now from ambivalence and emotional conflicts. Moreover, the climacteric places at her disposal energies that before were erotically bound and can now facilitate the link with her social environment in a new way. The destiny of the woman who grows old having achieved psychological maturation and complete gratification of her instinctual urges toward motherhood is contrasted with that of the neurotic woman who, suffering from her awareness that she has not fulfilled the goal of her sex, is often imprisoned by anguish with respect to a rapidly approaching old age and the imminent loss of her sexual attractiveness. Benedek demonstrates this thesis with more than adequate clinical material. Moreover, pointing to anthropological data, she asserts that, just as each woman's reaction toward her menopause is determined by her individual history, so too does it depend on society's attitude toward the mature woman. Obviously, attitudes differ in societies that value woman essentially for her erotic attributes and those, such as our contemporary society, in which, to some extent, growing old offers woman new possibilities based on her greater experience and understanding.*

Among the Mohave Indians, for example, George Devereux could not find any indication that menopause was from the point of view of the men or the women a depressing or traumatic passage. Among these people, women do not restrict their sexual lives during this time; on the contrary, new marriages occur quite frequently. A mature woman is often sought after by a younger divorced father who has been disappointed by his immature wife's incapacity to adequately care for him and his children. The older woman also enters a period in

---

*In later years Langer criticized the values in Latin American culture that tend to see postmenopausal women as asexual. She believed that in psychoanalytic terms, this propensity to condemn sexuality in the older woman "is the realization of an old infantile phantasy. Children demonstrate it quite often when they say to their mothers, 'You will see when I am big and you are small.' It has been confirmed scientifically that sexuality never ends, that until we die we have sexual desires; the need may be less intense, but the desire remains." ("Old Age, My Old Age," Fem, June, 1982). Langer spoke of her own experience of being an aging woman in Mexico and how there was hardly any possibility of having an intimate erotic relationship with a man, given the cultural taboos against it. So while she was able to actualize many of her aspirations in the social and political domain, she felt her chances of continuing to express her sexual desire as an older woman were unfortunately inhibited by social norms and expectations.

which she begins to take care of her grandchildren. Moreover, menopause liberates her from all restrictions with regard to her participation alongside the men in the life of the tribe. Although she still cannot exercise an official function, she occupies an important place in the social organization, based on the fact that she is considered to be a person who psychologically is developing new strengths and consolidating what she has attained during her youth and maturity.

It appears that in other primitive societies as well, menopause is not always traumatic but, rather, following Benedek's expression, is defined as an "evolutionary phase." In our society, in contrast, a menopause free of problems and depressive reactions is considered by many to be exceptional. The great frequency in the young woman of today of psychosomatic disorders in her reproductive functions leads us to conclude that she is not fully able to enjoy her femininity. It might be equally deduced from her reaction to menopause that her life has not been satisfactory. The reaction to menopause is like a litmus test that reveals whether or not a woman has felt privileged or unlucky, instinctually fulfilled or caught up in the continual search for inadequate erotic gratifications or sublimations throughout her childhood, adolescence, and adulthood. Unfortunately, in our society the results of the test are often negative.

Certainly, a woman will pass this test better if she has not ruined her chances for motherhood. However, the full attainment of motherhood is now almost impossible in our society. In *Male and Female*, her anthropological study of contemporary North American life, Mead claims that 25% of North American women arrive at menopause without having had a child. In general, mothers do not have more than one child, or two or three at best. Consciously, they do not even wish to have more. Even though it cannot be said that they have fully satisfied their maternal instincts, they do not want to have more children because raising them in the conditions that prevail today has already been difficult and full of sacrifices. The contemporary middle-class family is reduced to the father, mother, and young children. In contrast to earlier times, the woman no longer lives with her parents or in-laws or an aunt, unmarried sister, or widow who can help her raise her children. Thus, she is forced to renounce her work or her career if she cannot afford adequate paid help. She stays at home, working more than if she had a paying job but feeling inferior and insecure with her women friends who work outside the home and earn a living. Afterward, as the children grow up, the work slowly diminishes; finally, when they leave home, the reason for which she abandoned her career or profession is also gone. At this point in her life the woman is generally still too young to remain inactive but she is often now too old to resume the work she abandoned many years earlier or to dedicate herself seriously to new endeavors. It is not a question of age that impedes her capacity to study but, rather, the fact that she has not been involved in systematic training for years because of her time-consuming domestic obligations. Now that she has more than enough time, her mind has lost the habit and discipline. So she remains alone at home, unoccupied for the first time in many years. Whereas she once wished desperately for some free time to herself, now she does not know what to do with this freedom. Her husband returns home at noon and at night, but the mornings and afternoons suddenly seem to her to be endless. This critical period of her life generally coincides with menopause. According to Mead, depressive reactions are not due primarily to the physiological changes but to the critical sociological situation just described, which so many women in our society are obliged to experience because of their having renounced the creation of interests and work that belong exclusively to them in favor of raising their children.

This is the reaction of the woman who has had children and has dedicated herself to raising them. Surely, the reaction toward menopause of the woman who has not had children is more intense, even though she has firmly established her profession, social status, and other sources of gratification. In this book we have studied woman's most profound anxiety, her unconscious fear of not being physically intact because of the sins she committed in phantasy. The most convincing proof of her innocence is that she has not been punished, that she can give birth to a healthy child. The more a woman has consciously rejected motherhood, the more she will unconsciously need this proof, and the more it will evade her because of feelings of guilt and inadequacy. But as long as the woman does not reach menopause, consciously or unconsciously the phantasy of creating a child is stimulated during each menstrual cycle. Only with the disappearance of menstruation does she realize that all her phantasies are unrealizable, that they belong irrevocably to the past. This fact is so painful for her that sometimes she searches by whatever means possible to retain at least the illusion. I knew a childless widow, nearly 60 years old and menopausal for 10 years, who rejected a belated suitor because of the fear, as she explained it, of getting pregnant.

However, there are exceptions: The very repressed woman, who has suffered profoundly because of being sexually dissatisfied, is sometimes relieved by menopause, which finally liberates her from any obligation to fulfill her femininity, as, for example, in the case of the extremely infantile woman. If she did not have children because she wanted to remain the highly esteemed only child of her family, this woman will move quite well through menopause if she is able to secure an ongoing protective attitude on the part of others toward her.

The woman who concentrated all her energy on the cultivation of her physical attributes and the conquest of men generally suffers more with the approach of old age. When we studied frigidity, we saw that this kind of woman tries, through her sexual avidity, to compensate for her primitive oral dissatisfaction. For her, menopause has such a catastrophic character because it represents something like an irrevocable and definitive weaning.

But why is her physical attractiveness so important to woman? Freud explains that she compensates for her lack of a penis by eroticizing her entire body. But we repeat that it is not so much the lack of a penis as it is the impossibility of knowing what occurs inside her body that makes her depend, often quite anxiously, on the perfection of her beauty. If she is beautiful outside, then she must be so inside. And if so, this implies that she did not attack her internal objects and did not deserve to be punished, attacked, and destroyed. For the young girl, to be pretty or good are practically synonymous. The princess of fairy tales is young and beautiful, the bad witch is old and ugly. So, justifiably, the princess is loved and the witch is hated. The woman who suffers before the mirror with each new wrinkle unconsciously feels transformed from the good and loved little girl into the old and hated witch. She feels guilty for not having known how to preserve her beauty and mourns the loss of her physical attractiveness as an integral part of her identity and her ego (see León Grinberg's ideas about persecutory guilt and mourning by the ego). She no longer recognizes herself.

But, what is the witch? Snow White's stepmother was beautiful, only showing her wickedness and her bad deeds when upon becoming a woman the girl surpassed her in beauty. The witch is the internal image of the mother, transformed into a bad mother for having been conquered by the daughter and dispossessed of the father-prince and of every feminine sexual attraction. For that reason, she is characterized by phallic attributes (the long nose and the broom) that represent her union with the father's bad penis. In her unconscious envious attacks on her mother for all that she has, the girl anticipates her manic triumph over her mother and the mother's transformation into an old woman and bad witch for what she is doing to her. Because of this, when the girl actually becomes a woman through the arrival of her menarche, she often fears her mother because of experiencing herself as victorious. The older woman suddenly recognizes in the mirror the witch in her own face and feels hated and dispossessed as she hated and dispossessed her internal mother.

The senile psychoses are categorized by the existence of one or another overriding idea: (1) the aging woman's paranoid idea that she is persecuted and robbed, which expresses the identification of an eye-for-an-eye posture with the dispossessed mother from whom the girl stole both sex and the father; (2) the aging woman's depressive idea that nothing has value any more and now there is no reason to live, which expresses the conviction that she cannot survive change and time that have transformed her from her father's triumphant and preferred little girl into this image of the destroyed mother whom now no one loves or feeds.

Together with aging and the decline of sexual life, old homosexual desires and fears often return. Behind the revival of oedipal material, behind the man (the father) appears the woman (the mother). And this mother will be a witch—*vehini-hai*—and feared to the extent that the girl made fun of her when she was victorious over her in the process of growing up and leaving with the man. Here a nightmare, brief and impressionistic, of a woman of a "certain age" will be illustrative: She saw nothing more than a wood door and a bolt that very slowly retreated. She felt a kind of suspense and panic in the face of this door that was about to open soon, very soon, inexorably. Who was going to come through, once the door was open? She awoke, bathed in sweat and suffering from tachycardia. The door with the bolt made her remember a similar one belonging to an old house where she used to meet her lover. But behind this amorous association, expressed in symbolic terms, lay her anxiety with respect to aging. She was the old house and the bolt that retreated from the door was the penis that withdrew, leaving her genitalia open and defenseless, to which the mother would have access. The dreamer deduced from the climate of anxiety dominating the dream that the mother was a feared mother-witch. But the witch's invisibility anticipated another fear as well: the fear of nothing, of the death that was approaching.

We have underscored the conflicts and fears accompanying menopause but also the specific important achievements belonging to this period from which the woman can reap the benefits of accumulated experience and the serenity that comes from the resolution of conflict. If she has led a satisfactory adult life, this will have counteracted many of her infantile fears. However, we already pointed out that because of the great frequency of negative reactions to menopause even in a woman who has had a gratifying life with her husband and children, it is necessary to conclude that she remained unfulfilled during the long period of her life that was biologically destined to motherhood. This is understandable if we take into account the great social restrictions imposed on her. In order for the contemporary woman to avoid being frustrated with respect to her maternal instincts, she needs to adequately sublimate the part of her reproductive instincts that cannot be satisfied directly. She needs to work in something outside the extraordinarily reduced circle of the contemporary family. This need presents immediate social problems in that she must have assistance in raising her children while she is working and have her work schedule adapted to the requirements of her nursing infant. Until the government is willing to resolve these problems, each woman will have to search individually for the most acceptable solution for herself. I wish here to point out only one aspect of the problem: Just as a mother's satisfactory sexual life does not hurt but, rather, helps her child, so too does woman's work fail to conflict with motherhood but psychologically complements it. If a woman sacrifices for her children the gratifications that she now can attain in the social domain—for which her mother and grandmother as young women so often envied men—she will not accept her destiny as a woman and her children's welfare will be compromised as a consequence.

I have already cited the women of the Marquesas islands, who behave as if they believed that they have to pay a price for their social and sexual rights by renouncing the pleasures of motherhood. Women in our society often behave as if they shared this unconscious conviction. This phenomenon explains the current tendency of women, discussed throughout this book, to deprive their reproductive lives of all instinctual and pleasurable qualities. In place of abandoning themselves freely to their nature, they attempt to limit, direct, and suppress it. We have demonstrated these factors, especially when we discussed the practices of induced labors and bottle-feeding. But women very often go beyond this in their renunciation. They believe they must choose between motherhood and sexual pleasure on the one hand, and satisfactory and creative work or politically and socially significant activity on the other. But each renunciation has its consequences, with the result that the woman who has given up a good deal in order to take care of her children often will do it bitterly and with continual reproaches, expressed verbally or unconsciously through body language. Discontented with the destiny of her sex, she will also feel the same way about her daughter's fate. She will communicate to her in a thousand ways that women are inferior, that they are life's victims, that she would have preferred a son who would not have to suffer such a sad fate. Through the case histories in this book, we have seen the disastrous consequences a mother's rejection of her femininity has for her daughter.

What should be done about this problem? We cannot change our own childhoods. But we can attempt to raise our daughters, the mothers of future generations, so that they do not suffer this contradiction between their instincts and their ambitions, so that they do not envy men for having such a clearly defined future. In other words, so that they will be content being women. They will have no need to repudiate their femininity when they understand that it can give them a maximum of pleasure without preventing other achievements and that they can accomplish as much as men. They will come to see that their achievements in many domains will, because they are women, have a different quality than those of men, because rather than being the result of sublimations of the masculine sexual instinct, they will be sublimations of the feminine instincts, especially of motherhood.

When discussing the causes of the various psychogenic disorders, all of which reflect a woman's conflict with her femininity, we found almost as a common denominator certain factors and family constellations that represented a pernicious influence, especially during our patients' early childhoods. It was Freud's great merit to have made us aware of the nearly decisive importance of the first years of life for subsequent development, and it was Melanie Klein's merit to have included the first year of life in psychoanalytic research in order to show the complexity of early processes and their persistence in subsequent development. This thesis of the fundamental importance of infancy led to investigations in diverse terrains with a variety of methodologies, and the theory became indisputable. If we wish to raise healthy daughters who are accepting of their sex, we should assure them a positive childhood in every way possible. If the mother cannot give all the necessary warmth, affection, and milk (although it be with a bottle) to her infant daughter, adapting to her rhythm and her specific needs, the girl will later suffer the psychological consequences unleashed by these early frustrations. When nursing, the completely dependent infant expects the satisfaction of a vital need. If the hungry infant receives the desired and necessary milk without having to wait for a long time or having to force her mother with her cries of impotent rage to give her what she wants, if she can drink held against a warm body, embraced with loving affection by her mother's secure arms, she will have learned something very important for her future life that will remain fixed in her unconscious. This experience will serve as a model for her personal and social links to the world. It will influence her love for her father, and later will permit her to give herself confidently to her sexual partner in order to repeat on a more developed level the joyful experiences of her infancy. On the other hand, through her own experience she will have also learned the value of an appropriate and suitable active stance, developed by her mother in order to satisfy her.

When activity is later demanded of her, she will know how to actualize it, identifying with a good and active mother.

We are mortal. From the beginning, alongside the life instinct and the need to love, we also contain the death instinct within us, which is expressed through hatred and envy.* Because of this, the most well-disposed mother cannot save her child from a certain amount of frustration. But the child will be able to overcome its effects if it is counteracted by many happy experiences. Some might question my insistence that a mother retain her professional career or work at the same time that she maintains such a high degree of involvement with her infant. I have specifically insisted on the importance of the first period of infantile life because up to now it has not been sufficiently understood by the majority of mothers. They maintain that older children need a great deal of maternal attention when, in fact, it often would be advantageous for them to have more independence. And they believe that the infant does not need any more attending to than a diaper change and a bottle (prepared according to the most modern pediatric formula) every 4 hours. If the baby asks for something in the interval between two feedings, they argue that it is not necessary to pay

---

*A word is in order regarding the concept of the death instinct. It is one of the most controversial of psychoanalytic concepts, one that has not gained the acceptance of many of Freud's followers, especially in the United States. However, Melanie Klein and her disciples and successors have continued to argue in favor of the concept of the death instinct. While in later years Langer might have been more equivocal about the idea of an instinct of death, she continued to view the destructive tendencies as a central issue for human beings. The views of Langer and her Latin American Kleinian colleagues on this subject have been deeply influenced by the history and culture of Latin America, which since the 15th century with the brutal European conquest of the indigenous populations of the New World has been characterized by the intense and impassioned clash of different cultures and the violent imposition of European hegemony over millions of indigenous peoples and their counterparts imported from Africa as slaves. The disparities of opportunity and wealth in the past 4 centuries have been based on exploitative class relations maintained intact by custom and law that have empowered the wealthy to defend their privilege from challenges by the popular classes, through military repression when necessary. Such conditions have produced cultures that are highly politicized, in which class consciousness acknowledges the social order as composed of essentially antagonistic rather than harmonious interests. The traditional tendency toward violent solutions of conflict have been reinforced in the 20th century by U. S. interests, which have generally supported, trained, and armed the military forces whose role it is to maintain the status quo. The Latin American social milieu has been a "good fit" with some central concepts in Kleinian object relations theory, including the death instinct. Langer witnessed the intensification of the violence of everyday life under the terrorist state in Argentina and the legacy of human rights abuses by the repressive state in Guatemala and El Salvador among the population of exiles who had fled to Mexico from those countries. In the psychology of political repression and human responses to it, Langer found much to suggest the primary importance of destructive tendencies—if not the death instinct proper—in human beings.

any attention to her, that, on the contrary, she could become spoiled. They do not realize that the infant needs something beyond a full stomach and that because of the infant's lack of experience about the passing of hunger, pain, or time itself, the half hour during which she cries becomes for her an eternity.

But at her mother's side the small girl (like the little boy as well, of course) soon needs her father to become actively concerned with her. This will permit her to distribute her affection and to abandon, little by little, her primitive and total dependency on her mother. Moreover, we live in a world of two sexes. In order to orient themselves successfully in this world, especially with regard to their own gender identity, children need to learn from the beginning how to situate themselves with reference to both parents. They achieve this through the connection established between themselves and their mother and their father. This learning is successful when it is based on the example of parents who love each other, who know how to sexually enjoy one another, and who mutually respect one another's individuality. The daughter of a loved and happy mother will try to identify with her and the rest of her sex and will learn how to complement her mother's character with that of her father's, the first masculine representative for her.*

In this book we have also spoken a good deal about the damaging consequences of envy and hatred toward the pregnant mother and of sibling rivalry. But these sentiments, which naturally coexist with other feelings of love, will take on pernicious characteristics only when the young girl's ego is still too weak to elaborate them and her dependency on her mother too great for her to be able to share her. This occurs in the very young child.

Many women believe that it is an advantage to have their children close in age. "In this way they grow up together," they think, "and they are better friends and less work." For the younger of such children, the older child can indeed function as a model at the beginning, even becoming a good playmate later. But for the older child, the situation is different. During the beginning of life, we all need to be our mother's only and adored child. The restrictions that are imposed on the infant from the first moment by our culture—she is separated from her mother and changed and generally fed on a fixed

---

*In later years Langer stressed the fact that the masculine did not depend on the actual existence of the father in the family but, rather, that the father principle— patriarchy—would be transmitted to the child by the mother's unconscious and phantasized representation of the husband/father, by other members of the family or community of friends, and by the mass-mediated cultural representations of gendered social relations.

schedule—are so serious for her that they need to be compensated for by a maximum of love. The small child cannot cede her preferential place to another without retaining a lively resentment and a sensation of having been the victim of a great injustice. She will only be capable of overcoming her jealousy of a new arrival when she already knows how to find satisfactions outside her exclusive relationship with her mother. On the other hand, many mothers are inclined to pay more attention to the new baby, the younger sibling. Generally, it is enough for a mother to find herself pregnant again for her to reject her child. Her first measure will be to wean her, more or less suddenly, more or less precipitously, and prematurely. Generally, the mother is not conscious of her rejection, nor does she note that she becomes more impatient and more severe with her child. But she stops nursing or hurries toilet training, thinking, "I have to train her fast so that she is already a bit older when my baby arrives." Thus, she suddenly changes her 1- or 2-year-old child into "the older," from whom she now demands judgment and the ability, as much as possible, to take care of herself. The child does not understand the change in her situation. The only thing she intuits from the beginning and with great perspicacity is that her mother no longer loves her in the same way. She is rejected because her mother is expecting or has had another baby. It is the baby who receives the mother's breast, who is allowed to cry and dirty itself. The young child does not love or understand the baby, to whom she reacts with hatred and desperation. Because of this, in the case histories of our patients the hatred toward the pregnant mother, the mother giving birth, and the younger siblings always reappears. If we wish to save our older children from this suffering, we should wait until they are 4 or 5 years old before giving them a sibling. This is easy to achieve in the contemporary family, because parents now tend to regulate pregnancy and to have fewer children.

Of course, the child's development and transformation into an adult does not depend on these factors alone but on a complex interrelationship between her innate capacities, upbringing, social environment, and so forth. The child is integrated into a society that influences her and that she influences from childhood on. Providing a secure childhood offers the foundation for a positive development.

We live at a difficult moment and in a world undergoing constant change. We offer our children neither the external security nor the limitations of an earlier time. But thanks to Freud and the restlessness his discoveries awakened among researchers in his own and other disciplines, we have learned how to give our children a maximum of internal security. I should like to remind the reader once again of the experiment with monkeys carried out in Wisconsin [by Harlow and

Zimmermann]. The little monkey raised by a mother made from wire netting could not endure a confrontation with something unknown (the mechanical toy), because it saw *a priori* something bad in it and had no resources with which to modify this first impression. Its reaction was to withdraw and become psychotic. A young monkey that could seek refuge in the mother made of cloth learned to confront new things, to lose its fear, and to be curious, which, when applied to the human infant, means to firmly establish the basis for the capacity to adapt and to investigate. But only a monkey raised by a real mother could later know how to choose a partner and to successfully bond. Or, translating this again to human beings, in this world of ours with, in many regards, its unknown future, only the infant raised by a mother who is really present—and this obviously implies the real presence of the father—will be able to love life and to successfully embrace it. And if the child is a female, she will know how to transmit her mental health to the next generation.*

---

*In the past several decades, with the advent of the feminist movement, the meaning of the mother–daughter relationship has become much more of a focus within psychoanalysis, and feminist psychoanalysts have written specifically about the nature of this relationship. Langer's contributions to this discourse are discussed in the Afterword of this volume. For provocative analyses of feminist and psychoanalytic visions of the mother–daughter relationship, see the chapter "Feminist Discourse/Maternal Discourse," in *The Mother/Daughter Plot: Narrative, Psychoanalysis, Feminism,* ed. M. Hirsch (Bloomington: Indiana University Press, 1989) and J. Butler, "Gender Trouble, Feminist Theory, and Psychoanalytic Discourse," in *Feminism/Postmodernism,* ed. L. J. Nicholson (New York: Routledge, 1990).

Notes

Chapter 1

1. However, in some works, for example, " 'Civilized' Sexual Morality and Modern Nervous Illness," Freud attributes female intellectual inferiority to the greater educational coercion suffered by little girls in response to their sexual curiosity.

2. I use the term in the sense of psychological incorporation.

3. [Tr. note: This footnote was added in the 1964 edition of the book.] I add to this overview, written in 1951, a note in order to complete the discussion about penis envy and at least to mention the very important concept of breast envy.

In *Envy and Gratitude*, which appeared in 1955, Melanie Klein returns to the theme of envy. She describes how this destructive feeling emerges already in the dyadic relationship between the child and the mother and is directed against the breast. Because for the child the breast is the creative source of all that she lacks, upon feeling frustrated by it she believes that the breast feeds itself in place of gratifying her. She attacks and destroys it in her unconscious phantasies.

This primitive envy, difficult to understand without having studied the concept of unconscious phantasy and other Kleinian theories, can nonetheless be clearly observed in analysis within the transference relationship. In my work "Sterility and Envy," presented at the 20th International Psychoanalytic Association Congress, I demonstrated how this envy forms the basis of many of the disorders described in this book and established, as well, the distinct connections between breast envy and penis envy, as summarized in the following points: (a) As Melanie Klein already found in 1928, the voraciousness of the small girl and her envy of the breast lead her to envy and to desire the father's penis as well, because she believes that the possession of this organ makes her capable of receiving the mother's breast. Penis envy, then, is proportional in its intensity to the girl's voraciousness and her envy of the breast. (b) Given the fact that breast envy motivates the girl to attack the mother's body and to fear her retaliation and that she defends herself against the fear of the destruction of her femininity by adopting a masculine position that implies penis envy, this envy is, ultimately, the result of her breast envy. (c) Melanie Klein has demonstrated that the girl abandons the breast and turns toward the penis because in her phantasies she considers it to be an inexhaustible breast. But since her breast envy originates in the phantasy that the breast feeds itself instead of feeding her, she in turn reacts toward the penis with jealousy and envy, suspecting that the penis also feeds itself and her mother. In this way, her breast envy is transformed directly into penis envy. (d) Finally, the girl's lack of any creative organ, be it the breast of the adult woman or the penis, forms the basis of her envy of both.

Chapter 2

1. A significant part of this chapter appeared under the title "The Myth of the Stewed Child" in the *Revista de Psicoanálisis*.

2. I can add another clinical observation with a similar content, that of a hysterical conversion symptom. A mother who is breast-feeding her several-week-old baby one day feels an unexpectedly painful spasm in her breasts, which intensifies until becoming intolerable. The pain disappears suddenly when she relates it to an incident that had occurred several hours earlier. She had received a letter in which her mother communicated to her that it had become necessary for her to accept the economic aid her daughter had offered some time previously. What the patient expressed through her symptom was that she was willing to give her breast to her infant, with whom she identified, but not to feed her mother, because to do so would be to let herself be eaten by her. This condition was expressed and protested against through her pain, which disappeared when its significance became conscious.

3. A while ago I was told that a very wealthy woman, who was generally not stingy, used to take from the kitchen cupboard each morning a bag full of sugar cubes. She carefully counted out each of the many servants' share of the cubes for that day. Afterward she gave them to the cook and put the rest back under lock and key. At first I felt this attitude to be offensive because of its contrast with the economic condition and lifestyle of the family. But then I concluded that probably the good woman's mother did the same to her when she was a child and had asked for caramels or other inexpensive candies.

4. A 4-year-old girl who had a new baby brother asked her father, "What does one do to make a baby's heart stop beating? Is it enough to hold it down real hard?"

Chapter 3

1. I recommend, especially to physicians, *Psychosomatic Gynecology*, by Kroger and Freed, which contains an extensive compilation of the literature

and an exposition of the physiological and physiopathological mechanisms that underlie the various disorders that we will study in the clinical section of this book.

2. The English-speaking girl refers to her menses as the "curse." Even the more inoffensive word *indisposed* transforms menstruation into an illness.

Chapter 4

1. Some of the case histories presented in this chapter have been previously published. See Marie Langer, "Algunas aportaciones a la psicología de la menstruacion" ["Contributions to the Psychology of Menstruation"], *Patalogia Psicosomática*, Biblioteca de Psicoanálisis, Buenos Aires, 1948.

Chapter 5

1. Published under the title "Una sesión psicoanalítica." ["A Psychoanalytic Session"].

Chapter 7

1. Interview regarding a clinical history.
2. Benedek and her collaborators (1953) came to the same conclusion in their article.

Chapter 8

1. The symbolic meaning of the dream is not exhausted with this interpretation. The patient in the bath represents the experience of being inside the mother—inside a receptacle filled with liquid—as well as a typical identification with the fetus—her child inside of her. Thus, just as the patient's mother did not permit her to remain inside of her but threw her out by giving birth, neither does she permit her to relive, through a pregnancy and her identification with the fetus, her phantasies of returning to the maternal womb. Thus, the dream signifies the unconscious thought: "My mother did not love me, so she threw me out and doesn't want me to have children." We have also seen the phantasy of returning to the maternal womb as typical for individuals treated with indifference in their childhood.

2. Subsequent observations made in my private psychoanalytic practice and during my activity as a psychotherapist and director of a psychosomatic service in a hospital confirmed the importance, often fundamental, of the factors presented here.

3. I often observed through dream analysis of pregnant women that a woman unconsciously perceives the sex of the baby she carries within her.

4. Personal communication with Dr. David Liberman.

Chapter 9

1. Parts of this chapter were previously published in *Psicología Psicosomática* under the title "Aspectos Psicoanalíticos de Algunos Trastornos del Embarazo." ["Psychoanalytic Aspects of Some Disorders of Pregnancy"].

2. Vomiting that, because of its intensity, endangers the life of the pregnant woman.

3. A patient whose serious agoraphobia did not permit her to leave her house without being accompanied could do so perfectly well when she was pregnant. The fetus substituted for her mother's company.

4. Unfortunately, there exist some Pavlovians who, erroneously interpreting the concept of *Childbirth without Fear*, follow the same road. They simply substitute drugs and general anesthesia with suggestion and hypnosis.

Chapter 10

1. A part of this chapter has already been published with the same title in the *Revista de Psicoanálisis* (1945–46).

2. I am indebted for my awareness of this part of the experiment to a personal communication with Dr. Mirsky.

3. I would not completely discount the possibility that the rejection experienced by the mother through nursing unfavorably impacts on the chemical composition of the milk. But as of now, there are no studies that I know of with respect to this.

Bibliography

Abraham, Karl. (1927). A short study of the development of the libido, viewed in the light of mental disorders. In *Selected papers on psychoanalysis*. London: Hogarth.

Anselmino, Karl Julius. (1947). Schwangerschaften nach langjähriger,undehandelter Kinderlosigkeit. *Geburtshilfe und Frauenheilkunde*, Vol. VII, No. 1.

Anonymous. (1921). *Tugebuch eines halbwüchsigen Mädchens. Seltzer*. New York.

Bauer, Alfredo. (1957). *Aportes a la práctica del parto sin dolor [Contributions to the practice of childbirth without pain]*. Buenos Aires: Editorial Cartago.

Beauvoir, Simone de. (1953). *The second sex*. New York: Knopf. (Original work published 1949)

Benedek, Therese. (1950). Climacterium: A developmental phase. *The Psychoanalytic Quarterly*, Vol. XIX, No. 1.

Benedek, Therese, George C. Ham, F. P. Robbins, and Boris B. Rubenstein. (1953). Some emotional factors in infertility. *Psychosomatic Medicine*, Vol. XV, No. 5.

Benedek, Therese, and Boris B. Rubenstein. (1942). *The sexual cycle in women: The relation between ovarian function and psychodynamic processes*. Washington, DC: National Research Council.

Bergler, Edmund. (1946). *Unhappy marriage and divorce*. New York: International Universities Press.

Bonaparte, Marie. (1946). *Myths of war*. New York: Imago.

Brunswick, Ruth Mack. (1940). The preoedipal phase of the libido development. In R. Fliess (Ed.), *Psychoanalytic reader: An anthology of essential papers with critical introductions*. New York: International Universities Press.

Chadwick, Mary. Menstruationsangst. *Zeitschrift für Psychoanalytische Pädagogik*, Vol. IV.

Clifford, Stewart. (1948). Fetal anoxia at birth and cyanosis of the newborn. *American Journal of Diseases and Children*, Vol. LXXVI, No. 6.

Daly, C. D. (1928). Der Menstruationskomplex. *Imago*, Vol. XIV.

Daly, C. D. (1935). The menstruation complex in literature. *The Psychoanalytic Quarterly*, Vol. IV.

Deutsch, Helene. (1944). *The psychology of women*, Vol. I. New York: Grune & Stratton.

Deutsch, Helene. (1945). *The psychology of women*, Vol. II. New York: Grune & Stratton.

Devereux, George. (1950). The psychology of feminine genital bleeding. *International Journal of Psycho-Analysis*, Vol. XXXI, No. V.

Dick-Read, Grantly. (1944). *Childbirth without fear*. New York: Harper Brothers.

Dunbar, Flanders. (1932). The menopause and mental disorder. *Journal of Neurology and Psychopathology*, Vol. XII.

Dunbar, Flanders, and Raymond Squier. (1946) Emotional factors in the course of pregnancy. *Psychosomatic Medicine*, Vol. VII, No. VII.

Eastmann, Nicholson. (1948). Prevention of fetal anoxia. *American Journal of Diseases of Children*, Vol. LXXVI, No. 6.

Eisler, Josef. (1923). Uber hysterische Erscheinnugen am Uterns. *Internationale Zeitschrift für Psychoanalyse*, Vol. IX.

Engels, Frederick. (1972). *The origin of the family, private property, and the state*. New York: International Publishers. (Original work published 1942)

Freud, Sigmund. (1892–1893). A case of successful treatment by hypnosis. In J. Strachey (Ed. and Trans.), *The standard edition of the complete psychological works of Sigmund Freud*, Vol. 1, pp. 116–128. London: Hogarth Press.

Freud, Sigmund. (1905). Three essays on the theory of sexuality. In J. Strachey (Ed. and Trans.), *The standard edition of the complete psychological works of Sigmund Freud*, Vol. 7, pp. 135–245. London: Hogarth Press.

Freud, Sigmund. (1908). Civilized sexual morality and modern nervous illness. In J. Strachey (Ed. and Trans.), *The standard edition of the complete psychological works of Sigmund Freud*, Vol. 9, pp. 181–204. London: Hogarth Press.

Freud, Sigmund. (1909). Analysis of a phobia in a five-year-old boy. In J. Strachey (Ed. and Trans.), *The standard edition of the complete psychological works of Sigmund Freud*, Vol. 10, pp. 5–149. London: Hogarth Press.

Freud, Sigmund. (1917). Mourning and melancholia. In J. Strachey (Ed. and Trans.), *The standard edition of the complete psychological works of Sigmund Freud*, Vol. 14, pp. 243–260. London: Hogarth Press.

Freud, Sigmund. (1918[1917]). The taboo of virginity (contributions to the psychology of love, III). In J. Strachey (Ed. and Trans.), *The standard edition of the complete psychological works of Sigmund Freud*, Vol. 11, pp. 193–208. London: Hogarth Press.

Freud, Sigmund. (1923[1922]). Two encyclopaedia articles: (B) The libido theory. In J. Strachey (Ed. and Trans.), *The standard edition of the complete psychological works of Sigmund Freud*, Vol. 18, pp. 255–259. London: Hogarth Press.

Freud, Sigmund. (1923). The infantile genital organization: An interpolation into the theory of sexuality. In J. Strachey (Ed. and Trans.), *The standard edition of the complete psychological works of Sigmund Freud*, Vol. 19, pp. 141–153. London: Hogarth Press.

Freud, Sigmund. (1924). The dissolution of the Oedipus complex. In J. Strachey (Ed. and Trans.), *The standard edition of the complete psychological works of Sigmund Freud*, Vol. 19, pp. 172–187. London: Hogarth Press.

Freud, Sigmund. (1924). The economic problem of masochism. In J. Strachey (Ed. and Trans.), *The standard edition of the complete psychological works of Sigmund Freud*, Vol. 19, pp. 159–170. London: Hogarth Press.

Freud, Sigmund. (1930). Civilization and its discontents. In J. Strachey (Ed. and Trans.), *The standard edition of the complete psychological works of Sigmund Freud*, Vol. 21, pp. 64–145. London: Hogarth Press.

Freud, Sigmund. (1931). Female sexuality. In J. Strachey (Ed. and Trans.), *The standard edition of the complete psychological works of Sigmund Freud*, Vol. 21, pp. 225–243. London: Hogarth Press.

Freud, Sigmund. (1933[1932]). New introductory lectures on psychoanalysis. In J. Strachey (Ed. and Trans.), *The standard edition of the complete psychological works of Sigmund Freud*, Vol. 22, pp. 5–182. London: Hogarth Press.

Freud, Sigmund. (1937). Analysis terminable and interminable. In J. Strachey (Ed. and Trans.), *The standard edition of the complete psychological works of Sigmund Freud*, Vol. 23, pp. 216–253. London: Hogarth Press.

Grinberg, León. (1964). *Culpa y depresión [Guilt and depression]*. Buenos Aires: Editorial Paidós.

Hann-Kende, Fanny. (1933). Ueber Klitorisonanie und Panisneid. *Internationale Zeitschrift für Psychoanalyse*, Vol. XIX, No. 3.

Harlow, H. F., and R. R. Zimmermann. (1959). The development of affectional responses in infant monkeys. *Science*, Vol. 130, pp. 421–432.

Hartmann, Heinz. (1927). *Die Grundlagen der Psychoanalyse*. Vienna: Psychoanalytischer Verlag.

Horney, Karen. (1923). Zur Genesis des weiblichen Kastrationskomplexes. *Internationale Zeitschrift für Psychoanalyse*, Vol. IX, No. 1.

Horney, Karen. (1926). The flight from womanhood. *The International Journal of Psycho-Analysis*, Vol. VII.

Horney, Karen. (1931). Die Pramenstruellen Verstimmungen. *Zeitschrift für Psychoanalytische Pädagogik*, Vol. V, No. 5/6.

Horney, Karen. (1933). The denial of the vagina. *The International Journal of Psycho-Analysis*, Vol. XIV, No. 1.

Horney, Karen. (1934). The overvaluation of love. *The Psychoanalytic Quarterly*, Vol. III, No. 4.

Horney, Karen. (1967). On the genesis of the castration complex in women.

In H. Kelman (Ed.), _Feminine psychology._ New York: W. W. Norton. (Original work published 1924, in _International Journal of Psycho-Analysis_, Vol. V, Pt. 1, pp. 50–65.)

Hupfer, Susanna. (1932). Ueber Schwangerschaftsgelüste. _Internationale Zeitschrift für Psychoanalyse_, Vol. XVI.

Jacobson, Edith. (1946). A case of sterility. _The Psychoanalytic Quarterly_, Vol. XV, No. 3.

Jones, Ernest. (1938). Early female sexuality. In _Papers of psychoanalysis._ Baltimore: W. Wood. (Original work published 1913—various editions revised and enlarged in subsequent years.)

Kardiner, Abram. (1939). _The individual and his society._ New York: Columbia University Press.

Klein, Henriette, Howard Potter, and Ruth B. Dyk. (1950). Anxiety in pregnancy and childbirth.

Klein, Melanie. (1952). Notes on some schizoid mechanisms. In _Developments in psycho-analysis._ London: Hogarth Press.

Klein, Melanie. (1957). _Envy and gratitude._ London: Tavistock.

Klein, Melanie. (1975). _The psychoanalysis of children._ New York: Delta. (Original work published 1932)

Krapf, Eduardo. (1948). Contribución al conocimiento de la histeria de conversión [Contribution to the knowledge of conversion hysteria]. _Patología Psicosomática [Psychosomatic Pathology]._ Buenos Aires: Biblioteca Psicoanalítica.

Kroger, William, and Charles Freed. (1951). _Psychosomatic gynecology including problems of obstetrical care._ Philadelphia: W. B. Saunders.

Langer, Marie. (1948). Algunas aportaciones a la psicolgía de la menstruación [Some contributions to the psychology of menstruation]. _Patología Psicosomática ._ Buenos Aires: Biblioteca de Psicoanálisis.

Langer, Marie. (1948). Aspectos psicoanalíticos de algunos trastornos del embarazo [Psychoanalytic aspects of various disorders of pregnancy]. _Patología Psicosomática._ Buenos Aires: Biblioteca de Psicoanálisis.

Langer, Marie. (1948). Problemas psicológicos de la lactancia [Psychological problems of breast-feeding]. _Patología Psicosomática._ Buenos Aires: Biblioteca de Psicoanálisis.

Langer, Marie. (1949). El viaje al centro de la tierra [Trip to the center of the earth]. _Revista de Psicoanálisis_, Vol. VII, No. 1.

Langer, Marie. (1950). El mito del niño asado [The myth of the stewed child]. _Revista de Psicoanálisis_, Vol. VII, No. 3.

Langer, Marie. (1951). Una sessión psicoanalítica [A psychoanalytic session]. _Revista de Psicoanálisis_, Vol. VIII, No. 2.

Langer, Marie. (1958). Sterility and envy. _International Journal of Psycho-Analysis_, Vol. XXXIX, Parts ii–iv.

Langer, Marie, and Celes Carcamo. (1948). Psicoanálisis de las esterilidad femenina [Psychoanalysis of female sterility]. _Patología Psicosomática._ Buenos Aires: Biblioteca de Psicoanálisis.

Langer, Marie, and Raúl Park Ochandorena. (1953). El espasmo de las trompas como origen de la esterilidad [Tubal spasm as a cause of sterility]. *Revista de Psicoanálisis*, Tomo X, No. 1.

Lewin, Bertram. (1945). Ensuciarse con heces, menstruación y superyó femenino [To dirty oneself with feces and menstruation and the female superego]. *Revista de Psicoanálisis*, Vol. III, No. 1.

Lorand, Sandor. (1939). Contribution to the problem of vaginal orgasm. *The International Journal of Psycho-Analysis*, Vol. X, No. 4.

Lundberg, Ferdinand, and Marynia Farnham. (1947). *Modern woman, the lost sex*. New York: Harper Brothers.

Marañon, G. (1935). *Ginecología endocrina [Endocrinological gynecology]*. Madrid: Editorial Espasa Calpe.

Mead, Margaret. (1968). *Coming of age in Samoa*. New York: Dell. (Original work published 1928)

Mead, Margaret. (1935). *Sex and temperament in three primitive societies*. New York: William Morrow.

Mead, Margaret. (1949). *Male and female: A study of the sexes in a changing world*. New York: William Morrow.

Meng, Heinrich. (1931). Ueber Pubertätund Pubertätsaufklärung*Zeitschrift für Psychoanalytische Pädagogik*,Vol. V, No. 5.

Moulton, Ruth. (1942). The psychosomatic implications of pseudocyesis. *Psychosomatic Medicine*, Vol. IV.

Muller, Josine. (1931). Ein Beitrag zur Frage der Libidoentwicklung des Mädchensin der genitalen Phase. *Zeitschrift für Psychoanalyse*, Vol. 17.

Newton, Michael, and Niles Rumley Newton. (1948). The let-down reflex in human lactation. *The Journal of Pediatrics*, Vol. XXXIII, No. 6.

Racker, Heinrich. (1950). *Contribución al psicoanálisis de la neurosis de transferencia [Contribution to the psychoanalysis of the transference neurosis]*. Paper presented at a meeting of the Argentine Psychoanalytic Association.

Reik, Theodor. (1919). *Probleme der Religionspsychologie*. Leipzig, East Germany: Internationaler Psychoanalytischer Verlag.

Ribble, Margaret A. (1943). *The rights of infants*. New York: Columbia University Press.

Robbins, Lewis. Suggestions for the psychological study of sterility of women. *Bulletin of the Menninger Clinic*, Vol. VII, No. 1.

Salerno, Enrique. (1948). El aborto espontáneo emocional [Emotional miscarriage]. *Patología Psicosomática*. Beunos Aires: Biblioteca de Psicoanálisis.

Santayana, George. (1935). *The last puritan: A memoir in the form of a novel*. London: Constable.

Schmiedeberg, Melitta. (1931). Psychoanalytisches zur Menstruation. *Zeitschrift für Psychoanalytische Pädagogik*,Vol. V, No. 5–6.

Schwab, Max. (1932). Die Ursachen des unstillbaren Erbrechens. *Zentralblatt für Cunekologic*, Vol. XLV.

Spitz, René G. (1957). *No and yes: On the genesis of human communication*. New York: International Universities Press.

Steckel, Wilhelm. (1943). *Frigidity in woman, in relation to her love life*. New York: Liveright.

Sterba, Richard. (1968). *Introduction to the psychoanalytic theory of the libido*. New York: R. Brunner. (Original work published 1942)

Stieve, H. (1942). Die Zentralnervöse Steuerung, der Geschlechtsorgane. *Medizinische Klinik*, No. 1–2.

Stieve, H. Nervös bedingte Veränderungen and den Geschlechtsorganen Deutsche. *Medizinische Wochenschrift*, No. 34.

Velde, Theodore H. van de. (1957). *Ideal marriage: Its physiology and technique*. New York: Random House.

Winterstein, Alfred Robert Friedrich. (1928). Die Pubertätsritender Mädchen und ihre Spuren in Märchen*Imago*, Vol. XVI.

Zilboorg, Gregory. (1947). Masculino y femenino [Masculine and feminine]. *Revista de Psicoanálisis*, Vol. V, No. 2.

Zilboorg, Gregory. (1945). *Historia de la psicología Médica [The history of medical psychology]*. Buenos Aires: Librería Hachette.

Afterword

NANCY CARO HOLLANDER

Just as the fetishism of commodities conceals the fact that their value is produced by the labor of the working class, so too does phallic fetishism deny that behind the vulva, which it has reduced to a mere hole or wound, the vagina leads to the woman's reproductive organs. Thus, the working class and the female gender are deprived of the right over their products and of their legitimate power.

—Marie Langer

Marie Langer's life, which had for more than two decades been dedicated to career and family, would undergo a dramatic change in the years following the 1964 publication of *Motherhood and Sexuality*. Despite her promise in the 1972 prologue to write a sequel to her study, Langer never had time to write another book-length treatment of female sexuality and motherhood. Instead, her publications in subsequent years reflected concerns that emerged from her experiences as a politically engaged psychoanalyst and feminist. The sixties and seventies were a tumultuous period in Argentina, one in which revolutionary movements in culture and politics grew to represent a challenge to the old social and economic structures of underdevelopment that had condemned the majority of its citizens to an impoverished life. In the articles she published from the early seventies on, Langer's central concern revolved around the need to integrate aspects of Marxist, feminist, and psychoanalytic theories of the oppression of women. She studied the political strategies being developed by the new generation

265

of feminists in the United States and Europe, as well as the theoretical directions being opened up by feminists reappropriating psychoanalysis as a vehicle for explicating patriarchy and the reproduction of female subordination. Her clinical practice with women in Argentina, Mexico, and Nicaragua reflected her departure from psychoanalytic orthodoxy in response to the economic and political exigencies of the time. The shift in her intellectual and professional development was framed by her own political activism, carried out in the violent conditions of dictatorship and rebellion in Latin America.

A New Synthesis:
Psychoanalysis and Marxism*

In 1966 Langer's husband died and her children were growing up and pursuing their own interests and ambitions. As the sixties drew to a close, social and economic conditions in Argentina prompted the middle classes to a new political activism in which Langer participated. She felt free now to act in light of her political desires and interests without compromising her family. Argentina was suffering the legacy of a decade of failed economic policies perpetrated by a series of inept civilian governments and repressive military regimes. Escalating inflation, rising unemployment, and a concentration of wealth gave rise to heightened workers' struggles and a radicalization of students and middle-class professionals. These forces coalesced in the general strikes that broke out in many Argentine cities in 1969 in which workers and students, supported by neighborhood organizations, occupied major sectors of the capital and provincial cities until they were dislodged by army troops.[1]

The psychoanalytic community was directly affected by these events and became an important arena in which opposing political forces confronted one another in a heated ideological struggle. Langer, along with several of her peers, many younger colleagues, and a number of incoming candidates who were members of leftist political parties and movements articulated the need for psychoanalysis to embrace a social perspective of human suffering. These dissidents critiqued institutionalized psychoanalysis for its rigidity and elitism, arguing that the contributions of the Argentine Psychoanalytic Association (APA) were now overshadowed by its inhibition of true intellectual discourse

---

*All direct quotes, unless otherwise specified, are from taped interviews by the author with Marie Langer in Mexico and Nicaragua, 1983 through 1986, as part of the research for a biography of Langer.

and its unwillingness to critique the external limits on individual psychological change imposed by the exploitative class relations of Argentine society. The apolitical tradition within the APA, which argued for neutrality in the psychoanalytic enterprise and for a value-free scientific inquiry, was challenged by Langer and others who insisted that scientific endeavor was always guided by human subjectivity and that ideology, not neutrality, permeated the psychoanalytic experience.[2] These psychoanalysts argued for the integration of a psychoanalytic theory of human subjectivity with a Marxist conceptualization of class society and hegemonic ideology.

This sentiment was articulated internationally in a number of psychoanalytic associations by socially concerned candidates and senior analysts who were responding to the student and worker protests in many European nations and the antiwar movement in the United States. Anger at the hierarchical rigidity and noncommittal politics of the International Psychoanalytic Association (IPA) moved dissidents to organize parallel countercongresses at two IPA meetings, the first in 1969 in Rome and the second in 1971 in Vienna, in an attempt to develop a psychoanalysis relevant to the dramatic social crises affecting the world. Langer participated in both countercongresses but also presented a highly controversial paper entitled "Psychoanalysis and/or Social Revolution," at the official congress of 1971. In it she asserted the inevitability of radical transformation of contemporary society and urged her colleagues to use their psychoanalytic knowledge to facilitate rather than to oppose the process of change. She admonished them not to follow in the footsteps of the analysts who had left Cuba following the 1959 revolution or those who were preparing their departure from Chile in response to the election of the Popular Unity candidate, Salvador Allende, as President. "This time," she asserted, "we will renounce neither Marx nor Freud."[3] Langer was to say later that she considered her paper "a fitting farewell to her long years of participation in the International." She was saddened at the disapproval expressed by some colleagues but heartened by new friendships with others, "who expressed support for my critique of the politics of the International."[4] But, most importantly, in Vienna, where so many years earlier she had been unable to integrate her social concerns with her interest in psychoanalysis, she was now part of a movement within the profession that asserted the necessity of just such a project.

In October 1971 the Argentine dissidents broke with the APA, convinced that reform of the institution from within was impossible. They wished to make psychoanalysis responsive to the political drama facing their country. Viewing themselves in the tradition of Reich, Fenichel, Fromm and Marcuse—psychoanalysts with socialist convictions and social theorists with a psychoanalytic critique of bourgeois society—they set themselves the task of addressing in theory and practice the social domain of psychological pain.[5] As the national economic and political crisis in Argentina deepened, Langer and other dissidents wished to create "a psychoanalysis bound to an ethic of engagement in the struggle against a repressive society."

Langer took a leadership role among psychoanalysts, psychiatrists, psychologists, and social workers who aligned themselves with the progressive sectors of Argentine society fighting for political democracy and economic structures responsive to the needs of working people. These activities were carried out amidst growing violence on the part of military governments aimed at repressing popular unrest. Langer coedited two volumes called *Cuestionamos*,[6] collections of articles whose authors analyzed different aspects of the relationship between psychoanalysis and social change: the nature of violence and aggression within repressive societies; the character of mourning in societies where imprisonment, torture, disappearances, and assassinations touch the lives of a significant percentage of the population; and the role of reparation in revolutionary struggle. Langer's contribution to the second volume was an article entitled "Woman: Her Limits and Potential." The article explored the convergence of Marxism, psychoanalysis, and feminism in the conceptualization of the specific nature of woman's oppression. It was the product of Langer's theoretical development and a response to her professional and political contact with working-class women. This article deserves to be described in some detail not only because it demonstrates the direction in Langer's thinking but because it was what she chose to write in lieu of a sequel to *Motherhood and Sexuality*.

Psychoanalysis and Marxist Feminist Politics

Langer sought to explore the manner in which both Marxism and psychoanalysis offered a particular way of understanding the roots of the oppression of women. In both modes of thought, she contended, one could find a conceptualization of the "invisible" aspect of female existence, which was the consequence of biological forces (according to psychoanalysis) or socioeconomic factors (according to Marxism) that have marked the limits of woman's social role and determined the ideological representation of womanhood. Langer elaborated the three psychoanalytic perspectives of Freud, Horney, and Klein, all of whom relate woman's inferiority feelings and anxieties to anatomical causes, understood to be either the lack of a penis or the invisibility of the female genitalia. She reviewed the Marxist analysis of the historical oppression of women, focusing on the theory of "invisible labor," which suggests that female labor is characterized by the elaboration of products that have attributes of use value (rather than exchange value, a characteristic of commodities bought and sold for money in the market economy) and that are for direct and private consumption within the family. Woman is segregated from the world of surplus value, where the products of labor are economically visible and destined to create wealth through exchange value in the market. Woman's labor, essential to the economic system through its maintenance and reproduction of labor power, is invisible because it receives no monetary remuneration or status. The nature of domestic work is its repetitive quality, and the only visible product is the child.[7] While for both psychoanalysis and Marxism woman's anatomy has determined her destiny, from the Marxist perspective woman's specific character has emerged from the sexual division of labor in which she is condemned to the "invisible" labor of maintenance and reproduction of the next generation of workers; for the majority of psychoanalysts, woman's "invisible" genitals translates into the female child's ignorance of pleasure or her procreative capacity, which can be realized only in the distant future. Her lack of awareness of sexual potential represents the etiology of woman's sense of inferiority and conflict. Her failure to achieve psychological autonomy is rooted in her biology and manifested in the limited parameters of her life within the confines of domesticity. The family and her function in it become the only measure of her "normal" development.

Langer went on to demonstrate how the social restrictions of women to the domestic sphere and the cultural imperatives to adapt to it are internalized as part of the superego so that women remain divested of a critical conscious awareness of the structural source of their sense of inferiority and the conflictual relationship to their work and intimate relationships. She criticized the role that psychology has played in urging an attitude of conformity among women and in interpreting any gesture of rebellion against this oppressive situation as lamentable and dangerous.

In this article Langer recounted a research project initiated in a public hospital in a working-class neighborhood in Buenos Aires in the early seventies that illustrated how the shift in her thinking about women and her political activism had opened up new possibilities in her clinical work. The project's purpose was to examine the pathogenic conditions of the conflictual family structure among the working-class and the psychopathology of working-class housewives.[8] The presenting complaint of the majority of working-class housewives who came to the hospital seeking treatment was depression. Langer and her colleagues found that most of the women were characterized by immature personality development and reactive depressions while the rest suffered from less specifically defined conditions, including vague anxiety feelings, weepyness, exhaustion, and the lack of mature affective capacity and sexual responsiveness. Half of the women manifested various forms of hypochondria. Most had developed their symptoms upon marrying and becoming housewives and mothers, and they remembered with nostalgia the days when they had worked outside the home. Langer and her two cotherapists shared a political critique of the class and gender system that had withdrawn their patients from remunerated work and participation in political and union struggles. In the group therapy sessions with these patients, they grappled with the question of how a politically engaged psychoanalyst could remain faithful to a therapeutic intervention based fundamentally on interpretation, rather than assume a supportive or didactic approach. The issue of neutrality in the psychoanalytic endeavor was of interest as well, and Langer once again sought to demonstrate that every intervention on the part of a therapist carries with it an ideological perspective, conscious or unconscious.

The description of a specific episode in one group therapy session crystallized the change in Langer's clinical approach. She was the principal therapist and supervised the two female psychologists who were her cotherapists. One patient, pregnant with her first child, spoke about wanting to pursue a college education in order to avoid a future that duplicated her mother's frustrating life.

Langer analyzed the significance of three different interventions. She argued that the comment of one of the psychologists ("You are competing with your mother") was essentially an oedipal interpretation, one directed at the child within the adult woman who continues to compete for her father. She suggested that the other psychologist's interpretation ("You are competing with your husband") pointed to penis envy, that is, to the negative oedipal complex, and that its implicit goal was to help the patient work through this envy, discard it, and adopt a "feminine" attitude toward the husband-father, accepting the baby as a substitute for the penis. For this patient, it would mean renouncing first her studies and then, over time as her husband's work brought a degree of economic security, the opportunity for working outside the home. Langer believed that these two oedipal interpretations tended to transform a "rebellious" woman into a submissive housewife and future patient. Dedicated to the invisible labor in the home, this woman would live as her mother had, in total emotional dependency on her husband-father and on her child, the only visible product of her labor. Such a life would make her more infantile than her husband and less able to sublimate. Her own low self-esteem would provoke envy of her husband's involvements, including his political activity. Thus, these two interventions, made in good faith by individuals who consciously had little intention of supporting the existing patriarchal family, represented at the unconscious level an ideology supportive of the existing class and gender system.

Langer than addressed the significance of her own intervention, which she made taking into account the fact that the patient's husband was a student who also worked and engaged in leftist political activities. The first part of her interpretation ("It is true that you would like to go beyond your mother and have the same opportunities as your husband. And why not? It is your right") dealt with the oedipal material but tried to suggest that the patient discriminate between her infantile desires and her rights as an adult woman. The second part ("But there are two avenues to achieve this: the struggle for an individual solution or the struggle with others collectively, so that everyone can change these conditions of deprivation") pointed to another aspect of the oedipal drama and of human history. It alluded to the husband-brother rather than the husband-father. Langer summarized Freud's description, in *Totem and Taboo*, of the origins of the Oedipus complex. Freud argued that at the dawn of human history the horde of brothers allied themselves in the murder of the tyrannical father who had exploited them and who, in order to possess all the women, had expelled his sons when they reached sexual maturity. After the father's murder, the sons consumed his remains, thus introjecting his power as a superego. Then, obeying the superego injunction, incest with mothers and sisters of the horde was forbidden so that the crime would not be repeated. When we speak of the Oedipus complex, asserted Langer, we almost always refer to the prohibition against the desire of the son for the mother and his competition with the father. In so doing, she claimed, we ignore another important situation, equally prohibited and repressed by the superego, which is prior to the Oedipal crime: the alliance among the brothers. We can deduce, she maintained, that the most "criminal" activity, and thus the one that is the most severely prohibited and repressed by the paternal superego, is the conquest of the mutual jealousy among brothers in order to dethrone the father. Interpreted in terms of social organization, this activity would signify putting solidarity among comrades ahead of individual and family welfare and respect for the established authority. So, concluded Langer, to speak to the patient of the "second alternative" indicates to her implicitly that she should not confuse her husband with her father but symbolically see him as equivalent to her brother. Then she might ally herself with him and other comrades against the system.[9]

Langer took the position of many contemporary feminist theorists of the early 1970s that the family was, ideologically, the central mediating institution of the class and gender system. The family needed to be critically reevaluated in terms of its destructive impact on women, as well as in the light of its stabilizing role in maintaining the authoritarian values of class society. Sharing with radical feminists their emphasis on the right of women to control their own bodies in sexual pleasure and reproduction, Langer criticized as ideology and not science the traditional assumptions within psychoanalysis that condemned women to define themselves passively in relation to men and children. And, like her feminist counterparts in the United States and Europe, Langer was willing to entertain the idea of a profound alteration at the very core of personal relationships within the patriarchal family. For example, she critiqued her own prior conviction that breast-feeding in particular and an intense mother–infant relationship in general were essential to the mental health of both mother and child. She now argued that an individual's psychological health did not require a dependent relationship with the mother, who was, in fact, often unable to give psychologically to her child due to the multiple demands on her time and energy. She viewed the resistance to the idea of alternative forms of childrearing, such as the collective child-care centers in Eastern Europe and the Soviet Union, as a fear of losing the intense tie between mother and child, a sentiment based on the deeply held conviction that a child should love its mother above all other people. But, argued Langer, love was characterized by different qualities depending on the nature of the relationship. A child who did not depend solely on its mother and a mother who did not sacrifice all other interests to her maternal role learned from the beginning to engage in a more equal and balanced relationship. Langer emphasized the central importance of the psychological availability of the father in the rearing of children, especially in early childhood. The presence of adult males in general—teachers, caregivers, psychologists—was essential in the lives of young girls as well as boys, she wrote, for the healthy development of their sexual identity. Boys and girls needed the presence and early affective connection to both sexes in order to be able to identify with one and differentiate themselves from the other.[10]

Do we run the risk of destroying the family? asked Langer. Perhaps. But was it such a healthy institution? She believed it was difficult to question the mother–child relationship because to do so implied not only an attack on the basic unit of society but on our own most intimate and absolute relationship based on private property, that is, an attack on the most possessive kind of connection that exists, in which children belong to parents and learn from them an identity based on possession. When a woman could be creative in visible work, perhaps she would not need her child to be her unique product, better than all the rest, into whom she projects her own desires, ambitions, and anxieties.

Langer ended the article on an optimistic note about the human potential to build a society in which social relations would not be based on the idea of mutual possession. She believed in the necessity of committing oneself to the struggle against the great economic and social inequities of class society, and she argued that an authentically equitable society would not be possible without gender equality. She cited Freud's contention in "Civilization and its Discontents" that while the socialization of the means of production would eliminate one of the important roots of human aggression, the more significant source lay in the domain of sexual relations, in which jealousy, envy, and the need to possess the desired object provoked the most violent feelings in human beings. These relations were already being challenged, claimed Langer, by sexual liberation movements and by the new forms of the family emerging in the prior decade. In order for that process to advance, men, women, and children had to be willing to renounce their possession of one another, something of which Langer thought human beings were ultimately capable. "In describing a future I believe possible," she wrote, "I hope I am not straying . . . into science fiction or into the intellectual sin of idealism. I believe that if we continue forward in a manner consistent with what has already been laid down in the past—a past that is observable in the present—predictions based on what can already be glimpsed for the future become legitimate."[11]

Psychoanalysis as Political Activism

It was Langer's political activism that permitted her to believe in the possibility of a future so radically different from the problematic conditions of the present. "At last I could act in concert with my values and beliefs—with my ego ideal—and dedicate myself to the things that really mattered to me. Only this time, unlike in Vienna so many years earlier where I had to separate my professional interest from my politics, I could finally be an activist within my profession and utilize my training as a psychoanalyst in the service of the popular classes." Langer and other political psychoanalysts began to work in hospital services, health centers, and outpatient clinics. Langer became president of the Argentine Federation of Psychiatrists (Federación Argentina de Psiquiatras, or FAP), an organization that vocally criticized political repression and supported workers' and students' struggles. The potential danger of Langer, as the head of FAP, being exposed to violence from the political Right was constant. She also took a leadership role in the creation of the Organization of Mental Health Workers, which together with the Association of Psychologists strove to democratize access to psychoanalytic training by making it available for the first time to nonmedical members of the mental health community. The two organizations established the Research and Training Centers (CDI's), the most important of which was in Buenos Aires. Training included theoretical and clinical courses, supervision of candidates' clinical work in hospitals, clinics, and unions, and activism in mental health trade unions. Although a short-lived experiment because of political persecution of its organizers, the CDI's demonstrated that psychoanalytic training outside the APA could be acquired at minimal cost and that psychoanalytic technique could be utilized with all social classes in a variety of settings.[12]

Members of FAP and the Organization of Mental Health Workers went to working-class neighborhoods and squatter settlements to practice in public clinics and health projects initiated by progressive political organizations. It was here that Langer met many women whom she came to respect and admire: middle-class professionals and students who were willing to sacrifice their class privilege in order to participate in a larger social project; working-class women who were the backbone of community organizations and unions struggling to improve the physical and social conditions of their neighborhoods and redress the exploitative circumstances of their labor. On many occasions Langer and others were called upon to treat political prisoners who had been released from jail or been tortured by the military or paramilitary forces. Occasionally, they received requests to provide psychological evaluations of activists whose mental state might potentially jeopardize comrades in clandestine organizations. And as members of FAP, they continued to denounce the gross abuses of power exercised by the military and paramilitary forces bent on shoring up an unjust and inequitable social order.

The politically committed mental health professionals faced the same possibility as other activists of being imprisoned, tortured, disappeared, or murdered. In fact, the mental health professions became a specific target of repressive forces that ranked Freud with Marx as a pathological influence on the body politic. Many psychoanalysts were forced into exile to protect themselves and their families. Such was the fate of Marie Langer. In 1974, on the eve of the military's

Draconian 7-year "Dirty War" against the civilian population, her name appeared on a death list of the right-wing, paramilitary Argentine Anticommunist Alliance. Pressured by family and friends, she sought exile in Mexico, where she was joined by her two daughters. Once again a political refugee, she joined thousands of other exiled Argentines who faced the challenge of reconstructing their lives in order to give meaning to an existence far removed from their country, families and the political struggle which had given them a sense of personal value and purpose.[13]

Mexico: Vicissitudes and Possibilities

Mexico proved hospitable to Langer. Shortly after her arrival, she began teaching and supervising in the graduate training program at the National University of Mexico and soon became affiliated with Mexican psychoanalytic and psychological institutes. In response to the widespread need for therapeutic treatment among the exile community, Langer and other Argentine mental health professionals established the Mental Health Commission, which functioned as an integral part of the Committee of Solidarity with the Argentine People (COSPA). Often their work went beyond psychological intervention and included aiding families in locating new residences and jobs. This work soon included aid to refugees fleeing military dictatorships from the entire Southern Cone and Central American countries as well and included research on the psychological effects of political repression. Various members of the Mental Health Commission, including Langer, published papers documenting their findings. They noted a variety of symptoms among their patients who had lived under repressive conditions, including depression, listlessness, symptomatic fear, intellectual impairment, psychosomatic illnesses, insomnia, difficulties in social interactions, and paranoia. Some individuals manifested a syndrome of survivor guilt, with its attendant symptomatology similar to that of concentration camp survivors. A majority of patients suffered from what Langer called "frozen grief," a condition resulting from the inability or lack of opportunity to elaborate the loss of loved ones, in which the combination of personally troubled relationships and traumatic loss due to political violence impeded normal mourning. Mental health professionals found that patients who had been jailed and tortured had experienced a situation damaging to their core sense of identity. Imprisonment had included the violation of the victim's physical and psychological boundaries owing to the withdrawal of familiar sources of reference. The degradation resulting from imposed submission to torturers and guards had meant a traumatic loss of autonomy, capacity for judgment, and decision making. Torture, sexual humiliation, and, in some cases, collaboration secured under these mentally and physically debilitating conditions had put into doubt the basic psychosocial identity of the victim.[14]

Working with victims of government repression in Argentina as well as in exile demonstrated to Langer and her colleagues how important their own commitment to human rights and democracy was to their patients' ability to trust them. Extreme political repression had clarified the impossibility of neutrality, both in the political and the professional domains. Knowing that the therapist had not remained silent or complicit in the face of the destruction of civil society facilitated a bond—the patient's willingness to trust the therapist— and therefore the working alliance that underlies the analytic process. The working through of traumatic experiences, the problem of social reintegration, and the reformulation of present and future plans were tasks that affected patient and therapist alike.[15] Along with other analysts treating the thousands of political refugees in Latin America and Europe, Langer noted how difficult it was for those in exile to maintain coherence with the past through political activism, which was, she thought, a significant aspect of reparation.

Indeed, it was Langer's ability to continue to act in concert with her political principles that enabled her to utilize the conditions of exile as an opportunity for growth and enrichment. Exile meant other possibilities as well. She reestablished friendships with European psychoanalytic colleagues she had not seen for years. She made new friends with young feminists from Europe, the United States, and Latin America, who appreciated her rare combination of wisdom and openness to new ideas and ways of thinking. To them Langer was a model for how to sustain one's youth and *joie de vivre* even in one's sixties and seventies. Her agile body, kept strong by frequent walking and swimming, made her appear much younger than her years; her white hair framed a pretty, lined, and tanned face with engaging blue eyes; and her Viennese-accented Spanish and flirtatious airs, still very much a part of her persona, were a charming complement to her serious and purposeful attitude. For Langer, relationships with younger friends and colleagues were gratifying and stimulating, but she also suffered from the lack of close friendships with people of her own age able to remain involved in a similar life project. She lamented, as well, the loneliness she sometimes experienced because she had no ongoing primary love relationship. She felt victimized by the taboo against sexuality in older women, which she believed was even stronger in Latin American cultures than in Europe or the United States.

However, she derived much pleasure from her family, who remained a close-knit clan. Her two daughters, their husbands, and children lived in Mexico, and Langer saw them often. Her sons, who had remained in Argentina, came periodically with their families to visit her. As always, however, her family shared Langer with the other passions of her life. Her eldest son was able to capture this quality in his mother, with perhaps a mixture of respect and regret, when he once said to her jokingly, "Mama, you're not one of those full-time grandmothers, like my mother-in-law; you're a part-timer." To which she had replied, "That's right! Or perhaps you could say I'm more like a grandfather, because I continue to work." And work she did, her busy schedule incorporating both her professional and political responsibilities.

Dialectic of Women's Struggles

Throughout this period Langer maintained an interest in the specificity of female experience. But whereas in the early seventies her writings had focused on a theoretical elaboration of the family and woman's role in it as a mark of her oppression, her political activism in Argentina and Mexico with women committed to the struggle against dictatorship and underdevelopment had shifted her interest. Now she was concerned with how women could collectively empower themselves while struggling alongside men for a radical transformation of oppressive social and economic institutions. She was sought out by Mexican, Argentine, and Central American women interested in feminism and in understanding the relationship between the psychological and social oppression of women and the economically oppressive relations of class society. Her writings from this period of her life reflect these concerns.

In "Women, Madness and Society,"[16] for example, Langer argued that in each gender there are particular manifestations of mental illness directly related to an individual's violation or exaggeration of gendered social norms. She analyzed mental illness specific to female experience, noting that symptoms such as low self-esteem, infantilization, and postpartum and menopausal depression are linked to the social restrictions imposed by the wife-mother role. Romantic love represents another source of madness in women, functioning as a full-time occupation that absorbs their vitality and capacity for independence through the objectification of self. Women are condemned to madness, wrote Langer, unless they have access to a transcendent purpose beyond their assigned role of reproduction: biological reproduction, ideological reproduction, and the reproduction of the labor force.

Alongside the love for one's partner and child, one needs to be able to affirm oneself as a subject, as agency in history.

Langer pointed to the example of the "Mothers of the Plaza de Mayo," Argentine grandmothers and mothers who organized weekly demonstrations in front of the presidential palace demanding of the repressive military dictatorship that it return their disappeared children and grandchildren. These women were called by Argentines "*las locas de la* [the madwomen of the] Plaza de Mayo." Why? Langer asked. Were they mad to openly oppose a state that had squelched all opposition to its Draconian power? Were they were mad to persist in their confrontation with a state that had already arrested or disappeared some of them? Were they mad—"bad women"—because they did not fulfill their mission of subordination to husband and children? No, they were not mad, nor did they go mad like so many mothers who chose to suffer their losses individually and silently, not daring to become part of a collective struggle to share their pain with others who had been victimized in the same manner by a repressive state. The sanity of the "Mothers of the Plaza" came from their capacity to act.[17] "They have a project that belongs to them, but which they share with their children, their husbands and their *compañeros*. In other words, their existence, their vital project, although very personal for each one of them, engages them in the desire for and the common struggle toward the transformation of society."

Langer also wrote "Coda on the Subject of Women" as part of an autobiographical narrative, *Memoria, Historia y Diálogo Psicoanalítico*, created in concert with two collaborators and published in 1981.[18] In this piece Langer turned her attention once again to the meaning of motherhood in contemporary woman's life, taking the opportunity to review recent feminist theory regarding the origins and nature of the patriarchal family and woman's role in it. With respect to the prevailing ideology of motherhood as *the* noble female function, she was especially interested in the political uses to which scientific theory was put. She pointed out that the views of Klein, Spitz, and Winnicott, for example, though admirable for their discovery of the importance of the early mother–child relationship to the future mental health of the child, became popular in the postwar period because they psychoanalytically justified the era's social imperatives to reinvigorate the domestic ideal of womanhood following the wartime integration of women into the public sphere. These psychoanalysts, like the psychiatrists who spoke of the "schizophrenogenic mother," wound up supporting a position similar to that taken by researchers in postwar England who blamed working-class women for their children's hunger, their precarious state of health, and even the defeat of the Empire.[19]

Langer argued that this posture, which caused women to live with a constant state of guilt—" 'colonized from within' to use Franz Fanon's concept"—could be located in cultural tradition. Rousseau's view of the ideal woman in *Emile*—the self-sacrificing and devoted Sophie, the wife whose dedication to motherhood came "naturally" and "instinctively"—was the ideological underpinning of the psychoanalytic perspective on women. Freud, Deutsch, Klein, and Winnicott's views retained Sophie as the referent for the truly feminine woman while the father in psychoanalytic theory, from Freud to Lacan, was the father who legislates, rewards or punishes, and represents the outside world. Langer believed that Deutsch's feminine woman, characterized by the triad of narcissism, masochism, and passivity, emerged in the 19th century as an ideological construct of industrial capitalism, with its separation of home from the workplace, and though she continued to exist, did so "as a superstructure of a specific era, already condemned to disappear."

What about the "new woman" who was taking the place of Rousseau's Sophie? She who chose to have a career instead of children, or a career *and* children, or children on her own without a partner? She who had opportunities her grandmother never even dreamed about? Was she happy? "After several years of psychoanalytic practice I know her inside out," wrote Langer. "I would say that in any case she is happier than Freud's patients were. But she does have conflicts and I would ask young psychoanalysts and psychotherapists, especially male colleagues, to help her solve them." Langer appealed to mental health professionals not to undermine their female patients' efforts to express their creative and productive talents in the social sphere by interpreting them as symptomatic of penis envy. Unsure of their rights and abilities, she insisted, these women should not be castrated. "An important aim of therapy should be, in fact, to help a daughter understand her guilt for having managed to surpass her mother, which derives from the old rivalry with mother who has now been defeated."

While women did have opportunities not imagined by their grandmothers, still the percentage of women in decision-making positions in public life was minimal. Langer was interested in how real equal rights and opportunities could be achieved that "satisfied both members of the couple." While a staunch supporter of feminism, she believed that insights could be gleaned from psychoanalysis to help women develop a feminist movement not seduced and thus weakened by antagonism toward men.

What is the role of feminist movements in the struggle to change political and economic systems that undermine the human potential to create and to derive pleasure from life in the majority of men and women? Langer argued that an independent feminist movement mobilized to challenge class relations and patriarchal culture is a necessary part of revolutionary struggle, though she was critical of the current within feminist ideology and politics that she considered to be essentially anti-male. Indeed, she warned against confusing the battle against patriarchy with a battle against men. From her psychoanalytic perspective, women's hostility against men is a symptom, that is, a compromise formation between repressed thoughts or feelings and the defense against them. She believed that the anxiety and hostility that is provoked in the struggle for emancipation originates in the early relationship with the mother and is displaced secondarily onto the male. The elaboration of the original conflictual relationship is necessary to free women's political energies. Women who seek a connection exclusively with other women regress to a preoedipal relationship in the wish to become merged with the generous and omnipotent mother.[20] It is in this wish, argued Langer, that women deny their own hostility as well as the other image of the mother—the omnipotent and frightening one. This image is displaced onto the male and thus preserves the good internal mother. The possibility of autonomy and liberation, of the achievement of maturity, including motherhood, has been abandoned. Having said this, Langer reaffirmed the absolute necessity of a strong and independent feminist movement; feminism without a class analysis, she maintained, cannot achieve structural change, but leftist parties are not sufficient to carry out the struggle for the rights and needs of women. "One has to be a woman, she wrote, to have experienced in one's own guts our insecurity, our doubts, our overwork, and marginalization, in order to recognize just how much has to change."

During this period and in the years to follow, Langer's political experiences with women were to reinforce the shifts in her thinking with respect to some of the theories she had advanced in *Motherhood and Sexuality*.[21] For example, she came to doubt the existence of a maternal instinct but felt that even if a woman's desire to have a baby is instinctually based, the instincts are changeable, just as everything about the human being is changeable. She believed that the expression of woman's creative energy, including motherhood, has been and will continue to be dictated by cultural options open to the female gender. The new feminist historical research had taught her that, in fact, attitudes toward motherhood and parent–child relations were extraordinarily heterogeneous, illustrated by the diversity of socially endorsed family practices in premodern Europe and elsewhere in which for centuries parents willingly gave up their children temporarily or permanently through the practices of wet-nursing, fostering, adoption,

and abandonment. Langer became increasingly convinced that psychoanalytic theories of motherhood and the mother–child relationship
are the ideological product of a specific era, culture, and class. As she
saw it, in contemporary society women's biologically based biannual
reproductive cycle had been altered by the science of birth control, and
she believed that this momentous technological advance enabling
women to choose to bear and raise fewer or no children at all needed
to be complemented by society's acceptance of women's right to be
significant and creative actors in other domains. Moreover, Langer no
longer held that a woman was obliged to have children in order to be
completely fulfilled or to actualize her femininity; rather, she now
stressed the importance of recognizing the practical limits on a
woman's ability to realize herself in all terrains, especially in view of
the lack of enlightened social policy in most countries of the world. For
example, in the case of the middle-class professional woman in Europe
or the United States, where to have a child means to interrupt and
perhaps to lose a meaningful career, the price of being a mother may be
too high. In such instances, Langer came to believe, if a woman decides
not to have a child, she is renouncing one capacity, a biological one in
this instance, in favor of others. However, the cultural specificity of
female attitudes with respect to motherhood was something that
Langer learned firsthand from the late 1960s on through her connections with working-class and peasant women in South and Central
America. She was convinced that motherhood for the Latin American
woman—the Third World woman—reflects a different reality from
that in Europe and the United States. Latin American women still
aspire to have many children, an attitude that is rooted in preindustrial
patterns and traditional cultural values, which encourage them to
identify self-esteem and pride with their maternal capacities. In
addition, reproduction and motherhood are complex political issues in
Latin America in that they have been the target of population-control
strategies imposed by the United States, stimulating, according to
Langer, nationalist resentment that attributes widespread poverty and
economic stagnation to the draining of Latin American resources by
the industrialized countries rather than to overpopulation. The identification of motherhood as the central source of female fulfillment
among Latin American women has also been taken up by feminist and
politically progressive movements interested in the implementation of
social changes that would encourage women's equal participation in
the social sphere as well as their control over their own bodies through
programs of reproductive rights. Langer herself would be witness to
such efforts during the 1980s as part of her work with the Nicaraguan
Revolution.

The biopsychosocial approach that characterizes *Motherhood and Sexuality* continued to be Langer's fundamental lens through which she viewed gender. For example, though she supported the contemporary feminist vision of childrearing shared by both parents as a strategy for eliminating the reproduction of exaggerated gender differences and inequality between the sexes, she did not believe that gender difference would disappear because men as well as women parent. She continued to postulate that the fundamental biological difference between males and females would always translate psychologically into different kinds of intimacy with children. Barring future scientific discoveries that succeed in removing reproduction from the human body completely, Langer felt certain that the childbearing capacity of the woman gives her a specific relationship to children, even though one could speak of the "maternal environment" to refer to an attitude assumed as much by males as by females. Why, she asked, do some feminists wish to deny difference and to assert sameness between the genders? In the final analysis, the question is one of creating a discourse and social institutions that respect difference.

Langer's ideas about female sexuality changed dramatically over the years since she wrote *Motherhood and Sexuality*. The book, she later asserted, was framed and thus limited by the prevailing psychoanalytic ideology of the time. She thought in retrospect that in the context of her essentially Kleinian analysis of femininity her faithful Freudian conceptualization of female sexual inhibition was the product of her insecurity for having been critical of Freud. Thus, she felt she had written about the inability of a woman to accept her femininity narrowly, in terms of frigidity, and she had defined frigidity as the inability to have a vaginal orgasm. She now criticized not only this view, which subsequent research had demonstrated to be incorrect, but also the superego demands analysts had placed on female patients to measure up to a preconceived—and indeed mistaken—notion of normalcy. She agreed with the Masters and Johnson research that proved the centrality of the clitoris to female orgasm but suggested that their focus on physiological phenomena to determine female sexual sensation was restrictive. Psychological experience rather than behavior was, for Langer, the true key to female sexuality. Normalcy or abnormality could best be understood through an examination of phantasies—how they stimulate desire and excitement—during the sexual act. Even though Langer came to regard female sexual difficulties, including frigidity—which she now understood as the fear of sexual intimacy, penetration, or orgasm—in a different light, she thought her analysis of their psychogenesis in *Motherhood and Sexuality* continued to be essentially correct. On the other hand, she came to reject her assertions in the book that sex for the truly feminine woman is passive and that the assumption of an active role indicates her masculinization or rejection of femininity. The sexual act is different for every couple, she came to argue, and passive and active roles, independent of gender, may be assumed quite pleasurably.

With respect to her analysis of breast-feeding and childbirth, Langer arrived at the conclusion that there are a variety of psychologically healthy choices a woman may make with respect to these two experiences and came to reject the assumption that only one approach represents a woman's acceptance of her femininity. Recognizing the contemporary tendency to exalt the psychological as well as the physiological value of breast-feeding, she found this view too judgmental of women who are unable or choose not to nurse their infants. She acknowledged the importance of the social flexibility represented by bottle-feeding, in regard to both a woman's work schedule and paternal or other caregivers' participation in childrearing. A loving and engaging attitude while feeding the baby, she thought, is more important than whether the nourishment comes from the breast or the bottle. In the same regard, she believed that while what she had written in *Motherhood and Sexuality* about childbirth without pain was for its time at the forefront of progressive thinking on the subject, she now disagreed with the assertions that in the absence of organic obstacles a woman should be able to go through labor without pain and that pain represents psychological conflict about motherhood. Now she was concerned about the pressure that women experience to live up to unrealistically demanding expectations of the perfect delivery and the guilt they feel if they have to use anesthesia to stop the pain of labor. With the newer and relatively harmless anesthesias, a woman can, insisted Langer, enjoy the benefits of being completely conscious during labor without excessive pain. She viewed the expectation that a woman should be able to go through labor without having recourse to modern science a guilt-inducing cultural demand on women and an unfortunate return to an idealization of nature.

Finally, Langer continued to hold to her general argument in the book with respect to infertility. In response to the criticism that she had conceptualized the causes of infertility exclusively in psychological terms, she responded that her psychosomatic approach had never overlooked the importance of the physiological etiology of infertility but, rather, had attempted to explain infertility in terms of psychogenic factors in cases where there was no organic obstacle to pregnancy. While she acknowledged that medical science has advanced our understanding and detection of the structural causes of infertility since she wrote *Motherhood and Sexuality*, she maintained that her analysis, with its psychosomatic focus, elucidates the intimate relationship between psyche and soma, an approach that is very much in the forefront of medical research today. Langer felt that the psychosomatic aspect of the increasing incidence of infertility in the United States, for example, is underestimated and should certainly be taken into account when modern medical technology designed to treat infertility does not result in pregnancy. Though aware of the feminist concern that a predisposition to view female reproductive difficulties in psychogenic terms might reflect misogynist views of women or end up missing possible organic etiology, Langer nonetheless defended her psychosomatic perspective. She remained convinced that psychological conflict and stress produce physical illness and pointed, for example, to the discovery by contemporary medical research of the link between stress and cancer. Langer knew firsthand about the painful reality of elevated rates of cancer and other life-threatening diseases among political refugees and exiles, who are subjected to excessive stress marked by dislocation, loss, culture shock, and the anxiety of adaptation to a new and often inhospitable environment.

Women of our era, Langer believed, experience the profound stress that comes from being at the center of a variety of global social changes that demand too much of them. She thought her role as an analyst was to help women to explore their desire and ambition in order to make choices related to intimate relationships, motherhood, and work with as little guilt as possible. Langer's analytic practice in Mexico was composed mainly of middle-class women, and the political refugees she treated, who were increasingly from Central American countries, were often women as well. But from the early 1980s on, she no longer wrote or published essays or articles about women. In fact, just as *Motherhood and Sexuality* was enjoying renewed popularity in Latin America and being translated into Italian and Portuguese for European distribution, Langer's intellectual and political attention was captured elsewhere by the passionate social drama of revolution in Nicaragua.

Nicaragua: Psychoanalysis and Revolution

—"*Oh, to be able to go to sleep now*
And to awake within a hundred years, beloved . . ."
No, my love, not that; I am not a deserter.
My century does not frighten me.
My miserable, scandalous century,
My spirited, great, heroic century.

I never complained of being born too soon.
I am of the twentieth century. I feel proud of this.
I am happy to be where I am:
In the midst of our people
And fighting for a better world . . .
—"To be a hundred years from now, my love . . ."
—No: much sooner than that and in spite of it all.
My agonizing and renascent century,
My century, whose last days will be beautiful,
This terrible night that crushes the shrieks of dawn,
My century will be ablaze with the sun, my love,
The same as your eyes.
                                                —Nazim Hikmet[22]

Langer now entered a new phase of her life, one that she came to value as the true synthesis of her commitment to radical politics, feminism, and psychoanalysis. She and other Latin American psychoanalysts and psychiatrists living in Mexico during the 1970s had avidly followed the Nicaraguan people's struggle to overturn 50 years of the brutal Somoza dictatorship.[23] When the Sandinistas triumphed in July 1979, Langer's enthusiasm was like that of so many progressive Latin Americans who viewed the young revolutionary country as the source of hope in a continent plagued by the politics of suffering and poverty. People from all over the world—physicians, nurses, teachers, agronomists, engineers, filmmakers—rushed to help the war-damaged country initiate its social and economic reconstruction. Langer joined these efforts in 1981 as the Co-coordinator of the Internationalist Team of Mental Health Workers, a group of 12 Latin American psychoanalysts, psychiatrists, and psychologists living in Mexico who would travel monthly to Nicaragua to train a variety of professionals providing direct health and educational services to the people of Nicaragua. From their vantage point, these mental health professionals would witness firsthand the Sandinista program of development based on political pluralism, a mixed economy, and a nonaligned foreign policy.

Revolutionary Nicaragua was the first country undergoing radical social transformation to endorse a psychoanalytic psychology as a foundation of its first national mental health care program. From Langer's perspective, the primary objective was not to engage in a political discourse about whether or not Nicaragua was Marxist or how a Marxist psychoanalysis could be theoretically linked to the Revolution; it was, rather, to endeavor to be useful to Nicaragua with certain psychoanalytic concepts. Thus, the efforts of Langer and her colleagues were directed toward the elaboration of strategies for the adaptation of psychoanalysis to the social and economic conditions of extreme underdevelopment and the specific characteristics of Nicaraguan cultural tradition. In an article called "Psychoanalysis without the Couch," [24] she described how the Internationalist Team Of Mental Health Workers taught the principles of unconscious mental functioning and the technique of interpretation of symbolic meaning in dreams, phantasies, and delusions within the specific treatment models developed to respond to the cultural, economic, and political conditions of Nicaragua. Langer's friendship with some of the Revolution's famous women leaders taught her about the unique aspects of female experience in Central American culture. For the first time in her life, she had the opportunity to provide clinical treatment to female patients living in a society whose government supported the fight against the institutional oppression of women. In the female patient population who sought treatment for depression, anxiety, and psychosomatic illnesses, Langer observed the psychological manifestations of the problematic family structure in Nicaragua, characterized by a historical pattern of male abandonment of families.[25] The widespread pattern of female-headed and female-centered households had produced several contradictory patterns: on the one hand, as feminists from the United States and Europe had noted, this phenomenon had strengthened women by promoting qualities of independence and self-sufficiency that had enabled them to participate in large numbers and in leadership positions in the Revolution; on the other hand, women felt themselves to be disempowered by the widespread male practice of establishing more than one set of primary family relationships—la familia grande and la familia chica—either simultaneously or sequentially. Consequently, many women harbored intense feelings of resentment toward men, the result of which was their tendency to form their closest affective ties with their children, whose strivings for independence were often experienced by their mothers as a threat and thus resisted.

Langer's supervision of Nicaraguan mental health workers focused on teaching them to think in psychoanalytic terms about the meaning of their female patients' symptoms and to make psychoanalytically informed interventions. Consistent with her approach to mental health as both an individual and collective project, Langer encouraged them to remind their patients about their political resources, such as the Association of Nicaraguan Women (AMNLAE), a government-sponsored organization with a special interest in education, child care, family life, and employment for women that had spearheaded the struggle for women's legal and political equality after the Revolution. AMNLAE successfully fought for the legal obligation of men who abandon their children to pay child support and also secured a new law that calls on all family members, regardless of sex, to participate in household and childrearing tasks. Langer believed that involvement with AMNLAE would provide women with increased self-esteem and mutual support outside the home and thus give them a source, in addition to their families, of personal meaning and intimate relations. She believed a stronger sense of self would emerge from women's common struggle to challenge the legal, social, and economic traditions that had subordinated them and had framed the psychological impediments to gender equality.[26]

Working in Nicaragua, Langer was happy. For her, the daily frustrations and obstacles endemic to extreme underdevelopment were more than compensated for by the optimism and spirited energy of militants who viewed their revolution as a symbol of sovereignty and independence in Latin America and its social programs as their children's guarantee for a decent future. "I realized on my second trip to Nicaragua what the experience is for me. I realized that there I am not old or young . . . I am atemporal . . . and I live it as if the Spanish Republic, the old Republic, had won, and I am collaborating in the reconstruction . . . it is . . . a continuity . . . and finally, and suddenly, I am there." These sentiments she shared on her annual trips to Europe, where because of her European roots and professional prestige she was able to draw large audiences interested in learning about the Nicaraguan experience.

The Final Chapter

In December 1985 Langer was invited to present a paper on psychoanalysis in Havana, Cuba, at the annual meeting of an organization called The Encounter of Intellectuals for the Sovereignty of the People of Our America. Some of the continent's most prestigious figures from the arts, literature, and sciences came together to engage in a dialogue about strategies for Latin American economic and cultural liberation from the structures of dependency that had continued to exist since colonial times. In an emotional moment Langer was surprised by the public announcement honoring her as a newly elected member to the 12-person permanent commission of the organization. She was to replace a fellow Argentine, writer Julio Cortazar, who had recently died, to become the second woman elected to the commission and the only member so far to represent the sciences. She joined such noteworthy colleagues as Colombian writer Gabriel Garcia Marquez and Brazilian theologian Friar Betto. Langer believed her inclusion in the permanent commission represented the acceptance of psychoanalysis not only as a part of the intellectual movement for Latin American independence but as a scientific tool in that endeavor. Soon afterward, Cuba would open its doors to psychoanalysis; the Psychology Department of the University of Havana was to become host to a series of biannual meetings organized as encounters between Marxist psychology and Latin American psychoanalysis. Participants would come from Latin America, Europe, and the United States to share their ideas and experiences as mental health professionals interested in strategies for human emancipation.[27]

Shortly after the conference in Cuba, Langer discovered that she was suffering from inoperable cancer. During the following two years her pace gradually slowed, but her involvement in the work that she passionately loved continued. Experimental cancer treatments gave intermittent hope to family, friends, colleagues, and comrades that Langer would survive the illness that was consuming her. She alternated between her wishful desire to live and her rational acceptance of death. Finally, in the summer of 1987, realizing that she had very little time left, she returned to Buenos Aires, to the home she had been forced to leave 13 years earlier. Just before she departed Mexico, she received an invitation to participate in a conference, "The Driving out of Reason and its Return," organized by the Austrian government to honor prominent figures in the arts and sciences forced by Austro-fascism to leave the country in the late thirties. But by October she was too ill to travel to Vienna. Her letter expressing regret at not being able to attend this encounter with colleagues who had suffered a fate similar to her own at the hands of fascism was read publicly during the conference.[28]

As her symptoms worsened, Langer's desire to live became more powerful and the acceptance of death more difficult. Even as she became progressively weaker, she stubbornly resisted her doctors' orders to rest. She agreed to be interviewed at length on film about her work in Nicaragua and her concern for the survival of the Sandinista social experiment, which was being violently undermined by the United States. Although the experience drained her, it was, on the brink of her death, a gift permitting continuity with the ideals that had informed the choices she had made throughout her life.[29] On December 22, 1987, Marie Langer died as she had lived, an active participant in history.

Notes

1. For a detailed description of political events in Argentina during the sixties and seventies, see G. W. Wynia, *Argentina: Illusions and Realities* (New

York: Holmes & Meier, 1986); D. C. Hodges, *Argentina, 1943–1987: The National Revolution and Resistance* (Albuquerque: University of New Mexico Press, 1988); and J. Corridi, *The Fitful Republic: Economy, Society and Politics in Argentina* (Boulder: Westview Press, 1988).

2. For a more detailed discussion of the dissident movement within Argentine psychoanalysis, see N. Hollander, "Buenos Aires: Latin Mecca of Psychoanalysis," *Social Research* 57–4 (Winter 1990): 889–919.

3. M. Langer, "Psicoanálisis y/o Revolución Social," in M. Langer, (ed.), *Cuestionamos II* (Buenos Aires: Granica, 1973), pp. 257–269.

4. In an interview with the author (Mexico, December 1986), Langer recalled the shift in attitude toward her by prominent British Kleinian Hanna Segal, who, along with Klein herself, had several decades earlier rehearsed Langer before her presentations at the IPA, because she was one of the few identified Kleinians to give papers at the congresses; it was Segal, among others, to whom Langer referred with respect to colleagues' displeasure with her paper in Vienna in 1971.

5. Hollander, "Buenos Aires: Latin Mecca . . . "

6. M. Langer (ed.), *Cuestionamos I* (Buenos Aires: Granica, 1971) and M. Langer (ed.), *Cuestionamos II* (Buenos Aires: Granica, 1973).

7. North American and European feminists were interested in similar questions and pursued a similar analysis; Langer was familiar with the theoretical arguments of many contemporary feminist authors, some of whom, including Isabel Largia, Linda Gordon, Kate Millet, and Shulamith Firestone, she referred to in this article.

8. The details of this research project, including the psychological profile of the patient population and the researchers' psychosocial analysis, were presented by Drs. Marie Langer and Silvia Berman as a paper, "Patalogía Femenina y Condiciones de Vida," at a congress of the Federación Argentina de Psiquiatras (FAP), Cordoba, Argentina, 1973.

9. Although Langer was a feminist, there was not a viable feminist movement in Argentina at this time, in contrast to Europe and the United States. There were only very small and isolated feminist groups, including the Unión Feminista Argentina (UFA), composed mainly of middle-class women whose feminist practice did not address the issues that were foremost in the minds of most Argentines who were likely to participate in progressive and leftist political movements against the status quo. On the other hand, hundreds of thousands of working- and middle-class people had been mobilized by the mass-based leftist tendency of Peronism, which had created a special women's section called "Agupacion Evita" and was politically active in industrial unions, professional guilds, neighborhood committees, and university and high school organizations. Because of the absence of a tenable feminist movement, Langer understandably was inclined toward thinking in terms of the potential her female patients had for seeing themselves as political actors who could join in the mass-based political struggle alongside men and women fighting "against the system."

10. Langer's belief in the importance of altering childrearing patterns so that egalitarian parent participation would undo the psychological problems

attendant upon exclusively female parenting resonated with contemporary feminist psychoanalytic views, such as those of Nancy Chodorow and Dorothy Dinnerstein, whose work she greatly admired. She was unaware of Jessica Benjamin's perspective, which regards the father as an important identificatory (as well as libidinal) object for the little girl, but she would probably have found much to agree with. See Jessica Benjamin, *Bonds of Love* (New York: Pantheon, 1988) and "Father and Daughter: Identification with Difference— A Contribution to Gender Heterodoxy," unpublished paper.

11. M. Langer, "La Mujer: Sus Limitaciones y Potencialidades," in Marie Langer (ed.), *Cuestionamos II*, (Buenos Aires: Granica, 1973), 275.

12. M. Langer and I. Maldonado, *Nicaragua Libre*, unpublished manuscript; interview with M. Langer and I. Maldonado, Argentine psychoanalyst, Mexico, February 1984.

13. The political repression in Argentina produced a veritable "brain drain." Middle-class professionals who had been progressive political activists—and even those with little or no political history—became targets of repression and they, along with their families, represented a substantial number of the hundreds of thousands of Argentines who fled their homeland, forming large exile communities in Mexico City, Madrid, Barcelona, and Paris.

14. The military coup in 1976 ushered in 6 years of the most violent repression ever experienced in Argentina, rivaling in its brutality toward the civilian population the most repressive dictatorships throughout the continent. The military saw its mission as one of cleansing Argentine society of the "ideological criminals Marx and Freud" and set about in ruthless fashion to accomplish that end. Working-class people, who were the main target of the military, had fewer resources than the middle and upper classes, who could mobilize resources in order to abandon the country. The civilian government that replaced the military in 1983 supported an investigation into military crimes against civilians; see J. Corradi, "Terror in Argentina," *Telos* 54 (1982–3): 61–76 and "The Report of the Argentine National Commission on the Disappeared" in *Nunca Mas* (Farrar Straus & Giroux: New York, 1986).

15. See for example, A. Ornstein, "The Holocaust: Reconstruction and the Establishment of Psychic Continuity," in ed. A. Rothstein, *The Reconstruction of Trauma: Its Significance in Clinical Work*, (New York: International Universities Press, 1986); Rosario Dominguez and Eugenia Weinstein, *Aiding Victims of Political Repression in Chile: A Psychosocial and Psychotherapeutic Approach*, unpublished paper, 1985.

16. M. Langer, "La Mujer, la locura y la sociedad," in Silvia Marcos (ed.), *Antipsiquiatría y Política* (Cuernavaca, Mexico: Extemporaneos, 1978), pp. 181–192.

17. For an elaborate analysis of the relationship of political engagement to psychological health in the case of the Mothers of the Plaza de Mayo, see D. Kordon and L. Edelman, *Efectos Psicológicos de La Represión Política* (Buenos Aires: Sudamericana-Planeta, 1986); interview with D. Kordon and D. Lagos, Argentine psychoanalysts, Los Angeles, December 1989.

18. M. Langer, J. del Palacio, and E. Guinsberg, *Memoria, Historia y Dialogo Psicoanalítico* (Buenos Aires: Folios Ediciones, 1981). The book was translated into English and published under the title *From Vienna to Managua: Journey of a Psychoanalyst* (London: Free Associatio Books, 1989), with an introduction by N. Hollander and an 1986 interview with Langer by A. Varchevker.

19. Langer refers to a study by A. Davin, "Imperialism and Motherhood," in *History Workshop Journal* 5 (1978): 9–66.

20. Langer never changed her view regarding the psychological limits of activism carried out exclusively in a feminist movement isolated from general political struggles. She realized the implications her psychological analysis and political evaluation held for an assessment of female homosexuality and believed they would be unpopular with feminists. She said of herself that while she came to disagree with many of her own assumptions about homosexuality in *Motherhood and Sexuality*, she had not come to grips theoretically with the meaning of homosexuality. For an insightful review of psychoanalytic perspectives on homosexuality and a construction of paradigms for thinking about homosexual object choice that are not based on analogies to pathological conditions, see Maggie Magee and Diana C. Miller, " 'She Foreswore Her Womanhood': Psychoanalytic Views of Female Homosexuality" forthcoming in *The Clinical Social Work Journal*.

21. This material is taken from two interviews the author had with Langer specifically regarding the changes in her thinking about some of the concepts in *Motherhood and Sexuality*, Managua, Nicaragua, June 1984 and Mexico City, December 1986.

22. N. Hikmet, *Antología Poética* (Buenos Aires: Quetzal, 1968): This poem is cited by Langer in "La Mujer: Sus Limitaciones y Potencialidades" and was a favorite of hers. I have chosen to translate it and include it in this Afterword because it captures so well Langer's attitude of engagement in the world. Hikmet, a Turkish revolutionary whose passionate poetry made him one of the great international poets of this century, can be read in English. See for example, *The Epic of Sheik Bedreddin and Other Poems* (New York: Persea Books, 1982).

23. Many fine studies of the Nicaraguan Revolution have been published in the last decade; see for example, R. Harris and C. Vilas, eds., *Nicaragua: A Revolution Under Siege* (London: Zed Books, 1985); O. Cabezas, *Fire From the Mountain: The Making of a Sandinista* (New York: Crown Publishers, 1985) and E. B. Burns, *At War in Nicaragua: The Reagan Doctrine and the Politics of Nostalgia* (New York: Harper & Row, 1987).

24. M. Langer, "Psicoanálisis Sin El Divan," published in J. C. Volnovich and Silvia Werthein, *Marie Langer: Mujer, Psicoanálisis, Marxismo* (Buenos Aires: Editorial Contrapunto, 1989).

25. Female-headed families were the consequence of both cultural and economic factors. The attitudes embedded in *machismo* in Nicaragua accorded status and prestige to men who formed relationships and had children with more than one woman, either simultaneously or sequentially; thus, even

though married, most women experienced abandonment by husbands for some period of time during their marriage. High unemployment rates forced men to seek seasonal employment and to thus become part of the migrant labor force employed in planting and harvesting in different parts of Nicaragua, during which time they left their families; thus wives were forced to fend for themselves and their children. In the early eighties, over 50% of the households in Managua were female-headed.

26. AMNLAE functioned effectively from 1979 to 1989 in spite of the U. S. economic and military war against Nicaragua, which forced the Sandinista government to divert an increasingly large part of the national budget to defense, thus weakening social programs. Since the Nicaraguan elections in 1990, which the Sandinistas lost, AMNLAE has operated as part of the opposition and met a similar fate to other Sandinista social programs; while it maintains significant ideological support, it fights to hang on to its share of a constantly shrinking budget as the economy continues to deteriorate.

27. This organization is but one example of how Cuba is not as intellectually or politically isolated from other countries in the Western Hemisphere as we in the United States are led to believe. To a large group of mental health professionals from Latin America, the United States, and Europe, this bi-annual congress is an important vehicle for exchanging perspectives on the relationship between social, economic, and political conditions and mental health as well as for assessing the relevance of psychoanalysis to progressive social change. It has taken place twice and is scheduled to meet again in February 1992.

28. Interview with Rudolf Ekstein, Viennese-born North American psychoanalyst, Los Angeles, February 1987.

29. The interview was filmed by colleagues from the Internationalist Team who intended to make a documentary about their work in Nicaragua. The experience was very difficult for Langer, because she was so weak physically, but it lifted her spirits to see herself still able to contribute something meaningful to Nicaragua. (Interviews with Dr. Tomas Langer, Langer's son, and Juan Carlos Volnovich, psychoanalyst, Buenos Aires, August 1990; Armando Bauleo, Argentine psychoanalyst, Havana, February 1989).

Index